EVENSONG

EVENSONG

PEOPLE, DISCOVERIES AND
REFLECTIONS ON THE
CHURCH IN ENGLAND

RICHARD MORRIS

WEIDENFELD & NICOLSON

First published in Great Britain in 2021 by Weidenfeld & Nicolson
an imprint of The Orion Publishing Group Ltd
Carmelite House, 50 Victoria Embankment
London EC4Y 0DZ

An Hachette UK Company

1 3 5 7 9 10 8 6 4 2

A CIP catalogue record for this book is
available from the British Library.

ISBN (Hardback) 978 1 4746 1422 1
ISBN (eBook) 978 1 4746 1424 5

Printed and bound in Great Britain
by Clays Ltd, Elcograf S.p.A.

www.orionbooks.co.uk
www.weidenfeldandnicolson.co.uk

For Rosemary Cramp

CONTENTS

GLOSSARY OF TERMS

Angel: a messenger, intermediate between God and people

Anglicanism: doctrine and practice maintained by Christians in communion with the see of Canterbury

Ant[iphon]: sentence sung or said before or after a psalm or canticle

Archdeacon: cleric with an administrative role delegated by a diocesan bishop

Archdeaconry: group of parishes overseen by an archdeacon

Benefice: originally a grant of property in exchange for services, the term has evolved to signify an ecclesiastical office – normally a rectory, vicarage, or perpetual curacy – in which revenues assigned to it are used to support the holder's performance of specified duties (whence also 'beneficed' and 'unbeneficed'). Historically, a benefice was usually coextensive with a parish; today, it may embrace a number of pastoral units

Bishop: the highest order in Christian ministry. In the Anglican Communion, a bishop is held to be differentiated from a priest by the power to confer Holy Orders and to dispense the rite of confirmation

Canon (1): title of clergy belonging to a cathedral or collegiate church

Canon (2): in law, a term that distinguishes ecclesiastical from civil enactments. Today, Canon Law is used to cover the Church's organisational and administrative rules generally

Canticle: song or prayer derived from the Bible which forms a part of liturgical worship

Cathedral: church containing a *cathedra* (chair) that denotes the office and authority of a diocesan bishop

Chantry: an office or benefice endowed for the singing or saying of masses for the souls of the founder and others in the founder's circle. By extension, an altar or chapel at or in which such masses were said

Chapel (1): church subordinate to a parish church, often provided for the ease of parishioners living in outlying parts or where access to the parish church is difficult

Chapel (2): space within a church with a separate altar, often dedicated to its own saint

Chapel (3): place of worship reserved for an institution (e.g., college, royal household)

Chapel (4): term used in contradistinction to 'Church' to denote members of dissenting denominations (as in 'Church and Chapel')

Chaplain (1): priest who serves a chapel

Chaplain (2): priest appointed to serve an institution (e.g., hospital, branch of armed services, prison)

Chapter: body of self-governing clergy

Church Assembly: body made up of Houses of Bishops, Clergy and Laity, brought into being by the Enabling Act 1919 to 'deliberate on all matters concerning the Church of England' and make provision for them. Replaced by General Synod in 1970

Clerk in Holy Orders: formal term denoting a bishop, priest, or deacon

Close: enclosed area around a cathedral, originally walled and gated, containing ancillary buildings, houses for clergy, and a bishop's palace

Collegiate church: church served by a self-governing body of secular (i.e., not monastic) clergy under the charge of a dean or provost

Confirmation: rite whereby grace of the Holy Spirit is gifted and ratifies vows taken at baptism

Crypt: in original sense, somewhere hidden; now: a chamber, usually subterranean or semi-subterranean, beneath the main body of a church

Curate: the word today denotes an unbeneficed cleric – often newly or recently ordained and under training – who assists an incumbent. In earlier use it denoted any clergyman who had the cure of souls

Deacon: one ordained into the lowest of the three ranks of Anglican ministry (deacon, priest, bishop)

Dean (1): head of a cathedral chapter or collegiate church

Dean (2): a rural dean assists the bishop in administration of a group of churches that form a subdivision of archdeaconry

Diocese: basic territorial unit of ecclesiastical governance, administered by a bishop

Eucharist: act of thanksgiving in Christian worship, and focus of controversy at the Reformation as between those who upheld the doctrine that Christ's body and blood coexist in consecrated bread and wine, and those who regarded the Lord's Supper either as commemorative or as a transfer of virtue

Evangelicalism: outlook founded on the tenet that salvation comes only by divine grace, awarded in response to faith, not as something a sinner may earn through merit

Faculty: legal grant of permission enabling work to a church or churchyard to be done

General Synod: Church of England governing body (from 1970), which considers and approves legislation, frames new forms of worship, debates matters of importance, and approves the Church's annual national budget

Glebe: land assigned for the maintenance of a parochial incumbent

High Church: tendency in the Church of England that puts weight on continuity from Catholicism, and upholds the nature of the sacraments and exceptional role of bishops. High Church opinion can be traced from the sixteenth century, but following abeyance from the late seventeenth through the eighteenth century it was restored to prominence from the 1830s by the movement centred on Oriel College, Oxford, which produced Tracts for the Times (whence 'Tractarian')

Incumbent: holder of a benefice

Liturgy: a formal set of words, music and actions prescribed for use in worship

Lych-gate: (from OE *lic*, a corpse) covered gateway into a churchyard

Mass: an early medieval term for the Eucharist which in Anglican usage has become associated with High Churchmanship

Minister: (from Latin *minister*, 'a servant') one who is authorised to perform spiritual duties in the Church

Monastery: community living under religious discipline; by extension, the site and buildings so occupied

Ordination: consecration that translates an individual from lay to clerical status and authorises the performance of particular rites and ceremonies

Parish: territorial unit for the cure of souls, which today may be served by a rector, vicar, priest-in-charge, group, or team

Parson: originally and strictly, the holder of a benefice who possesses its rights – that is, the rector (from Latin *persona*, literally 'the person' to whom God's property in a parish was assigned)

Parsonage: house assigned for the use of a rector or vicar

Patron: in Anglican use, an individual, office, or institution with the right to appoint or present a member of the clergy for a vacant benefice. In the past, this right could be bought, sold, or gifted

Priest: one who has been admitted to the order of priesthood by a bishop, with authority to celebrate mass and provide cure of souls

Priest-in-charge: one who is in charge of a parish but is not its incumbent

Real presence: doctrine that Jesus is present sacramentally in the Eucharist

Rector: an individual or body in receipt of the income of a rectory. The rector may appoint a vicar (from Latin *vicarius*, 'a deputy') to perform the duties of the rectory

Rectory: the rights and duties of a rector; by extension, the rector's house

Saint: one who has a close and special relationship with God, and by extension may be regarded as a protector or advocate – for instance, of a nation, place, or family

R[esponse]: congregational reply to a versicle

See: (from Latin *sedes*, 'a seat') in ecclesiastical use, a chair that symbolises the authority of a bishop

Stipend: money paid to enable work to be done, but not in commercial proportion to it

Suffragan: in the Anglican Church, a bishop under the authority of a diocesan bishop

Tithe: former tax of one tenth on produce or earnings taken for support of clergy

V[ersicle]: sentence sung or said by a minister to which the congregation responds

Vicar: (from Latin *vicarius*, 'a deputy') one who is appointed to undertake the parish duties of a rector

Vicarage: the rights and duties attaching to someone appointed as a vicar; by extension, the vicar's house

After the day there cometh the dark night;
For though the day be never so long,
At last the bells ringeth to evensong.

STEPHEN HAWES, d.1523

Oerder yn yn amser ni,
Y ria glas ywr eglwysi.
On'd oedd dost un dydd a dau
I'r llawr fwrw'r allorau?

Cor ni bydd yn y byd,
Na chennad yn iach ennyd.

SIÔN BRWYNOG, C.1550

Christus est stella matutina,
Qui nocte saeculi transacta,
Lucem vitae sanctis promittit
Et pandit aeternam.

BEDE, C.710

PREFACE

Evensong contains three overlapping groups of memoirs about the Church of England. The first describes life in post-war parsonages. Discoveries in and about churches make up the second. The third is a search for what it was that drew my father and others towards ordination as they came home from war in 1945. That is, why did I find myself growing up in parsonages?

It may be asked why anyone would want to know. By any measure, parsons, parsonages and Anglicans are generally these days on the edge of things. Most of the older vicarages and rectories have been sold off, and surveys say that fewer than two in a hundred people go to Anglican services. Collapse has been generational. Few under forty now identify with the Church of England. As older citizens die, church buildings are becoming husks, outwardly part of the local scene but functionally meaningless. There are places where the trend is bucked, often in areas where arguably the Church is needed least, but it would be no wiser to see them as signs of general renewal than it would be to take a shower of snow as evidence for the reversal of climate change.

Historians agree that decline has been going on for a good while. They are less decided about how long, or why. Different theories of secularisation are debated; very likely a number of processes have been operating at different speeds. Yet however we explain or measure the falloff, it is in contrast with the status that the Church continues to occupy in law and national life. That standing seems even more marked when we recall how much of it has already been done away with. England's main features as a confessional state were dissolved in 1828–1837 and through subsequent reforms. The Church in Wales was disestablished in 1914, and Anglican claims over people's lives and pockets were brought to an end long ago by dissent and secular challenge. Yet for all that, and even though Britain is now among the least religious countries in the world, Church and State remain bonded like metals in an alloy.

To give but a few examples: the Church of England passes its own laws; diocesan bishops are appointed by the Crown; some of them sit in the House of Lords (and when new Lords Spiritual are introduced to the House, their apparel, like that of Yeoman Warders of the Tower, goes back to the sixteenth century); the archbishops are Privy Councillors; there is a Second Estates Commissioner in the House of Commons; sittings of both Houses of Parliament begin with prayers. Chaplains are met in every sphere of life. About a million children are educated in schools run under Anglican auspices. The Archbishop of Canterbury has the authority to confer degrees. New monarchs are initiated by the Archbishop of Canterbury. The monarch is supreme governor of the Church of England, and coins in your pocket tell you (in what was once the Church's international language) that she is FIDEI DEFENSA-TRIX, 'defender of the faith' and reigns 'by the grace of God'. It goes on.

In a largely faithless Britain, after decades in which Anglicans have been unable to agree on important moral and theological issues even among themselves, it is reasonable to ask by what test the Church of England continues to lay claim to public authority and national embodiment. How much of its theatre and gesture can be taken seriously? Indeed, how much of it do we need? Maybe just enough to put on a good show at national moments? Despite the incongruities, observers of these things say that the establishment will last for a good while yet, because the uncoupling of Church from State would be so complicated that no one in a position to embark on it has the interest or will to do so. We are left with an equation in which indifference tinged by nostalgia equals inertia.

One answer to the 'Why *Evensong*?' question, then, is that regardless of what we think about the Church, it is there and continues to affect us. As the theologian William J. Wolf put it: 'Anglicanism, coming from an establishment position as a national church concerned with all types and people, has always been deeply rooted in a cultural context.' Kevin Gardner, writing about Anglicanism and the poetry of John Betjeman, points out that this gives it a social and cultural worth beyond its spiritual role. Looking more widely, modern conservatives identify Western culture with Christianity and the Bible, and in the parlance of their populists – Trump, Orbán, Kaczyński, Johnson – civilisation and 'way of life' have replaced democracy or social justice as their touchstones for allegiance and selfhood. This reminds us that irrespective of what we believe as individuals, all history is in some sense religious history, and we ignore it at our peril. Church and Bible pervade our tongue, literature, music, education, and law; to ignore them is to neglect bits of ourselves. Indeed, the leaching out of Anglicanism and participation in worship from general experience arguably gives rise to a crisis in which cultural meanings become masked, areas of experience are rendered inaccessible, and new inquiry is disabled. Very likely this is one reason why new and alternative religious movements now multiply so readily, and why some of them are a bit like subatomic particles orbiting around the old ones. But staying with the Church of England, if it does not much matter to its few remaining members why a Roman soldier who might have been born in Turkey around 1,700 years ago should have come to stand for far-right English nationalism, for students of far-right nationalism, perhaps it should.

One measure of the void being left by the Church's collapse is the extent to which its own hierarchy has lost interest in – in some ways even misrepresents – its own story. Indifference to history is a grave business for a historical religion. Paradoxically, however, the very lack of curiosity suggests that a relationship between Church leaders and their historical inheritance must in some way still matter, for why else should so many of them be wary of it? When a senior Anglican uses the phrase 'heritage fascism' to describe a funding body's insistence that its grants to churches be conditional on the involvement of a wider range of people in heritage, it is hard not to wonder if he feels engagement with the past to be not just outside the Church's concern but a threat to its mission. A corollary of that conjecture is another one: how other than through a sense of entitlement could someone expect a heritage funding body to grant-aid a church *without* such a condition?

Such aloofness is distinct from the concerns of those in the front line of the parish system in which they find themselves. 'Here's the thing,' writes a vicar in Somerset:

> Half of our churches, 8000 of them, have 26 adults or fewer on a Sunday. If you had 26 people to form a Christian presence in a community, you wouldn't start from here. You wouldn't have a listed building which costs thousands to heat and insure. You wouldn't have the protocols for running the church written into law. You wouldn't have so many aspects to Sunday worship (warden, verger, organist, reader, prayer leader, vicar, sides-person) that there's barely anyone there who isn't there because they're on a rota. You wouldn't open an Anglican Extra, you'd have an Anglican Express. In fact, you probably wouldn't open a building at all.

No, you probably wouldn't. But 16,000 places of worship are where we start.

Why so many? The origins of England's local churches are mainly the result of two bursts of activity: the first centred around a thousand years ago (c.950–c.1150), the second in the nineteenth century, lasting just eight decades (1820–1900). The means and motives of the founders have been described in other books. Less often discussed are the reasons why so many of the buildings put up in the first wave are still there. Martin Renshaw suggests they are found mainly in the dynamics of England's Reformation, which in several ways differed from religious revolutions elsewhere. For one thing, it was slower, with determinative stages that ran across several decades; for another, he says, it was led by rulers, not by people in general. At the time, indeed, the largest expressions of popular opinion were against it. These factors together meant that parish churches tended to escape the fiercer kinds of harm that result from populist upheavals. More than this, although people acceded to enforced reform, their initial reluctance sometimes lessened its impacts – for instance, where banned items were sequestered rather than destroyed. Hence, while reformers ordered the defacing of images, it was often, literally, just the face that was struck off or one quarry of glass that was removed, just enough to break eye contact. England's parish churches and carved angels hovering beneath their ceilings were left largely whole, and when Puritans did gain control for a time in the seventeenth century, their tendency to simplify existing churches rather than replace them again acted to conserve the legacy. A further factor was that England's churches were not much touched by the zeal for classical revival which overwrote so many religious buildings elsewhere in Europe after the counter-Reformation. In result, says Renshaw, there are more intact medieval churches in England and Wales than in most other European countries put together. In what follows, I suggest that cherishing them is not devotion to ashes but the transfer of fire.

Evensong is mostly anecdotal, and in writing it I did not set out to give a recent history of the Church, or to give an account of the ever-evolving tensions between its different parties, or to write a biography of my father. Nonetheless, the book touches things that give rise to reflections on or episodes of all three. It also bumps into topics about which I never meant to write. I imagined that writing a memoir would mainly involve setting down things remembered but should have realised that experiences are just moments and flashes, and that to be of use to anyone else they need to be contextualised. Contextualisation means mugging up on unfamiliar topics and sources, and it can take you in unforeseen directions. Cold War interactions between the Church, the Foreign Office and the Security Service, early Thatcherite experiments in privatisation, and the bush war in Zimbabwe–Rhodesia were not things about which I expected to write when I picked up the pen. Nor did I foresee the extent to which I would come upon the trashing of lives well lived for the good of others. A. N. Wilson's description of Stuart Blanch as 'the most undistinguished Archbishop of York in the 1300 years or so of the province's history' is readily parried by pointing to his disregard for the enormity of the competition. Much more disconcerting is the extent to which history's processes are being threatened by rumour and gossip conveyed and burgeoned through social media and the internet. Debate on many issues is now being shaped regardless of critical skills, and the seepage of resulting 'facts' into the aquifers of public and academic discourse (all those things 'everybody knows') is well under way. This is not simply a matter of whether something is true or supportable; it affects history's agendas and ways in which debate is structured; it puts the mob that bawls *Barabbas!* in place of source criticism.

Context of another kind was provided by SARS-CoV-2, which reached Britain shortly after the book was started and had taken three million lives worldwide by the time it was finished. The countermeasures closed archives, put some primary sources out of reach, and barred travel to revisit places first seen when the events in this book took place. The virus has a cruel aptitude for targeting things people do together, and since to a large extent churches exist through fellowship and shared endeavour, something more than web resources of prayer will be needed to see them through into whatever world lies ahead. Another reason, then, to look back at the one we have just left.

A word on usage. 'Church' is capitalised when used in an institutional sense simply to differentiate it from 'church' as a building. No other privilege is implied, and in both instances the underlying meaning of 'church' as a body of believers is respected. I have tried to be careful with 'England', 'Britain', and their derivatives, which mean different things at different times, and to different people, and have very particular meanings today. Historians have long been trying to warn us off the phrase 'Celtic Church'. I have used it as little as possible, and – I hope – only when quoting or in the idiom of others.

Last, a word on debts. For encouragement and much patience while the writing was in progress I am in the debt of my friend and mentor at Orion, Alan Samson. Warm thanks go to friends and colleagues who answered questions and gave advice or help along the way: Philip Birtles, Angela Ambrose, Tim Blanch, Wendy Childs, Anne Deighton, George Demidowicz, Anna Eavis, Bill Flynn, Rebecca Hiscott, David Keen, John Longstaff, Kenneth Neil McKenzie, Keith Merrin, Robin Mitchell, Harold Mytum, Robert Owen, Henry Owen-John, Ian Paul, Martin Pickard, Martin Renshaw, Julian Richards, Rev Canon Tony Shepherd, Martin Sharp, David Stocker, Ian Wood, and Christopher Young. My foremost debt is to Jane, my wife, for her frank comments and criticisms at every stage, and for her original suggestion that this book be written.

Third Sunday after Easter, 2021

PROLOGUE

NIGHT PRAYERS

Nineteen . . . maybe . . . was it 1958? If so, I was ten, and that was the year when the choir went to Wadderton House. Wadderton was large and rambling, in twelve acres amid hilly wood-pasture on the edge of the Worcestershire village of Blackwell. Years later, I found that it had been built in 1870 by a family that pioneered the mass production of pen nibs. The Diocese of Worcester bought it after the second great war and turned it into a place of retreat. And there we were.

We were led by a with-it director of music in his early twenties with whom lady members of the congregation serially fell in love. There was new music to learn each day. We rehearsed from ten until noon and again in the late afternoon, preparing for choral evensong in Blackwell's parish church of St Catherine. St Catherine's had been built just before the war. It was white-walled, airy, roofed with pantiles, felt new, and had a curious smell, a mixture of furniture polish and lilies. Looking it up, I see that it was built in a style called 'Scandinavian free Gothic'. Whatever it was, it felt right. I quite liked weekday choral evensong, too, not because I enjoyed church services, but because of all the ones I was made to attend it was the least tedious – lots to sing, no sermon, and few of those droning prayers that went on for hours on Sundays. (I tried to avoid Sunday evensong altogether, because it clashed with *Take It from Here* on the BBC Light Programme.)

Wadderton offered a lot to a ten-year-old. For one thing it had a pond, fed by a miraculous, quivering mound of clear water that welled up through the grass. I spent the first free time each day trying to build a raft. Then there was the Lickey Incline. Blackwell is atop the steepest mainline railway gradient in Britain. Ascending trains were assisted by tank engines known as Lickey bankers that pushed them the two miles up from Bromsgrove and dropped back when they passed the summit. There was no footbridge at the station, so you could stand right on the edge of the barrow crossing and watch the approach of a train, black smoke blasting from front and rear. Long, heavy-laden trains pushed by two bankers made for drama as they thundered past, inches from our faces.

Similarly wanting in health and safety were the battles. Church choirs are divided into halves called Cantoris and Decani, after the places of the cantor and the dean who sit facing each other in a cathedral choir. In the Middle Ages, the singers on each side led in alternate weeks; during great festivals the alternation was daily; psalms and canticles were sung in rotation. The names survived the Reformation and have been used ever since. Cant and Dec make ready-made sides for football, cricket, or any other kind of contest – like a running fight with acorns. A well-aimed acorn hurts, especially if the leathery cupule at the end is still attached. The Battle of Acorn Hill on the last afternoon involved everyone – choristers, organist, curate, and vicar. It seemed to go on for hours, through woods, across fields.

By the end of a day, then, we were beneficially knackered. After supper, we collected fallen branches, lit a fire, and sat round it as the vicar read us a ghost story. The stories came from M. R. James's *Ghost Stories of an Antiquary*. Two of them shook me. One was 'The Ash-tree', concerning the trial of a witch in 1690 and a 'curious series of events' at a small country house in Suffolk. Another was 'Oh, Whistle and I'll come to you, my lad', in which a young academic on a golfing holiday by the east coast finds a whistle 'of some considerable age' on the grassy site of a Knights Templar preceptory. By blowing it he summons up a succession of fearful things. We listened spellbound, as sparks from the burning branches shimmered upward and merged with the stars.

The day ended in the house chapel with Compline. Compline is the last of the daily offices. It is calming, and brief. As furry moths loomed out of the warm darkness and bumped against the windowpanes, the minister began:

The Lord almighty grant us a quiet night and a perfect end.

I did not then grasp the symbolism of 'a quiet night and a perfect end' in which a day stands for a lifetime and sleep foreshadows death. We replied:

Be sober, be vigilant; because your adversary the devil, as a roaring lion, walketh about, seeking whom he may devour; whom resist, steadfast in the faith.

We waited for the verse from Psalm 17:

Minister: Keep me as the apple of an eye.
Us: Hide me under the shadow of thy wings.

At the end of the week, we took a last look down the Lickey incline, and went back to our homes in the industrial suburb whence we had come. In my case, that meant the vicarage, because my dad was the vicar, but for most it was a post-war council house, or one of the new flats on Turves Green, or maybe a pre-war semi up Coombes Lane. Looking at it all now, I am struck by how many of the 1950s estate roads were named after places in Shropshire, like Clee, Titterstone, Clunbury, Culmington; was there someone in Birmingham Corporation who thought that by bringing these names into the city, some magic or memory would travel with them?

Maybe it did. Just before we went back to school, there was a choir outing to the Malvern hills. We met outside the church and walked the mile or so to the A38 between Longbridge and Rubery to catch the 144 Midland Red bus which ran between Birmingham and Malvern Wells. Midland Reds were posher than Corporation buses. Their seats were better, and the conductors used a different kind of ticket machine that produced thin white tickets rather than the coarse paper ones you got on city services. Midland Reds also stopped less often and so were faster. The bus stop was close to the city boundary, overlooked by a water-pumping station like a brick cathedral. The main road running past had been widened thirty years before and planted with lines of trees. We waited in their shadows.

Wychbold and Martin Hussingtree were places through which the 144 passed on its way to Worcester, where the bus crossed the Severn and turned west. On Worcester's edge, if you knew just when to look, you could catch the gleam of a silver Spitfire parked beside some playing fields. Ron, one of the tenors, said the fields had been a landing ground in the war, but we had no idea how the aeroplane had got there, or why.

Worcester offered other absorbing things. One of them was a bone from King John's thumb, which was on show near his tomb in the cathedral. The tomb of Arthur Tudor was another. Arthur (1486–1502) was the eldest son of King Henry VII and Elizabeth of York. He is remembered today, if at all, as a Tudor might-have-been, but in 1486, after years of vicious civil war, he was England's hope. Married to a Spanish princess, appointed Warden of the March, Prince of Wales, domiciled at nearby Ludlow, raised to be King Arthur, his sudden death at the age of fifteen put the House of Tudor on a different path from the one his father had hoped for. After the funeral, a chapel like a cage spun from stone gossamer was raised over his grave, and in it priests sang masses for his soul.

A few months before, I had stood nearby in Worcester's chapter house and auditioned for the choir school. I sang a couple of verses of an Easter hymn to the organist, David Willcocks, which went well, followed by an arithmetic test, which did not. So that was that. But on the Malverns, who cared? There were rocks to scramble, slopes to roll down, drifts of broom into which to fall. In the evening, worn out, looking back from the bus, the hills seemed blue. We got off beside the water tower and walked home in twilight, dust between our toes.

A similar kind of halcyon feeling surrounds our time at St Davids, to which we went to sing while the resident cathedral choir was on holiday. St Davids is at the far end of Wales, and since the top speed of the elderly coach with faulty brakes in which we travelled was no more than thirty-five miles an hour, it took some getting to. The M5 had opened just three weeks before, and for a few minutes we enjoyed the unfamiliar glamour of a four-lane highway with little traffic and long clean curves. However, in 1962 the M5 only ran for twenty-eight miles, and we were soon back on old roads, among Herefordshire's riverside meadows and hopyards. At Brecon, we joined the A40, highway to the Arthurian west, through Llandovery and Llandeilo to Carmarthen, where the tidal river told you that the sea must be somewhere close. From here to Haverfordwest there were glimpses of the purple Preseli hills, and a sense of expectancy stirred by the way the road rose to a series of tree-crowned ridges, each one suggesting something rare on the far side. Beyond Haverfordwest, we saw it: the sparkling arc of St Bride's Bay, rimmed by headlands, havens and islands, and the headland and city of David himself.

Pentir y Sant, St David's peninsula, is a mosaic of marshy grassland, relict dunes, isolated farms, and secluded hollows, all overlooked by craggy knolls that reminded you of the dorsal plates of some primordial monster. Place-wise, St Davids was just a village. Its cityhood stemmed from the cathedral, which stays hidden until you reach the valley crest and find yourself looking down at its tower and outspread roofs. Purple, green, and salmon-pink stones in its walls tell the story of the Cambrian age – from Cambria, the Roman name for Wales – when life on earth burgeoned. Their layers, since twisted and upended by earth movements, are visible in nearby cliffs. Around the cathedral are mansions for its clergy, remains of a medieval college, a bell tower, ruins of a bishop's palace, all enclosed by an ancient wall that winds across the valley. The valley explains the place, for tradition says it was here that David established a religious community in the sixth century, and around his grave that a famous centre of pilgrimage grew up. By the eleventh century, if not before, it was being said that David was a grand nephew of the fabled King Arthur.

We camped on the floors of a primary school overlooking the Close. Ron the tenor impressed everyone by the romantic progress he made with the resident organist's daughter, and there was at least one run-in with local lads who stalked us among the ruins of the bishop's palace. We sang each evensong in stalls under the central tower. One of the anthems was by Thomas Tomkins (1576–1652), a composer we were told had been born in St Davids and who as a boy had sung where we stood now. During his long life, Tomkins was appointed organist at Worcester Cathedral, became a member of the Chapel Royal, wrote music for James I's funeral and for the coronation of Charles I, lived through the Civil War, and saw his organ smashed by Parliamentary soldiers. After Charles's execution, he composed *A Sad Pavan for these Distracted Times*, and retired to Martin Hussingtree, on the route-to-be of the 144 Midland Red.

If things got dull during services, you could lose yourself by staring at the oaken ceiling above the nave. Everything about it – the textures of bleached gold, pendants with dolphins, the interplay of arcs and lines – is a wonder. Tree rings measured since show that it was carpentered during the reign of Henry VIII, and that it was finished on the eve of the issue of the first *Book of Common Prayer* – the founding document of the Church of England. And to remind us that the Church of England had a Welsh stem, the tomb of Henry's grandfather, Edmund Tudor, first earl of Richmond (1430–1456), stands nearby. It is a panelled chest with a black lid of polished limestone fetched from Dorset. The tomb's position in front of the high altar, a nuisance for clergy, recollects its original place in the Franciscan friary at Carmarthen, whence it was brought when Edmund's grandson shut it down in 1538: one among the thousand or so religious houses in England, Wales, and Ireland which were disbanded on Henry VIII's orders between 1536 and 1541.

Edmund Tudor's wife was Margaret Beaufort, a descendant of Edward III. It was through her that their son Henry's claim to England's throne ran after his victory at Bosworth. David was part of that victory, for in imagination he was the ever-present leader of the *Cymry*, the people of Wales, and it was Bretons and Welshmen who made up the nucleus of his force that defeated Richard in 1485. Henry Tudor now became Henry VII, founder of the dynasty under which, say English historians, and with God's approval, England blossomed as a proud nation with an imperial destiny. Certainly, this was the impression given at the time. Look at this legend on a gold sovereign of Elizabeth I:

> *ELIZABETH D G ANG FRA ET HIB REGINA*
> Elizabeth by the Grace of God Queen of England, France, and Ireland
> *DNO FACTU EST ISTUD ET EST MIRAB IN OCULIS NRIS*
> This is the Lord's doing and it is marvellous in our eyes

Or this on a silver crown of Edward VI:

> *POSUI DEUM ADIVTORE MEUM*
> I have made God my helper

Whoever said religion and politics do not mix?

Our main pastime outside the cathedral was swimming. Whichever beach we went to, there were reminders of David and his world. If we walked south to Porth Clais, we passed a chapel named after St Non, David's mother. At Porth Clais itself were traces of a chapel used by pilgrims to his shrine. If we went west, there was a ruined chapel dedicated to Justinian, one of his companions. A bit further north, among sand dunes at Whitesand Bay, was the site of yet another chapel. The map said it was dedicated to St Patrick. Locals told us that human bones were sometimes washed out by winter storms.

Whitesand was the best swimming place. The forty-minute walk to get there began in a deep lane, set between tall hedge-banks wreathed in honeysuckle, past a farm called Pen Arthur (which had been the childhood home of Thomas Tomkins's stepmother) and a caravan occupied by a family to whose daughter I longed to speak but was always too self-conscious to try. From there it was out onto tussocky common land overlooked by the largest of the rocky knolls, Carn Llidi, and the last mile or so to the beach.

There was a lot to take in when you got there. Up on the nearby headland was a great hunk of rock propped on a slender upright stone, a bit like the raised bonnet of a Flintstone car. The stones were the innards of a prehistoric tomb called Coetan Arthur. (Arthur again – why him?) On the beach itself, very low tides revealed trunks of trees and bones of bear and aurochs from a land that had been drowned thousands of years ago. And there was that chapel dedicated to St Patrick.

Patrick was a fifth-century Briton who worked as a missionary in Ireland. What was he doing here? The short answer is probably nothing, or at least, nothing directly. Patrick got into the story because a clerk at the cathedral called Rhygyfarch (1056–1099) wrote him into it in a biography of David he composed around 1080 – that is, about six hundred years after Patrick's lifetime. Rhygyfarch opened the biography by saying that Patrick settled hereabouts until an angel told him that the place had been assigned to one who was not yet born – David. Patrick was not pleased, but the angel granted him a vision of Ireland, saying that this was to be his promised land. Patrick duly surrendered the site and took ship from Whitesand Bay.

Rhygyfarch's motives for this bit of elaboration were probably several: by depicting one great national saint as the herald of another he was presenting his subject in a way that boosted his standing through a most favourable comparison. The fact that the chapel was built around the same time as Rhygyfarch was writing might even suggest that it was put there to corroborate the story. However, while there is not a smidgeon of evidence to connect the historical Patrick with this part of Britain, there is plenty to connect his world and David's. For one thing (as the angel knew), you can see it: in the right light the Wicklow Mountains are visible from Carn Llidi, while nearby cliffs can be seen from Ireland by mariners coming the other way. This sense of association is reinforced by things found under the chapel, which was put in an existing graveyard where funerals had been taking place since at least the sixth century. In other words, some of those buried here were contemporaries of David, if not of Patrick, and among them were people who went to the grave with Irish customs. Other things give pause. For instance, ocean-going trading ships in the early Middle Ages worked off gently shelving beaches rather than from jetties or docksides. With their long, level keels, shallow draught, and upswept bows and sterns, such vessels could be pushed up beaches by waves when they came to land and floated off by the tide when they departed. Whitesand is such a beach, and sure enough, in the eleventh-century life of David it is called Portus Magnus, 'the great harbour'. Objects found nearby – coins (a lot of coins), Irish metalwork, crucibles for working metal, glass and amber – confirm that it was. Looked at this way, far from living in a marginal place that no one else wanted, David and his community were at the pivot of an international network connecting Ireland, Scotland, Wales, south-west England, and western France.

Whitesand is exposed, and when weather blows from the south-west waves can be large. Keith Wyer, one of our basses, fair-haired, amiable, wore his glasses in the sea, where they were held on by a thick elastic band until the evening when a large wave knocked him over and pulled them off. Keith's mates immediately gathered at the spot and felt around with their feet – but they were only just in their depth, and amid curling rollers and dragging currents there was little chance of finding them. Eventually, they gave up and came in.

Dad now did a strange thing. For a minute or so he stood still, then he walked in a straight line down the beach and out into the surf. When the water was up to his chin, his toes were touching Keith's glasses. Years later, a thought crossed my mind: what was he doing during the quiet minute or so before he set off in a straight line? Had he been praying? St Anthony of Padua is the patron saint of searches for lost objects; did David have a niche role as the patron saint for things lost in surf?

Patrick and David had me a bit foxed. It is near certain that both were real people, but where did they fit – and into what? The story we were told at primary school in the 1950s was nothing like the joined-up world we see now. Back then we were taught that the Romans left Britain at the start of the fifth century, that the English who came after were pagans until St Augustine arrived to convert them, and that areas like Wales had been cut off from the rest of Christendom in the meantime. The O level history curriculum did nothing to amend this, chiefly because it did not start until 1066 and so left the whole thing out. We were left with a blurry impression of the early British church as being a bit like the Galapagos, where everything evolved separately. Presumably this was why we needed a Synod of Whitby, to get things back in step. The isolationist story went back a long way. It suited evangelicals in the days of Edward VI (1547–1553) and Elizabeth (1558–1603) because it allowed them to trace the ancestry of their new reformed Church of England to the early days of Christianity without going through Rome.

After a week in warm sunken lanes, the flitter of butterflies you never saw anywhere near Birmingham, and not a word exchanged with the girl at the caravan, we were sorry to leave. The mood on the bus was a bit like the hollow feeling you got on a 1950s Sunday, when everything was closed, it was raining, and there was nothing but the week ahead. The feeling deepened as we passed in reverse the landmarks that had raised our spirits on the way out: the Towy at Carmarthen, the Black Mountain, Herefordshire's land of slow rivers and wooded valleys. We gave a raucous cheer on a hill as the bus overtook a vehicle that was travelling even slower than we were. Near Leominster there were signs to Ludlow, home of the forgotten Prince Arthur, where his household had been based at the start of the sixteenth century.

Arthur Tudor exemplified the proverb that nothing is more certain than death, and nothing more uncertain than its hour. On the first day of April 1502, he was well, and by the end of the second he was dead. The abruptness posed challenges: the organisers of his obsequies needed time to inform officials, agree plans, summon nobles and bishops, arrange relays of public mourners, and rehearse choristers. Ceremonies to be staged across the best part of a week called for the purchase of timber, canvas, pigments, hundreds of yards of cloth, six thousand pounds of beeswax, and the commissioning of sawyers, joiners, weavers, painters, and chandlers. Hundreds of black cloaks and hoods were needed for members of Arthur's household. Banners, horse trappings, coverings, valances, and palls called for black velvet, damask, gold beaten on buckram, sarsnet, and black silk. A wagon and relays of horses to draw it would be wanted for the procession to Worcester, with accommodation and supplies along the way. Several dozen craftsmen were called to erect and adorn intricate structures to support arrays of candles and heraldic flags.

A few hours after his death, Arthur's organs were removed and replaced with spices. His corpse rested in his chamber for the next twenty days, always watched. On the afternoon of Saturday 23 April, St George's Day, yeomen of the Prince's chamber bore the coffin into the castle hall, whence it was taken in procession the four hundred or so yards to Ludlow's parish church of St Laurence. In the procession were gentlemen of his household, Carmelite and Austin friars from the town's friaries, abbots and priors from surrounding religious houses, Ludlow's parson and chaplains, the prince's Man at Arms and officers, members of Princess Katherine's Spanish household, the bishops of Coventry, Salisbury and Lincoln, and eighty poor men clad in black and bearing candles. Gentlemen and yeomen of the March shires walked behind.

The coffin was taken into the church, where it was set upon on a specially made hearse aglow with candles and heraldic emblems. The coffin rested in the choir overnight, attended by mourners. A *Dirige*, part of matins for the dead, was celebrated in the early hours. Next morning, masses of Our Lady, the Trinity, and the requiem were performed in succession by the bishops of Coventry, Salisbury, and Lincoln. Another *Dirige* was recited in the small hours when vigil again was kept. In the morning, Monday 25 April 1502, after a second requiem, Arthur's corpse was transferred to a black wagon drawn by six heavy horses, and the cortège left for Worcester.

The day was cold, windy, and very wet. Bystanders marvelled at the passing of the great wagon, its hooded outriders, the company of 120 torch bearers, the three bishops, and gentlemen who carried painted banners of the Trinity, Our Lady, and St George. Blazoned pennons bearing symbols of Britain's mythical founders stirred thoughts of a heroic past. Bells of parish churches tolled in salutation. The company paused overnight at Bewdley and continued to Worcester next day. Sir William Uvedale, the head of Arthur's household, rode ahead to ensure that no one entered the city before his master.

At Worcester the coffin was processed through the town. Citizens lined the route but did not make offerings: an epidemic was in progress – very possibly the same mysterious disease that had killed Arthur – and there was fear of contagion. Sir Gruffydd ap Rhys, the master of Arthur's horse, bore a banner embroidered with his lord's arms as the coffin was led into the cathedral precinct by the abbots, priors and monks of religious houses in the March shires. The coffin was received into the cathedral and watched through the night. Around 2 am, the cathedral's monks left their dormitory and processed into the church to celebrate matins for the dead. In shadow and by the glimmer of candles, the dead Prince before them, they began: *Dirige Dominus Deus meus, in conspectu tuo viam meam* (Direct O Lord God my way in thy sight). Later:

> *Requiem aeternam dona eis Domine: et lux perpetua luceat eis.*
> Give them eternal rest O Lord: and let perpetual light shine on them.
> Ant: *Nequando rapiat ut leo animam meam, dum non est qui redimat, neque qui salvum faciat.*
> Ant: Lest he snatch my soul as a Lion, while there is none which may redeem it, nor which may save it.
> V: *A porta inferi.*
> V: From the gates of hell.
> R: *Erue Domine animas eorum.*
> R: Deliver their souls O Lord.

Next morning, perhaps a thousand were present in the cathedral as the three masses were reprised. During the requiem, officers of Arthur's household assisted the surrender of his coat of arms, shield, helm, and sword. In a *coup de théâtre*, Arthur's Man at Arms rode the Prince's caparisoned white courser along the nave and into the choir, all the while holding a downward-tilted poleaxe. The Benedictus was sung as he dismounted, and Uvedale presented him to the Bishop of Lincoln. The Man at Arms offered the horse to the bishop, who gestured his acceptance by touching its muzzle. Later, when Arthur was in the grave and holy water and earth had been sprinkled upon his coffin, Uvedale led members of the household in snapping their staves of office and throwing the pieces into the pit. At the day's end, Arthur's household was disbanded. Seven years on, Arthur's younger brother Henry married his widow, so starting the chain of events that led to the Church of England.

One of those who witnessed these ceremonies was Thomas Cooke, a wealthy gentleman who had been a member of Arthur's household and Ludlow's bailiff in 1489 and 1499. Eleven years later, Thomas made his own will. He asked to be buried in the parish church, where his executors were to 'lay a stone upon me of 2 yards and almost a foot long and one and a half yards broad with three images of laten'. Thomas was describing what we call a monumental brass: a sheet of latten metal (an alloy of copper, tin, lead, and zinc) let into the pavement bearing an engraved memorial. He asked that one image should depict himself; another, his wife; and the third was to represent the *danse macabre*. The dance portrayed encounters between people of all degree with themselves-to-be as cavorting, rotting cadavers. Peasant, merchant, emperor, knight – all must submit to death's equalising power. The cycle had deep roots, but the version Thomas Cooke knew had appeared a few years before in the cloister in the Pardon Churchyard of St Paul's, and had become known as 'the dance of Paul's'. By Cooke's day, knowledge of its images and accompanying verses (put into English by the poet and monk John Lydgate, c.1370–c.1451) had been widened through woodcuts, books, wall-painting, and monuments. Cooke asked that the figure beside him and his wife should have this text in his hand:

> Man behold so as I am now, so shalt thou be
> Gold and silver shall make no plea
> This daunce to defende, but follow me.

The dance fed more images. At Hickleton near Doncaster, three skulls still peer out at you from a barred alcove in the lychgate. Above them is an inscription: *Hodie mihi, cras tibi* – today for me, tomorrow for you.

The point of this tradition of meeting death in person was to bang home the urgency of your need to seek salvation. Life may end at any

moment; be ready. Being ready meant preparing your soul for purgatory: the place or state of punishment between death and the general
judgement. Smaller sins could be forgiven at death through confession
and purged through punishment. Purgatory's mildest pains were said to
be greater than the worst pains on earth, but suffering could be eased
and shortened by prayers and masses. Thomas Cooke's wish to speed
his ordeal is shown by the two priests he hired for two years to sing
Dirige three times a week and masses 'for them that I am indebted to
or have taken any goods wrongfully in buying or selling or in any other
way'. Souls were particularly vulnerable at the moment of death, when
demons might try to intercept them as they left the body. St Michael,
airy saint of high places, was the protector of departing souls, but
to be on the safe side Cooke set the prayers going before he died to
cover his crossing. Thereafter, Cooke left income for a priest to sing
a daily mass for the souls of himself, his wife and children for ninety-
five years.

In later medieval England, then, the living and the dead kept in
touch through community which took in both. Those unable to pay for
priests to sing personal masses could club together to do it jointly. Forebears and benefactors were remembered daily by people in the places
where they had lived. The sight of things given – like the vestments,
cloth of gold copes, and monthly doles to Ludlow's poor bestowed by
Thomas Cooke – stirred thoughts of their givers. When you looked at a
tomb, the image of the person beneath it put you in mind of him or her
in life, and prompted your prayers for their soul.

And yet: a puzzling thing about Arthur Tudor's tomb is that it bears
no image. A monument without a portrayal was a contradiction, so the
first thought must be that an image was provided and that it was later
removed. The lid of the tomb, a flat slab of dark Purbeck stone, suggests a plan to depict him in brass – like Gruffydd ap Rhys (d.1521), his
friend and Master of Horse, the man who bore the Prince's banner at
the funeral, who was buried under a similar Purbeck-lidded monument
nearby. Indeed, it looks as though Gruffydd's tomb was envisaged as a
companion to the tomb of his lord. (The Purbeck slabs add to a sense of
old bonds recollected: the quarry that produced them was on the land
of one of Sir William Uvedale's relatives.) There is another harmonic
here, for Gruffydd's father, Sir Rhys ap Thomas (d.1525), was the man
who earlier had been in charge of Edmund Tudor's monument – the
tomb that was moved to St Davids when his grandson abolished the
Carmarthen Greyfriars. It too was a chest-tomb with a dark Purbeck lid

and a brass image, and in its position before the altar and black marble it recollected the purported tomb of King Arthur himself in Glastonbury Abbey.

There is another possibility: a plan to provide an image that was unfulfilled. The chapel in which Arthur's tomb stands was meant as a place for priests to sing masses for his soul until the end of time. In the event, the priests were silenced within a generation. Scepticism about Purgatory was already simmering in evangelical circles in the 1520s. The Ten Articles of doctrine issued under Henry VIII in 1536 declared Purgatory's existence to be uncertain. Under the government of Arthur's young nephew, King Edward VI, doubt hardened to denial: masses for the dead were declared not merely worthless but unlawful. Purgatory was annulled. Arthur's priests were pensioned off. His chapel was redundant.

Worcester was in the thick of this: its bishop between 1535 and 1539 was Hugh Latimer, who promoted reform and iconoclasm. We do not know when Arthur's tomb was made, but the signs are that it was some years later than the chapel, while its similarities with the nearby tombs of Gruffydd and of King John, who was reburied before the high altar in 1529, point to a date in the later 1520s. When the time came to commission the image, did it coincide with the intensifying attack on prayers for the dead? Did the project lose its path in those few years when the idea of community was redefined, the forgotten prince coming to be symbolised by an unfinished memorial?

This was where I had meant to start, where the Church of England itself started, and in border country – the March between England and Wales, and between one mental world and another. But stuff happens, and the obligations of the living to the dead are again being rethought. Nearly five centuries on, in March 2020, a new virus is in the wild. On the morning of the third Sunday in Lent, the parish choir in which I sing meets as usual to rehearse for matins. The parish is one of only a few left with a choir that still sings prayer-book matins and evensong all the year round. The appointed psalm, Psalm 46, opens 'God is our hope and strength, a very present help in trouble', which seems appropriate in the circumstances. When we reach the verse 'He breaketh the bow, and knappeth the spear in sunder', the organist adds a smouldering low pedal crescendo, which seems to crackle when we reach 'and burneth the chariots in the fire'. The anthem is 'Wash me throughly' by Samuel Sebastian Wesley. (The words are from Psalm 51: 'Wash me throughly from my wickedness'.) The last time we sang it the curate got a laugh when he misread it as 'Wash me thoroughly'. The congregation laughs again today, but this time it is gallows humour.

Early in the evening, we come back to rehearse for choral evensong. Anglican evensong has been described as a home for the hesitant, a service for those who put store by doubt as well as belief. Such people, writes Angela Tilby:

> don't want to be jollied along, made to shake awkward hands with their neighbours, or sway their bodies or clap their hands. They are not looking for sermons or for instruction in the Christian faith. They come for God, I think, relieved that no one is going to get at them. The music is important, of course, but so is what the rhythm of speech and music does for them: that slowing of the heart rate and breathing, the quietening of the mind, the sense of space and mystery and presence.

The word itself – from Middle English *æfentīd* (evening time) – already begins to do that.

The word 'evensong' was in the language before the Reformation, but the man who gave us this office for the tentative was Thomas Cranmer, the youngest son of a minor Nottinghamshire gentry family who was installed as archbishop of Canterbury in 1533 and became England's guide through the early stages of the Reformation. Cranmer drew up the English liturgy of the reformed Church: *The Book of Common Prayer*, published in 1549 and much revised three years later – the edition that abolished Purgatory. The 1552 book never entered general use: Edward VI died seven months after its release, and it was banned by his successor, Mary, who reinstated the Latin rites of the Roman Church and burned Cranmer. The revision nonetheless had lasting effect. After Elizabeth's accession in 1558, the Anglican Church was restored, and the Prayer Book issued in 1559 followed its predecessor in all but a few details.

The matins and evensong of these successive prayer books were derived from the Catholic Liturgy of the Hours, the sequence of prayers recited by all priests at different times of every day. By giving prominence to offices connected with the devotional life of the clergy, Cranmer and his helpers shifted attention of the laity away from the Eucharist. The new prayer book's 'order for Evensong throughout the year' was created by combining parts of vespers and compline, the last two of the canonical hours, and putting their Latin texts into English. Some passages were borrowed (the translations of the Magnificat and Nunc Dimittis, for instance, were taken from a recent devotional collection called *The King's Primer*); others were translated from scratch. William Tyndale's (c.1494–1536) translations of the Bible in the 1520s and 1530s gave a wealth of phrases that remain in daily use: 'signs of the times', 'a moment in time', 'let there be light', 'a law unto themselves', 'filthy lucre', 'the powers that be', 'knock and it shall be opened', 'the spirit is willing but the flesh is weak'. Wherever the words came from they were unified by Cranmer's ear for the ways in which language works and the rhythms of speech. *The Book of Common Prayer* has soaked into the groundwater of English-speaking culture: 'peace in our time', 'the world, the flesh and the devil', 'in the midst of life we are in death', 'ashes to ashes, dust to dust'.

Cranmer considered that his prayer book's purpose was 'the styrring of people to more devotion'; even when it was new its lexis was not exactly everyday. Nowhere do you catch that better than at evensong, where the words have outlasted all efforts to find new ones. That has not been for want of trying: since 1966 there have been at least seventeen attempts to find fresh words for different parts of the Anglican liturgy. Behind that struggle lie differences of aim. Some believe that new forms of service should embody contemporary thinking about faith as well as updated language; others say that old-time religion is as good now as it ever was and all it needs is a better image and simpler words.

Suspicion of tradition and complexity are reflected in the café church movement, in which inherited buildings and forms of worship are abandoned in favour of commercial cafés or community spaces. The church at Kingswood on the northern fringe of Hull, for instance, has no building and no services. Instead, you are invited to 'drop-ins' at a local school. (Anglican leaders have a knack for appropriating outdated jargon.) Kingswood's 'Sunday Sesh' promises 'crafts, mindfulness spaces, reflection spaces, interactive prayer zones, Sunday papers and some great coffee' – a format 'born out of a natural need of people wanting to connect in a way that doesn't mean we have to visit a different planet'.

Back on Planet Cranmer, 6.30 comes and in we go. Arriving in the choir stalls there is the usual quick shuffle of the music into order of need, a glance at the weekly newssheet for the number of the first hymn, and a search for its page during the play-over. Like the morning's psalm, the hymn is topical:

> As now the sun's declining rays
> At eventide descend,
> So life's brief day is sinking down
> To its appointed end.

We sing it to an old Irish tune, wondering when, or if, we will all sing together again.

Next day, Monday 23 March, the Prime Minister orders the closure of playgrounds, libraries, outdoor gyms, and churches. The Archbishops of Canterbury and York suspend public worship. Church House say that baptisms and weddings must cease, and that funerals are to be limited to brief outdoor services with only closest relatives present. Before long, some councils ban even these. This goes further than the last occasion when sacraments were withheld, the interdict imposed on England by Pope Innocent III in 1208 (uncannily, on the same date, 23 March), when baptism and confession for the dying were still permitted. For the first time in maybe fifteen hundred years, you can enter the world without being admitted to the Church and leave it beyond the touch, sound, or sight of anyone who loved you.

And a lot of people are about to leave. In the months ahead, the new virus will be more than a match for Bernardino of Siena (the patron saint of respiratory ailments), run rings around Theobald and Benedict (patron saints of dry coughs), thumb its nose at Edmund King and Martyr (patron saint of pandemics), and outwit St Barbara (patron saint of anaesthesia and intensive care). Politician, airline operator, lockdown sceptic – all will kneel before it. Joseph (patron saint of departing souls) and Anthony of Padua (patron saint of the elderly) will be rushed off their feet. Exercise classes for the old and frail in care homes will be the new *danse macabre*, and since deep breathing in close company for several hours a week is about as close to an ideal environment for transmission as you can get, choir practice is the new Russian roulette. *A Sad Pavan for These Distracted Times* would be fitting to play for the rows of patients with sodden lungs who lie in induced comas like white chrysalises, each awaiting one transformation or another, but live musical performances are now forbidden. If ever there is a return to the way things were, devotees of St Cecilia, patron saint of music, will be among the last to reach it.

It is almost as if God, the Creator of all things, set out to invent a disease to prevent Himself being worshipped. Given the state of the Church of England, one wonders why He went to the trouble. But then, God moves in a mysterious way. Whatever His plan, He made a cracking job of Covid-19.

Part One

PARSONAGE YEARS: 1950–1975

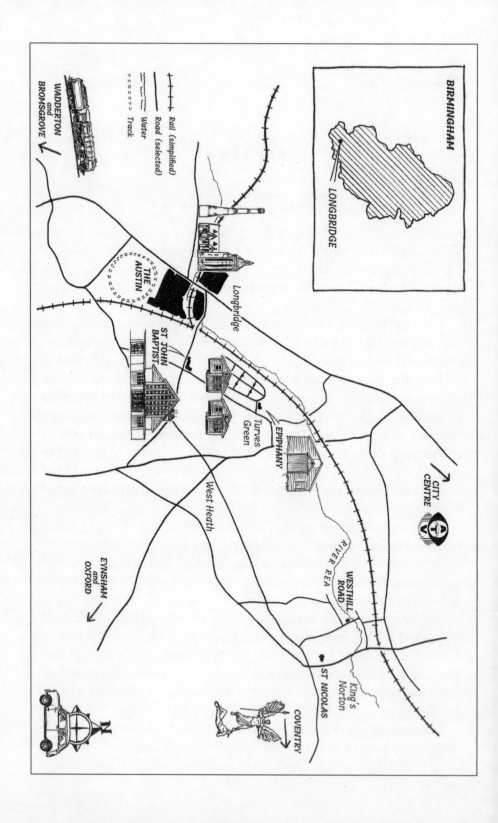

1

BIRTH OF A PARISH: LONGBRIDGE AND BEFORE

'This is a Church paper. We hope you will be glad to receive it as a link (or contact) with your Church.' So began the first issue of *Contact*, the Longbridge Church Monthly, published in April 1956, four pages, price twopence.

On page three was an artist's impression of the new church, adjoining hall, and vicarage to be built on land where Longbridge Lane, Turves Green, and Culmington Road met. The church was to be dedicated to St John the Baptist, Jesus's herald. Brick-walled, an undivided space under a continuous roof, marked by a lateral tower capped by gables sheathed in copper, it recalled the Festival of Britain. Readers were told, 'The new vicarage is "nearing completion" – something which it appears to have been doing for some time. First started at the end of 1954, begun again in April 1955, and still far from finished in March 1956, it is hoped that this job is not a fair sample of British building industry at its fastest and most efficient.'

The handover was eventually scheduled for 26 May. When the day came, it was still not finished. We moved in anyway. The builders eventually struck camp in mid June, leaving mashed-up surroundings, ideal for making dens, dugouts, and other activities forbidden to an eight-year-old in a proper garden.

The site was a few yards back from a sunken lane, beside land earmarked for the new church. The emerging complex was a part of a diocesan campaign to establish new parishes in outlying parts of Birmingham where estates had been spreading since the war. The campaign was called 'Circles without Centres'. Fresh paint and optimism were in the air.

Longbridge's new vicarage was a copybook post-war design. It stood for economy and egalitarianism. No front and back stairs, no fancy materials, no china closet, no chapel, nor even a bell cote, and no ostentation. The days when a new parsonage might be one of the most elegant buildings in a parish were gone. But tradition was kept by putting it next to the church, to enable the parson to come and go for daily offices without taking up too much of his time, and its layout reflected the underlying fact that a parsonage is both a workplace and a dwelling. The copybook said that the two should be linked by an entrance that is welcoming but keeps the functions apart. At Longbridge this was achieved by a glass-fronted lobby facing the street which enabled passers-by to see into the central bay of the front half of the house. The entrance was put towards one end, opposite the door of the parson's study, the idea being that someone wishing to meet the parson could do so without coming into contact with anyone else in the family.

A parson's study is for private interviews, small meetings, administrative tasks, books (usually, a lot of books), preparation for services, and storage of robes. Longbridge's study was lit by windows on two sides, one of which looked out on the west end of the church, the other into the back garden. My father put his desk in the angle between the windows. Sermons, letters, *Contact*, and, in due course, newspaper articles and broadcasts were written upon its enormous dark-polished surface. It was so large that to move it you had to take it apart, and when you did that, stencilled lettering on its underneath reminded you of the late 1940s when furniture makers recycled wartime crates.

Other rooms followed the post-war vicarage norm: at the other end of the house were two rooms for family use and a kitchen which had a back door into a small service yard. Upstairs were four bedrooms with sleeping space for up to seven people. The Commissioners reckoned on a notional standard clerical family of five. The additional space was intended for occasional visitors like visiting preachers; at various times ours became the lodging for a visiting clergyman from Nigeria, and a member of the Committee of 100 who arrived in mysterious circumstances, being either disowned by her family or sought by Special Branch, or possibly both.

The floor area of the living room was about a quarter larger than an average new-build house. This was to give the parson space in which to offer hospitality to parishioners. The Commissioners emphasised that the large room was not meant to be a substitute for the parish meeting room, but rather to recognise that some kinds of gathering work better in informal surroundings. On Friday evenings, there was often an 'At Home', when a dozen or so parishioners arrived simply to get to know each other. Each kind of meeting made its own sort of sound; I learned to tell a marriage preparation group by its hum and laughter. The fact that many people came through the vicarage made it a collecting point for forgotten umbrellas, gloves, and hats.

The 1950s Church of England was still a coal-fired organisation, so the opportunity to provide the new vicarage with central heating and insulation was passed over in favour of a coal fire in the living room, a coke-fuelled range in the kitchen which gave off choking fumes when you opened it, and two-bar wall-mounted electric fires in some other rooms. None of these arrangements ever actually warmed a room, and in winter they were boosted by a paraffin heater. The living room fire was a proprietary system that was meant to draw air through an underfloor channel. The air supply was supposedly controlled by a knob in front of the grate, but for months it produced little more than smoke. I walked in one day and found the architect, the foreman, my father, and several others standing in a semi-circle looking at it in silence. At length, one of them knelt down, reached into the underfloor duct, felt about and pulled out a brick that had been left behind by the installers.

A parsonage differed from an ordinary dwelling in the further respect that it was meant to form part of the allowance that enabled the parson to live while doing his job. A clergyman in the 1950s was not an employee but the holder of an office who received a stipend rather than a salary. The difference is that a salary represents payment for work done, whereas a stipend is intended to enable someone to fulfil a role the worth of which cannot be measured. A clergy stipend was also supposed to reflect the fact that the parsonage is provided free of rent, water charges, repairs, insurance and council tax (in those days, rates), and that approved parochial expenses are reimbursed. This improved on arrangements in the nineteenth century, when most clerical incomes depended on the state of agriculture, and rose and fell accordingly.

For comparison with Longbridge, consider the vicarage into which my godparents, Stuart and Brenda Blanch, moved four years before. Stuart and my father had met during the war, when their paths crossed in the RAF. As newly married undergraduates in 1946, they shared a house on the outskirts of Oxford, where Stuart went on to serve his curacy. By 1951, he was looking to take his next step. The living of Eynsham was vacant, and Canon Julian Thornton-Duesbery (1902–1985), the Principal of Wycliffe Hall, invited him to consider it. Stuart had studied at Wycliffe Hall, the living was in Wycliffe's gift, and Thornton-Duesbury's suggestions were 'not to be taken lightly'. Stuart and Brenda caught a bus and went to look.

They found a limestone village beside the Thames. Before the Reformation, Eynsham was the site of a religious house, of which the scholar-theologian Ælfric (c.955–c.1010) had been abbot. Streets and house-plots ghosted the outline of an early medieval town beside the abbey; the parish church was on the boundary between the two. Having explored it, Stuart and Brenda went in search of the vicarage, which Thornton-Duesbury said might seem 'a bit unwelcoming'. They found it behind lofty elms and a wall with gates at either end. Passing through, they were faced by a three-storey mansion of c.1707, since doubled in volume, with large outbuildings, in overgrown grounds. The front door was up a flight of twelve steps at the base of a full-height pedimented central porch.

Stuart and Brenda Blanch and family with Phyllis Sutton (left) and visitors in front of Eynsham vicarage, October 1953

Houses like this were sometimes built by clergy themselves, back in days when rural clergy were on a par with minor aristocracy. Their upkeep was challenging, and if neglected, even briefly, expensive dilapidations could ensue. Faced with a decaying parsonage, up until the 1850s it was not unknown for an incumbent to sue the estate of his predecessor for the costs of its repair. The previous incumbent at Eynsham was a bachelor, who over the years had retreated into two or three rooms and abandoned the rest. There was no electricity, gas only on the ground floor, no bathroom. Beetle attack in the basement kitchen was so advanced that cupboards and shelves crumbled at the touch. Cobwebs hung in great black swags over the Queen Anne central staircase. Window frames rotted. Momentary dark traces on the edge of vision marked the darting of rats. With three children under five, and a likely stipend of around five hundred pounds a year, this did not look promising. But after thought, prayer, and an assurance from Thornton-Duesbery that electricity would be installed, Stuart accepted. Even so, on arrival only three rooms were habitable, the worm-ridden basement kitchen was unchanged, and although Thornton-Duesbery had kept his word about electrical wiring, no electricity yet ran through it. For the first nine months, the Blanches took their baths in the homes of sympathetic parishioners.

Eynsham vicarage was great for children: it had big grounds, trees to climb, and a coach house with a real cart in it on which you could sit and imagine you were riding. But on balance, Longbridge's vicarage seemed the better deal. Despite its slow beginning, it had a bathroom, warm water came out of the taps, and the lights worked. Leafing back through *Contact* is as good a way as any to recall some of the things that went on in and around it, and how the parish took shape.

Within living memory, Longbridge had been pasture interspersed with heath, bordered by old hedges, lines of oaks, and streams that cut through red earth. Hardly anyone lived there, and the few who did dwelt in a thin scatter of isolated farms, some of which were enclosed by moats that went back to the Middle Ages. The name came from a farm beside a bridge across the little River Rea, which with its causewayed approaches looked quite long. The causeway-bridge carried a road connecting Birmingham's centre, seven miles to the north, and Bromsgrove, a market town six miles to the south.

The original boundary of Bromsgrove's parish was forty miles long and surrounded a substantial tract of north Worcestershire. Very likely it was the ghost of some Anglo-Saxon sub-kingdom; in the later Middle Ages, subsidiary chapels were planted to serve parishioners who lived in its far-flung parts. One of them was at King's Norton, a former royal manor two miles from Longbridge where a large church of red sandstone with a tall steeple overlooked a village green. It was dedicated to St Nicolas, and in 1846 it became a parish church in its own right,* with Longbridge inside its bounds. The Longbridge district was two miles

---

* So did a lot of other places. On the principle of binary fission, further parishes formed from St Nicolas, Kings Norton, included St Mary Moseley and St Paul Balsall Heath (1853); St Agnes Cotteridge (1916); and parts of Christ Church Yardley Wood, All Saints Kings Heath, The Ascension Stirchley, St Francis Bournville, and St Mary Magdalen Hazelwell.

from St Nicolas, but since few people lived there, it was not felt necessary to provide a chapel for their ease. The only faith group to come to
Longbridge before the Great War were the Quakers, who in the 1870s
built a meeting-house on Longbridge Lane.

In the later nineteenth century, a number of Birmingham's firms relocated from its smoky, densely settled centre to purpose-built premises
on the edge. An example was the cocoa and chocolate business of the
Quaker brothers George and Richard Cadbury, which from the 1870s
was moved by stages to a greenfield site between Selly Oak and Stirchley. The site had good access by canal and rail. George Cadbury added a
purpose-built village to house the workforce and called it Bournville. In
1894, this example was before William White and Frederic Impey, partners in the printing firm of White and Pike, who decided to establish
an out-of-town works to pursue a recently invented process of colour
printing onto tin-plate boxes. Impey and his family already lived in
Longbridge. He and White, like George Cadbury, were Quakers, and
the three knew each other through political and philanthropic activity.
Impey and White took a leaf out of the Cadbury book and put their
new factory at a nodal point for road and rail transport by the bridge
over the Rea, opposite Longbridge Farm. It immediately became known
as the Longbridge Works; it soon failed, but in 1906 the vacant premises
were taken over by an engineer, Herbert Austin. By 1918, Austin had
20,000 workers; by 1956, 'the Austin' was the biggest car plant in Europe.

One of many challenges the Austin company faced during the Great
War was how to minimise the need for its employees to spend a large
part of each day trekking to and from distant lodgings. Local newspapers carried notices inviting householders in surrounding places to rent
spare rooms. Hostels were built. In 1917, Austin took a step towards a
more permanent solution by buying two farms, and laying out a garden
village of some 250 timber houses bought in from the United States. The
estate was laid out with drainage, gas, mains water, surfaced roads, and
avenues of trees. By the end of the war, around a thousand people lived
there, and although Birmingham's City Council saw the project as temporary, and viewed wooden houses with deep misgivings, it was all still
there forty years later, by when the trees and families had grown. The
estate remains now, a fragment of Michigan hybridised with England.

Such a community evidently did merit its own chapel, and one
was duly provided – a wooden hut (thousands of which were being
sold off by the government at the end of the war), leased to the parish,
that became the Church of the Epiphany. The first service was held on

Christmas Day 1918, and when the parish church of St John the Baptist was consecrated in December 1957, its congregation formed the nucleus of the new parish.

During the years between, the Epiphany had been served by clergy from King's Norton, latterly by my dad, who since his arrival as curate in 1952 had been assigned to this part of the parish. The curate's house in King's Norton was a 1920s semi. It stood on Westhill Road, a hillside lane which near its crest was shaded by oaks and elms and ran down to the little River Rea. From the 1890s, Westhill Road was gradually suburbanised with brick villas. They were all put on one side; fields on the other side were merged to make a park, and although a row of war-time prefabs stood on its edge the area still had a sense of greenwood. Greener still was Wychall Lane, which led towards West Heath and Longbridge and was overhung by ancient trees. Since Longbridge was several miles away, my dad spent a lot of time walking or cycling. I sometimes walked with him. It was a journey of binaries: along old footpaths and roads so new the Ordnance Survey had not yet mapped them, past houses half built and others falling down, and a question about where you were when you got there: Longbridge had no obvious centre, no natural edges, and until then its only unifying feature was the Austin factory that had brought it into being, where nobody lived. But then, a parish is as much people as territory.

Epiphany people included stalwarts, eccentrics, young and old. Among the stalwarts was Jim McCracken, a toolmaker and Old Time Dance enthusiast who was one of the church wardens. Jim had been in the area since 1930. He was friendly, youthful, the church's treasurer, and helped organise the estate's football club. Then there was Mrs Tristram, quiet and self-effacing, who for years had delivered King's Norton's parish magazine to its outlying parishioners, and now saw to the distribution of *Contact*. Mrs Tristram had a round face that always wore at least a half smile, and until Christopher Scarf arrived in 1955 she played the piano for services.

Chris (or 'The Scraff' as he became privately known in the vicarage) was twenty-one when he offered to play for a carol service. His studies at Oxford had been curtailed by conscientious objection to military national service, which led to his service as an orderly in a local hospital whence from time to time he brought glamorous nurses. Chris was fun, a talented musician who for the next four years raised and trained a choir until Ely Cathedral recruited him to be its deputy organist. Musically, however, he was a traditionalist, and he was aghast when my father invited Geoffrey Beaumont to preach. Like others, we shall meet Beaumont near this book's end. For the moment, it is enough to say that he, too, was a gifted musician who, in the words of Malcolm Williamson, was creating 'a deep incision in the face of contemporary church music'. While working as a curate in London's East End, he had written *A Twentieth-Century Folk Mass* which drew on cabaret, music hall, and American stage musical. It went round the world, and no amount of huffing, puffing, and academic disapproval 'had been able to stem its exuberant progress'. Beaumont's hymns, likewise, were 'distinguished pieces of writing without a trace of vulgarity in the usual sense, but are vulgar in the 1611 sense'. In the 1950s, the discovery that popular music and inherited texts could be combined was joyous to many but discomfiting to those who equate tradition with repetition, or for whom the worldly in worship is a kind of sacrilege. Hence the slash across the face. A few minutes before Beaumont arrived, a Woodbine in the corner of his mouth, Chris made the gesture of a handshake which might crush Beaumont's fingers.

Moving to the eccentrics, I think of the man whose fixed stare used to terrify me during evensong, the piano teacher whose limited success had to do with the force with which she hit the hands of young pupils with a ruler if they made mistakes, and the famous Miss Leech, who until a few years before had run a well-attended school in her house on Hawkesley Drive. Miss Leech had been present at the first service in the Epiphany in 1918. She was unmistakable outdoors: tall, with a slight forward lean, conspicuous in a dark green mac and red beret. Close to, the combination of her beret, long face, and a slight side-to-side quiver of her head reminded me of a hen, which was uncanny because along with her four cats she shared her house with poultry.

Before Dad's arrival, the Epiphany had been served for several years by a retired clergyman, and before that by Wilbert Awdry (1911–1997), who from 1940 to 1946 had been King's Norton's curate. I became aware of Awdry around 1953, by when he was vicar of Emneth in Norfolk's fenland. We were told that *The Three Railway Engines* (1945) had begun in a series of stories he thought up in 1943 to entertain his son during an attack of measles.* Critics since have grumbled about plodding writing and alleged class and gender typing (disorderly proletarian trucks, male locomotives, female coaches). It is questionable whether the first books

---

* It may or may not be relevant that the given name of King's Norton's vicar during Awdry's curacy was Thomas (Shelton-Dunn), and that he left in 1948.

would have held young audiences as they did without their illustrations, but they were well-crafted and work well when read aloud. Their world is not the golden sunset of steam railways, but an ordered, imagined England of neatly kept farms and villages, stations staffed by willing employees, diligent technicians, capable managers, and locomotives willing to be good pupils. It was in contrast to experience of the real British Railways, which so surprised some American visitors to the new vicarage that their perplexity made it to the front page of *Contact*:

> The Americans wanted to know why we put up with inaccurate information and routing, with poor and discourteous service from railway personnel, and with trains that are filthy dirty.
>
> That the long-suffering British public does put up with these things cannot be denied ... But why do we stand for it? ... If the travelling public asserted its rights and insisted on proper service there would be a miraculous change. But no. We go passively, apathetically on our weary way. As the Americans used to say of us during the war: 'These British sure know how to take punishment.'

Awdry was a real railway scholar and industrial historian. He belongs in that tradition of clerics who combined a specialised interest with religious calling – like John Michell (1724–1793), rector of St Michael, Thornhill, first proponent of black holes and seismic waves; the parson-naturalist Francis Orpen Morris (1810–1893); Northumberland's county historian, John Hodgson (1779–1845); or Charles Druce Farrar (1856–1932), author of *Birdroom and Aviary: Trials and Triumphs of a Yorkshire Parson* (1927), whose delight was the keeping and breeding of exotic finches. Many factors favoured their pursuits. Clergy were social equals of medical men, lawyers, gentlemen landowners, and industrialists who formed philosophical societies. They held degrees, in subjects like history, mathematics, or natural sciences, as well as classics or theology. Parsonages provided stable vantage points from which to make observations in different fields – natural history, meteorology, astronomy, railway photography, the list goes on – and over a term of years. Most of them had space for collections, laboratories, and darkrooms. Clergy were free to organise their own time, and the intellectual challenges of, say, place names or botany offered more intellectual stimulation than might otherwise be forthcoming in remote parishes. Place names and parishes often went together; a number of the first county studies of place names were written by clerics; the names of their parishes – France Lynch, say, or Yardley Gobion, of both of which the historian, Celticist and parson Arthur Wade-Evans (1875–1964) was incumbent – are poetic in themselves.

I read *The Three Railway Engines* while recovering from chicken pox, possibly in the same room in which the stories had first been told. The stories made immediate sense. This was not because of the illustrations' brochure colours, or the ways in which the engines' different personalities were visualised, or even (looking back) the artful way in which different parts of an imagined pre-war England were edited together.* Rather, it was because when the window was open they formed an extension of the world I was actually in – the ringing of shunted trucks, trains passing on the line from Birmingham to Gloucester (about which Awdry later co-wrote an academic study), locomotives stuck on the Lickey incline, the few days in the year when the smell of lilac drifted in, and the ceremony of lamplighting. A lamp post stood outside, and each evening towards dusk a lamplighter arrived by bicycle with a ladder and rod balanced on his shoulder. He used the rod to pull a chain to open the supply of gas, which took flame from a pilot light. Around sunrise he returned to shut the gas off. The ladder – a slender isosceles triangle, just long enough to rest on the crossbar – was carried in case anything needed to be fixed. The thing about the chain was its sound: when it was pulled, it made a gentle, silvery chime; on evenings when the bellringers practised, the silver mingled with King's Norton's ring of ten.

Across in Longbridge, the new parish took shape. Its emergence from the world of Anglican process was slow. The first step involved a formal recommendation from King's Norton's parochial church council (PCC) and the diocese that Longbridge should become a Statutory District; that is, no longer part of the existing parish of King's Norton. When this was finalised, the proposal was sent to the Church Commissioners, who

---

* The visual history of the early railway books was intricate. A different artist was hired to illustrate the first edition of each of the first three, and their respective contributions have sometimes been confused. C. Reginald Dalby illustrated the third in the series (*James the Red Engine*, 1948), and went on to illustrate eight more, until his relationship with Awdry broke down. In parallel, Dalby replaced William Middleton's muted artwork for the first edition of *The Three Railway Engines* (1945), and in result has been credited with the overall look of the series down to 1956. This is fair, but much of that spirit and style came from the work of Reginald Payne (confusingly, another Reginald), who illustrated the first edition of the impetuous but optimistic *Thomas the Tank Engine* (1946). It was Payne who introduced the brighter colours and more stylised eye expressions that came to characterise the whole of the early canon.

spent some months thinking about it. The Church Commissioners then prepared legislation which joined a queue of parliamentary business awaiting attention. Next, when the new church was completed and consecrated for worship, the Commissioners prepared further legislation to give the Statutory District the status of an independent parish. When this point was reached in February 1958, the Commissioners were still havering over part of its boundary. In Longbridge itself, the emergence of the parish as a community can be watched in the forming of clubs for young people, the recruitment of sidesmen, events, visiting preachers, the creation of routines, a manner in worship, music, and atmosphere.

Stuart, meanwhile, had left Eynsham and gone back to Wycliffe Hall to be its vice-principal. Here we note that he was being placed on a particular path. The normal career itinerary for a parson runs through a small number of parishes, perhaps with some additions like an honorary canonry or special chaplaincy towards the end. However, the route to high office did not then usually pass through many parishes. Rather, after serving a curacy, and perhaps a year or two as a parish priest, it was common for men destined for greater things to be called back into academic life, typically as an Oxbridge college chaplain or as a principal or vice-principal in a theological college. Stuart's early return to Wycliffe Hall suggests that he had already been singled out for preferment.

Stuart's gentle sense of humour was a valuable ice-breaking tool which enabled him to pursue the Pauline objective of being all things to all men. He sometimes brought groups of ordinands to Longbridge for a taste of parish life. On one occasion, their visit coincided with the public baptism service, when once a month up to twenty babies and their families would be gathered at the font with a large congregation in support. When they reached the individual baptisms, my father turned to Stuart and asked if he would like to do some of them – perhaps in turns? Thinking perhaps that this was a task best left to the parish priest, he tactfully declined. 'No, no,' he said. 'You wash and I'll dry.'

Back in Oxford, the Blanches now lived at 4 Blackhall Road. It was narrow but tall – I think on four floors, which meant that moving around usually involved stairs. After the initial shock of Eynsham vicarage, Brenda had enjoyed the thriving friendships of its parish, the village's legendary families like the Pimms, and missed them when they returned to Oxford. No parishioners called at Blackhall Road, there was next to no garden, Stuart was out in college for much of the time, and a student and his wife were occupying the top floor. Their dog missed Eynsham so much that he kept walking the eight miles back to it, on

one occasion turning up during a meeting of the PCC. Nonetheless, for
a visitor, there was a kind buoyancy about the place. Susan, the eldest
daughter, was already a formidably accomplished pianist; her chromatic
scales a sixth apart might thunder out from the next room. Meals in the
basement kitchen began with a grace sung in canon, which after hearing several entries you could pick up and join. And there was Stuart's
voice. I loved its warmth, and the sense of shared feeling he brought to
whomever he was talking.

The journeys back to Longbridge ran through Long Compton,
Great Rollright, and Alderminster, villages Shakespeare knew from
journeying between Stratford and London, where the limestone walls
of churches are pale yellow and ginger. But around the age of ten I had
read no Shakespeare. The road itself had an essentialist being. It was
lined by elms. On the back seat of Chris Scarf's elderly Ford Popular,
wherein rust enabled you to watch the spinning nearside rear wheel, it
was the elms that held me.

And so vicarage years began to turn. There were no set working
hours. A conscientious parson might work all day and on into the
evening. Before a holiday, Dad would be up into the small hours, trying
to anticipate tasks and duties so that the parish would run without him.
Weekends were busy; there were four or five services on a Sunday, so we
ate Sunday lunch on Saturday. Christmas was wearing, a time of touring schools, hearing the same hymns, readings, and random inflections
('And in *those* days . . .') over and over again, and trying to counter the
commercialisation that dragged a liturgical season that did not begin
until Christmas Eve ever further back into autumn.

Neither the diocese nor the stipend then took account of the contribution made by a vicar's wife. Mum answered the incessant phone,
triaged messages, provided food and drink for visitors, talked to one
parishioner if Dad was tied up with another, coped with the unforeseen
(a beggar, someone distressed on the doorstep, a call from someone in
crisis), entertained, and accommodated visitors, some of whom stayed
for weeks on end. All this, and more, was done in tandem with her own
work as a drama teacher. One of the few occasions I saw her really angry
was when a local newspaper referred to her as 'the wife of the vicar of
Longbridge'.

In the early days, young mothers arrived on the vicarage doorstep
asking to be 'churched'. Irrespective of whether a family went to church,
there was a widespread belief among industrial workers (usually passed
down from mother to daughter) that after childbirth a woman must

undergo the purificatory rite of churching before she could go out shopping or enter other people's houses. 'Are we somewhere back in the age of Black Magic?' *Contact* asked, going on to explain that churching was an expression not of cleansing, but of thanks. The doorstep was also a place to collect malapropisms, as from those who arrived asking to be added to the 'electrical roll'.

From the first, my dad had had the help of a lay reader, Ernest Hobson, who moved about with an air of solemnity and spoke in a gravelly voice. In complete contrast was Peter Wagner, who joined us as curate in the autumn of 1960. Peter's arrival in the vicarage was like a gust of wind, sometimes accompanied by a line from last night's *Goon Show*. Peter was an aficionado of Maigret, and often cast himself as Lucas, the fictional detective's right-hand man, calling out '*Patron!*' as he breezed into the study. He was extraordinarily agile. After Chubby Checker released 'The Twist', Peter astonished members of the youth club by dancing it while gradually leaning back until the back of his head nearly touched the floor. I loved him for his ebullience, frankness, and easy manner.

Peter Wagner, Longbridge, 1961

The lay volunteers without whom no parish runs mostly had day jobs, which means that planning, discussion, fundraising, and liaison with other denominations and organisations were generally done in the evening. For an individual, this might occupy one or two evenings a month; for the parson, it meant almost every evening. And while he was out, the calls came in. Some of the calls at all hours, I now realise, were from families in distress. Nothing about this was said to me directly at the time, and nothing at all, ever, by my father; but as I grew older, and from things hinted by my mother, I gradually pieced together the fact that in some homes there was violence. Among the wife beaters, I now see, were fathers of great outward rectitude. Not all the aggressors were men. Periodically, we went to lunch with a clergyman and his family in a neighbouring parish. I never knew how his wife tormented him, but plainly in some way she did, and I came to suppose that our visits were contrived for peacekeeping purposes.

Another kind of distress concerned men who were gay and who until the decriminalisation of homosexual acts in 1967 were at their wits' ends to know what to do it about it. Several of them became frequent visitors – the vicarage was a safe, emotionally warm place, and great friendships ensued. There was one man whom I admired greatly – a talented pianist and composer. I loved his visits and was puzzled when they stopped. I was told that he had killed himself.

Misfortune attended another visitor whom at the time I took simply to be a family friend. This was the Rev Richard Amphlett, who in the early 1950s was rector of Bourton-on-the-Hill, a parish in the Cotswolds overlooking Moreton-in-Marsh. Richard was aristocratic and a little eccentric in manner, with large eyes set far apart (the better, it seemed, to triangulate you), a buoyant smile and an infectious enthusiasm that was occasionally interrupted by a stammer. I was told that I had been named after him, but had no idea why, or how he and my parents had met. I had no idea, either, why Richard's marriage to Joan Gibbs in late 1955 should have led to his departure from Bourton-on-the-Hill. Until the year before, Joan had been the wife of Norman Gibbs, Fellow of All Souls, and Oxford's Chichele Professor of the History of War. Gibbs's affections had passed to a young departmental secretary whom he soon married after divorcing Joan. In 1955, the Church of England had not yet reached the point at which it measured the moral worth of a relationship by its quality rather than the marital status of its parties; by choosing Joan, Richard hastened the end of his own parish ministry.

On the outer edge of things were occasional diocesan visitors like archdeacons and of course the bishop himself. Sidney Harvie-Clark, Archdeacon of Birmingham, spoke in a deep, rapid, staccato way. When he led the Lord's Prayer, he said it in a kind of arc, starting low and quiet, rising to a high point, and then subsiding again. He was also tone deaf, and if asked by Chris upon what note he would like to intone the responses, would reply tartly, 'You can give me any note you like but I shan't sing it.' Archdeacons undertake tasks to do with parochial and diocesan governance, buildings, and property; they are key players in the operation of faculty jurisdiction and sit on committees like the Diocesan Parsonages Board. At Parsonages Board meetings, when a new vicarage was under discussion, Harvie-Clark's abiding interest was in its drains and plumbing; it was rumoured that in his own parsonage in Harborne there was a poltergeist that periodically flushed the lavatory.

Birmingham's bishop from 1953 was Leonard Wilson, a north countryman whose career thus far had taken in soldiering during the Great War, curacy of the parish of St Michael in Coventry, teaching in Cairo, parish work in the Durham coalfield during the hungry thirties, and the deanery of Hong Kong. In 1942, he became Bishop of Singapore, which was seized by the Japanese shortly after his arrival. An operation by Allied special forces in the following year led the Japanese to suspect that they had received local help; Wilson was among many who were interned and tortured. At the end of the war, his influence on captors and captured alike lifted him to worldwide view.

Leonard Wilson, Bishop of Birmingham 1953–1969

Wilson found the Diocese of Birmingham short-handed. Its parishes were being overwritten by new housing, and after the long episcopate of his predecessor Ernest Barnes, its clergy and congregations were divided. Barnes's science-based opinions about miracles had estranged him from evangelicals and Anglo-Catholics, while the defeat of Nazism placed his eugenicist views in a light that increasingly divided him from scientists. Wilson tackled both by fixing on pastoral and social purpose. St John's Longbridge was one of the first results. Its pastoral success, coupled with like-mindedness with my father on issues such as the ordination of women (for), capital punishment (against), or whether there is a moral as well as practical dimension in the possession of nuclear weapons (there is), made for friendship.

Wilson's biographer depicts a man in a love–hate relationship with the establishment, wary of ecclesiastical formality, liable to poke fun at false pomp, uncomfortable in committees. Wilson himself said his faith was not ready-made: 'I've always been questioning.' Unlike many visiting clergy who simply ignored children, Leonard actually liked them and would go out of his way to talk. Characteristics that came across were informality and spontaneity. The Leonard Wilson who was never happier than when in crumpled old clothes, incognito at a cricket match, was the same man who appeared in coped splendour each November before the nation and the Queen. His wartime experience identified him with the Royal British Legion and the Burma Star Association, and from 1956 until 1968 he led the Anglican contribution to the annual British Legion Festival of Remembrance at the Albert Hall. My father was his chaplain on these occasions, from which he returned with tales about the sign language used by the bandmaster to keep the broadcast on schedule.

From 1958, a third notable figure in our circle was Nicolas Stacey, who arrived from a curacy in Portsmouth to be Leonard's domestic chaplain. Stacey was famous as a former Olympic sprinter, who when at Oxford studying history had been a member of the extraordinary athletics team that included Chris Brasher, Roger Bannister, and Chris Chataway. Stacey told us that running came naturally to him; it was said that before running the 220 he liked to light a cigarette and hand it to a colleague, who handed it back when he crossed the finish.

Nick came from a wealthy family; his first career had been in the Royal Navy; his wife was the daughter of Shropshire's lord lieutenant; he had presence: a high forehead with plastered-down hair above, large ears, and a crinkly smile that revealed a slight but eye-catching gap between his front teeth. He was forthright and impatient for progress. If you were in his vicinity, you knew there was work to be done and no time to lose in doing it. When he left Portsmouth, the local newspaper described him as the 'initiator of numerous functions and events'.

Within weeks of his arrival, he was embarked on a project to reach tens of thousands of non-churchgoing people in a new way. 'Most parish magazines are pathetic,' he said. Many of them had remained unchanged for seventy years, and they were uneconomic to produce for fewer than five hundred readers. His plan was to produce a monthly small-format newspaper of twelve pages, the outer eight of which would cover significant regional and national issues in simple, down-to-earth style, with an inner four pages specific to each parish that joined the scheme. To join, a parish needed to take a minimum of one thousand copies. When *Birmingham Christian News* first appeared, he pulled no punches about the state of the Church: 'At the moment, her leaders, both clerical and lay, have their feet buried in history and their heads buried in the sand. The result – almost total paralysis.'

Nicolas Stacey

Such frankness made him an inspiring leader, and an unsettling subordinate. At the outset, around thirty-five out of Birmingham's 180 parishes joined the newspaper syndicate, Longbridge and *Contact* among them. A notable absentee was the city-centre church of St Martin in the Bull Ring, Birmingham's original parish church, whose rector, Bryan Green, a noted preacher and evangelist, was known as the Anglican Billy Graham. A few weeks after the launch, Stacey gave a talk to the Birmingham Rotary Club at which Green was present. Behind his winning manner, Green considered that Stacey was on his turf, and while Stacey was pitching *Birmingham Christian News* to the city's businessmen Green murmured an aside to his neighbour which caused Nick to turn and tell him to 'shut up'.

Nick did not stay long. He was eager for challenges, and in 1960 he was given a large one when Mervyn Stockwood, the Bishop of Southwark, invited him to revivify the urban parish of Woolwich. That is where we shall meet him again, but his impact on us before he left was strong for another reason. In the closing months of the war, he had served as a midshipman on the battleship HMS *Anson*, which with other Allied vessels had accepted the Japanese surrender of Hong Kong, and proceeded to Tokyo Bay for the formal Japanese capitulation on 2 September 1945. Several weeks later, he visited Hiroshima and walked its ruins. Thirteen years on, he was one of the few people in the land who had seen at first-hand what a nuclear weapon does, and what follows.

Nuclear weapons had increased in potency a thousand-fold since 1945, and even before we moved from the Epiphany to St John's, an invitation to a public meeting to hear from scientists about the effects of the hydrogen bomb was one of two international issues that had appeared on the front page of *Contact*. The other was an appeal for funds to support the legal defence and families of 156 opponents of apartheid accused of high treason in South Africa. The items were put before Longbridge parishioners in successive months in 1957. It was fitting that they appeared side by side: apartheid and the nuclear threat were to be defining concerns of the next thirty-five years, and they had entangled roots. South Africa's National Party claim that many of those it had put on trial were communists mapped onto two beliefs then widely held in the West: that Christianity and communism were incompatible, and the State-generated idea that the Cold War was a campaign against evil.

The two issues were further united in the person of Canon Lewis John Collins, whose campaigning causes since the end of the war had included relief for starving Europe, Anglo-German reconciliation, the abolition of capital punishment, and now – and in tandem – unilateral nuclear disarmament, and the Defence and Aid Fund to support victims of apartheid. Since 1948, Collins had been a canon of St Paul's Cathedral. Before that he was dean of Oriel College, Oxford, where he was my father's tutor. The two had kept in close touch and become firm friends. Wherever Collins went politically, my dad was usually at his elbow. This became evident in 1958, when Collins became the founding chairman of the Campaign for Nuclear Disarmament (CND), and came to Longbridge to preach against apartheid.

Jacquetta Hawkes, Sir Richard Acland (co-founder of Christian Action) and Canon John Collins (centre) marching from Aldermaston to London, 1959

Christianity for Collins was about action, not meetings. In the pulpit, he drew a congregation in with his energy and plain words. In private, he was much the same. Andrew Brown and Linda Woodhead might have had him in mind when they recalled the days when the 'Church of England was still run by men who smoked pipes', and most bishops wore spectacles with 'weighty, emphatic dark frames' that gave emphasis to their pronouncements. Except, of course, that Collins was not a bishop, and with his flair for publicity harnessed to a growing list of humanitarian causes he was never going to be one. The Anglican leadership looked upon his campaigning 'with the deepest suspicion'.

To go back a step, in mid-1950s Britain there were many who agreed with the clergyman (a former public prosecutor in Pretoria) who wrote to *The Times* in January 1955 to say that apartheid had 'an unassailable foundation in biology', and that the Anglican Church was unable to take a proper view of the subject because it lacked the necessary scientific grasp. There were many, too, who recognised this as tosh and wrote to *The Times* to say so. It took Trevor Huddleston properly to contextualise a relationship between apartheid and the Cold War. Huddleston was a member of the Community of the Resurrection, an Anglican religious order, and had just returned from thirteen years in South Africa, where he had worked and lived in the African township of Sophiatown. On 10 December 1956, he wrote to *The Times* to point out that South Africa's Suppression of Communism Act contained definitions of communism which were so fantastic that it was possible for the Government to intimidate or smear anyone who spoke out against apartheid. This Act, he said, was notably effective in deterring those White South Africans who, while critical of apartheid, lived in dread of being identified with communism.

There were communists in the African National Congress (ANC), and they were the only political group which stood for universal suffrage, and accepted Africans and Indians as political equals. The ANC was a broad church – it embraced the Indian National Congress, the white Congress of Democrats, and the Coloured People's Organisation – but as Nelson Mandela explained to Collins in 1954, the irrationalities of the Suppression of Communism Act were having the opposite effect to the one intended. Oliver Tambo, an Anglican, told Collins, 'If you are drowning and someone throws you a rope, you don't ask much about his political beliefs.' Collins's ensuing activism on behalf of the ANC in raising funds and consciousness did not please Archbishop Geoffrey Fisher, who to some seemed more exercised by Roman Catholic exceptionalism than communism. In 1954, he was reproached for describing the refusal of Catholics to say the Lord's Prayer with non-Catholics as 'apartheid'.

The Church of England did a better job opposing apartheid than it did in reaching a coherent view about nuclear weapons. In 1948, a Commission appointed by the archbishops produced *The Church and the Atom*, which in its fifteen conclusions remained undecided on whether circumstances could be envisaged in which the use of nuclear weapons might be acceptable. The report restated the doctrine of just war, saw that nuclear weaponry probably made it obsolete, but declined to address the ensuing question about what a new moral theology of war should look like. 'The Report thus concludes,' sighed a reviewer, 'where, to be of any present use, it should have begun.' An editorial in the *Manchester Guardian* regretted that the authors had 'drunk so deeply of the Church of England's well of masterly compromise' that they had persuaded themselves that there was 'nothing inherently unchristian in the manufacture, possession and use of atom bombs'. Canterbury's 'Red Dean', Hewlett Johnson, dissented. So did Bishop Ernest Barnes of Birmingham, who read the report with 'absolute dismay'. In June, he asked his diocesan conference, 'how can anyone read Christ's teaching and feel that our Lord would approve atomic warfare? I know the answer is commonly given – if others use such weapons, we must use them or perish. If that reply is true, Christianity is false.' But by this time Barnes was a marginal figure, better known for his scepticism about miracles, and for his advocacy of euthanasia for 'defective infants' and sterilisation of 'inferior stock'.

The Church and the Atom thus mirrored the spread of public opinion about nuclear warfare, and the tendency to follow rather than lead opinion on the subject continued in following years. That it did so had to do both with leadership and preoccupations within the Church, and with external events. William Temple's death in 1944 had removed Britain's leading Christian social reformer, while the post-war Church was preoccupied with domestic overhaul. Fisher, his successor, boosted clerical spirits by taking steps to improve clergy stipends and conditions of work, and reorganised what from 1948 became the Church Commissioners to do so, but he blocked the path of radicals to higher appointments, and the main project during his pontificate, incredibly, was the revision of Canon Law.

Looking outward, the 1948 Lambeth Conference tilted Anglicanism away from its pre-war hope for transnational ecumenical ties, and towards British anti-communist policy. The Korean War heightened public consciousness about the atomic bomb as a deterrent. Importantly, Korea reinforced an existing complicity between some senior Anglicans and the Information and Research Department (IRD) of the Foreign Office, which had been formed in 1947 as an anti-communist instrument. The IRD's stock in trade was grey propaganda – the discriminating use of selected factual material to reinforce pro-Western and anti-Soviet perceptions – and although it was distinct from MI6 and the Security Service it had links with both. Members of the Church's Council on Foreign Relations were among the channels that the IRD used to put preferred material and opinions into circulation.

Anglican acquiescence to the maintenance of nuclear weapons persisted after the US H-bomb test at Bikini Atoll on St David's Day 1954. The weapon was far more powerful than its makers had anticipated, and its fallout across the world stirred international reaction. On the St David's Day following, it was announced that Britain itself now possessed the H-bomb. When the *Church Times* asked 'Why is the Church silent?' Archbishop Fisher replied that it was not for the Church to tell statesmen by what methods peace should be achieved, nor do anything that might weaken their power to resist 'Communist threats to civilization'. Fisher mused that a thermonuclear war might even form part of God's greater purpose: 'For all I know it is within the providence of God that the human race should destroy itself in this manner.' As usual, his colleagues were divided. The Bishops of Chichester and Exeter were among those who pronounced the H-bomb to be morally indefensible, but the Bishop of Winchester spoke for a majority in the Anglican hierarchy when he said, 'It might be better to perish than to submit to the parody of civilization which seems to be the alternative presented from the other side of the Iron Curtain.'

My dad's view, printed in the *Birmingham Post*, was that it was 'not the job of the Christian Church to keep in step with public opinion but to change in accordance with the mind of Christ'. Following CND's first public meeting in 1958, he became closely identified with its cause, on one occasion chairing a mass meeting in Birmingham town hall that was addressed by Collins and another of the campaign's founders, the archaeologist Jacquetta Hawkes. Peace-mongering came to a head in 1962, when he was invited to represent the Midlands CND branch at the World Peace Congress in Moscow. Such assemblies had been staged every three or four years by the World Peace Council (WPC) since 1949.* Most of those attending were members of Soviet and East European communist parties, representatives of other Soviet-backed groupings, and Third World countries. But participation by non-communists and Western peace groups was encouraged to enhance the standing of the event, and criticism of Soviet nuclear testing was tolerated to foster an impression of free speech. The WPC went out of its way to seek support from Africa and Asia by playing the part of an autonomous, anti-colonial body that sought to promote a new international economic order and foster liberation. Few Western leaders went to Moscow in July, but 2,469 guests, delegates, and observers from 121 countries did.

My father came back exhilarated. He brought with him a small silver-covered religious icon, Picasso's dramatic congress poster with its sunlit dove in triumph over junked weapons, and a record of the Russian national anthem which he played first thing in the morning for weeks afterwards to remind himself of waking up in the Moscow Hotel. The organisers cannily encouraged delegates to go wherever they wished and talk to anyone they liked. Out in the streets he met people who

---

* The preceding Congresses had been held in Stockholm (1958) and Helsinki (1955).

were eager to talk, and since English was taught in Soviet schools there were many well able to do so. He recognised the possibility that the openness was a contrivance to lend credibility, but his personal experience told otherwise. He was introduced to Russian Christians, visited well-attended churches, went to the monastery at Zagorsk, and met Yuri Gagarin, recently returned from the first human journey into space. An emotional peace concert and performance of *The Sleeping Beauty* at the Bolshoi lifted his heart. Khrushchev's two-and-a-half-hour speech, wreathed in anti-imperialist rhetoric, drew no corresponding response from a senior Western leader. 'Can it be,' my dad wrote in the *Birmingham Post* when he came back, 'that when we confront one another's policies we see the mirror image of our own?' He told the *Post*'s readers that the experience of Moscow made him less inclined than ever to resign himself to nuclear policies that threaten the destruction of entire populations.

This was like IRD propaganda in reverse – factual, but selectively deployed. No doubt it did not go down well in the Foreign Office, or at Lambeth, which kept a blacklist of left-wing clergy. I do not know if my father's name was on it, but his closeness to Collins, and Collins's proximity to figures like Priestley, Jacquetta Hawkes, and the Marxist physicist John Desmond Bernal, all of whom were monitored by the Security Service, suggest that in this period he was not far from a threshold across which he might join them.*

James Cameron reflected that CND began as a concept, became a

---

* The extent to which CND's leaders were under surveillance in the later 1950s and early 1960s is a not yet fully answered question. Cabinet Office records show a distinction between the CND (essentially law-abiding) and the Committee of 100 (seen as subversive and for practical purposes indistinguishable from 'Spies for Peace' which from 1963 worked to put official secrets about civil defence into the public domain). However, it was recognised that many members of CND sympathised with direct action. Moreover, while many personal files of left-wing activists of the 1930s and 1940s are now in the public domain, few later files have so far been released. In May 1964, the Cabinet was told that 'Neither the Security Service nor the police have a systematic or comprehensive record of unilateralist activities', and the considerable work of making one would produce only 'a limited and haphazard return'. By then, the unilateralist movement was in disarray, and the Cabinet was further advised that public sympathy for it might be revived if measures taken against it were to come to light. This does not contradict evidence that watch was kept on *some* unilateralists, and by cross-referencing incidental references to individuals in those personal files which have been made available, we can see that it was.

cause, and for a while was a large influence on the political scene: 'The initials went into the language; the rather stark badge became a symbol.' The high point was probably in 1960, when the Labour Party conference voted to renounce nuclear weapons. Thereafter, solidarity was weakened by the breaking away of the Committee of 100; the outcome of the Cuban Missile Crisis appeared to some to be a vindication of deterrence; opposition to US involvement in the Vietnam War began to replace unilateralism as a cause; and there was organisational disarray within the campaign. By the time Collins stepped down in 1964, Dad's involvement had already begun to lessen.

In tandem with all this: on a map, the Birmingham I knew would look a bit like an elongated dumbbell, with Longbridge at one end, the city centre at the other, and an eight-mile strip running between that took in what you could see to either side from the top deck of an 18a bus. When I went with my dad to take a load of donated toys to some other part of the city in that empty, flat time just after Christmas, it all felt strange. But there was an exception: a salient from Corporation Street which led towards Aston Cross, where Associated Television had their studios.

ATV was launched in 1956 to serve the Midlands on weekdays. It was the first Independent Television station outside London to broadcast to a region, and within two years its bright confidence and varied programming had captured most of the Midland audience. ATV was fronted by personable announcers like Jean Morton and Pat Astley with whom the public felt affinity, and it did new things – like daily bulletins of regional news, live coverage of topical events, and light entertainment at midday. The pioneering included religion. My father was recruited to a roster of ministers from different denominations who were sent on a broadcasters' course and opened each day's schedule at 12.45 with a 'Thought for the Day', and ended it with an 'Epilogue' towards 11 pm.

For the next six years, parish routine was punctuated by Dad writing these TV homilies and going back and forth to the Alpha Studios in Aston to give them live to camera. At first, ATV provided a car and driver to collect and return him. By 1959, the broadcast fees enabled him to take driving lessons and buy an old Austin Westminster. As the Bristol Road was empty around midnight, the temptation to drive faster than the law allowed on return cost him several fines. The car also revived a matter that had literally been left hanging since 1954: the short vicarage drive that led out into Longbridge Lane was about twelve feet above the road, and no one on the Diocesan Parsonages Board had bothered to think how to link the two. Eventually, an access ramp was cut into the bank, although such was the acuteness of the angle with which it met the gate that using it led to much scraped bodywork. Meanwhile, the diocese responded to the broadcast fees by reducing his stipend.

Jean Morton drove an Austin Healey, and once or twice turned up in it to lend her fame to opening parish events at Longbridge. By 1959, she and Noele Gordon were probably the best-known women in the Midlands, and on the occasions when my dad took me with him to the studio, they shepherded me around. In those pre-*Crossroads* days, Gordon presented the midday magazine programme *Lunchbox*; Morton was one of the main station announcers but also presented programmes, including a late-evening jazz and cabaret show called *Rainbow Room* which featured upcoming young singers like Cleo Laine and Billy Fury. Common to both were Jerry Allen and his TV Trio, who were booked by Lew Grade for *Lunchbox* in 1956 and played every weekday for the next eight years. They were more than jobbing musicians; years later, I discovered that Allen had toured with Tommy Trinder and Syd Field, and that Lionel Rubin, his drummer, had been a member of Nat Gonella's band.

TV work was a good antidote to the risk of developing 'the clergy voice': that mannered way of speaking, sometimes sepulchral, sometimes sing-song, in which so many parsons intone prayers, read sermons, or in some cases talk in ordinary conversation. My father never spoke like this (it was seldom guessed that he was a parson because he never sounded like one), but the voice can be heard in any old Ealing comedy or sitcom with a vicar in the cast (think *Dad's Army* or *All Gas and Gaiters*). For many, the clergy voice was a deterrent to churchgoing, particularly among the young. It is unclear where it came from. One suggestion is that in days before electronic amplification, slow delivery, exaggerated diction, and variation of pitch were ways in which a parson with no vocal training would attempt to project his voice to members of a small congregation scattered around a large church. Another is that parish clergy are isolated from their peers and feel a need to put their identity as 'the vicar' before their own individuality.

The isolation exacts personal costs. Parish priests usually have no close colleagues to tell them when they do well or encourage them if things are going badly, or even with whom to compare experiences. The job has no borders. The homes and workplaces of others who regularly see death, sickness, or family violence – doctors, social workers, police

– are usually in different places, whereas the vicarage is public, and if someone rings its bell or telephone, you do not leave it unanswered. 1727, 1366, 2250, 3484: the telephone numbers of successive vicarages and rectories will be the last things to pass beyond recall. In the days before mobiles, the telephone was always ringing, and callers to vicarages did not ring on the cycle of work or leisure, although they had an uncanny gift for knowing when you were about to sit down to eat. But then, if your husband has just smacked you across the face, or you are an obsessive who for the third time in a week wants to know if the Church is about to impose a new prayer book, time is the last thing on your mind.

Parsons' incessant emotional giving to others taxes what they can give to their own families. The strains are of different amplitude, ranging from large or acute crises through to tiny irritations such as may arise from regular dealings with a well-intended but bothersome parishioner. Taken individually they may be manageable – but for a conscientious parson, they never are, because the pressures are overlain and relentless. In time, they can erode the ability to focus on routine tasks. The working week is at least six days, and duties on most evenings – like governors' meetings, PCC business, liaison with other denominations – can push the hours beyond sixty. After years of combining ministry with encounters with congregations which, week by week, are ever smaller, ever older, it is not difficult for a conscientious parson to become demoralised. Stuart recalled the strain he felt towards the end of his curacy. His doctor said, 'You can't go around carrying people's burdens on your own shoulders all day – you must leave them with the Lord.'

I do not know where my father left his burdens. He seldom watched television (indeed, until we reached Longbridge we never had one), but he had an eye and ear for what challenged the establishment. When *Z Cars* began in 1961, its harsh regional world of new estates and ear for inconsequential and fragmentary dialogue struck a chord in Longbridge. He was an instant devotee of *That Was the Week That Was* and was delighted by its consumer guide to religion which used the style of *Which?* to compare the relative merits of faiths, their inputs and outputs. The sketch drew 178 formal protests, an inquiry by the BBC, and was even (*Daily Mail* readers were primly told) criticised by David Frost's father. *TW3* went out late on a Saturday evening, and during its all-too-brief *floruit* he reorganised his routine to finish the next day's sermon before it began.

Around midnight, his mind whirring with some problem or train of thought, he tried to unwind by reading. He often fell asleep with the book open, on one occasion reawakening to be faced by an owl looking in from the sill of the open window. The books were usually detective stories (Victor Canning, Mickey Spillane, Ed McBain, Georges Simenon – he worked his way through the whole crime canon), but there was a moment in 1962 when he came home from the library with *Catch-22*, and I wondered why he was so animated.

He was a committed chess player and organised a small chess club which met at the vicarage. He also played chess by post; on any given day there were usually two or three games on the go, and he had a library of books about games, gambits, and moves which he studied using a small travelling chess set with folding covers. The set had been given to him in gratitude for the time he spent visiting a man in hospital, with whom he played, until the day a stranger walked into the ward and for no known reason shot him dead.

He was rigorous about taking his day off. From 1959, when we got the car, I sometimes kept him company on his rounds visiting the sick. We had a road atlas (Johnson & Bacon, three miles to the inch, relief attractively mapped in colour), and while he was in someone's house, I read it like a book, immersing myself in surrounding counties which I visualised from the map, imagining places to which we might go on the following Tuesday – like Coughton Court near Alcester, heartland of the Catholic Throckmortons in the sixteenth century; Titterstone Clee, where the spectres of Prince Arthur's hooded outriders might be passing; or the Vale of the Red Horse, where V-bombers from Gaydon, Peter Hennessy's 'great white ghosts of deterrence', skimmed the Cotswold edge. Indeed, thinking further about the Second Horseman of the Apocalypse, there was that day when we caught a bus into town and took a train to visit the nearly finished cathedral in Coventry.

2

A COVENTRY CAROL

> A stocky water tower built like the stump
> of a super-dreadnought's foremast.

There it is! Geoffrey Hill knew the Longbridge brick pumping station by the bus stop where we stood waiting.

> It could have set
> Coventry ablaze with pretend
> broadsides, some years before that armoured
> city suddenly went down, guns
> firing, beneath the horizon, huge silent whumphs
> of flame-shadow bronzing the nocturnal
> cloud-base of her now legendary dust.

The spread-out roof glittered with frost under a full moon. Flares began to fall before young Geoffrey's bedtime. If he went outside to look on that November evening, momentary bubbles of energy and light flickered on his eastern horizon.

The story we were told in the fifties was that the attack was pointless barbarism. When J. B. Priestley visited Coventry for *English Journey* (1934), he was enchanted by its great churches and the timber-framed, jettied buildings crammed in its centre. The fact that not many of them were there twenty years later seemed to confirm the tale of wanton destruction. Its seeds were sown immediately afterwards, when newspapers printed photographs of the roofless cathedral of St Michael with heavily ironic captions such as 'NAZIS' "MILITARY" OBJECTIVES'. But, of course, you have only to read to the bottom of Priestley's page to be reminded why, as targets go, Coventry was so alluring: the medieval centre was surrounded by factories making vehicles, aircraft, engines, radios, electrical equipment, magnetos, machine tools, and half a hundred other things with which to fight a war.

The narrative of 'unfathomable barbarity' (as the *New York Herald Tribune* called it) ran in counterpoint with another: that in the eyes of progressive planners and campaigners for social justice, England's historic provincial cities were polluted problems awaiting sweeping solutions. Worcester, York, Coventry, and places like them were sooty jumbles of narrow, crooked streets that were no good for cars and lined with shoddily constructed, insanitary buildings. One of the reasons why Coventry burned so well was that many fire engines became trapped in narrow streets with bomb craters at each end. If such places just happened to be opened out by bombs, enlightened renewal could follow. There were quite a few in wartime Britain who thought like this. One of them was the architect and champion for a strengthened planning system, Clough Williams-Ellis, who shortly after the raid wrote to John Reith, formerly ruler of the BBC, now minister for reconstruction, to suggest that bombing could be a blessing in disguise. Five hundred dead and a charred cathedral was some disguise for a blessing, but bomb damage offered a simplified way to exchange old cities for new.

Reconstruction in the 1940s was more than an idea; it was a new kind of air. You can still breathe it at the end of a guide to the cathedral's remains which was published in 1949. The booklet was written by the provost of the old cathedral, the Very Rev Richard Howard; on its last page is a drawing entitled 'A look into the future' which shows the cathedral's surviving steeple in a new setting: at the end of a spacious, grassy, rectangular precinct enclosed by multistorey concrete buildings.

Twelve years later, we sat at the front of the bright new British Railways DMU that rattled from New Street towards Coventry, looking ahead down the track, breathing that new air. It was a Tuesday, Dad's day off, and we were going to look at the new cathedral. It was nearly finished, and one of his friends from Westcott House days would be there to show us round.

The friend was Simon Phipps, who since 1958 had been the Bishop of Coventry's Industrial Chaplain. This seemed interesting: a clergyman whose parish was the world of work rather than a piece of territory, and who lived in a council flat rather than a vicarage. Among Phipps's pulpits were media like the *Sunday Mirror*, and ATV, to which he gave advice on religious broadcasting. Except that, looking back on what he was saying, he thought the division between 'religious' and 'secular' was spurious. Anyway, there he was, waiting on the steps leading up from Priory Street, tall, long-necked, poised, a little like a heron with an umbrella. As we met, bracketed by the steeple of old St Michael's and Jacob Epstein's sculpture of St Michael and the Devil, he seemed to wield the umbrella like a dance cane. We shall find that Phipps had been a war hero, that his ordination was some loss to musical theatre, and that he was a close friend of Princess Margaret.

He led us between workmen and noisy machines. We marvelled at John Hutton's engraved glass screen, with its floating images of angels and saints, stood before the boulder from Bethlehem that was to be the font, peered into the Chapel of Christ in Gethsemane, with its heraldic angel mosaic and metallic crown of thorns, and looked out at factories from the Chapel of Industry. I was struck by the quiet intensity of Phipps's explanations. There was a kind of ardour in his feeling for the new building and the things it stood for – renewal, unity, reconciliation. A similar mood seemed to hang over the new city that was rising outside. How had this happened?

Coventry Council set up a city redevelopment committee within a month of the great raid, and by the following February two renewal schemes were ready for consideration. One of them was put forward by Ernest Ford, the City Engineer, who wanted to retain the existing street-pattern and surviving buildings in the central area. Donald Gibson, the city's architect and planning officer, was author of the other. Gibson's scheme was more radical: a staged transition towards entire replanning of central Coventry through a gridded road system. Gibson explained that he was responding to 'the opportunity, which may never recur, to build a city designed for the future health, amenity and convenience of its citizens'. In doing so, he was led by Le Corbusier's principles that renewal should decongest city centres, increase their density, add to ways of moving about, and expand parks and green spaces. While embracing these, Gibson was wary of following Le Corbusier's proposal to enhance compactness and open space by building upwards: Coventry was a small city centred on three soaring medieval steeples with which it would not be desirable to compete. A denser yet more open centre could be achieved by organising hierarchies of zones and multilevel precincts for business, commerce, culture, and recreation.

Gibson's plan was adopted by a large majority. St Michael's was at its heart, in a close on the east–west axis of the replanned city. The close had once been a huge space containing the Benedictine cathedral priory of St Mary together with the parish churches of Holy Trinity and St Michael, and several freestanding chapels – a kind of holy land at the city's heart which also functioned as its burying place. The priory was demolished after the Dissolution, and the great enclosure had since been blurred by encroachment; nonetheless, it remained a recognisable space, wherein Holy Trinity and what was left of St Michael (which had been elevated to cathedral status in 1918) still stood. At this point, however, no one knew what a rebuilt cathedral was going to look like, or even where it would stand.

In March 1941, the Cathedral Council agreed to rebuild the cathedral 'on or near its present site'. It appointed a Rebuilding Commission consisting of twelve of its members to explore questions about the site, the appointment of an architect, and the design. Over the next nine months, the Commission considered whether the new cathedral should be a replica, of modern design, or made to fit with the ruins externally while being original within. Ernest Ford, the City Engineer, believed the new building should evoke the old one even if it was not an exact copy. Donald Gibson, the City Architect, observed that medieval builders had always been forward-looking and spoke in favour of a modern design.

Early in 1942, the Commission gave its view: the new cathedral should either incorporate or stand in close relation to the surviving medieval steeple. Provost Howard invited Sir Giles Gilbert Scott (1880–1960) to produce a design which might be 'a bridge between Gothic and modern traditions'. Scott was famous as the author of Liverpool Cathedral, Battersea Power Station, and the red telephone box, and at first sight the scheme he submitted during 1944–1945 looked like a traditional cruciform building with a massy central tower. In reality, it was radical, and full of distinctive contemporary expression: Scott proposed to build on a north–south axis, impaling the body of the old cathedral with a long, centrally planned building which used the surviving five-sided apse as a transept and treated the old steeple as a campanile. Its focus would be a central altar. The press talked of a 'people's cathedral' and liturgical innovation. Many of the windows were small, Scott's aim being to use shadows, and pools and shafts of light to foster a sense of mystery and drama.

Unease hovered. Scott's early sketches had coincided with the arrival of a new bishop, Neville Gorton, a virtuous eccentric whose previous career as the headmaster of Blundell's School seems to have prepared no one for his determination to see a spacious, well-lit building in the spirit of an airy modern factory. Scott responded by redesigning the interior in a more forward-looking manner, the great hall now formed around vast concrete inverted catenary arches.

Scott's design was exhibited at the Royal Academy's 1945 summer exhibition. There was a bleakness about it, like something out of *Gor-menghast*, and it was not well received. In December 1946, the Royal Fine Art Commission urged Gorton and Howard to drop it. Scott resigned the following month, complaining about interfering commit-tees and commissions that fettered the hapless artist and hampered the production of good work. The Cathedral Council duly appointed another Commission, this time under the chairmanship of William Ormsby-Gore (1885–1964), the fourth Lord Harlech, whose qualifi-cation seems to have been his service as the minister for Works and Public Buildings in Stanley Baldwin's government. Sir Percy Thomas, a past President of the Royal Institute of British Architects (RIBA), was among its members.

The Harlech Commission reported in July 1947. It recommended a cathedral 'not copied from the old, yet not in violent contrast' with it; that is, not necessarily Gothic, but in the Gothic tradition. The steeple should be retained, but the outer walls of the old nave could be sacrificed. (Bishop Gorton was suspicious of ruins, fearing that the sentimental pleasure people took in them might override their responses to a living church.) The new cathedral should be built as nearly as practical on the site of the last, and externally be of the same red sandstone. The Commission further recommended that in the interests of thrift, and to avoid any sense of competition between the new cathedral and nearby surviving medieval buildings such as Holy Trinity and St Michael's steeple, the architect 'should avoid excessive external decoration and concentrate instead upon internal richness'. The architect should be selected by an open competition, organised by RIBA.

A special diocesan conference was now convened to consider the Commission's advice. In summing up, Bishop Gorton drew attention to the views of RIBA, Donald Gibson, and others that the requirement for a design in the Gothic tradition should be set aside. The conference was not pleased by this, considering its own viewpoint to be the only one that mattered. Nonetheless, RIBA and Gibson stuck to their guns, and the conference was cautioned that unless competing architects were given stylistic freedom, many of the best of them would refuse to take part. The conference accordingly gave its 'general approval' to the Harlech report. Harlech advised the Cathedral Council to form a Reconstruction Committee to produce a detailed brief, purchase adjoin-ing land and organise the competition. When the Committee's brief was announced in January 1950, it was said to be in line with Harlech's advice save for one 'modification': style would be left to the judgement of the architect. The stipulation for a building in the Gothic tradition had been dropped.

Seven months later, the three expert assessors sifted 219 entries, and hesitated. When the result was announced on 15 August 1951, the general standard was said to be 'disappointing', although there was a group of designs of 'great merit' and one of 'outstanding excellence'. The assessors' selection of the design by a forty-four-year-old Scottish architect, Basil Spence, seems at least in part to have been influenced by pragmatism. A pioneering scheme would likely be attacked by the Reconstruction Committee, Anglican diehards, and townspeople alike, whereas Spence's proposals stood between tradition and innovation, and this may have raised the assessors' hopes that it would win acceptance across different factions.

Uproar ensued nonetheless. The architect and teacher Sir Albert Richardson (1880–1964) considered it 'frightful to look upon'. The Rev G. Cloudesley Shovel, a Methodist minister in Bude, wrote with plodding irony to suggest that the medieval steeple be demolished and replaced by a mill chimney, which would be 'more in keeping with the design . . . and with modern art – falsely so called'. Sneering traditionalists likened it to a cinema, an 'outrage', and 'pagan'. Spence received hate mail. But his scheme had responded to the brief, and to the place.

Spence, like Scott, put the new cathedral on a new, nearly north–south axis, but whereas Scott's church would have passed through its predecessor, Spence placed it to make a right angle. He also kept most of what was left of old St Michael, figuring its nave as an open-air narthex, juxtaposing it with the new nave to symbolise the Provost's theme of sacrifice and resurrection. The new nave would be noble within, its walls angled in a series of vertical bands, a bit like the radiator shutters of some great engine, slotted with windows full of colour. To east and west, Chapels of Unity and of Industry would stand apart from the main structure, their likeness to tents maybe stirring thoughts of temporary homes, or people on the move. On 1 September 1951, the *Illustrated London News* quoted Spence's explanation of his design as 'growing out of the old cathedral and incomplete without it'. And ten years later, here it was. Back on the steps into Priory Street, was Simon Phipps really an industrial chaplain, or was his umbrella an archangel's spear?

The dispute about revivalism versus innovation was not the only argument that taxed the energies of Gorton and Howard as they strove to bring the new cathedral into being. There was debate in the press and at meetings about what a late-twentieth-century cathedral was for.

Should it be an auditorium, built for capacity, or chiefly for prayer and sacrament? If it was an auditorium, would it compete with the work of existing parishes? What kind of liturgy should be said and sung inside a new building – surely not the language of Cranmer inside a church of the space age? Where, exactly, should it stand? J. B. Priestley put his oar in by urging that the old ruin be left alone and the new church put somewhere else. Some went further and asked whether it should be in Coventry at all. For a time, the Reconstruction Committee met opposition from members of the City Council who argued that the cathedral would divert scarce skills, labour, and materials away from housebuilding. In their view, priority should be given to renewal of the city and housing, and let the cathedral wait.

Aback of it all, in June 1951 readers of *The Stage* were told:

> Although, as the Bishop of Coventry recently stated, the ruins of Coventry Cathedral may be gathering false sentiment, it affords in its present state an aesthetically excellent setting for religious plays. There is also a deep historical significance in the presentation of the ancient Guild plays in Coventry.
>
> Originally performed on Corpus Christi Day, it was the custom for the craft-guilds to ride in procession round the ten wards of the city and for one or more of the guilds to present a religious pageant on a wagon. The scenes ranged from the Annunciation to Domesday. The words of only two of the plays have survived. The first, given by the Shearmen and Taylors' Guilds, is world-famous as the Coventry Nativity Play; and the other, given by the Weavers, has not been fully performed since Queen Elizabeth's visit in 1580. These two are combined, with fragments of a prophet-play, and form a 90-minute dramatic piece. Following tradition, the players are anonymous. The first presentation was on 24 May, before a selected audience, and it will be performed on a further 15 afternoons and evenings . . .

The 24th of May in 1951 was the feast of Corpus Christi, the festival which before its abolition in England in 1548 had celebrated the presence of the body of Jesus Christ in the Eucharist. Corpus Christi originated in the thirteenth century; by 1400, it had become an extravaganza marked by processions, music, holidaymaking, and biblical plays performed by laity. Its popularity partly had to do with its place on the Thursday after Trinity Sunday, a last hurrah of the old ritual year before the long haul through the ordinary time of summer and autumn that brings us back to Advent.

Until recently it was thought that the civic and guild plays from Chester and York were survivors from a genre of long, serialised urban play cycles that tell the world's story from its beginning to the last judgement. However, it is now realised that these cycles, and fragments of possible cycles like the one from Coventry, were exceptions rather than the norm. Since the 1980s, the systematic sifting of pre-Reformation accounts has pieced together a new normal for late-medieval drama in which playmaking was widespread, parish-centred, and embraced many religious and moral themes. Parish performances ranged from grand spectaculars with elaborate sets and special effects through to cycles played across a term of years. Parish plays could be occasional or annual, long or short, in church or out, and at different seasons – Christmas, Easter, the feasts of particular saints, but notably at the great summer festivals. Of these, none was greater than Corpus Christi.

The first written allusions to Coventry's civic Corpus Christi drama are met around the turn of the fourteenth/fifteenth century. Coventry in the late fourteenth century was fabulously wealthy; the city's economy was England's fourth largest after London, Bristol, and York; in 1397, it accounted for 6 per cent of all cloth sold in the country; it enjoyed special trading privileges. Merchants in wool, clothiers, dyers, and drapers led a supply chain of weavers and fullers, craftsmen in metal (wiredrawers, needlers, pinners, goldsmiths, pewterers), associated trades in leather and fur, and stimulated travel that spurred demand for wheelwrights, blacksmiths, and saddlers. Such a noble scene of industry made fertile ground for industrial chaplaincy, and whereas in 1961 there was but one Simon Phipps for the whole diocese, five centuries before most of the city's industries had chaplains of their own. In 1522, at St Michael's alone, besides the vicar, there were some eighteen priests and six chantry priests. By the fifteenth century, St Michael's covered the best part of half an acre and was honeycombed with altars bearing different dedications and special spaces associated with groupings like the Cappers, Mercers, Drapers, Girdlers, and Dyers. St Michael and Holy Trinity also had dependent chapels elsewhere in the city, and some of these, too, acquired industrial links: the Shearmen, Tailors, and Fullers, for instance, were centred on a chapel of St George above Gosford Gate; the guild of Corpus Christi, founded 1348, had connections with the suburban chapel of St Nicholas.

Everyone took part at Corpus Christi – watching, bystanding, eating, acting, drinking. Analogy is elusive, but the solidarity surrounding a great football team might give an inkling. Late-medieval guilds and fraternities combined diverse purposes – cartel, dining club, social network, health insurance – with the care of their members' souls. One effect of this was to interweave business and devotion in ways that could not be told apart. Another was to boost clergy numbers in towns where industry and trade prospered. In places like Coventry, religion was an industry in its own right and an economic driver. Such places were accordingly rich in people who could read, write, copy music, and owned books.

Coventry's two survivors have reached us via copies made by a certain Robert Crow in 1535. One, the pageant of the Shearmen and Tailors, portrays events immediately before, during, and after the Nativity. The other, the pageant of the Weavers, covers the Purification of the Virgin Mary, the presentation of Christ in the temple, and young Christ with the doctors. Crow's manuscript of the Weavers' play still exists (as do two leaves which miraculously survive from a fifteenth-century working playbook of the same play); his copy of the play of the Shearmen and Tailors was lost in a fire, but by then a transcript had been printed.

Puzzles surround the Coventry plays. Why were there so few of them? Any one subject in the pageant of the Shearmen and Tailors – the Annunciation, Mary's visit to Elizabeth, Joseph, the journey to Bethlehem, the Nativity, the shepherds, the Magi, the flight into Egypt, the Innocents – might have been a play in itself in York or Chester. Was the cycle always confined to the New Testament, in contrast to the northern cycles which covered the history of the world from Genesis to Revelation? Did the composite plays exist from the start, or did they emerge through successive adaptations and amalgamations, perhaps in response to epidemics and the recession which desolated much of the city's commercial life in the late fifteenth and early sixteenth centuries?

Another enigma is why the plays stopped. The old idea that Protestant reformers shut them down does not quite square with what happened. If it was possible to deny the real presence in the Eucharist through legislation, the abolition of civic drama on the day in the year that celebrated the real presence would surely have been more straightforward – yet performances continued on and off into the 1570s, in Coventry's case until 1579. It is the case that demands were made for cuts and rewrites, and in places we can watch bishops and cathedral deans leaning on guilds and corporations, as in York, where in 1572 all copies of the Corpus Christi plays were called in by Archbishop Grindal. But this looks like piecemeal influencing rather than coordinated policy. An accelerating factor might have been the growth of Calvinism.

In the eyes of Puritans, the kind caricatured in Malvolio, dressing up and disguising were 'undecent and uncomely' – whence the significance of the sting in *Twelfth Night* whereby Malvolio is gulled into dressing up his legs. Puritans wanted to suppress not only religious drama but theatre in general. If the attenuation of civic religious drama is to be understood as part of an overall attempt to 'obliterate the memory of traditional religion', we need a deeper understanding of what its threat was perceived to be, and how the attempt was organised. Were reformers of different degree looking over their shoulders at each other?

Fifteen-year-old William Shakespeare might have watched the last performances. Stratford-upon-Avon is just down the road, and there are plenty of hints in his work that he was there. The reference in *Hamlet* to an actor who out-Herods Herod is well known. Henry V's warning to the citizens of Harfleur about what will follow if they do not submit recalls the Herod who 'rages in the street' in the pageant of the Shearmen and Tailors:

> Your naked infants spitted upon pikes,
> Whiles the mad mothers with their howls confus'd
> Do break the clouds, as did the wives of Jewry
> At Herod's bloody-hunting slaughter-men . . .

And when in *Richard II* Mowbray and Bolingbroke are called to a trial of arms at Coventry, city records tell that the place of their actual meeting was Gosford Green, outside the city's east gate. The plays were presented in order on wagons in different parts of the city; their procession began in Gosford Street, suggesting that this, if not Gosford Green outside, was the assembly area where the wagons formed up.

Spectators could pay for pitches around playing places – upper rooms with views, rooftops – where sellers of drink and snacks would congregate. The routes mattered. In York and Lincoln, performance places lay along ancient processional paths. York's route linked the city's two great collegiate churches; it can be traced in the entry pageants of Norman and Angevin kings, and since the plays spanned the history of the world, from Creation to Doomsday, in a sequence linked to liturgical readings that were heard in the city's churches between Epiphany and Palm Sunday, on performance days the city became a model of the universe and a figure of time.

Was it like this in Coventry? We do not know. Coventry's medieval layout was oddly amorphous, reaching out into pastures to the west and north along long streets that led from a walled and ditched core, where shops and workshops fronted streets and market spaces, with long, narrow yards and garths behind. It is suggested that the ten composite plays corresponded with the city's ten wards, and that each was performed at a traditional site. Some of the playing sites are known, and we hear of several pageant-houses in which guilds kept their costumes, props, and play wagons. But if there was a connecting symbolic geography, it has been lost; and even if we knew it, Donald Gibson's post-war replanning rubbed most of it out.

The legacy of the Coventry cycle, then, is one of its songs. 'Lully, Lulla, Thou Little Tiny Child' is a lullaby for dead children, victims of the paranoid Herod. In history, Herod was a client ruler of the Roman province of Judea between around 37 and 1 BC. In the Shearmen's play, he is 'the mightiest conqueror that ever walked on ground', prince of Purgatory and chief captain of Hell. The elegy is sung by three mothers.

> Lully, lulla, thou little tiny child,
> By by, lully, lullay, thou little tiny child
> By by, lully, lullay!

We know it as the 'Coventry Carol'. The music was written down in 1591. It may be original. At any rate, its three-part harmony, with an acid false relation in the penultimate bar of the refrain, might have been composed between the later years of Henry VI or Henry VII. The lie of the parts shows that the innocents' mothers were played by men.

The bombing, too, took innocents. Among them:

Marion Grace Billings	5 months
Geoffrey James Elden	9 months
James Matthew Doney	2
Arthur Edward Haddingham	16 months
Anthony Peter Hands	4 months
Margaret Hoare	5 months
David John Jenkins	4 months
Noel McCrea	22 months
Patricia Mary Pickering	2
Roger Edward Smith	12 months
Patricia Snow	12 months
Arthur Derek Todd	2

Those present when the roof of St Michael's burned recall how molten lead sizzled, hissed, and spat as it met water sprayed by firefighters. It took a while for firemen to get there. The city's fire service was busy elsewhere, and it was not until around 9.30 pm that the fire brigade from Solihull, twelve miles away, arrived at the vestry door. By then, Provost Howard and his three helpers were dog-tired by their efforts to tackle a series of incendiaries with buckets of water, stirrup pumps, and sand. The incendiaries had fallen in different places, in successive showers; a number penetrated the outer lead and were burning on the upper surface of the fifteenth-century oak ceiling below. The firemen ran out long series of hose lengths, but before long, pressure fell and the water ceased – high explosive bombs had shattered the mains. As the cathedral burned, the bell of the clock in its tower continued to tell the hours, encouraging some within earshot to think that the church was still intact.

The following Sunday was the twenty-seventh after Trinity, a fortnight before Advent. During Advent, Christmas, and Epiphany, the period covered by the play of the Shearmen and Tailors, rain and snow soaked into the unroofed walls. In March, as the Cathedral Council met to discuss what to do next, colours were noticed gleaming from a stretch of wall high up between the former chapels of the Girdlers and the Drapers. A fall of plaster had exposed older plaster bearing a painting of the Virgin Mary holding the infant Jesus on her left arm, his hand raised in blessing. The scene was painted in the fourteenth century, around the time that Edward III granted the city a charter of incorporation. After six centuries, here was the holy family, revealed.

3

SANDERSTEAD MAN

I n 1964, we moved to Sanderstead, an outer London suburb in north-east Surrey, on a chalk hill, in the Diocese of Southwark.

Southwark was the cradle of a 'south bank religion', the workroom for tomorrow's parish, some of whose clergy wore jeans. Southwark summons up the Anglo-Catholic Edwin in Barbara Pym's *Quartet in Autumn*, drafted in 1971, who recoils from long-haired guitar-playing priests, yearns for the days of cloak and biretta, and is 'doubtful about the "Kiss of Peace"'. The diocese had only been created in 1905. Before that, Sanderstead had briefly been in the Diocese of Rochester, into which it was transferred in 1877 from its birth mother, Winchester.

In the eleventh century, Sanderstead's lord was Winchester's abbey of St Peter of Hyde. The hamlet's position only three miles from Croydon shows what a wide-flung realm the diocese of Winchester then was. The city of Winchester was England's capital from the age of Alfred to the Norman Conquest, its kudos still called up by the position of its bishop as one of the five Anglican prelates who automatically hold the rank of Lord Spiritual in Parliament. And if you care for Edward III's world of chivalric fantasy, Winchester's bishop is *ex officio* a prelate of the select fellowship dedicated to the image and arms of St George, the Most Noble Order of the Garter.

As a parish, then, Sanderstead was old. Whereas Longbridge had been formed eight years before, Sanderstead had been around for at least eight hundred.* But they had things in common. Until recently, both were very thinly settled, each had since been overrun by a nearby city, and although they had become built-up, each remembered its

---

* Like many churches, All Saints Sanderstead is first mentioned in writing in the Taxation of Pope Nicholas (1291). The oldest recognisable fabric in the building is around sixty years older than this. The earliest reference to Sanderstead itself is a bequest of land in the will of an *ealdorman*, Alfred, AD 871 x 889.

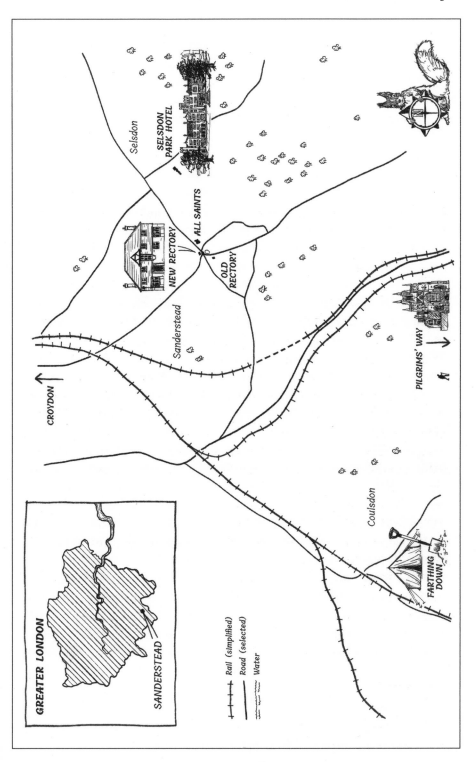

former self. Like an adult looking back to a childhood, Sanderstead in the 1960s still thought of itself as a village, and in Croydon's art gallery there were paintings by a Sanderstead artist, William Henry Hope (1835–1917), depicting hilly, purple heathland, oak and birchwood, ponds and commons.

Red squirrels still flourished in Sanderstead when a new rectory was built c.1929 to replace the Georgian predecessor that was considered to be over-large and too expensive to keep. The new rectory was put in a plot bought across the road from the old one, close to the point at which a road called Sanderstead Hill emerged from a tunnel of trees and met the road to Addington. The classical symmetry, size, and proportion of the old rectory represented a society upheld by local gentry and clergy. The new one continued to embody conservative objectives by harking back to an imagined England, somewhere between the days of old John of Gaunt, time-honour'd Lancaster (1340–1399), and the accession of James I (1603). In general shape it resembled a Wealden hall house, thereby evoking a prosperous yeomanry, while its oriel window, tile-hung walls, and tall chimneys suggested good Queen Bess and the religious settlement of 1559. Within, however, the allotment of space had the same underlying scheme as Longbridge. There was a central lobby in which to welcome visitors (hence the oriel, facing south, to light it), with study and family rooms at either end, a kitchen behind, and four bedrooms along an axial landing above. The rear garden, cut out of woodland, was close to half an acre. This was larger than Longbridge, partly because it had included a grass tennis court: a feature that enabled the rector to reciprocate in the tennis parties which at the start of William Temple's pontificate were still a part of middle-class interaction. Below the court on the hillside was a wilderness, shaded by trees living on from older woodland. When the dog who had been Dad's chum since King's Norton died, it was at the foot of one of these that he buried him.

Soon after our arrival, Dad launched a new parish magazine: *Signpost*. It was bimonthly, glossy, and really three magazines in one because it served two daughter churches, St Antony Hamsey Green and St Edmund Riddlesdown, planted in the 1950s, as well as the mother church of All Saints. *Signpost*'s twenty pages carried the usual things you expect in parish magazines – paragraphs on forthcoming events and meetings, the Mothers' Union, Young Wives' group, retirements and arrivals, activities and services, a sprinkling of adverts – along with regular pieces from the clergy, a letter from the bishop (syndicated through the diocese), and occasional articles contributed by outside authors.

Signpost carried a regular 'The Rector Writes' column that called for six hundred words. Whether finding them came easily was one of many questions I never asked. We have seen that he knew the craft: his columns for the *Birmingham Post* and TV work had honed skills in writing accessibly, and to length and deadline. But fluency on the page does not always mean ease in composition, and to judge from the amount of time he could put into a five-minute sermon or the density of pipe smoke in his study at the end of it, the skill came as much from graft as flair.

He had a keen eye for a hook on which to hang an article. His farewell column, written on the eve of the 1970 general election, took its cue from events five months before when Edward Heath and his shadow cabinet met in the nearby Selsdon Park Hotel to thrash out policy. The free-market, libertarian, law-and-order manifesto which emerged drew the taunt of 'Selsdon Man' from Harold Wilson. When Heath abandoned it in the face of the 1973 oil crisis, recession, and industrial unrest, the way was prepared for Margaret Thatcher's succession.

'Selsdon Man' prompted kindly musings on 'Sanderstead Man' and 'Sanderstead Woman' by the rector, who found them to be nothing like the materialistic 'gin and Jag' Surrey commuter stereotype. Sanderstead People were decent, industrious, compassionate, and responsible, who looked after their gardens, turned up at school open days, supported the arts and religion, and took a conscientious interest in community affairs. Many of them worked in banks, insurance, or in specialised professions, and if anything needed doing – a new cover design for *Signpost*, a fund-raising campaign for a new project – or an office-bearer was wanted for the PCC, there was always someone qualified and willing to take it on.

The roster of parishioners with special skills included Godfrey Talbot, the BBC's 'Voice of the Desert' during the Eighth Army's progress through North Africa and Italy between 1942 and 1945. After the war, he became the BBC's court correspondent, commentating at national events, reporting from faraway places during royal tours, and advising on media handling of the amours of Princess Margaret. If there was a lesson to read on a special occasion or a speech to be made at a parish function, Godfrey was there. He was genial, mannerly, and, as George VI noted at their first meeting ('BBC does make 'em tall, don't they?'), imposing. He was also funny, with a fund of reminiscences about his emergence as a 'news observer' in the days when the BBC had no reporters of its own.

In Sanderstead, then, some talent or gift lay around every corner. The parish even employed a part-time verger, a gentleman called Price, who wore a black cassock, spoke in deep, grim tones, walked with a limping lurch, and used a private language he had invented down the years to describe his duties. On ceremonial occasions, he spoke such lines as 'Will it be *full* verge you're wanting this evening, rector?' The place epitomised Nick Stacey's suggestion that outer suburbs were the one kind of environment in which parsons and the parochial system could make a go of things. As we shall later see, Stacey and some of his inner-city colleagues were having a hard time, but the mood I sensed on arrival – caught, I suppose from the manner of visiting preachers, Dad's asides about diocesan plans, news of Southwark's ordination course for men (and later women) who were unable to study full time, and occasionally through full conversations – was one of buoyancy. Southwark in the 1960s contained some of the most able clergy in England – figures like Douglas Rhymes (1914–1996) whose book *Layman's Church* had appeared the year before; Eric James (1925–2012), canon with special responsibility for inner-city areas; and the New Testament scholar and secular theologian John Robinson (1919–1983).

Mervyn Stockwood and John Betjeman sparred publicly about responsibilities for the care of churches. In private, they were friends.

Southwark's bishop since 1959 was Mervyn Stockwood, an outspoken, colourful figure whose way of dismissing a teenager's slack thought ran you down like a train, while the fact that he wore a broad smile while doing it enabled him to tilt the conversation towards whatever it was he thought you really ought to be talking about. As often as not this was himself. A conversation with Mervyn was often one-sided (this came over in the famous debate with John Cleese and Michael Palin about *Monty Python's Life of Brian* (1982), when for considerable stretches neither they nor Tim Rice, the programme's chair, could get a word in). So unceasing was he that when he wished his glass to be recharged with the bone-dry *fino* sherry he expected to be on hand when he came to preach, he simply held it out at arm's length while carrying on without pause. His flair for self-advertisement was once teased by a fellow bishop, who when Stockwood arrived at a subdued gathering in the magnificence of a purple cassock and episcopal bling, murmured, 'Ah, Mervyn: incognito, I see.' But he was just as likely to wear street clothes, as in the tale of him being shooed away by the wife of a vicar he had come to see on the grounds that her husband had an appointment with the bishop. Mervyn also stood for simple things, and for justice. After the Six Day War, he encouraged Southwark's parishioners to join his frequent diocesan pilgrimages to the Middle East not only because he wished others to be moved as he was by places like Jacob's Well and the Church of the Nativity, but to boost the Palestinian economy, bring support to those with scanty livelihoods, and help the small Arab Anglican Church.

Stockwood, it has often been pointed out, was a bundle of opposites: an egalitarian who kept a liveried servant; a left-wing councillor who hobnobbed with the titled rich; a chauvinist who battled hard for the ordination of women; ruthless yet an outstanding carer; a progressive who sometimes acted on the advice of reactionaries. He worked best when acting on intuition. Michael De-la-Noy caught him well when he said that he worked with whatever materials lay to hand. 'You are doing a great job,' Archbishop Fisher once told him, 'though very often in the wrong way.' Dad was a good mimic and studied the manner in which his confident drawl came from the side of his mouth. The affection in which Dad held him was not shared by all Sanderstead's parishioners, one of whom – a grammarian and lay reader – reinvented him as Vermin Woodstock. I was never told, or perhaps never asked, what it was that drew Dad into his orbit. It is possible that he was recommended by someone like Nicolas Stacey, but equally thinkable that the suggestion came from the person and place through whom, as we shall later see, very many things connected: John Collins, and Westcott House, where Collins had been vice-principal when Stockwood trained for ordination.

Stockwood's entry in the *Oxford Dictionary of National Biography* points out that in his forty-four years of ministry, the Church gave him only three jobs. The first two, everyone knew, established him as one of the outstanding parish priests of the twentieth century. In 1936, he became assistant curate, later vicar, of the large parish of St Matthew, Moorfields, in Bristol. At first, 'Stockwood was assigned scarcely habitable accommodation attached to the parish's mission church, St Saviour's, a building that doubled during the week as a rehabilitation centre for the unemployed. The local football team made use of his bathroom on Saturdays while Stockwood had to make use every day of a public lavatory.' Moorfields was twinned with Blundell's School in Devon, whose boys visited the parish to assist, and whose headmaster, Neville Gorton, we have already met in his next post as bishop of Coventry. After nineteen years at Moorfields, Stockwood became vicar of Great St Mary's, the university church in Cambridge, where he combined his incumbency with service as a left-wing councillor. Over the next four years, Sunday congregations rose from two hundred to one thousand.

Despite his maverick reputation, Stockwood's faith was traditional. This was in contrast to John Robinson, another who trained at Westcott House, and who served his curacy with Stockwood at St Matthew, Moorfields (1945–1948) before going back into a productive academic life. In 1959, Stockwood invited his old colleague to accompany him to Southwark. After some hesitation, and reflection on advice from many colleagues who told him to decline, Robinson agreed. Three years later came *Honest to God*.

Robinson's pitch was that the New Testament's supernaturalist framework was an artefact of its time – a temporary form of expression of deeper truths, not something fixed or inherently self-sufficient to be toted down the centuries regardless of other cultural or intellectual developments. If symbols and images are fixed, he warned, they become idols. He argued for the uncoupling of Christianity from symbols stuck in a pre-scientific era, and for discarding the notion of God as a superhuman being who by definition would be confined by the religion which had called him into being. He invited a new conception of God as ultimate reality, a 'window through the surface of things into the very ground of our being', and a morality founded on love in which evil is love's absence.

John Robinson, Bishop of Woolwich (1959-1969), afterwards dean of Trinity College, Cambridge, in 1979

One of the book's reviewers was C. S. Lewis, who in an artfully patronising article wondered what all the fuss was about. Lewis asked why one set of symbols should be preferred to another – and how a God who is not a person could yet be personal? Archbishop Ramsey denounced the book. Another likened Robinson to a new Martin Luther. But in that kind of comparison lay a risk of confusion, for 'reform' can run in opposite directions: it can signify desire to go back to an unspoiled past, or forward into the unknown. If the Church was on the brink of a new reformation, which was it to be? And how would a new reformation relate to the old one?*

A week after *Honest to God* appeared, its publisher said, 'Free speech is what the Church of England needs, not a heresy trial.' A trial, nonetheless, was more or less what followed. Many bought the book to find out which side of it they were on. Many more took this decision without bothering to read the book. The '*Honest to God* Debate' became a phenomenon in itself. The initial frenzy was partly in reaction to the

---

* *The New Reformation?* was the title of Robinson's following book. The question mark seems significant.

headline of a pre-publication article Robinson had written for the *Observer*: 'Our Image of God Must Go'. These were not words Robinson used, but their reception blew like a hurricane. The initial print run was six thousand; within a few days, the publishers ordered forty thousand more; by the end of the year, it had sold three hundred thousand; in 1967, sales passed a million.

Honest to God prompted years of argument about the nature of Christian belief in a largely secular society that was ever more ruled by science. The book is also held to have epitomised a revolutionary mood abroad in the 1960s in which things hitherto taken for granted in religion, politics, social and personal behaviour began to disintegrate in the face of radical challenge. In fact, much of the book was led by the recent thought of several Lutheran theologians, hence not much in it was new, while the scale of its immediate influence had a lot to do with the ways in which launch publicity caught its sail. Continuing debate also reflected media suppositions that it was part and parcel of the larger phenomenon of 'south bank religion' – a theological agenda to partner reform of a failing parish system. However, while the presence of *Honest to God* alongside Southwark's other activities (and arguably along with the Second Vatican Council) did foster a sense that one age was drawing to a close and another beginning, on the ground it was not clear what this meant. The kind of renewal being advocated by Robinson was outside the Church, which raised the question what purpose the reform of Church structures might serve. Parishioners who hitherto had worked hard to keep the show on the road in places like Sanderstead were beginning to ask themselves what the show actually was.

There was a large, attentive congregation when Robinson came to preach. Afterwards, at supper, my main impression of him was his softness; he seemed very shy, said little, and when he did speak did so with a quiet precision. Sanderstead's usual response to radicalism was to listen with polite interest and then carry on as before. It was thus with *Honest to God*. The closest Sanderstead congregants got to anything new was the Series Two communion service and singing Patrick Appleford's jazzy congregational *Mass of Five Melodies*. Appleford's music was from the same stable as Geoffrey Beaumont, who had been his chaplain when Appleford was an undergraduate at Trinity College, Cambridge; the two were among those who around 1960 founded the Twentieth Century Church Light Music Group. His mass worked better with a piano than an organ, and if you were playing it, there were images either side of the east window about which to think if the

service got boring.* They were painted as a pair in the fourteenth century. One depicted St Edmund, the Anglo-Saxon king martyred by the
Vikings. The other showed a bishop, probably Thomas Becket, who was
martyred by four of Henry II's knights in 1170.† Everyone knew that the
road to Thomas's shrine at Canterbury passed Sanderstead just a short
distance to the south, but a larger point was being made by juxtaposition
of the two figures. Edmund and Thomas were England's most powerful
martyr cults, Edmund from the earlier Middle Ages, Thomas from the
later. Together, they packed a punch. Before the Reformation, their joint
presence behind the main altar, looking out over the priest towards the
congregation, was a way to project protective force into the community.
Reformers considered such holy energy to be treacherous, not because
they believed in it, but because they regarded it as a kind of infection,
transmissible by sight, which gullible people might catch if the saints
caught their eye. Which is why the images were painted over in the
1540s. Since then, they had waited, blindfolded behind limewash, until
conservators released them back into our view, and us to theirs.

Sanderstead liked to remember its roots, and in 1956 a society to
extend knowledge of them was formed. It was called the Bourne
Society, the name being taken from the unpredictable streams that
issue now and then from the North Downs, where old channels provide
routes for the A22 and A23, and meet at Purley to flow northward into
the River Wandle. The Bourne Society fostered identities of villages like
ours that had been removed from Surrey into the London borough of
Croydon.

A name often on the lips of Bourne Society members was Brian
Hope-Taylor (1923–2001), a son of Sanderstead whose excavations at
nearby Farthing Down were celebrated by *Picture Post* in October 1948:
'Its history has been traced back 4,000 years. Its flanks were ploughed
into fields by Iron Age Celts in the 1st century BC. It was occupied
in Roman times. Now, archaeologists discover Saxon burials along its

---

* In fairness to Series Two, at the age of seventeen it was a lot less dull than the
1662 communion. Stockwood said that if he and his chaplain omitted all the op-
tional sections, they could crack through it in less than fifteen minutes. De-la-Noy
has since quoted Stockwood: 'I don't mind if it's High Church or Low Church, as
long as it isn't Long Church.'
† Or is this Edmund of Abingdon, who became Archbishop of Canterbury in
1234, clashed with Henry III, died and was buried at Pontigny in 1240, and was
canonised six years later? Several institutions were dedicated to him, and it is possible that the images were intended to evoke a pair of Edmunds.

spine.' *Picture Post* printed photographs of burials being uncovered by eager volunteers from Sanderstead, of every age from four to sixty, all shorts, slacks, open neck shirts, and smiles. One of the captions jumps straight out of the eugenic world of Ernest Barnes: 'Skull-measurements can tell a lot. Saxon skulls are longer than Romano-British. But racial mingling evolved a new type.'

Brian Hope-Taylor (back row, second from left) and members of his excavation team at the Mote of Urr, 1951

Since then, Hope-Taylor's work at Yeavering in Northumberland had transformed understanding of early Christian England, and his TV series *Who Were the British?* (1966) and *The Lost Centuries* (1968) were much admired. Impressive, too, was his ITV broadcast on Christmas Day 1967. It was called *The Fight for York Minster*, and told how analysis of cracks and warping in the cathedral's structure called for engineering remedies that were likely to take half a decade to complete and would destroy 750,000 cubic feet (21,200 cubic metres) of archaeological deposits in the process. If I had known that, four years later, I would be one of the people helping to rescue the deposits, I would have paid more attention.

Brian Hope-Taylor has variously been described as an engraver, illustrator, broadcaster, and archaeologist. He is best thought of as an artist. With that ran traits with which artists are often associated: perfectionism, self-criticism, difficulty in letting go of things, fixation with whatever might be over the next skyline, vulnerability, and strategies to cloak it. What formed him is an open question. He left school at sixteen. His natural gifts were prodigious, but it is not always clear whence, or when, came the technique. In a few respects, we can work it out. His skills as a broadcaster were learned through freelance toil for the BBC in the later 1950s, writing and presenting schools history programmes in series like *Listen and Learn*. He had no first degree; when he reached his thirties, friends encouraged him to study for a doctorate to enable his entry to academia; the schools income helped to fund it.*

Other expertise is harder to locate. Where, for instance, did his techniques as an excavator or wood engraver come? His strategy at Farthing Down shows that he was aware of the pre-war work of the Prehistoric Society, when he was in his early teens. How did this reach him? On engraving, it has been said that he trained with George Mackley (1900–1983), author of *Wood Engraving* (1948) and teacher at the Central School of Arts and Crafts. There is no reason to doubt this – Mackley himself mentioned it – but when and how did the study take place? Hope-Taylor's engraving skills were well developed when he provided woodcuts for an English edition of Mikhail Prishvin's *The Lake and the Woods* in 1951, so we can put it before then; immediately before the war he was working as a clerk, and in 1948 he was described by the *Daily Herald* as a 'London advertising man and spare time archaeologist'.

The likely context for mentoring was the war itself, when Hope-Taylor's artistry was harnessed by the RAF's Central Interpretation Unit at Medmenham, by the Thames in Buckinghamshire. Medmenham's work was the interpretation of aerial photographs. From 1941, it also had a Section V which produced finely detailed, closely scaled terrain models of forthcoming targets to prepare aircrew and troops being sent to attack them. Such work called for artists in different media – sculptors, engravers, illustrators, craftsmen – who were recruited from staff and students at art schools. It appears that Hope-Taylor was being mentored by Mackley, and through him was drawn to Medmenham

---

* During the later 1950s and early 1960s, Hope-Taylor also appeared in, and sometimes presented, thematic programmes on aspects of archaeology and history on the Third Programme and Home Service, and with Glyn Daniel on TV.

when in 1941 he reached the age to enlist. Another modeller in Section V was the leading wood engraver, James Henry Govier (1910–1974), who worked alongside Hope-Taylor from 1942 to 1944.

Medmenham also provides the setting for Hope-Taylor's archaeological education. Air-photo interpretation drew extensively on archaeological skills, and around him were archaeologists and members of the Prehistoric Society who were only too glad to talk about their subject, regardless of rank. Further, many of the interpreters and model-makers were women, including a number with notable professional or social backgrounds, such as Charlotte Bonham Carter, Dorothy Lygon, and Sarah Churchill, who in turn attracted celebrated visitors with special skills – like Cecil Beaton, whose signed photograph of Sarah Churchill was found among Hope-Taylor's papers after his death. Medmenham was Hope-Taylor's cultural university.

Hope-Taylor, we shall see, changed our conception of what England is and how its Church began. But there are things about him that are not quite in focus, or at any rate not quite what they seem. For instance, his first name was not Brian. It was Kenneth. Brian was his second name, and around 1945 he decided to transpose them. Likewise, the surname he was born with was Taylor. Hope was his mother's maiden surname, and he combined them to rename himself as Hope-Taylor. It was as if he was reinventing himself. Name-shifting ran in the family. While his maternal grandfather is remembered as William Henry Hope, his alternative, and perhaps original, surname was Hodgkins. Artistic ability ran in the family too, for this William Hope (or Hodgkins) was the artist whose paintings of Sanderstead's prelapsarian red-squirrel days of heath, woodland, and heather have already been noted. Or again, it is said that he remained unmarried because he never recovered from the death of his fiancée in a road accident. But the only source for this story was Brian himself, and those of us who knew him could envisage other reasons why he might wish this side of his life to be downplayed – and perhaps why Cecil Beaton gave him a photograph of Sarah Churchill signed by himself at Medmenham.

In 1970, Stockwood put a test larger than Sanderstead before my dad. The south London parish of Battersea had fallen vacant. In all kinds of ways – its civic life, deprivation, problematic housing, the speed of change – Battersea was a formidable challenge. When John Betjeman visited a few years before, he found it 'a terrifying district' where 'the churches are barricaded with padlocks, and all the telephone booths are wrecked, so that one cannot ring up the vicars'. The inner city was Dad's natural habitat, and he agreed to go. For this to happen, the Church of England being what it is, the recommendation of the living's patron was first needed. Since 1763, the patronage of Battersea had belonged to the Earls Spencer, so to complete the formalities my mother and father were invited to Althorp to be interviewed by the Eighth Earl, former equerry to George VI, Johnny Spencer. They spent the night as guests, amused by the butler who showed them to adjoining rooms and coughed discreetly to indicate that there was a connecting door. Spencer coached them in his pronunciation of 'Althorp' ('Alltrup'), thereby keeping up that minor tradition whereby certain aristocrats insist that the names of their seats be spoken in a particular way (like 'Harwood' instead of 'Harewood') while everyone else apart from their friends and the BBC pronounce them normally. Having passed such tests, the way to Battersea was open.

A few weeks before they left, I arrived at the rectory on a late June afternoon. It was hot, and the house was empty. My parents were away. I had borrowed their car to collect books and clothes from Oxford, where I had just finished. The garage was behind the rectory, at the top of a bank overlooking the old tennis court. On the grass, in the stillness, were four fox cubs. They stared at me. Then they resumed play – somersaults, mock battle, springy jumping. After maybe a minute, trying not to break the spell, I looked around. On the far side of the lawn, in shadow, stretched out, watching, was the vixen. Eventually, she rose, flicked her tail, and the family withdrew.

There is no sentiment among the Church Commissioners or Diocesan Parsonage Boards, and Sanderstead rectory, like its predecessor, has since been sold. In 2018, permission was granted for its conversion into four flats, and the building of four houses in the garden and wilderness where the fox cubs played. There were objections, but neither the local people who put them nor the planners and councillors who set them aside knew about the resting place of the dog under the tree.

4

JOURNEYS AND MARGINS

———————

What, meanwhile, of Stuart? We left him at Wycliffe Hall, his family in the four-floor house in Blackhall Road, and Brenda pining for Eynsham. They were observant godparents. No birthday passed without a card bearing a thought-through message in Stuart's attractively formed hand, and few godchildren can have received Christmas presents on so wide a spectrum as a book of Clive Sansom's poetry at one end and a government surplus box kite at the other. The kite, quite large, yellow sail cloth on a demountable tubular aluminium frame, was a piece of wartime kit for ditched airmen, to hoist an aerial to radio a distress signal from a dinghy. Wind and weather were among Stuart's interests, appropriate for a student of the Old Testament, acquired I think during his days as a navigator in the RAF.

In 1960, he was appointed as the principal of a new theological college, attached to Rochester Cathedral. Its syllabus and routine were aimed at students with established careers – in industry, the police, self-employed, whatever – and no necessary academic background. Rochester was too distant for day trips from Longbridge, but when we moved to Sanderstead it became accessible. Indeed, on one of Dad's days off, we walked there.

The route we took was a twenty-five-mile stretch of the Pilgrims' Way – the path from Winchester to Thomas Becket's shrine in Canterbury that Hilaire Belloc imagined in *The Old Road* (1904). The idea was conjured again by Michael Powell and Emeric Pressburger in their film *A Canterbury Tale* (1944). The place we started was not far from locations in the film's opening, where medieval pilgrims ride through heathland on the Surrey Hills and a falcon cast by a knight match-cuts to a Spitfire.

The Pilgrims' Way in the 1960s was thought to have originated as a prehistoric track that became a route taken by pilgrims from Winchester to Canterbury following Becket's assassination. At its end was Becket's crown, at once the sword-sliced top of Becket's skull and the rotunda at the east end of the cathedral built 1179–1185 to contain it. Becket's crown was but one of the things that pilgrims came to venerate. Others were the site of the archbishop's martyrdom in the north-west transept, the marble tomb in the crypt where he was first interred, and the shrine in the Trinity Chapel to which he was translated in 1220. The shrine was a jewelled golden casket lifted high on a marble base, sheathed under a wooden cover, topped by the image of a ship, which could be lowered or lifted by a system of cables to the accompaniment of silvery bells.

The saint's concealment added to the awe with which he was contemplated. Wonder would be deepened by the creamy-grey and reddish-brown stones used to form the pairs of columns that flank the space: aside from a splash of Becket's brains, these colours recollected those of Christ's tomb in Jerusalem, and by using them here a comparison was being invited. The glazing of the vast windows of the Trinity Chapel is both monumental and intricate; it has impact from afar and yet draws you in. The glass dates from about two decades after Becket's murder. It is full-colour (there is hardly any white glass) and provides a kind of gemmed surface around the shrine which extended the palette of the masonry. And because the windows pre-date tracery, the glass is held within an iron armature, itself arrayed in decorative shapes, which vary from window to window. Hence, from a distance, there is beauty and rhythm in the colour and form, and the shrine is one jewelled casket inside another.

Up close, the windows tell of miracles which had already taken place at Becket's tomb. A number of them were recorded soon after his death and were used to support the case for his canonisation. Each is represented in a series of scenes, a bit like a comic strip, that show the ailment or crisis, the journey to the tomb, the cure. Inscriptions explain who is whom. Monks acted as tour guides for pilgrims, pointing to the various miraculous episodes with long sticks.

It has recently been found that several of the scenes depict people from Kent: William of Dene, a paralysed knight; Goditha, a crippled woman from Canterbury; and Saxeva, a woman from Dover, who had pains in her stomach and arm. What is really tantalising, then, is that pilgrims to the new shrine might well have known – or would certainly have known of – some of the people depicted in the windows. Another discovery concerns a panel of glass depicting a group of pilgrims on the road to Canterbury. Until recently, this was thought to be the work of a late Victorian glazier, but it is now realised that the portrayal is substantially medieval: it is the earliest known representation of Canterbury pilgrims, and was made less than twenty years after Becket's death. Yet more remarkable is a discovery made while the glass was out of the window under study in the studio: faint traces of letters on the white road which under a microscope and raking light resolved as 'PEREGRINI ST', 'pilgrims of the saint'.

Becket eclipsed Cuthbert and Edmund as England's leading saint. His shrine became Britain's most visited place. Metal detectorists find souvenirs sold to pilgrims far afield. 'Thomas is the best doctor for the worthy sick' reads the inscription on one of them. Secondary Becket relics – things like pieces of alleged vestments, swords, bits of his shroud – are recorded all over England. However, the route we walked that day probably had little to do with him. Canterbury-bound travellers from the south-west very likely did tramp existing routes along the North Downs, but the 'old way' is now regarded largely as a product of imagination, a joining of hitherto un-associated lengths of footpath, bridleway and quiet lane to make a surmised route. In the nineteenth century, the Ordnance Survey labelled it 'Pilgrims' Road' (in confirmatory antique lettering), thereby giving the idea credence, which in turn elicited things like signposts, pub signs, and house names. By such means can fallacies reinforce themselves.*

Pilgrimage was believed to alter your state of mind: far from friends and home, pilgrimage took you to a boundary between different worlds, freed your mind in time and space, and brought encounters with the unknown. The old road as something imagined rather than found connects with this view of pilgrimage as a state of heightened consciousness – like being in the back of Chris Scarf's car looking up at the elms. The attack on Becket's cult launched by Henry VIII in the autumn of 1538 was thus a bold move. If the saint was as powerful as most people had assumed, how might he react? But Henry had no choice but to take him on, for in the veneration of Becket lay the threat of papal authority over princes.

The un-sainting that followed was akin to the kind of erasure of

---

* That said, there was a pilgrimage route in the later Middle Ages, but not here: the later fourteenth century Gough Map (undated, made maybe in the 1370s, revised in the earlier fifteenth century, conceivably based on an older representation) shows a route from Southampton to Canterbury along the foot of the South Downs, presumably a course taken by religious tourists from overseas, or by English pilgrims bound for continental shrines who took in Becket on their way.

personality practised in Soviet Russia. During September, the shrine was dismantled, its treasures carted away, and the bones secretly disposed of. The prevailing rumour at the time was that the bones were burned, but there has been conjecture since about an unmarked reburial. (The discovery in 1888 of one candidate set of remains included a skull which was said to show clear phrenological signs of 'large perceptive qualities, much intellect, and indomitable energy': another instance, like the Pilgrims' Way, of an identity projected onto an assumption.) In November, a proclamation ordered that Thomas Becket must 'not be estemed, named, reputed, nor called a sayncte, but bysshop Becket'. Images and pictures of him throughout the realm were to be 'putte downe, and avoyded out of all churches, chapelles, and other places'. Days 'used to be festivall in his name' were not to be observed. Where his name occurred in services, antiphoners, collects, and prayers, it was not to be read 'but rased and put out of all the bokes'. Side by side with Becket's elimination from sight, sound, and word, Thomas Cromwell produced a revised narrative in which the blame for Becket's murder was laid on the bishop himself.

The superstitions surrounding popular devotion towards saints and shrines were repudiated by the Forty-two Articles of religion, a set of doctrinal tenets largely drafted by Cranmer which were issued in 1553 a few weeks before Edward VI died. Mary promptly revoked them, but they reappeared nine years later, with revisions, as the Thirty-nine Articles which finally defined the dogmatic position of the Church of England. Article 22 deals with the notion of saints as special intercessors: 'The Romish Doctrine concerning Purgatory, Pardons, Worshipping, and Adoration, as well of Images as of Reliques, and also invocation of Saints, is a fond thing vainly invented, and grounded upon no warranty of Scripture, but rather repugnant to the Word of God.'

That looks clear enough, but the Church of England did not get where it is today by being clear. The actual position is still debated. Some take Article 22 to be a flat rejection of the invocation of saints. Others point to passages in the New Testament – St Paul, for instance, describing members of the Church as 'fellow citizens with the saints, and of the household of God' (Ephesians 2.19) – and say the intention was not to ban saints altogether but to outlaw notions unwarranted by Scripture; for example, that saints continue to exert power or influence events from their graves. A similar debate surrounded angels, references to which in burial services were dropped in early Anglican prayer books. Angels were viewed by Reformation thinkers with great suspicion, but they survived in popular culture because Protestants 'simply could not afford to live without them'. And while angels took human forms when they needed to make themselves apparent, their inherent condition was invisible energy. Angels 'appeare not nowe as in former times' said the leading Puritan William Perkins (1558–1602).

The Church of England has dealt with such differences by absorbing into its calendar a number of historically attested medieval saints from different denominations and churches, combining them with notable figures – teachers, spiritual writers, social reformers, pastors – from other backgrounds and times, but does not call them saints nor credit them with heavenly properties. The result is an interdenominational list in which Brigid of Kildare (c.451–c.525), William Wilberforce (1759–1833) and the poet Christina Rossetti (1830–1894) rub shoulders. The list includes John Wycliffe (c.1328–1384), morning star of the English Reformation, and martyrs like William Tyndale (c.1494–1536), translator of scriptures; Nicholas Ridley, the Diocese of Rochester's reforming bishop (1547–50), burned by Mary in 1555; and Óscar Romero (1917–1980), fourth archbishop of El Salvador, campaigner for social justice, assassinated while celebrating mass, the twentieth century's Becket.

Stuart was at ease with scriptural saints, but to judge from his books, he shared Cranmer's scepticism about the kind of figures at whom Article 22 took aim – like William of Perth (d.1201), the murdered baker whose shrine at Rochester became enormously popular just after Becket's cult got going, perhaps not coincidentally because most people on their way to Canterbury went through Rochester to reach it. In Stuart's eyes, the Church for which the Reformation martyrs died was founded on Scripture and love, not dodgy miracles or dogma. He had little interest in Church organisation, and was suspicious of the kind of Anglicanism in which, like Judaism in the early first century, rules and professionals to enforce them are to the fore. In a Lenten meditation, he wrote, 'Maybe you will have to find Christ down the street, before you learn to find him in the Church.' However, if he was not much engaged by ecclesiastical process, he was absorbed by the history of spirituality. He was fascinated by the desert-seeking men and women of fourth-century Egypt and Syria who saw desolate places as the domain of demons, and went to live in them as a way of being militant in the cause of the gospel. Desert-seeking became the model for Christian monasticism. Stuart repeated a saying of Carlo Carretto (1910–1988), who for many years lived and prayed alone in the Sahara: 'Find yourself a desert in your life.' Desert can be time as well as place: Stuart kept a cut-off time each day when he stopped whatever he was doing and turned to study the Bible.

Britain's deserts in late antiquity were symbolic places like moors, remote valleys, and islands. There were plenty of those in west Wales, and the year before we walked to Rochester Stuart and Brenda invited me to join their family holiday in southern Pembrokeshire. This took me back into the world I had glimpsed when the choir went to St Davids. Indeed, it was Chris Scarf, on his way to another such visit, who drove me down. His car was now a battered 2.4 litre Jaguar, and as we ascended the tree-crowned ridges between Carmarthen and Haverfordwest, there came again the sense that something rare must lie ahead. And it did, although it has taken me nearly sixty years to begin to make sense of what it was.

The Blanches were at Orlandon, a clump of farm cottages and out-buildings amid trees, at the base of the small headland which forms the southern tip of St Bride's Bay. Orlandon's position put four beaches within walking distance in different directions. Musselwick and Mar-loes Sands lay on either side of the peninsula to the west. Dale was forty minutes' walk to the south. To the north was St Bride's Haven, a narrow rock-flanked channel with a sheltered stony beach.

Orlandon days began with Stuart quietly moving round the edge of things – making a morning cup of tea, cleaning boots, preparing sand-wiches. Over breakfast there would be discussion about which beach to walk to. The decision was usually determined by wind and tide: if it was blowy on one side of the peninsula, it was sheltered on the other, and Musselwick's sands only appeared below half tide.

St Bride's was nearest. The inlet is overlooked by a church, dedicated of course to St Bride. From it, if you looked up from the small copper butterflies that flew like sparks on the haven's grassy margins, you could see across to St David's peninsula and Ramsey island off its end. Pretty much everything you see here evokes the spirituality of a Hiberno-Welsh world that existed hereabouts fifteen hundred years ago. Tradition said that Ramsey had been home to Justinian, a Carlo Carretto-like figure who was David's confessor in the sixth century. To the island's west are rocks and islets called the Bishops and Clerks. The sight of Ireland from Ramsey's highest point brings Bride herself to mind. Brigid of Kildare, protector of pilgrims, variously Brid, Bridgit, Brigid, or Ffraid in Welsh, is Ireland's second patron saint.

Some years would pass before I became aware of arguments about whether Bride existed, or was the Christianised personification of an

Iron Age goddess, or both, and over half a century before airborne laser scanning would reveal Justinian's surroundings. If I had had my wits about me, I might have spotted bits of bone dropping out of the sandy soil eroding at the top of the haven, perhaps even the marks of a sub-circular enclosure running under the churchyard, but these signs that we were holidaying in the midst of an early medieval religious community all went unnoticed. The nearest we wittingly came to anything to do with early spirituality at St Bride's was matins from the 1662 Prayer Book.

Matins can be dreary, especially on a sunny morning. With at least one psalm, three canticles (one of them long), and lengthy liturgical prayers, it has a power-to-weight ratio that often seems heavily stacked towards the weight. One of the few things a parson can do to make it bearable is to bring it in under the hour by limiting the intercessions and keeping the sermon short. On that August Sunday, the rector at St Bride's did neither. Moreover, his sermon was odd. Incumbents usually preach on texts taken from readings for the day, which are prescribed in a lectionary. However, on this occasion the rector announced that he was going to explore a sentence in the prayer of general confession: 'We have left undone those things which we ought to have done, and we have done those things which we ought not to have done.' (If you say this aloud, you can hear how Cranmer balanced the sentence, tempting speakers to put a slight stress on 'ought' in the first half, and upon 'done' and especially 'not' in the second.) I remember nothing of the sermon. However, the next year there we were again, and the rector began, 'I take for my text a sentence from the general confession: "We have left undone those things which we ought to have done, and we have done those things which we ought not to have done."' We were virtually the only people in the congregation; one of Stuart's daughters caught my eye. Evidently, this rector had fifty-two sermons, and if you went to his church at St Bride on Sundays exactly one year apart, you would hear the same one. I glanced at Stuart, but of course he was looking attentive, as if it was all new.

Occasionally, we went further afield, as on the following day when we walked to Monk Haven: a secluded rocky inlet on the north shore of Milford Haven. You reach it along a path from the church of St Ishmael (variously Ismael or Isfael) through a narrow stream valley that leads down to the foreshore. The church is on its own, away from the village, and the path was overhung by trees, shadowy, a little ominous, like something out of a fairy tale. The path went past the vicarage, which from its dereliction we assumed to be abandoned, save that there was a milk bottle by the back door.

At the foot of the valley, we met a high wall that divided the beach from the area where the path emerged from the trees. It was built of red sandstone rubble, and embodied a central opening, spanned by a hefty oak lintel, through which we went. After a swim and game of beach cricket, we collected driftwood and lit a fire.

I climbed the wall. It was crenelated. Clumps of pink thrift and gold hawkweed had taken hold in the joints between the stones. Glancing down after a few minutes, I was surprised to see a man standing in front of the gap in the wall – surprised, because no one had seen him arrive. He was middle-aged, wore a faint smile, and was looking around. At length, I said hello. He did not reply, nor even seem to register my presence. Eventually, he turned and walked back through the gap. I looked to see him appear on the other side, but there was no one there.

I wondered if our silent visitor might have been living in the run-down vicarage; perhaps, indeed, he was the vicar. But nothing explained his disappearance – and there is no point in trying to account for the unaccountable. More can be said about the surroundings. Nineteenth-century maps and records tell that the gloomy woodland through which we walked had originated as the pleasure ground for a country house which stands about a third of a mile back from the shore. The house is called Trewarren, it overlooks the Monk Haven valley, and it was built in 1845 for Gilbert Warren Davis, who commissioned it on the proceeds of his supply to the Royal Navy of cattle, which he drove on the hoof from Pembrokeshire to Portsmouth. The family turned the valley into an ornamental park, with groves, terraced paths, pools and waterfalls, follies, and trees planted in patterns of contrasting colour and kind. The crenelated wall was part of this. By 1950, the house had changed hands. The grounds became neglected; saplings spread; the ponds choked; bramble took hold; the ornamental park reverted to the wild.

Lost gardens are uneasy places. On the edge of this one was the parish church of St Ismael – medieval, but heavily restored. Looking around inside, the font, carved maybe during the reign of King John, is the oldest recognisable thing. Yet the place goes back before the font at least as far as we come after.

Dyfed's ruling dynasty between the fifth and seventh centuries was Irish. Their realm was divided into territories known as *cantrefi*. Seven such areas can be recognised in the kingdom of Dyfed. They differed in size, but as an order of magnitude, the *cantref* of Rhos, between Milford

Haven and St Bride's Bay, covered around one hundred square miles. Each *cantref* had a bishop, whose community was often on its margin. It was so in Rhos, where the mother church of the *cantref* was at St Ishmael, on the edge of its territory, and of Dyfed.

Ismael in tradition was a sixth-century Breton prince, and one of David's three most faithful companions. More than half a millennium lies between their day and the earliest sources that talk about them. The gap stirs worry that nothing useful can be said. And yet, since we were there, archaeology has recognised graves from Ismael's age, an enclosure for a religious community, and an inscribed stone brought from David's vicinity on the far side of St Bride's Bay. Here, did Ismael find a desert in his life?

5

BATTERSEA AND AFTERWARDS

The Thames-side church of St Mary's, Battersea, is an ancient foundation. Dad liked to sign himself as its fifty-ninth vicar, but it was only in the fifth of his eighteen years as its incumbent that he was able to live there. There was a parsonage, a handsome building – late eighteenth century, three storied, brick, elegant railings, listed, with an LCC blue plaque saying that the naturalist and polar explorer Edmund Wilson had lived in it. However, it had been neglected, and the Church Commissioners, local authority, diocesan architects, and solicitors quarrelled about what to do. Meanwhile, the diocese rented a flat for the new vicar in Cranley Gardens, over a mile away in South Kensington.

Cranley Gardens was unsatisfactory even as a holding measure. It was inaccessible to parishioners, and much of Dad's time was spent in fruitless trekking to and fro, and in trying to unscramble the inherited problem for which nobody would take responsibility. When he wrote to thank friends in Sanderstead for their send-off back in August, he added, 'I have a new game which adds zest to life to see how close to the house I can get my own car. I have only once so far succeeded in getting a bullseye (right outside the door), but I am childishly pleased when I score an inner (anywhere in the same road).'

By 1939, there were seventeen Anglican churches in Battersea, all but two of them created between the 1840s and 1902, when the population rose twenty-five-fold.* The presence of so many nearby parishes put other vicarages in the vicinity, and sure enough after a few months they were moved to a vacant vicarage in the adjoining parish of Christ Church, on Candahar Road: one of a number of streets in the neighbourhood named after British colonial feats of arms in the Second Afghan War and Zulu War.† The area whirred with crime. My mother's handbag was whisked off the kitchen table while she was hanging out washing;

---

* In round figures, from 6,800 in 1841 to 169,000 in 1901.

† Kambala Road, Kyhber Road, Musjid Road, Nepaul Road (originally, Square), and Zulu Crescent were among the others laid out between 1879 and 1881.

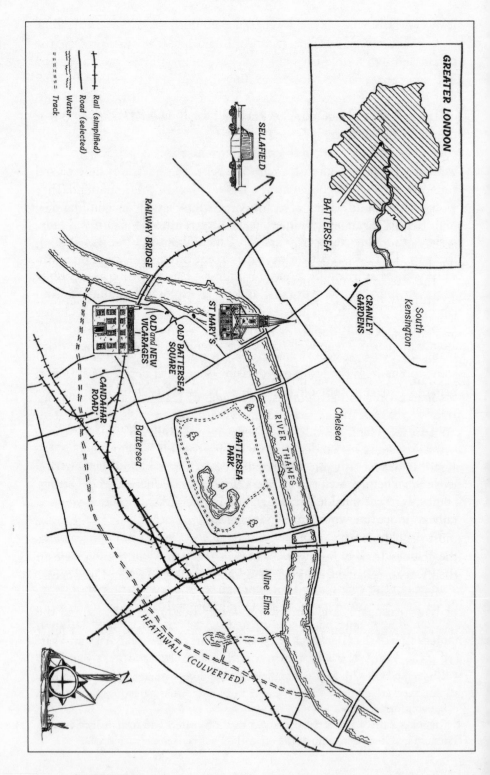

it was advisable to lock the back door even during a trip to the dustbin.

Candahar Road was closer than Cranley Gardens but still outside the parish and half a mile from the church. Douglas Jay, Battersea North's MP since 1946, gave advice. According to Dad it was 'well worthy of a first in Greats, a fellow of All Souls and former President of the Board of Trade. You must, he said, get them all together in the same room at the same time.' With Jay's help, this was achieved. They all met on a cold and wet afternoon, in the old vicarage itself. The building had been vandalised. Water poured through the roof. The buck was duly passed round. After a while, cooperation was offered and a solution found. They would sell the old vicarage, retain part of the garden, and build a new one. The old vicarage was auctioned in 1971. House-price inflation was accelerating; by the time the new vicarage was finished in 1975, the old one had changed hands several times and more than doubled in value.

The site left for the new vicarage was quite small. Its design was accordingly organised around a vertical axis rather than the kind of lengthwise plan we saw at Longbridge and Sanderstead. Tall, square, it was built around a winding staircase that gave first onto the study, with living and bedrooms above and a utility room below. Eccentric spaces in some rooms were the result of a decision, taken just before construction began, to shave a foot off one side to bring its cost back within the original budget.

Vicarage neighbours were a microcosm of Battersea. At the back, council flats. Just across the cul-de-sac passing the door, Old Battersea House, the early Georgian London home of the American billionaire Malcolm Forbes. Across Vicarage Crescent, the Thames, where sailing barges were occupied as homes. Two hundred yards to the south was a railway bridge across which trains rumbled in the early hours. In the 1970s, most people supposed there to be no direct north–south rail link across the Thames. In fact, there was this one, and the trains in the night were on their way to Sellafield, carrying spent nuclear fuel rods from Dungeness.

Battersea is first heard of in the late seventh century as Batriceseg or Badoricesheah.* The word translates as 'Beadūric's island',† and the island emerges when you look at the terrain. Until the 1860s, a relict

---

* The name occurs in land grants dated AD 677 and 693 that survive only in later copies; their authenticity is debated, but most authorities agree that they contain original information.
† In other early sources the personal name was often Patric, as in Patricesy in Domesday (Great DB folio 32r).

channel of the Thames branched eastward just upstream at Battersea
Creek, flowed along the foot of Lavender Hill and old Clapham, turned
north-east and rejoined the Thames at Nine Elms. The river was called
the Heathwall, and the low-lying, muddy area between it and the
Thames was the island. The Heathwall explains why there were so many
mills in Battersea; as early as 1086, there were at least seven, presumably
tide-mills, and although the river was culverted in the 1860s its former
course still forms the Lambeth–Wandsworth boundary.

Down to the 1800s, much of the area was water meadow and tidal
marsh, dissected by creeks, ditches, and cuts made at different times, in
places overhung by willow and poplar. Stretches of fertile alluvium and
silt were divided into strips ('shots') upon which were grown such things
as lavender (whence Lavender Hill), carrots, and asparagus ('Battersea
Bundles'), which were shipped downstream to Westminster, the City,
and Southwark. Mingled with the shots were orchards and plots where
niche crops like apricots grew. Other island pursuits were pig-keeping,
and the digging out of riverine clays for bricks. By 1750, Battersea
was a realm of contrasts: a residential London suburb centred on the
waterfront church of St Mary, with market gardens and common fields
raising crops for London markets.

St Mary was the first parish church. Until the sixteenth century, it
was held by Westminster Abbey, and its position on London's fringe,
between Westminster and Hampton Court, was suited to incumbents
of minor note, like Robert Cromwell (d.1517), the twenty-ninth vicar,
who was Wolsey's agent and probably introduced the cardinal to his
cousin, Thomas – with consequences met throughout this book. Battersea's patronage passed with the manor to the St John family, and from
them in 1763 to the Earls Spencer. Suburban villa dwellers and owners
of manufacturing concerns along the riverside provided impetus for the
complete rebuilding that followed. Its airy, light interior hums with cultural echoes. Benedict Arnold (1741–1801), the general who managed to
fight on both sides during the American Revolutionary War, is buried
in the crypt. J. M. W. Turner (1775–1851) lived just over the Thames in
Chelsea; in evenings, he liked to sit in the west-facing bay window of
the vestry, watching the river in different weathers and lights. Catherine
Boucher (1762–1831), the daughter of a Battersea market gardener, was
nineteen when William Blake (1757–1827), visionary painter, engraver,
and poet, met her in 1781. The two were married in St Mary's the following year. Catherine went on to become an accomplished printer, helping
to produce, colour, and sell her husband's illuminated books, the first to

see a proof of the page with *Jerusalem*. Blake is said to have drawn her on his deathbed: 'you have ever been an angel to me'. Literary Battersea is indeed a formidable place. Edward Thomas (1878–1917) attended its Grammar School for Boys; E. M. Forster (1879–1970), Seán O'Casey (1880–1964), Graham Greene (1904–1991), Mervyn Peake (1911–1968), and Roald Dahl (1916–1990) all lived and worked in the area at different times.

By the 1850s, Battersea's waterfront was thronged with dyeworks, maltings, concerns involving oil, grease, crucibles, and candles. Over the next thirty years, London-bound migration from Ireland and other parts of Britain turned north Battersea into one of the poorest, most over-crowded, and insanitary districts of London. After the Second World War, there was some slum clearance, municipal building of housing and flats. By the time Dad arrived, deindustrialisation was under way, and privatisation – more on this below – was about to begin. From the early 1980s, old factory sites were replaced by housing. In ten years, Battersea went from somewhere heavily industrial, red-lined by building societies, to an affluent residential area. In the 1990s, after Dad left, the surround-ings of the church were transformed again by the demolition of nearby flourmills, and the arising of Richard Rogers's Montevetro building.

Soon after his arrival, Dad became chairman of the Battersea Churches Housing Trust. The Trust was one of a number of church-based housing associations which benefitted from the 1974 Housing Act that fostered a middle way between council housing and the private sector. The private sector was then still rent controlled, generally in a poor state, while local authority housing was characterised by restrictiveness. Battersea came under Wandsworth Borough Council, which until the early 1980s had a housing policy that chiefly catered for families. Single mothers, unmarried parents, and individuals made up a large part of Battersea churches' clientele. In parallel, there was a pushback against the clearances, high rise, and emptying out of traditional communities that had dominated the 1960s.

Wandsworth in the 1980s was at the forefront of experiments in the privatising of functions like street cleaning, park keeping, refuse col-lection, and housing management that until then had been carried out by local government as a matter of course. In 1978, the Conservatives gained control of Wandsworth; from 1979, a right-wing tendency led by Christopher Chope began to reshape Wandsworth into a labora-tory for finding new ways to provide services. For a time, Dad was in the thick of this; following Mervyn Stockwood's example of being on the side of the poor through political action, he was co-opted onto Wandsworth Borough Council as a Labour alderman, and served as a Labour representative on the Inner London Education Authority until its reorganisation in 1986. On return from Council meetings, often in the small hours, he would give vivid accounts of angry exchanges and accusations shouted at Chope by Labour councillors around whom, for the most part, Chope ran rings.* One of the Wandsworth privatisation projects involved the large blocks of 1930s council flats behind Battersea vicarage. Wandsworth removed their tenants, oversaw their renovation, and then sold them into private hands. When Michael Heseltine arrived to open one of them, Dad was there with a banner bearing a text from Isaiah: 'What do you mean by grinding the faces of the poor?' The poor, meanwhile, had been moved on, and Battersea's face was changed.

Dad's arrival at Longbridge and at Sanderstead was on each occasion followed by a new parish magazine. At the time, it was there to be a channel of communication between parish and parishioners; looking back, it was also a mirror to the kind of place each of them was. *Contact* originated while the parish was actually being born; a good deal of it was used to explain what the Church was for, how it worked, and why workers at the Austin and Bournville might wish to join. *Signpost*, well produced, glossy, reflected middle-class preoccupations, well-established parish institutions, and, sometimes, external opinions.

Riverside Review was different again. It resembled *Private Eye*, black and white with a scissors-and-paste typescript layout; it even carried cartoons by some of the *Eye*'s cartoonists. There was tabloid vividness, snappy subediting, and it tackled street-level topics: housing, bus services, vigilance over planning applications, the Morgan Wall, Battersea memories, introductions to new politicians, residents' opinions. *Riverside Review* was produced on behalf of all North Battersea's churches. It was free. Its topicality, verve, social conscience, care for the place itself, and passing of its neighbourhoods reached a circulation of ten thousand. Behind it was Tom Hartman, the business partner of the publisher Leo Cooper, who used his skills, connections, and a lot of his own time to bring it into being and keep it going.

Since Christian action and politics went hand in hand, political

---

* And sometimes did so with progressive effect. One consequence of the privatisation of street cleaning was that the firm which did it employed staff from all backgrounds, whereas Wandsworth Council had operated a colour bar.

friendships ensued. One, with Douglas Jay, has already been mentioned. Jay was very well liked in Battersea; there was real affection for him, and behind his rather cerebral political reputation and prowess as an economist, Dad found a man in love with the landscape and literature of deep England. Jay had been in Attlee's government; we shall meet him again. Another was Alf Dubs, who was introduced to parishioners in *Riverside Review* when he took the seat of Battersea South at the 1979 general election. Dubs was one of the Jewish refugee children who were brought to England from Czechoslovakia in 1939 by Nicholas Winton. He, too, was admired by Dad, and although he was a humanist, he did much for the work of the parish. Not all Dad's political friendships were on the Left. His pastoral concern led him to involve himself in all areas of community life, and this naturally created bonds with people whose views differed from his. One of them was a Lord Coleraine, of whom I had not heard when I walked into the vicarage and found him drinking a cup of tea, although the name of his father rang a bell: Bonar Law, who became Prime Minister in October 1922 and resigned 209 days later because of throat cancer. His young son Dick was at his side during the days when power passed to Stanley Baldwin, and one day in May exactly fifty years later there he was.

Dick Coleraine become a frequent visitor, calling for a chat or game of chess once or twice a week. If I had had the wit to ask him about Lloyd George's government after 1918, or his boyhood in Downing Street when his father was Chancellor of the Exchequer, his subsequent twenty-seven-year career in the House of Commons, or membership of Churchill's wartime government, I would have done so – but being a Tory of the old school, he was far too polite to refer to himself without being invited to do so, and I was too thoughtless to give him the opportunity. We did talk about other things, and I was struck by his stillness as we did so; he was a keen listener, always polite and diplomatic, but liable gently to cross-examine if he sensed careless thinking. I tried to introduce him to music. We once listened to part of Holst's Choral Symphony, a mercurial, scampering setting of Keats's 'Folly's Song'. He was mystified: it might as well have been by Stockhausen.

Dick Coleraine's quietude belied his influence. In December 1971, he gave my parents an inscribed copy of his second and latest polemic book, *For Conservatives Only*, published the year before (its cover price nostalgically printed in both £sd and decimal formats). Coleraine said he wrote it to clear his mind about what conservatism stood for. It has two themes: first, that in the wake of global upheavals that had demanded centralising authority, government's task was not to increase its efficiency but to restrain itself; and second, that politics should be driven by principle and conviction, not by appeal to centre ground.

Dick was Aaron to Margaret Thatcher's Moses. Since 1945, he had argued for individual freedom, free-market economics, and small government. By thinking of the unthinkable, he influenced a political generation which had never known him in office or in the House of Commons. He helped to identify the themes that came to dominate Conservative thought after 1979; his was the inspiration for the Selsdon Group of young libertarian Conservatives which formed in 1973 in reaction to Heath's backsliding.

Behind the chess and chats in the kitchen, something else was going on. Dick Coleraine's friend Enoch Powell, author of his entry in the *Oxford Dictionary of National Biography*, explains what it was:

> Right at the end, in the presence of bereavement and infirmity, Coleraine made the last discovery. He was not only a Conservative and not only a Tory; he was also, and therefore, an Anglican. In his last two or three years Coleraine became a regular communicant and valued member of the congregation of the Thames-side parish church of Battersea. It was there that his friends took leave of him when he died in London on 15 November 1980.

Powell was in the congregation when Dick Coleraine's funeral was held five days later – the feast day of Edmund the Martyr, patron of pandemics, torture victims, and wolves. It is a day we shall come back to.

Battersea in the 1970s still contained a number of long-established families, the kind for whom shopkeepers and residents around Battersea Square would line the pavements to salute when one of them died and the hearse pulled away after the funeral. Few were more closely associated with Battersea than Arnold Taylor, whose father, grandfather, and great-grandfather were consecutively headmasters of Sir Walter St John's Grammar School for Boys. Arnold's father, John George Taylor, was author of *Our Lady of Batersey* (1925), a 442-page book with the heft of a brick which recounts the story of the church and its parish from original sources.

I first met Arnold in Christ Church vicarage, in 1972. He was famous for studies of the Welsh castles of Edward I in which his use of written records coupled with field observation had led to the realisation that Caernarfon and Conwy, with their town walls, and other castles were the work of one of Europe's great mason-architects, the Savoyard

Master James of St George. Aside from the inherent importance of his discovery, it paved the way for the inscription of these structures as a World Heritage Site. When we met, Arnold had just retired from his post as Chief Inspector of Ancient Monuments in the Department of the Environment. The Department had just been formed, when the Ministries of Housing and Local Government, Public Building and Works, and Transport were brought together. The office of Chief Inspector had previously rested in Public Building and Works, where Arnold had served intermittently since 1935.* In the world of conservation, architectural history, and archaeology the post of Chief Inspector was spoken with a kind of reverence; its title went back to the days of Augustus Pitt Rivers (1823–1900). I had recently joined this world, or at least its outer periphery; since the previous autumn, I had been a member of the team that was working flat out to complete the recording of 750,000 cubic feet of archaeological deposits under York Minster – fulfilment of the work begun by Brian Hope-Taylor at the start of the structural emergency four years before. Arnold struck me as gentle and wise. Then a penny dropped. Our frantic work under York Minster had had a thin start, and Taylor was one of those in charge of it.

Since Hope-Taylor's reconnaissance in 1966, the Dean and Chapter seem not to have shown much further interest in archaeology. Their wish to save the cathedral from collapse never led them to see that a grasp of how the building had evolved would enable the aim to be achieved. Instead, repair and rescue archaeology were separated. Having been warned that the life expectancy of the central tower was no more than fifteen years, in April 1967 the Dean and Chapter launched an appeal to raise £2 million (about £37 million at today's values) to pay for urgent repairs, and ruled out applying any of these funds to the support of archaeology. Rather, any work to understand the cathedral historically was regarded as an indulgence, ancillary to the repairs, to be organised and funded by archaeologists themselves. Luckily, the consulting engineers from Ove Arup realised that to save the Minster they needed to know its story, and that archaeological skills would be necessary to piece it together. In due course, it was they who helped to phase the work in such a way that some degree of recording could take place.

At first, however, relevant skills were in short supply. In 1967, a

---

* In Chapter 14, we shall see that in 1945 Taylor and my father knew each other while on active service with the RAF in Italy. During their companionship in the 1970s and 1980s, I do not think either of them realised this.

ten-strong archaeological advisory committee was formed to counsel the
Dean and Chapter. Sensing urgency, for the first year they acquiesced
to the contractor digging out the top six feet of the central crossing
under the eye of one archaeologist, loaned by another body, armed with
a pencil and notebook. There was no one even to hold the other end of
his tape. Part of the rationale for this decision, whereby a committee
of ten monitored the work of one, was a belief that the more recent
history of York Minster was already well understood, and hence that
limited resources should be husbanded for older and deeper deposits.
The committee was wrong. Arnold Taylor was one of its members. He
looked at me across the vicarage living room, no doubt wondering why
I had gone quiet.

By the time I arrived in 1971, a practised and reasonably well-
equipped archaeological team was in existence, ably led by Derek
Phillips, a young archaeology graduate from the University of Durham
who had arrived in 1968 and been working round the clock ever since.
The team had grown around his sturdy presence and had a special solidarity, not experienced since, because of him. By the late 1960s, it was
becoming clear even to the committee of elders that some degree of
independent resourcing was going to be needed, and its chairman, Sir
Mortimer Wheeler, duly coaxed a succession of grants from bodies such
as the Pilgrim Trust and British Academy to meet the growing costs.
When the main repairs came to an end in early 1972, Derek fell ill and
was off the scene for a few weeks; he had not paused for five years, and
since he lived in a caravan in Chapter House Yard (or as he had it, 'No. 1
Charnel Gardens') he had been on site all day every day. His permanent
availability to solve problems and deal with crises meant that dinner
dates were often broken, and his social circle shrank accordingly.

Alongside the shaky funding, incessant demands and physical
discomforts, Derek had faced and met an extraordinary intellectual
challenge. On an ordinary open site, archaeologists will work down
from most recent layers to the oldest, at their own pace. At York Minster
there was no control over pace, while the work and its timing were led
by engineering and constructional need, which over six years involved
some two hundred separate excavations. If you imagine a glass brick
roughly 174 yards (160 metres) long, 74 yards (68 metres) across, and
5.5 yards (5 metres) deep, randomly fragment it into several hundred
sub-volumes, examine the interiors of each, separately, at a different
time, then reassemble the resulting data, you get an inkling of what
was happening. The challenge was intensified by the fourth dimension,

time: what was known about a given layer or structure in 1968 differed from what was understood when you met it again, a few inches away, but three or four years later.

For all the talk about urgency, the Dean and Chapter did not entirely help themselves. The logical way to tackle repairs to a cathedral involving excavation twenty feet below the floor, the insertion of new substructures, and works of all kinds up to the vault, is to close the building while you do it. The Dean and Chapter did the opposite. Amid thickets of scaffolding, the hiss of welders' blue-white fire, the clamour of drilling, and our disinterment of the bones of many, many dead, the cathedral was kept open not only for daily worship but also for traditional secondary uses like public concerts. On one day in December 1971, I was eventually driven out of a deep trench in the north transept as the area darkened under the construction of temporary tiered choir seating for a performance of *Messiah*. Removing to the central crypt, a verger added a hundred or more yards to the route of our barrow run out to Chapter House Yard on the grounds that crumbs of earth were falling on the north choir aisle pavement, and the dean's wife did 'not like it crunchy underfoot'.

The continuation of services amid the mayhem meant that each afternoon the clamour subsided, the organ played, and the choir arrived to sing choral evensong. They called it the 'four o'clock miracle', and it was. On a few occasions I deputised for one of the choir men, rushing from wherever I was digging to the song room for rehearsal, then processing with the choir into the stalls to sing the service. My overalls were hidden beneath a cassock, but I recall the shock on the face of a neighbour when he glanced down and saw my boots. The sub-organist, Geoffrey Coffin, sometimes came in to practise late in the evening. Geoffrey had been the organist and choirmaster at Sanderstead a few years before; when we worked through the night it became a custom to send requests up to the organ loft. On one evening, Geoffrey got through a substantial part of the score of *The Sound of Music*.

By 1972, the Dean and Chapter were still not showing much interest in their archaeology. Only one of those who spoke to me showed any sense of ownership of what had been done on their behalf: a new story involving a Norman cathedral of a kind no one had imagined; archbishops who had been groomed as saints; a graveyard paved with the sculptured memorials of York's Anglo-Viking elite; inscribed stones from the age of Bede; the headquarters of the legionary fortress from which a Roman province had been run. They seemed to regard York

Minster's archaeology, essentially, as our business, not theirs, and that perspective was symbolised by a rumour – which may well have been true – that they were charging us rent for storage of their own finds. I did not know it then, but the thrust of my next job would be to help ensure that no dichotomy like this would occur again.

Members of our advisory committee were seldom seen, but there were some whose visits we welcomed. Top of the list was Wheeler, partly because we were in awe of him as British archaeology's greatest achiever and influencer of the mid twentieth century, and partly because he took us to the pub. Brian Hope-Taylor, nominally the 'Director of Research', was affable, ready to talk regardless of who you were, a casual yet slightly nervous smoker. Brian's visits were occasional, but his presence was felt through Derek, whose style of field drawing, calligraphy, writing, and ways of problem-solving reflected Hope-Taylor's idiom. In contrast was Courtney Arthur Ralegh Radford, last of the gentlemen antiquaries, aloof, much of whose career had been spent in attempts to use archaeological evidence to corroborate legends and traditions. Wheeler (for reasons we did not understand) held in him in high regard, but Radford's field technique was messy, and his interpretations of places like Tintagel and Glastonbury have not endured.

More on the edge of things, although he lived nearby, was John Harvey (1911–1997), who was then regarded as Britain's greatest living historian of Gothic architecture. Harvey saw later English Gothic, the world of Henry Yeveley and Chaucer, as a supreme artistic achievement, and the Tudors and Renaissance as its destroyers. By the early 1970s, his interests had begun to shift towards garden history, but he readily gave his time and erudition when we asked for it; there were meetings in which he helped to put our discoveries into wider context, and his prodigious bibliographic memory was put at our disposal. We devoured his *The Mediaeval Architect* (1972) and the revised *Cathedrals of England and Wales* (1974).

In all kinds of ways, then, John Harvey was our pin-up. But within his books were odd statements: 'the flowering of mediaeval culture upon the highest plane, putting it in the thirteenth and fourteenth centuries on a level with any of the most exquisite achievements of mankind [was due to] the arrival of biologically better blood in families of the ruling dynasties of Western Europe'. Harvey said that aesthetic discrimination 'has always been the possession of a minority of the human race, a relatively small number of men and women concerned with quality rather than quantity. All great art has been produced in response to the demands of this minority, and is the outward and visible sign of the presence – recognized or not – of a well-bred biological caste.' In Harvey's mind, then – and in Britain's broadly accepted and as-yet largely uncontested view – Gothic art flowed from well-born families and eugenics, not from anything else, like the spread of ideas through trade, and social or industrial change.

None of us knew that before the war he had been a virulent anti-Semite, an enthusiast for 'Nordic culture', a participant in neo-medievalist ceremonies, a close companion of Arnold Leese, leader of the Imperial Fascist League, or that his idolisation of Edward I mapped onto Hitler because of the actions both had taken against the Jews.

Going back to Battersea, for continuity, let us follow Dad into retirement in June 1988. The day of his last service was sunny; the church was full; there was a baptism in which two youngsters were welcomed; Tom Hartman read one of the lessons; the congregation sang Samuel Sebastian Wesley's great hymn 'O Thou Who Camest from Above'. Before the final prayer came Sidney Carter's 'One More Step Along the World I Go'. Carter (who collaborated on various projects with another Battersea resident, Donald Swann)* wrote it for an end-of-term service at Southwark Cathedral School in 1971. By the early 2000s, it had been republished over thirty times and copyright returns showed that its singing in schools was more popular than any other item. But it did not mention God, and it was described as 'almost devoid of content'. The potency of the song is in its context of moving on:

> And it's from the old I travel to the new,
> Keep me travelling along with you.

The new in Dad's case was Archbishop Holgate's Hospital, a group of almshouses outside Hemsworth in Yorkshire, where he would serve in semi-retirement as Master for the next ten years.

Archbishop Holgate's Hospital consists of twenty-four cottages set in thirteen acres with lodges for a master, a porter, and a chapel. Holgate was Robert Holgate (1481/2–1555), a son of Hemsworth and key player in England's religious commotions between 1530 and 1555. Holgate was appointed Archbishop of York in 1545 and a member of the group that produced the revised Prayer Book of 1551. Mary deprived him of his see. For a time, he was imprisoned. A small contemporary painting of him on a wooden panel hung just inside the chapel door.

---

* Swann was parishioner of another Battersea church, St Mary-le-Park.

Schools and almshouses became classic objects for endowment after the Reformation. With chantries abolished and prayers for the dead forbidden, they enabled commemoration by other means, whereby names of benefactors were spoken, sung, and remembered by those they helped or supported.

Mervyn Stockwood, meanwhile; how had he been travelling? In 1974 the sees of Winchester, York and Canterbury fell vacant.

Stockwood was never a serious contender for Canterbury but he was deeply disappointed not to be offered the archbishopric of York, an appointment which in many ways he deserved and which he would have filled with suitable gravitas. The following year he was smitten by deep depression which did not lift until in 1980 he resigned the see of Southwark.

In 1974, in fulfilment of his recall from Eynsham to Wycliffe Hall in 1954, it was Stuart who was consecrated Archbishop of York.

6

GETTING LUCKY

Tuesday 11 June 1974 was hot. The *Guardian* that morning carried an advertisement that caught my eye. The Council for British Archaeology (CBA) invited applications from 'suitably qualified persons' for the post of Secretary to its Churches Committee.

The CBA was a small but energetic archaeological charity, well known for its cyclostyled calendar of excavations which told you where you could go to dig, and for valuable work in confronting threats and highlighting needs. The impacts of unchecked development on historic towns were among the current threats; churches were among the needs. I wrote off for details. They said that the work would include research, administration of policy, and 'liaison with Church authorities'. The post-holder would also be expected to write a book to explain why churches were worth study.

Some of this sounded a bit desk-bound, but maybe there would be ways around that – and after three years working on one church there seemed to be logic in moving to churches in general. The job would be based at the University of Leeds, which was good, because I could commute by bus, and I and my family would not have to move. The post was only guaranteed for one year, albeit with a 'strong commitment' to 'at least' another two. Not secure, then, but no shakier than the job I already had. The salary was at the bottom of the university lecturer's scale: £1,929 to £2,118, 'with superannuation benefits'. I applied.

Derek asked if I had thought this through. The post looked admin-heavy; if I got it, I would be answering to a group of academics and heritage bureaucrats, not all of whom he admired. One of them was Arnold Taylor, whose acquiescence to the destruction of medieval deposits in York Minster had not been forgotten. And would it lead anywhere? Might I not be better off staying put? Derek was my guru. I ummed, ahhed, and withdrew the application.

A few weeks later, Derek was told that funding for York Minister's archaeology was to be cut. I was taken aside and advised to look for another job.

Mulling this over on Bridge Street, I heard my name called. Across the road stood Peter Addyman. I knew Peter slightly; he was the Director of York's recently founded Archaeological Trust, soon to embark on the epic excavation that would lead to the Jorvik Viking Centre. He was also chairman of the CBA's Churches Committee. He asked how I was. I explained that I was being made redundant. Ah, he said, well, in that case we should talk further, because the successful candidate for the churches job had just pulled out. Would I like to resubmit my application? I did. There was an interview. The post was offered. I accepted. I had got lucky.

I read up a bit on the context. Aback of it was an ever-widening disparity between the Church's needs and resources. In 1960, around thirty-five million of England's forty-one million people lived in towns, whereas roughly ten thousand of her seventeen thousand churches and chapels were rural. The imbalance came about because almost everyone had lived in the countryside when the medieval parish system came into being. This being so, many parish clergy were tied to places where few people now lived. In December 1963, *The Times* sent a correspondent into eastern England to see the problem at first hand. In part of Suffolk, he found 'as dolorous a collection of white elephant churches as you might find in a small compass'. Deep in rural Essex, he met the Rev George Henry Marsden, rector of Berners Roding and Willingale with Shellow, whose two medieval churches stood within yards of each other. At Berners Roding, 'in the silence of a Sunday afternoon', Marsden held evensong for a congregation of two. A nearby rural dean shepherding eighteen parishes reflected that if they could only get all the regular churchgoers into one congregation, they might fill one church.

Mismatches between means and wants were even greater in towns. Medieval provincial cities with small modern populations were crammed with old churches, whereas millions living on post-war estates had none at all, and churches built after 1800 to serve working-class industrial districts – a number of which had been indiscriminately thinned by wartime bombing – were being stranded by slum clearance. Many of them had been stranded all along. The nineteenth-century inner-city churches, each operating independently of its neighbours, were often a result of overbuilding. A legend has taken hold that they were once full, but the clergy who encouraged them were motivated more by optimism and competition than actual demand, and perhaps above all by a sense that a new urban church ought to look as though it was capable of seating its parishioners if they should all decide to come at once. The result was that church attendance as a proportion of the population was falling even before they were built.

More fundamentally, Victorian efforts to carry the medieval parish system into industrial cities were misjudged. Parishes had arisen in and belonged to a world of face-to-face community; their units of space and ministry were ill-adapted to bringing pastoral care to dense working-class populations. Some recognised this at the time. In 1836, John Henry Newman wrote prophetically that 'great towns will never be evangelized merely by the parochial system', because an 'unstable multitude' was beyond the reach of any one parson. The idea of the parish priest depended on his relationship with everyone in his parish, not just churchgoers, nor even Anglicans, and upon everyone's acceptance that this was the case. As Betjeman had it:

> It doesn't matter that there's no one here
> It doesn't matter when they do not come
> The villagers know the parson is praying for them in their church.

That kind of relationship was not possible in densely occupied, deprived, and rapidly expanding places like Liverpool, Manchester, and Bradford. In 1855, the Earl of Shaftesbury told the House of Lords, 'The parochial system is, no doubt, a beautiful thing in theory, and is of great value in small rural districts; but in the large towns it is a mere shadow and a name.'

New inner-city churches that did work often did so because they were supported by middle-class people; when the middle classes moved to suburbs in the later nineteenth century, impracticably large and near-empty buildings were left behind. The Church of England thus entered the twentieth century with many more pews than occupants, and its failure thereafter to close churches in line with the rate at which congregations were shrinking now led to a crunch. In 1967, a policy sub-committee formed in the Diocese of Southwark to consider 'Tomorrow's Parish' reported:

> The current state of affairs may be illustrated . . . by reference to the Deanery of Battersea. Of its fifteen parishes no fewer than five are investigating schemes for the redevelopment of their property. The fact that they should be acting with no reference to a coordinated

master-plan is only less surprising than the fact that no such master-plan exists.

The superimposed crises aroused tensions and stirred vehement exchanges. In the 1960s, as now, there were many more who admired churches for their own sake than actually attended them, and this was resented by churchmen in whose eyes they were 'obsolete plant'. The Southwark sub-committee considered that 'the preservation of buildings on purely aesthetic grounds' was 'not the responsibility of the Church as such but of the community at large to which individual church members belong'. Mervyn Stockwood said he would like to demolish half the churches in his diocese. When champions of inherited things like John Betjeman protested, Stockwood replied that he did not wish to remain the manager of a preservation society for the rest of his life. The Provost of Coventry Cathedral called for mass church demolitions, the sale of their land, and use of the proceeds to build new purpose-built multidenominational centres in which different social functions – like probation, health, religion – could be housed side by side. Apparently without realising what they were wishing for, Church leaders cried out for an 'ecclesiastical Dr Beeching'.

Problems were not confined to where churches stood. While England's population rose by nearly fourteen million between 1901 and 1961, the number of clergy under sixty-five years of age fell by over five thousand. Fewer clergy were being ordained than were about to retire, yet there was no mechanism to send younger men – and back then it was just men – to places where they were most needed. There was no mechanism either to enable early retirement for those dispirited clergy, 'isolated in unresponsive parishes with little support from their superiors', whose ministries had become counterproductive. Until lately, there had not even been a mechanism to enable poorer clergy to retire at all. Hitherto, many parsons with backgrounds in the gentry had had private means upon which to fall back and a house to go to in later life. But where they did not, the combination of paltry pensions and parson's freehold meant that elderly incumbents sometimes lived on in their parsonages until they died – and since the parsonage was a tied house, a parson's wife could be evicted if her husband predeceased her. As *The Times* put it in 1963, 'There are numbers of clergy clinging to their freeholds because they have not the means to do anything else and are continuing to minister with increasing ineffectuality.' In that year, I sang in a choir at the funeral of a vicar's wife. The vicar was in his eighties. He took the service and became distressed in doing so. As the choir wound out into the rainswept churchyard for the committal, the processional hymn got out of kilter with itself, so that by the end we were a full verse in front of those still inside. The ensuing dissonant canon seemed to stand for the inertia of an ageing institution run by highly educated yet somehow impractical people.

In 1964, a searching report by Leslie Paul on *The Deployment and Payment of the Clergy* addressed these questions and made brave recommendations. In doing so, Paul surveyed the backgrounds from which clergy came. Parish clergy, he found, were mainly from the middle to upper middle class. Nearly all deans and bishops were from the high upper middle and upper classes. More than this, since the end of Victoria's reign all but a few bishops had been educated at the same ten public schools, while since Palmerston's day all but fifteen of them had been alumni of Oxford and Cambridge. Given the scarceness of universities before 1900, perhaps that is no surprise, but what is telling is that a quarter of them had been members of just three colleges.

One of those in the forefront of pioneering new patterns of ministry was our old friend Nick Stacey. Stacey had not attended Marlborough, Winchester, or Eton; rather, he had been through the Royal Naval College at Dartmouth. He was now impatient for progress, and we recall that in 1959 he left Birmingham to be rector of Woolwich in the Diocese of Southwark. For the next four years, he pioneered a form of team ministry, closing several churches and focusing effort through one: the Georgian church of St Mary:

> which we converted into a multi-purpose centre for worship shared by the United Reformed Church, with offices for housing the homeless, the Samaritans, local voluntary bodies and a disco in the crypt for youngsters, many of whom were on probation. A number of the team, which included Anglican clergy, ministers from three different free-church denominations and a Roman Catholic priest, earned their living working in local state schools.

They even opened a bar, which of course attracted more attention than the pastoral project itself.*

Stacey had a gift for incisive writing to tight deadlines. In 1964, he

---

* Protests overlooked the fact that medieval churches and taverns often stood side by side, occasionally even in the same building, and that it had been normal and convivial for parishioners to drink together as a way of raising church funds.

ceased to draw his stipend, thereafter supporting himself (and several others in his team) through freelance journalism. The team thought there was an opportunity to reverse the decline of the Church, and raised money to send Eric James to tour England to test the Church's attitude to their plan for reform. When James returned, he reported there was no vision or enthusiasm for such reform.

Stacey was beginning to feel that they had played every card in the pack to no avail. St Mary's Woolwich was in many ways a success, but many of the newcomers in the congregation were middle-class people who had driven in from elsewhere. The work was like crawling over broken glass – at one point Stacey was told that his inter-denominational plan was illegal – and the Anglican hierarchy was unsupportive. Among their proposals were a destructured Church, the offloading of most church buildings, new multipurpose multidenominational urban centres serviced by teams, and self-supporting clergy working in secular jobs. Stacey noted that the Welfare State and voluntary bodies like the Samaritans and Citizens Advice Bureau now undertook many of the roles that had once fallen to parish clergy; in the new kind of ministry he envisaged, ordained men would enter and be paid by relevant secular professions such as psychiatric social work in which up to now they had just dabbled. Stacey urged that theological college curricula be revised accordingly, noting that expertise in such fields as New Testament Greek and Old Testament theology was no longer needed because 'we no longer accept that the Science of God is an exact science'.

Little of this made him popular, and calls for radical action at scale went unheeded. Stacey deplored the lack of any sense of urgency. On the last Sunday in January 1965, BBC1 broadcast a programme titled *Failure in Woolwich* in which Stacey declared they had done everything possible to make the parish a success and had failed. Stockwood disagreed, but his flag-bearer for parish renewal was close to giving up. In May 1965, when the Convocations of Canterbury and York accepted in principle proposals for eventual Anglican–Methodist reunion, but postponed any decision for at least another five years, he wondered aloud (in the *Observer*) whether the union would be a marriage of corpses. In 1968, Nicolas Stacey left Woolwich to become deputy director of Oxfam.

One part of the new job, then, was to help coordinate an archaeological response to on-the-ground consequences of a Church which was changing too fast for the liking of some, and far too slowly for the liking of others. Another part of it was exemplified by the old one. York

Minster was one of the most looked-at, written-about buildings in the world, yet our recent work had shown that much of its story had been misunderstood, and that quite a lot of it had been missed. If that could happen here, it could happen anywhere, and there were growing signs that it would. A long-standing sense that churches were evidentially secure, that their historical pith was safe, was being shaken. Alongside threats arising from closures, it was dawning that the unmonitored repair and alteration of the thousands of churches still in use was gnawing away at evidence for when they had come into being, how they had been used, and the mortal remains of nearly everyone who had lived in England between the tenth and nineteenth centuries. Hence the need for 'liaison with Church authorities'.

So it was that on the first Monday in January 1975 I took the bus to Leeds, walked up the hill to the university, and presented myself at the Department of Archaeology. More luck followed. To explain, we need to wind back a bit. The University of Leeds began as a medical school in the early nineteenth century, grew into a college of science, and became a full university in 1904. Down the years, it expanded across an area about the size of Monaco, absorbing entire Georgian and Victorian cobbled streets, rows of red-brick mansions, former schools, and chapels as it did so. If it had all been kept like that, the University could now be funding scholarships by renting itself out for filming period drama.

The archaeology department was small, housed in a worn-out nineteenth-century building on the campus edge, between a post office and a pub where at lunchtime you could get a pie and strangely luminous green peas. The three academic staff had rooms on the ground floor. My mentor was Lawrence Butler, who wore a beard in a style that reminded me of Solzhenitsyn, and combined a wry wit with an uncommon knowledge and feel for early things. On the first floor, at the end of a dark staircase, there was an outer room used as a drawing office by Lawrence's research assistant, an office for the secretary, and an inner room which no one wanted because it had no windows. The windowless room was to be mine, and it was to be the making of me.

For one thing, it was proof against day-dreaming: aside from a few streaks of brown fungus on the pale blue ceiling, there was nothing at which to stare, although in bad weather rainwater sometimes dripped in, and on really wet days the wiring emitted an ominous burr. (The building was so decrepit that on one occasion I was approached by an Asian gentleman who wanted to buy it on the spot, and offered me a carrier bag containing high denomination bank notes.) For another, this was where Lawrence kept his journals. In the room were complete runs of *Medieval Archaeology*, the *Journal of the British Archaeological Association*, the *Archaeological Journal* and *Antiquaries Journal*, together with a complete set of the CBA's British Archaeological Abstracts. After three years at York Minster, I was fairly proficient in fieldwork but knew little about historical framework, theories, debates, style-critical dating, or research questions. I began to work through the journals one by one, picking out articles that looked relevant, and using the fifty-minute-each-way daily bus journeys to read them.

I got lucky in other ways. The Brotherton Library had one of the best local history collections in the kingdom – ideal for churches. Elsewhere on the campus were Ian Wood, a newly arrived young historian who specialised in early medieval Francia and missionaries; Maurice Beresford, who was putting medieval settlement at the forefront of historical inquiry; and Peter Sawyer, the historian who more than any other had divided opinion about the Vikings. From 1979, two doors up in Theology, there was David Jenkins, who smiled across their departmental photocopier when you went to use it. Five years later, as bishop-designate of Durham, Jenkins would tell an interviewer on Channel 4 that 'no single historical fact can prove anything' and that 'there is absolutely no certainty in the New Testament about anything of importance'. Next day, under the strap 'TURMOIL THAT HITS AT HEART OF GOING TO CHURCH', the *Daily Mail* spoke of 'a major controversy' which had been started by a bishop who said that 'Jesus did not walk on water and he was not born to a virgin'. The gospels of Mark and John said nothing about a virgin birth either, but Christological source criticism has not always been a tabloid strength.

There I was, then, surrounded by inspiring, sometimes controversial elders, being paid to read, visit, and in due course encourage others to be interested in the story of England's churches. My impressions of the Church of England hitherto had been vicarage-based. I now began to look at it from the top down, and sideways on. An early question was where the top and sides were; indeed, whether it had any shape at all. The Archbishop of Canterbury was a leader, but not a chief executive – there was no management structure in a business sense, although George Carey (Archbishop of Canterbury 1991–2002) tried to establish one. (In 1978, Stuart reflected, 'The church discovers the virtues of centralisation just when others are beginning to experience its vices.') In looking for where to make contact, each diocese and cathedral was largely a self-governing entity, and since there were forty-two of each, 'liaison with Church authorities' meant establishing eighty-four sets of relationships. Nor was that the end of it. Dioceses and counties had never entirely coincided, and after the reorganisation of local government in 1974 the divergences became even greater. This mattered, because from the later 1970s it was through local authorities that archaeological influence on development projects was increasingly being exercised.

Archaeologists Peter Fowler and Philip Rahtz (left & right) with Harold Taylor (centre) at the Anglo-Saxon church of St Mary, Deerhurst, 1973. Taylor was then working to put the study of Anglo-Saxon architecture on a logical footing. Taylor, Rahtz, and Lawrence Butler had embarked on a project to understand the church.

The archaeologists we recruited to advise dioceses and cathedrals were from many backgrounds. Archaeology was then little profession-alised, with few posts and no career structure. A few held positions in museums or the newly emergent city and regional rescue units. Some were experienced amateurs. A good number were from university extra-mural departments and branches of the Workers' Educational Association. There was something in this world, at that time, that fos-tered original work. Richard Hoggart and E. P. Thompson produced *The Uses of Literacy* (1957) and *The Making of the English Working Class* (1963) while working as adult education tutors, and there were inspirational archaeologists like Philip Barker at Birmingham who revolutionised thinking about post-Roman Britain and excavation technique, Peter Fowler at Bristol working on landscape, and Charles Thomas, the leading theorist of early Christian Atlantic Britain, in Cornwall. Since part of my job was to be a channel through which experience gained by one could be shared by all, this meant travelling around the country to meet them. One of the great encouragers and outstanding excavators was Philip Rahtz, another of Birmingham's tutors, who had just embarked on a study of the Anglo-Saxon church at Deerhurst. Our first meeting was in a cafeteria lunch queue; by the time we reached the food, he had commissioned a paper from me on whatever it was we had begun to talk about when we joined the end. The aims and funding of extra-mural education were changed in the 1980s, and this wonderful culture has faded.

'Liaison with church authorities' meant getting to know parts of their law. The Church is represented in the UK's legislature through its archbishops (who are Privy Councillors), the bishops of London, Durham, and Winchester, and twenty-one other bishops, all of whom are members of the House of Lords. This falls well short of theocracies like Iran and Saudi Arabia, but in many ways the Church is a parallel state, passing its own laws (known as 'Measures', which are then enacted through Parliament), while mysteriously managing to remain exempt from a number of statutes which govern the rest of us – like those on conservation, or (at that date) discrimination on grounds of sex, or (since) freedom of information. Clergy are appointed to benefices by legal as well as spiritual means. In each diocese, decisions on what happens in and around churches are taken by a judge (known as the chancellor) who is a barrister-at-law and acts as the bishop's legal other self, and issues licenses (known as faculties) for work to be done. Since most chancellors know little about wall-paintings, bells, heating systems, medieval sculpture, damp-proofing, tree-ring dating, medieval glass, human remains, or any of the other matters upon which they are called upon to pass judgement, each of them is advised by a committee which is supposed to contain the necessary expertise.

The competence of the advisory committees varied, as did the degree of willingness of clergy, patrons, or in some cases even the bishops themselves, to take any notice of them. Stockwood gleefully confided that it had been 'a point of honour' not to apply for faculties when he had been vicar of Great St Mary's. A Lord Lieutenant who organised unauthorised drainage works around the eleventh-century church of which he was patron was displeased when I pointed out that the work was illegal. Some of the committees were go-ahead, friendly, and ready to embrace new expertise; others lived in a Trollopian world where elderly archdeacons joshed each other about who would 'bat first' at meetings, where handwritten minutes were read aloud from a leather-bound book, and the book was shaken to see if any faculty petitions dropped out. A handful were indifferent. One or two were hostile. A member of Worcester's DAC reacted to my attempt to introduce his committee to an archaeologist by describing such people as blind to beauty, likely to destroy beautiful things like wall-paintings for the sake of laying hands on bits of muddy pottery. If I had known that this view of archaeology as disreputable was once widely held in higher gentle circles, I might have better appreciated the experience of meeting its late flourish. As it was, some DAC members were then fighting among themselves about the risks (or not) to wall-paintings of new chemical methods of conservation.

Church closures came under different legislation. In 1968, the General Assembly passed a Measure to enable it to form new parishes, alter boundaries, substitute one church for another, create team and group ministries, and shed churches that dioceses did not wish to keep. This was usually known by its General Assembly title, the Pastoral Measure 1968, but is better understood under its parliamentary endorse-ment as the Redundant Churches and Other Religious Buildings Act 1969. At least twenty-nine earlier acts or measures were repealed or modified through the Church's new mechanism to rid itself of 'obsolete plant'. The mechanism was intricate, for each or any church involving statutory reference to two diocesan committees and five national bodies, two of which were new quangos formed for the purpose. In due course, we found that each case passed through so many pairs of hands that there was a limit to the number of cases the system could handle in a year.

Two features of the 1968 Measure exemplified the ability of the Church to convince itself of one thing when, in the eyes of most others, reality lay somewhere else. One was the question of 'de-consecration': if a church had originally been separated 'from all profane and common uses' and set 'apart in solemn manner to the performance of the several offices of our religious worship' in a ceremony of consecration, how could it be sold into secular use? The media assumed there must be some ritual of cancellation.

Dissenting Churches had never been much troubled by this since they saw sacrality either as associational, a function of use, and hence temporary, or else as non-existent.* Anglo-Catholics, on the other hand, held a dualist world view in which things that are sacral call into existence things that are profane. Hence, for the drafters of the Pastoral Measure the effect of consecration was both independent of what went on in the building and irreversible – a kind irradiation that left the building in a permanently altered state. In logic, then, no form of service could undo it. So far, so clear. However, there was a loophole. The Church saw the spiritual and legal effects of consecration as separable. Just as it taught that marriage was irreversible yet could accept the reality of divorce in the eyes of the state, so could it annul the legal effects of consecration while leaving the theological effects unaltered. A declaration of redundancy under the Pastoral Measure 1968 was thus the moment at which the legal effects of consecration were revoked – which is one reason why it came late in the process: until then, regardless of whether the building was actually being used or cared for, the theological effects of consecration still applied. Hence, the church remained outside the control of legislation on listed buildings and archaeology until the point at which it was offloaded. The gift for doublespeak was further evidenced by the protestation that parish churches could indeed be listed (most of them are); it was simply that for as long as they remained in use, the listing had no effect.

In the 1970s, this Anglican parallel universe seemed to present an opportunity, for in contrast to secular control (which for historical reasons was split between 'architecture' – listed buildings, overseen by local authorities – and 'archaeology', then primarily overseen by central government), it was both seamless and extended to contents and surroundings as well as structures. Looking back, however, Anglican unwillingness to be bound by mutual responsibilities for stewardship is hard to defend. Aside from fairness and justice, it rests on arguments that are casuistical (that cherishing inherited things might impede mission) and sometimes unworthy (that people who cherish are the 'dead hand of bureaucracy'). It is the case that rural church congregations spend upwards of £55 million a year on listed church buildings, nearly all of it raised through local efforts. However, it is doubtful whether anything like this figure would become available for

---

* According to the 1644 Puritan *Directory for public worship*, 'no place is capable of any holiness under pretence of whatsoever Dedication or Consecration', while the Quaker leader George Fox (1624–1691) said that the Lord dwells in human hearts, not in buildings.

alternative forms of ministry if the churches passed into other hands.

Which brings us to another pair of hands: the Church Commissioners'. The Commissioners support the work of the Church of England by managing its investments. Today there are thirty-three of them, some elected, others appointed (by the Crown, the Archbishops), all accountable to the General Synod, Parliament and the Charity Commission. They are exempt from Freedom of Information law. Their investments today include a property portfolio worth about £2 billion. Assets include the freehold of Gateshead Metrocentre, 585,000 acres of mineral rights, and 103,000 acres of forestry in the UK, Australia, and the United States. In 2019, asset value stood at £8.7 billion.

The Commissioners promote the ministry and mission of the Church of England, chiefly by contributing to diocesan costs in poorer areas, by paying for the ministry of bishops and some cathedral costs, running the legal framework for parish reorganisation and settling the future of unwanted churches, and the clergy payroll. In 2018–19, the minimum clergy stipend was £24,280, and £25,950 was the national benchmark. Comparable figures for deans and diocesan bishops were £36,930 and £45,270. Over the same period, just nine asset-management staff received payments totalling £1.08 million, the largest of them £256,000.*

I am running ahead. In 1975, my impression of the Church Commissioners was formed mainly through a few tangential experiences, two of which have already been described: the fates of Battersea vicarage and Sanderstead rectory. A third was in Bishopthorpe Palace, around which I was shown by Stuart shortly after his arrival. The main rooms of the Palace were for work, meetings, and the hosting of large gatherings in the central hall. Stuart and Brenda lived in a small flat in one wing. Stuart had a table-tennis table in the great cellar upon which the Palace stands. After a couple of games, Stuart gestured to two electricity meters and fuse-boxes, mounted high on the wall to avoid the waters of the river Ouse when they rise during winter floods. A typed notice was pinned over each: 'ARCHBISHOP'S POWER' and 'COMMISSIONERS' POWER', respectively.

Lastly, I got lucky with a small camera. The new job would involve

---

* My only meeting, I think, with anyone in the Church Commissioners was in the early 1980s, when we talked about a mechanism to enable someone with special expertise to present a conservation argument in an ecclesiastical court. The drawback, it was explained to me, was that they could think of no one other than the witness who could pay the chancellor's costs.

taking pictures, for reference and talks. Derek was an accomplished photographer. I asked him: what kind of camera? 'Do you want one with multiple functions, or a notebook?' I thought for a moment. 'A notebook.' He took me to a camera shop and pointed to a Yashica 35 – small, chunky, with an aperture-priority function and a large, clear viewfinder. It was virtually idiot-proof, and for the next fifteen years I used it to photograph church architecture, sculpture, excavations, and conservation atrocities. Most of the time I used slide film.

The slides became a diary. Looking at them, I am back among Norfolk's extraordinary muster of ruined churches in the summer of 1975. There are more than a hundred of them, almost a diocese's-worth, built of lustrous flint, or iron-rich carrstone the colour of gingerbread. Some of them had been ruined for centuries, although in the never-never world of Anglican legislation, the fact that they had not been declared redundant through the Pastoral Measure (which had made 'redundant' a legal term) meant that in the eyes of the law they were still in use. They are of every size and shape, from a shard of a round tower on the beach at Eccles to lofty East Somerton where trees growing inside the nave turned the sky green. Over the border in Suffolk, were craggy part-ruined churches like Covehithe and Walberswick in which art and geology seemed to have been hybridised.

Another thirty-five millimetre image between finger and thumb puts me back in a ransacked burial vault (ransacked by whom, and why?), rain dripping in on the putrefied face of a man whose coffin has been hauled out of its recess, stood on its head, and levered open.

And then there was that hot June afternoon in 1983 when I took the winding, empty road out of Rosedale, through heather creased by rocky gulleys, to meet the Rev John Clark, incumbent of the moorside parish of Egton with Grosmont, in Yorkshire. Mr Clark explained that late in the nineteenth century the medieval church of St Hilda had been replaced by a building closer to the village centre. Remains of the old church were still standing in the former churchyard, and he wanted to know what to do with them. This was a fair question, but our discussion somehow turned into a conversation about civil defence. Cold War paranoia was then widespread, but I was taken aback when Mr Clark confided that since the south wall of the Victorian church was thicker than the north, St Hilda would protect his flock in the event of the Soviet nuclear strike that sooner or later would befall the nearby early warning station at Fylingdales. He described the alarm system he had devised to call them in to safety.

Our talk of last things and the world aflame naturally led to York Minster's roof, part of which had been destroyed by fire two nights before. I mentioned the theory that the blaze had been started by lightning. Oh dear, did I really think so? No, it was obvious: this was God's response to the ordination of David Jenkins as Bishop of Durham the previous Sunday. I thought of David's smile across the Theology department's photocopier and wondered about God's priorities.

Other slides bring other parsons to mind. The tower of St Michael and St Laurence at Fewston in the Yorkshire Dales was not in good shape when the vicar led me up to look at its roof. Decking at the top rested on hefty beams which stretched from side to side, their ends embedded in the walls – save that on one side the ends had rotted, leaving the beams dangling from the covering they were meant to support. As the vicar put his weight on the ladder and the beams began to flap, I pointed to the likelihood of a catastrophic collapse. The vicar sneered at my faithlessness, and when he reached the top and nothing had happened, I wondered whether it was God who had protected us or whether it was simply that we had got lucky.

Slide projectors went out of production in the mid 2000s. Even if you still have one, bulbs and spares are no longer made. But when you hold a slide up to the light, you are back in the moment. Reaching into the box, here are six.

Part Two

A BOX OF SLIDES:
1975–2000

7

HEAR ME WHEN I CALL

The hour bell at Westminster, the bell we know as Big Ben, was cast in the Whitechapel foundry on the second Saturday in April 1858. Thirteen and a half tons of molten metal were poured to make it, and the metal took nearly three weeks to cool. Sixteen heavy horses then drew the giant on a trolley to New Palace Yard at Westminster, whence in October it was hoisted into the tower belfry. The following autumn it cracked. Cracks in bells are usually irreparable, but the damage here was mitigated by rotating the bell and substituting a lighter clapper that struck in a different place.

One hundred and sixty-two years later, a campaign began for Big Ben to be rung to mark the moment of the UK's departure from the European Union. Sir Iain Duncan Smith, the first Roman Catholic to serve as a Conservative leader, spoke for many when he said it had marked the hour at many national turning points, and should sound for what was 'arguably the biggest decision we have made since the end of the war'. Appropriately enough, the weights used to adjust the swing of the clock's pendulum were pre-decimal pennies. However, there was a problem: in 2017, the bell had been silenced to allow repair to the Queen Elizabeth tower. House of Commons authorities estimated that temporary works to enable it to speak for one evening would cost between £320,000 and £500,000 and take two weeks to put in hand. Parliament declined to fund this. In mid January, the Prime Minister said that the government was working up a crowdfunding scheme 'so that people can bung a bob for a Big Ben bong', but this went nowhere and time ran out. Leave supporters then urged that parish church bells be rung. Arron Banks, the co-founder of Leave.EU, claimed that the 'vast majority' of churchgoers were 'patriotic people' who would want to hear the bells 'ring out for freedom'. Independent research has since found he was right: most Anglicans did indeed wish to leave the EU. However, when a bell rings, everyone hears it, and for the near-half of the population who had voted remain, the sound would have come across as triumphalist rather than celebratory. When clergy pointed this out, Banks retorted, 'We've just about had enough of sandal-wearing, vegan-eating, virtue-signalling clerics.'

The leaving date came and went, and within a month the world had other things on its mind; within two, bell ringing was temporarily banned. Covid-19's uncanny ability to search out physical and social vulnerabilities extended even to change ringing, in which peals of differently tuned bells are wheel-swung to strike in ever-varying sequences. The rules – each bell sounding once in each iteration, no bell moving more than one position in each change, no row repeated – originated during the seventeenth century. Fabian Stedman and Richard Duckworth explained them in *Tintinnalogia* (1667) and *Campanalogia* (1677), when Britain was known as 'the ringing island'. Like a kind of piano roll, the Anglican Church of William Laud is still audible through its bells. But since the companionable teamwork of ringing involves sustained exertion by people in close proximity, in March 2020 the steeples fell silent.

The hush that followed reminded us of the many meanings with which bells are charged. Change ringing is life-affirming – think weddings, anniversaries, victories. Bells have been rung in high towers to catch the ear of God. Medieval bells were invested with characters that spoke when they were rung. Inscriptions around their mouths remind us of things they said:

> *AUDI ME INVOCAMTEM*
> Hear me when I call

> *CUM VOCO VENITE*
> Come when I call

> *SURGE AGE*
> Arise and come

The sleepy head I rouse from bed

The summons to matins and evensong was often rung for a given period, followed by two minutes of 'tolling in' on one bell. Special ringing would attend great festivals:

> *VITAM METIOR MORTEM PLORO*
> I measure life, I bewail death

During the last hours of a life, the far-carrying sound of a passing bell alerted neighbours to pray for the soul during its passage:

DEFUNCTOS PLORO VIVOS VOCO FUNERA CLAUDO
I weep for the dead, I call the living, I close funerals

Back in the days when gender was binary, the deaths of men and women, adults and children, were told apart by different numbers of strokes ('Nine tellers mark a man' – whence Dorothy Sayers's *The Nine Tailors*). In some places, the journey to the grave itself was charted in sound. At King's Cliffe in Northamptonshire, a winding bell was rung as the body was wrapped in its shroud. At Aldwincle St Peter, another church in that county, the tenor bell was tolled until the procession came into sight, whereupon three bells were chimed until it reached the gate, when the knell passed back to the tenor.

Such customs recollect forms of medieval funeral. A study of the sixty-odd surviving church towers put up in Lincolnshire during the forty years after the Norman Conquest shows that nearly all of them were built to cater for a form of burial service that was introduced by newly arrived Norman bishops. The ground storeys of the towers were spaces in which the body rested during the overnight vigil; these spaces were provided with west doors, through which the procession entered on the funeral's eve, and departed into light when the body was taken out for burial. A doorway above the arch in the east face of the tower shows how the ringer could enter the bell chamber without intruding on the area containing the body and funeral party below. A recurring feature is an upper window overlooking the main area of the churchyard which enabled the ringer to time his strokes to the second during the committal. In this way, the Archangel Michael, protector of souls, could be alerted to escort your soul to judgement, safe from interception by demons. Michael's association with the passage of souls led to his further connection with air, sky, and hills. In some churches, the top stage of the tower itself was known as 'St Michael'.

The simple wooden frames from which bells were hung before the fourteenth century seldom survive, usually because they were removed to make way for the larger, stronger, deeper frames needed for full-circle ringing. However, the upper part of a tower is often the least visited and least altered part of a church (no one forgets that moment when you teeter atop a vertical ladder, pushing upwards with your shoulder against a trap door that has not been lifted for years, and pigeon guano pours down your neck), and if you climb enough of them, you find things. At South Leverton in Nottinghamshire you can see a medieval ladder; in the belfry walls of St Michael at the Northgate in Oxford there are ammonite fossils which an eleventh-century mason set beside the sound openings. The tower of the church at Little Ouseburn in Yorkshire sprang a surprise when I climbed it one afternoon in 1987. Clambering about on the Victorian bell-frame, I looked up and realised that the two parallel timbers from which a medieval bell had been hung were still there – the newer bell-frame had simply been inserted below, leaving the original in position. A closer look revealed one of the timbers to be a reused rafter, recycled from the roof of an earlier nave. Looking closer still, the semi-circular chafe marks left by the swinging of the bell were visible. Out came the Yashica 35. In a synaesthetic moment, I was listening to a vanished sound:

> *INTACTUM SILEO PERCUTE DULCE CANO*
> Untouched I am a silent thing
> But strike me and I sweetly sing

In fact, a struck bell does not sing on one note. It is a bundle of sounds. Acousticians have found that the dominant pitch, known as the prime or strike note, the note you would write down if you were notating it as music, is but one in a gamut of frequencies generated by the vibrating metal. These sounds are known as partials, and the main ones have names – like the hum (an octave below the strike – this is the sound you hear lingering after the strike has died away), the tierce (a minor third above the strike – a pitch that contributes a trace of melancholy), the quint (a fifth above), nominal (octave above), and so on. Apparently, each of us hears them differently; moreover, we hear some of them in our own heads: acousticians find no active frequency in the spectrum that actually tallies with the strike note, which seems to be generated subjectively by the way we hear three of the partials. Part of the skill of a bell founder lies in the ability to bring the partials into tune with themselves, achieved by casting the bell to a particular profile and shaving off small amounts to fine-tune the harmonics. The partials of medieval bells were sometimes less exactly tuned, and the hum note was sometimes a seventh below the strike, which explains their dryer, more spangled sound. There are two localities in England where you can still hear it: St Lawrence in Ipswich and St Bartholomew the Great in the City of London. Both have rings of five pre-Reformation bells that enable you to hear the past. St Bartholomew's bells are rung before evensong twice a month, and if you stand within maybe half a mile, maybe on a wet

November evening, you will hear them as did Londoners in the days of Henry VII.

A bell's mingling of sadness and joy, its ambiguity and certainty, helps to explain why across the world its sound is regarded as propitious, why bells are believed to ward off evil, and why they help us to fix our minds on the divine. In medieval England, bells were rung during the mass to signal the approach of the moment of consecration. In an age lacking other rural mechanical noises, a bell may have caught and held attention in ways we have forgotten, and are unappreciated by incomers who complain about noise nuisance from chimes that have struck the quarters for a hundred years. It is as well they did not move into medieval provincial cities like Lincoln or Winchester, where within c.150 acres there were at least as many bells in the towers and turrets of two score parish churches, a cathedral, friaries, and religious houses. Around the hour such places reverberated in a rich haze of pulsing sounds. But parishioners knew the voices of their own parish churches, and when they spoke, they were reminded of parents and relatives gone before, and the life to come.

Urban bells did public as well as religious duty. They announced hours of trade, letting locals have preference or discourage forestalling (buying from incoming traders to sell at a higher price at the market). Fire alarms were signalled by bells rung backwards, or ting-tang striking (the predecessor of today's two-note emergency sirens). In areas susceptible to flood, there were places where bells were rung annually to summon the parish jury for inspection of drains and dykes. If storms and floods did come, bells were rung to ward them off:

> The winds so fierce I do disperse
> Lightning and thunder I break asunder
> Man's cruel rage I do assuage

The 'I' in these pithy inscriptions shows that bells were invested with personalities. Some were anonymous:

> *VAE MIHI SE NON ENVANGELISAVERO*
> Woe unto me if I proclaim not the gospel

Some were archangels:

> *MIKAELIS CAMPANA FUGIANT PULSANTE PROPHANA*
> The bell of Michael strikes to drive off evil

MISSI DE CELIS
Sent from heaven

HABEO NOMEN GABRIELIS
From Gabriel I take my name
Who messenger from heaven came

Many were humanised:

JOHNNES EST NOMEN MEUM
My name is John

VOX AUGUSTINI SONAT IN AURE DEI
Augustine's voice sounds in the ear of God

SUM ROSA PULSATA MUNDI KATERINA VOCATA
When struck, I am called Catherine the rose of the world

MARIA MATER DEI EST NOMEN MEUM
Mary the mother of God is my name

A lot of bells speak for Mary, who makes her home everywhere and anywhere: -in-the-Marsh, -le-Moor, -on-the-Hill, even in Norfolk, where her appearance in Walsingham in the eleventh century twinned the village with Nazareth.

The antiphon *Asperges me, Domine* forms part of the entrance ritual of the mass, with sprinkling of holy water. It was commonly sung when a bell was blessed. The verse, from Psalm 51 ('Purge me, O God, with hyssop, and I shall be clean: wash me, and I shall be whiter than snow'), shows that a bell was not thought of simply as a fitting: 'It was a participant in the rites made sacred by holy water.' The wetting of the bell was held to infuse its sound with the Holy Spirit: 'A bell, in effect, was ordained to be a bell in a ceremony, somewhat as a priest was ordained to be a priest.'

The baptism of bells introduces more associations, between the casting and ringing of bells, and fonts. Fonts are generally found at the west end of churches, near the main public entrance, which is generally a south-west door, and a little forward of the arch into the tower. The connotations are to do with arrival and admission, and through them their opposites, departure and death: baptism is a ritual funeral in which you are 'buried in Christ' and death is your rebirth.

By no coincidence, then, did these rites usually take place not only within a few feet of each other but also next to the places where the bells were made. On the north side of York Minster's nave there is a window that depicts bell-founding, glazed in the 1330s at the expense of local goldsmith and bell-founder Richard Tunnoc; its position may be close to a place where Minster bells had been cast. Until long-distance transport of heavy items was made possible by canals and railways, bells were normally cast inside the churches for which they were intended. The method used a mould made with loam, water, and horse manure, in four main parts: a core (which determines the pitch), a cope (an outer 'false bell'), a waist, and a crown. The mould was clamped together in a pit, the traditional place for which was under the tower floor, so that a finished bell could be hoisted straight up into the belfry. A temporary furnace was created nearby to heat the metal to the required temperature of around 620°C. This could take several days. More symbolism: fire purifies.

The symbolic and physical proximity of things to do with birth, death, and bells in a parish church brings us back to Big Ben. *The Times* recorded on 22 October 1856 that 'All bells, we believe, are christened before they begin to toll, and on this occasion it is proposed to call our king of bells "Big Ben"; in honour of Sir Benjamin Hall, the President of the Board of Works, during whose tenure of office it was cast.' This was two years before the date of the bell with which we began, the reason for this being that the first bell failed. The originator of both was Edward Beckett Denison, the first Baron Grimthorpe (1816–1905), whose description as a 'lawyer, mechanician and controversialist' in the 1912 edition of the *Oxford Dictionary of National Biography* rather played down his accomplishments. Beckett was a polymath who in his long, opinionated, and combative life combined careers as a commercial lawyer, ecclesiastical judge, moralist, horologist, authority on locks, and architect.

In 1851, Beckett produced a design for the mechanism of the great clock to be installed in the new Palace of Westminster. Progress on the Palace had been slow: begun back in 1840, it was not until the mid 1850s that the clock was needed. The firm of Warner in Cripplegate was awarded the contract to cast the bells, but there was insufficient space in their London foundry to cast the hour bell, so this work passed to the firm's foundry at Norton, near Stockton-on-Tees in County Durham. Two furnaces were prepared, and on the morning of 6 August 1856 copper and tin were loaded into them in the proportions specified by Denison's recipe. When the furnaces were tapped, metal flowed into a pool; a shutter was lifted, and in five minutes the bell was cast. It was nearly a third as large again as York Minster's Great Peter, to whose swelling reverberation I thrilled when it sounded noon every day while we dug beneath the north-west tower.

The bell was taken by road to West Hartlepool, where the plan was to hoist it aboard a ship for London. The vessel was the *Wave*, a billyboy-schooner, suited to the task by its box-like form, round bow and stem, and good sea-going characteristics. At the dockside, however, things did not go well. While the bell was being lifted, the chain jammed in the pully block, the timber shears gave way, and the bell fell into the hold. Two steam tugs towed the *Wave* out of the dock and ran her onto a sandbank lest she sink. When the bell eventually arrived at Maudslay's Wharf near Westminster Bridge, it was transferred to a special wagon and taken across to New Palace Yard, where it was hung for testing. It gave tongue for the first time just after eleven o'clock on Thursday 13 November 1856, when a note described as pure and natural was carried towards Chelsea and Battersea on a north-east breeze. And what a tongue: the clapper alone was about the same weight as an Austin Mini; perhaps the force of its swing explains the four-foot crack that appeared in it the following year. Amid reproach and argument about respons-ibility, the first Big Ben was broken up and its fragments recycled to cast the bell with which we began.

Alongside his controversial and opinionated role in relation to the new clock and bell at Westminster, Edmund Beckett Denison took an energetic, disputatious, and often vituperative part in Anglican affairs. He had no time for the idea that priests are mediators between God and the rest of us. His standards of ritual and doctrine derived from the principles of the Reformation (whereat, he said, the mass, the confes-sional, and sacerdotalism had been put aside), the 1662 *Book of Common Prayer*, and the Acts of Uniformity. He believed that the state should take precedence in authority over the Church in ecclesiastical matters. When the revised version of the King James New Testament appeared in 1881, he launched a book-length attack on it. In other books, he took issue with David Hume and Thomas Huxley over their rejection of mir-acles, and with John Ruskin on the aesthetics of Gothic architecture. His contributions to the abbey church of St Albans (1878–85), made at his own expense, autographed by a sculpture of angel-winged St Mat-thew near the west door that bears his features, have been little loved.

The later-nineteenth-century Church of England, like many of Beckett's dealings, reverberated with conflict. Beckett was a ferocious opponent of ritualism, and in 1889, now ennobled, he played a prom-inent part in the formation of a Protestant Churchmen's Alliance to do battle with the spreaders of Anglo-Catholicism, who in his opinion sprang from aristocratic and clerical circles rather than public opinion ('Nine out of ten of the clergy are High Churchmen, and nine out of ten of the Laity are Low'). Around one thousand people attended the inaugural meeting, over which Beckett presided. They agreed upon a campaign to alert the middle and working classes to the delusions being foisted upon them:

PLEBEM VOCO
I call the people

ADMONEO CUM MOVEO
I admonish when I move

Bells for Beckett meant summons, warning, the marking of occasion, and the passage of time. He did not accept them as saints and intercessors, not like this:

SANCTA MARGARETA ORA PRO NOBIS
St Margaret, pray for us

But it is, of course, how we hear that makes the difference between whether we are listening to Margaret or metal, prayer or physics.

In time ahead, whether or not bishops are still voting on economic policy in the House of Lords, whether even there is a Church of England, there will be ringers. On New Years' Eves they will stand in circles in ringing rooms, one aback of each rope. The best part of a second will elapse between the pull and the sound, so it will start as it does now, the ringer of the Treble calling the others to readiness with 'Look to!', then, at the beginning of the pull, 'Treble's going', followed by 'She's gone', the 'gone' coinciding with the strike, the other bells following in rhythm, down the scale, their out-rolling harmonics riding the air for a mile or more. In such sound we can imagine John Betjeman, brooding about the betrayal of his wife:

> On the windy weedy platform with the sprinkled stars above
> When sudden the waiting stillness shook with the ancient spells
> Of an older world than all our worlds in the sound of the Pershore
> bells.
> They were ringing them down for Evensong in the lighted abbey
> near,
> Sounds which had poured through apple boughs for seven
> centuries here.

8

POSTCARDS FROM KELLINGTON

There was no reason to go to Kellington on Christmas Eve, but it felt right. The team had been excavating the parish church since October. All of it. Latterly, in two shifts, around the clock. The work was at the behest of British Coal, and it was driven by the need to stabilise the structure before mining subsidence caused it to fall.

I remember the weather as mild; at any rate, there were sunny intervals, and while a storm was forecast it was still calm. I'm not sure how much work got done. The mood was cheerful, a bit giddy; one or two colleagues wore clip-on antlers or Santa hats; I suspect something stronger than Nescafe was being added to hot drinks during the coffee break.

The excavators were from all over the country, and they wanted to go home. Some had trains to catch, so around noon we decided to call it a day and send the vans back to York early. Since I had driven down independently, I offered to stay on to mind the site until the security guard turned up at 1.30 pm.

The vans pulled away; there was singing aboard; the voices faded. I walked back into the churchyard, reflecting on the seven-hundred-odd cubic metres of earth we had removed by hand since October. What to do for the next hour? I thought back to how it had all started.

March 1975

After three months in the room with no windows, I take a day out to look at churches. You do not have to go far from Leeds to find wonderful things, like Lead, a tiny chapel with ancient furnishings alone in a field; or the alabaster tombs of the Waterton family at Methley.

I take the Yashica, an Ordnance Survey map and a copy of Pevsner's *West Riding*. Church archaeologists at this time are a bit sniffy about

Nikolaus Pevsner, because almost every church they investigate seems to produce something new that contradicts what he says. A case in point is the church of St Mary at Rivenhall in Essex, described by Pevsner as Victorian and of 'little interest', which turns out on closer study to be Anglo-Saxon (and to contain some of the finest twelfth-century European window glass now to be found in England).* But *The Buildings of England* is not to be belittled. Its first volumes coincided with the Festival of Britain; the last, on Staffordshire, in 1974, with the three-day week and the coal miners' victory at the Saltley coke depot. In between lay forty-four volumes, thirty-two of them by Pevsner himself, ten more jointly. One of his helpers said that by being so well informed he had robbed the word 'specialist' of meaning. Betjeman saw him rather as an 'ambitious impresario' who was often adrift on his facts. Anyway, there the West Riding volume is: plump, black, with an upholstered cover, already in its second edition, on the seat beside me as I head into the endlessly level world around the lower reaches of the Aire, the Went, and the Calder, where industries, power stations, and washlands mingle. The washlands flood when the rivers are high; animals graze them when they fall. The churches thus tend to be on higher ground, although 'high' hereabouts is relative, sometimes just a matter of a few feet.

I go first to Birkin – famous for being a near-complete Norman village church, with an apse and fancy decoration with dragons, woven strands, giant birds, monsters, and zodiac signs. The south door includes a rudimentary form of the arms of Adam de Birkin (d.1185) who paid for it. This is Ur-heraldry. Adam's symbol, on a capital near eye level, invited the prayers of parishioners as they entered and left, and would have adjoined passing sacramental processions. Is that why when a south aisle was added two centuries later the entire doorway was taken apart and re-erected in the new outer wall?

Behind the organ, in the tower, is a hybrid between staircase and ladder: the rungs/treads were formed from a slender tree-trunk that had been quartered lengthwise. Is this medieval? At the other end, in the apse, the removal of an eighteenth-century memorial plaque has revealed an oblong of creamy plaster on which is painted a brickwork pattern in dark red lines. I recognise this from York Minster: the red lines were stylised masonry joints; when the church was new in the twelfth century most of the interior would have been painted like this.

---

* In 1840 panels of stained glass in the east window were brought from the village of Chénu (Pays de Loire) by the rector, Bradford Hawkins.

This patch has survived because it was sheltered behind the plaque when the rest was stripped by the Victorians.

Buoyed up by these discoveries, I head south along Intake Lane and over the Aire, through the village of Beal, to see the church of St Edmund at Kellington. Pevsner describes it as 'somewhat bleak-looking', and it is. It stands alone among fields, its nearest companion the windmill tower a quarter of a mile away.

I stop the car short of the church and get out to look around. It is chilly, coming up to Easter. A few daffodils nod by the roadside. An odd smell drifts; later, I learn that it comes from the Croda chemical works at Knottingley (Croda, because when Mr Crowe and Mr Dawson joined forces in 1925 to produce lanolin by refining wool grease, they named the company by combining the first two letters of their surnames).

All churches have secrets. Lonely churches have deep secrets: of what is it that they are bereft? Maurice Beresford over in Economic History says they often signify a lost village, or a settlement that has moved, or that we are in an area where there were no villages, just a scatter of farms. But none of that seems likely here, for there is a village, small and neat, centred about a quarter of a mile away, and to judge from its plan it has been there a good while. This means that the church and village have been apart for centuries, and yet there is not even a road between them. I mark St Edmund down as a church to come back to.

Wednesday 1 August 1990

Lawrence asks if I will stand in for him at an up-coming meeting about Kellington. He says there are plans for some engineering works.

Friday 3 August 1990

The meeting, convened by British Coal, is led by Malcolm Webb, a chartered surveyor whose fabulous job title is Head of Subsidence. Among those present are the vicar, the Rev Barbara Lydon, and one of her churchwardens; the church architect; and several people from the engineering/contracting world whose names I do not catch.

Malcolm is cheery, dark-haired, with a moustache and smiling eyes behind a large pair of glasses. He is also firm, and he's in a hurry. The intended 'engineering works' are to offset the effects of mining subsidence from the colliery at nearby Kellingley. Locally, it's called 'Big K': a jumble of towers, sheds, muck heaps, and overhead conveyors that serve one of Europe's largest deep coal mines. Big K has taken so much coal since it opened twenty-five years ago that the miners half a mile beneath us are six miles away in horizontal distance: they travel to the face by electric train. Most of the coal goes to nearby power stations, at Ferrybridge, Drax, and, looming over us, Eggborough. From afar, their cooling towers look like clusters of skittles; on cold winter mornings their rising plumes, tinted pink by the low sun, can be seen from as far away as Ripon and Lincoln. Such is the volume of coal being shovelled into them that British Coal wants to open a new production face north-east of the colliery. The only obstacle is Kellington church: it stands on a low, barely discernible knoll of sand, it is in poor repair, and over the years the tower has cracked and shifted. When Malcolm pointed this out to British Coal's economic planners, he assumed they would think again. Instead, they say that the choice lies between opening the new face or closing the colliery. Two thousand jobs, or the church. Which is it to be?

Consulting engineers have come up with a solution: underpin all the church walls with a ring-beam, construct underground jacking chambers to allow for post-subsidence adjustment when the mine working has passed, and provide a suspended ground-floor slab within the nave. But the tower is too fragile for any of that. Instead, the recommended plan is to take it down stone by stone and re-erect it on a new substructure.

We're all open-mouthed. Malcolm turns to ask about archaeology. In my head, I am thinking that this is another York Minster. Aloud, I say that such a project would call for the three-dimensional recording and numbering of every stone in the tower; that the manoeuvring of heavy equipment and contractor's machinery will require every gravestone within about ten metres of the church to be recorded and removed to safety for the duration of the work; and that the entire interior and a strip around the outside will have to be archaeologically excavated down to natural subsoil. Why? Because traces of earlier buildings and ritual features will be beneath the present church – and there will be hundreds of burials, the removal of which would otherwise call for a cemetery clearance company. How much time needed? Many months for the excavation, years for analysis and publication of what it finds. Ah, says Malcolm, we don't have many months. We have three. Counting back from the arrival of the subsidence, the engineers and contractor will need to be on site no later than the beginning of January. Most of the archaeological work needs to be done by the end of December.

This is a lot to take in. Others in the room do so in different ways. For the incumbent, the Rev Barbara Lydon, and her churchwardens, it means leaving their church for up to two years and joining forces with another congregation. All the pews, furnishings, the organ, monuments, and heating system will have to come out. Some of that will involve arcane skills. The heating system, for instance, is a piece of Victorian industrial archaeology; the pipes and collars are held together by run lead, which needs to be gently melted to pull it apart. The paving must be lifted and stored in safety, and before it is taken up it must be exactly drawn so that each slab can go back where it came from. The neighbouring farmer will be asked to make his next-door fields available for the contractor's compound, a village of huts, spoil, and storage of the dismantled tower. The parish's architect and treasurer are trying to come to terms with a scheme in which millions are about to be spent on work they did not ask for when the parishioners cannot afford to fix leaks in the nave roof. I am wondering how, or indeed whether, a project like this can be done in twelve weeks. Time with no money is the norm in rescue archaeology. In this case, we have money but no time.

4–10 August 1990

I look at written sources for medieval Kellington. Like most places in England, it is first heard of in Domesday Book – a survey of landholding and assets made in 1086 on the orders of William the Conqueror, who wanted to know what he had conquered and who held it.

The survey shows that the area's main assets were ploughland, meadow, and wood pasture. Under the heading 'Kellington', there were five townships, each a self-contained agricultural community ruled by its own lord: Roall, Beal, High, and Low Eggborough, as well as Kellington itself. The English lords on the eve of the Conquest were Wege, Baret, Gamal, Ulfkil, and Alric. The area then passed into the hands of Ilbert de Lacy, to whom the Conqueror entrusted the feudal barony of Pontefract, of which these lands formed a part. Ilbert was the son of an old Norman family, member of a dynasty whose descendants would run a large part of England for the next three centuries. At Kellington, however, there was some continuity at township level. While Beal was now held from Ilbert by 'a certain thegn', the Anglo-Saxon lords Alric and Baret each continued to hold portions of Kellington, and Baret continued to hold Roall.

The first written hint of a church comes about eighty years later, in 1166, when the record of a land transaction mentions Henry the clerk (*clericus*) of Kellington. Other documents from the de Lacy empire show that Henry was one in a line of hereditary clerics. His brother John was rector of Kellington by 1185; when John died in 1202, he was succeeded by his son Thomas, and Thomas was followed by his son, Alexander. Kellington church in the twelfth and early thirteenth centuries looks like a family business.

In late-Anglo-Saxon England, it was common for priests to own churches and to bequeath them to sons. Norman reformers discouraged that. They demanded clerical celibacy, while lay owners were pressed to pass rights in their churches to religious houses, who were felt to be more appropriate owners. In theory, this is what happened here, for by 1185 Henry de Lacy had given Kellington church to the Knights Templar. However, it is a question whether anyone told this to Henry the clerk or his brother John, or if they did whether they took any notice. Possession is nine tenths of the law, and it was many years before the Templars gained full control.*

The late arrival of reform hereabouts very likely had to do with the enormity of the diocese of York and associated difficulties of enforcing rules, or even of explaining what they were to people in out-of-the-way places.† It may further have reflected the background from which Kellington's clerical dynasty had emerged. The de Lacy archive shows that Henry the clerk and John the rector were sons of Humphrey de Ruhale – that is, Roall, another of the Kellington townships. In 1166, Humphrey held half a fee of Henry de Lacy – a fee being a kind of tenure, which could be heritable. Where this was so, the sense of continuity it conferred could encourage a lord and his successors to invest in the renewal of a church that they came to see as their dynastic resting place. In this connection, it is telling that Humphrey's mother was one of the granddaughters and co-heirs of Baret – the late-Saxon lord who had held Roall and Kellington back in the days of Edward the Confessor. If the church existed in Baret's day, it looks to have passed by descent,

---

* In 1223, the Master of the Templars in England presented Robert de Melbourne as Kellington's incumbent – with Alexander's portion of the living reserved to him until his death.

† There are other oddities. John, for instance, was described in one document as *decano de Kelingtona* ('dean of Kellington') and was simultaneously 'dean' of Pontefract. But at that date, in this area, 'dean' seems simply to have been a local usage for 'incumbent'.

remaining with the family until the Templars eventually took control.

The Knights Templar were an order of fighting monks formed around 1120 to shield pilgrims travelling to Jerusalem. Henry de Lacy was a keen supporter. He himself went on crusade twice, and he had a brother who joined the order. Templars' prayers were believed to be powerful. The Order was accordingly popular among lay donors from whom it attracted large gifts of land, until the early fourteenth century when it was dissolved by the papacy, in murky circumstances. Templar estates were managed by regional officials known as preceptors, each of whom ran a group of manors, farms, fisheries, and churches. The preceptory here was based at Temple Hirst, about four miles away.

In 1202, the Knights Templar fell into dispute with the Benedictine monks of Selby Abbey about the tithes from worshippers at a nearby chapel. The chapel stood about two and a half miles distant at Whitley Bridge, and the argument was about to whom the tithes were owed. Whitley chapel was served by the incumbent of Kellington, but the neighbouring parish church of Snaith (which was held by Selby) claimed the tithes as theirs. The argument was settled by agreement that each church should take the tithes in alternate years, that Kellington should pay 4s a year to Snaith, and that Whitley's parishioners should attend the church of Snaith at Christmas, the Purification, and Whitsunday. This shows that Snaith was remembered as Whitley's mother church but conceded that for practical purposes it was being served from Kellington. This was partly because Snaith was over five miles away, and partly because Whitley and Snaith were often cut off from each other by floods. The arrangement did not last, and by the end of the Middle Ages everyone had forgotten what it was. In 1548, when Edward VI's commissioners recorded the chapel's purpose as being 'to pray and to celebrate masse to the aged impotent men, that for waters cannot resort to the said paroch church', the parish church was assumed to be Kellington.

A parish with five townships . . . an Anglo-Norman family . . . ownership by the Knights Templar: how might any of that translate into whatever lies under the floor at Kellington?

11 August 1990

Another question is who is going to find out. I explain to Malcolm that it is open to British Coal to select an archaeological contractor, and that

North Yorkshire's county archaeologist will provide him with a list of appropriate candidates. Malcolm asks, 'Will you do it?' I say of course not. I now hold a half-time post with the University of York while the other half of me continues to work for the CBA. I am busy. And a new university term is about to start.

Mid August 1990

Malcolm is persistent. I mention Kellington to our head of department. A plan emerges. The department already has the nucleus of a field team. We could hire Warwick Rodwell – the doyen of church archaeologists – as a consultant to advise on strategy.

Later August–early September 1990

Warwick agrees to take part. He recommends Caroline Atkins, a buildings archaeologist, to lead the team to record the tower, stone by stone, and then oversee its dismantling. The excavation team will be led by Ian Lawton and Andy Jacobs. With Warwick's guidance, a phased plan emerges. A photogrammetric record of the tower will be made to provide a base for stone-by-stone recording. The university will undertake payroll and associated administration. A budget is agreed with Malcolm Webb. British Coal undertakes to provide funds for analysis and publication of results after the site works are finished.

Later September 1990

Ian and Andy have hired huts, which are craned in over the churchyard wall. Supplies of power and running water are laid on. A team of experienced excavators is recruited. Minibuses are hired to bring them to and from York each day. Cameras, survey instruments, drawing film, bone boxes arrive. A photogrammetric record is made of the exterior elevations of the tower. Gravestones are recorded prior to removal; furnishings and fittings are taken out; a record is made of the paved floor, which is lifted by a contractor and taken away to store. One warm afternoon, Tim, an undergraduate who is helping the churchyard survey, spots an enormous puffball – creamy white, like a moon rising through the churchyard grass. Tim is an expert on edible fungi. 'My supper,' he says as his pocketknife comes out.

Monday 8 October 1990

The excavation team moves in. Limewash and dirt must be removed from the interior elevations of the tower before the photogrammetrists can begin. This takes a week.

Later October 1990

The diggers outside the south side of the church are uncovering a lot of graves. Counter-intuitively, some of the oldest of them are not far under the surface; medieval sextons did not dig deep. Many of the graves interrupt each other – that is, when one grave was being dug, the sexton went through one or more others. In doing so, bones from different people mingled, and over the years they became very mingled indeed. The fact that some of them are still articulated shows that gravediggers were sometimes turning up body parts from graves that were only a few years old.

On the north side, there are hardly any graves at all – it is all very quiet. But there is one, and it is strange: it lies from south to north, at right angles to everyone else. We have no idea what this means, who it was or how old, except that it is older than anything else on that side of the church. It could be early medieval. It could be prehistoric. There are signs that originally it was under a cairn of stones.

A few yards away, just inside the north door, we find the grave of a knight. He lies beneath a slab let into the floor in the north nave aisle. The location, level with the floor, invites you to step on it – a gesture of self-abasement, maybe, or another prompt for you to pray as you came or went. But to judge from its condition, it was not walked on: it is near pristine, a thick rectangle of creamy limestone, the curves of a stylised calvary at its foot, new life budding from the head, a subtly tapered shaft, a hefty fourteenth-century sword. Archaeologists can become uneasy in the presence of beauty, not because they lack an eye for it, but because they like to come across as being motivated by evidence rather than feeling. But it is hard not to be moved by this stone. The answer to its position, surely, is that church north doors were key places for processions, and that being buried under the path of a sacramental procession was a spiritually valuable place to be. Beneath, the knight's bones lie in an earth grave dug to resemble the inside of a stone sarcophagus. In his right hand is a white quartz pebble. As work continues, we find many stones clasped like this.

Early November 1990

The decongestion of graves outside the south wall continues. It is slow work. Why so many? Why so crammed? There's an old rhyme about this:

> Here lie I by the chancel door;
> They put me here because I was poor.
> The further in, the more you pay,
> But here I lie as snug as they.

The rhyme is wrong. Or, at least, it's only half right. Until the creation of the Protestant Church of England, hardly anyone was buried inside the church. Before 1550, people of every station – priests, peasants, local lords in their stone coffins, women who died in childbirth – were gathered outside the south side, and especially around the porch. Hence, it was not just the poor who lay by the door – it was everybody. The answer to the cramming thus has something to do with community. Like the knight, like the arms of Adam de Birkin on the south door up the road, Kellington's dead were gathered so that when their successors entered or left, they did so through their community's midst. Being together mattered. And of course, when a sacramental procession entered or left, it passed through the entire historical community. After the abolition of Purgatory, when it became everyone for themselves, those who could afford it began to bury their relatives inside the church.

As for why so many, thinking back to the work on written records in September, Kellington was the burying place for people from five townships.

Later November 1990

Inside, we find traces of an older nave, the base of an earlier tower, and an earlier aisle. All stood on strip footings formed of river cobbles

about the size of a fist. The subsoil into which the footings were let is
sand: the church was put on a low sandy eminence – perhaps a former
sandbank of the Ur-Aire, or the outwash from a pro-glacial lake. Under
the first nave, we come upon traces of a rectangular platform. It is made
of bits of flaggy white limestone and has been much cut about by early
modern graves. When we come to take it to pieces, there are swirls of
discoloured sand below which Warwick recognises as marks by the cuts
of spades. Hence, before the platform was laid, someone dug the area
over. A fragment of tooth is found, and a penny drops: there were graves
here, and they were moved to make way for the platform.

The fourteenth-century chapel on the north side of the chancel
reveals a secret that sets us back on our heels. We have already found
that in the eighteenth century a local family used it as their burying
place – just under the floor were the outlines of their coffins, wide-
shouldered, a bit like the carrying cases of orchestral double basses. Since
then, going down, we realise that the side chapel originally stood over
an underground room. The subterranean chamber was reached through
a door behind the altar and down steps. What was it? In its north wall,
about waist height, is a small recess, a bit like a miniature fireplace. Is
this where consecrated things that had been spoiled were consumed?
The door was blocked at the Reformation.

Monday 19 November 1990

A long-running hiatus between the photogrammetrists and the architect means that only today have photogrammetric plots of the internal
elevations of the tower been delivered. This has thrown the carefully
planned phases of recording that were meant to mesh with the programmes of the scaffolders, the dismantlers, and the engineers.

Tuesday 20 November 1990

Kellington church is dedicated to St Edmund, the patron saint of
torture victims, wolves, and pandemics. Today is his feast day, and the
anniversary of Dick Coleraine's funeral. Next to nothing sure is known
about Edmund. The *Anglo-Saxon Chronicle* for 869 says, 'In this year
the host went across Mercia into East Anglia and took winter-quarters
at Thetford; and the same winter St Edmund the king fought against

them, and the Danes won the victory, and they slew the king.' Coins issued during his reign show that he existed, but that's about it.

By later repute, Edmund was a teenage East Anglian king who in November that year was captured by Danes. The great Danish army was real enough; led by sons of Ragnar Lodbrok, it had been in England and causing mayhem since 865, and recent archaeological study of the places where it camped show that it was indeed great. In the 1960s and 1970s, a fashion grew in some historical circles for numbering the Great Army in the hundreds and explaining its effect as through replacement of parts of the Anglo-Saxon elite rather than through mass force. We now know that it was a mass force. It was probably also impossible to bargain with, since each of the leaders headed his own faction, and making a deal with one meant nothing to the others.

One account of Edmund's death, written down over a century later, says that he was beaten, tied to a tree, and lashed with whips. Rather than crying with pain, he called out to Christ. This seems to have vexed his assailants, who redoubled their efforts by showering him with arrows. Yet still he called to Christ. Infuriated, the Danish commander ordered him beheaded. The head was dumped in a wood. When Edmund's followers later came to search for it, they found the head between the paws of a wolf who was guarding it against carrion-eating animals. The head was reunited with the body, which was moved to the Suffolk town of Beodricsworth (later, Bury St Edmunds), where a religious house was founded around the grave. The place became the centre of one of England's foremost cults; by the late eleventh century, it was one of the richest monasteries in England.

Saints lived on in their tombs; we have already seen how the Normans made sure to earn the approval of the ones who mattered most. Cuthbert at Durham, Etheldreda at Ely, Swithun at Winchester – within a generation of the Conquest, all these and dozens more were being translated into fine new homes. No one did they try harder to impress than Edmund at Bury. George was not yet on the scene; for practical purposes, Edmund was the patron saint of their new-won kingdom. What was he doing at Kellington?

Thursday 22 November 1990

A few members of the team are away during the day, doing a small job at another church on behalf of British Coal. They return just before

4 pm. None of them had heard any news during the day. When they are told of Mrs Thatcher's resignation, there is a frenzied outbreak of shouting. One of the returnees flings his shovel into the air, yelling 'Maggie! Maggie! Maggie! Out! Out! Out!' as it spirals upwards. Handling tools safely is one of the basics in archaeology; it is an iron (*sic*) rule that when picks, mattocks, or shovels are not in use, they are always placed so as to avoid mishap, and they are never thrown – let alone thrown as high as this one. It seems an age before the shovel falls back out of the dusk.

2 December 1990, Advent Sunday

The first day of the Church's year, when the great collect is spoken:

> Almighty God, give us grace that we may cast away the works of darkness, and put upon us the armour of light, now in the time of this mortal life, in which thy Son Jesus Christ came to visit us in great humility; that in the last day, when he shall come again in his glorious majesty to judge both the quick and the dead, we may rise to the life immortal, through him who liveth and reigneth with thee and the Holy Ghost, now and ever. *Amen.*

But not here, not today. However, one of Kellington's three bells was cast in the fifteenth century, and around its waist:

> *ISTE CAMPANA SONET JOHANNES*
> This bell sounds John

Is this the John of John 1:1, *In principio erat verbum* ('In the beginning was the Word'), or is it John the Baptist, the Jewish prophet who heralds Christ? Either way, he is appropriate to the day, and he reminds me of Longbridge. Going past Big K, through the chemical vapours, over the Aire and Calder Navigation, on through Knottingley to Ferrybridge, John is in my mind.

A word about Knottingley. On the face of things, it is a bit of a mess, a scatter of housing estates laid out in different directions at different times, dispersed shops, with nowhere you could call a centre. But down the years it has done skilful things, like making glass (which it still does), pottery, ships (over three hundred vessels were launched here), not to mention producing a succession of rugby-league stars. It's a real place, and like all places it is full of memories, hopes, and mysteries – like its church of St Botolph, a saint whose name often attaches to churches on boundaries, as it does here, on the edge of the wapentake of Osgoldcross, beside the river Aire.

Knottingley's decorations are already up. They are very simple, all of one colour, a washed-out pale mauve, fixed high on lamp posts along the main road. The designs include a star that flashes on and off, an angel, and a bell. The bell should appear to flash from side to side, but half its lights have failed, and it is thus permanently in midswing. On this day of renewal when the voyage towards Easter begins again, there is a sadness in the stuck bell.

Monday 3 December 1990

The work is too slow. Technically, we think it is good, but at this rate we will not finish by the handover date. Some of the excavators say we should demand an extension, but Warwick and I know that this won't be practical. After discussion, we have agreed to work continuously, in shifts. Fluorescent tubes, colour-matched to allow for photography, are hung from the roof to light the work at night.

We begin work inside the porch. We have postponed this for as long as possible, because digging in the porch gets in the way of going in and out. But it has to be done, and a planked bridge is built over the excavation to enable people to come and go. Excavation under the threshold of the south door uncovers a notable thing: a long, oblong piece of sandstone with a run of plant scroll carved on one face. The leaves and stems are well cut, quite classy. At some stage the stone had been broken lengthwise and at either end, and the face adjoining the plant-scroll panel has been cut flat, with a smooth chamfer along the angle where they meet.

Neither Warwick nor I have seen anything quite like this. We wonder if the decoration is of the twelfth century, but no parallels spring to mind. The chamfer and undecorated surface give rise to a suggestion that it started out as a door-head, and that it was laid to rest here when the original south door was superseded by the addition of the south aisle.

Thirty years on, I think again about this stone. The study of medieval sculpture and the micro-archaeology of worked stones has come a long way since 1990, and I consult a friend who specialises in these things. Within two hours, back comes the answer: it is part of the shaft of a freestanding cross that was later cut down for some secondary use. The date? The leaf form is a simplified version of a form that is normally dated to the late eighth or early ninth century. But it could be later, say, in the range 900–1100.

An Anglo-Saxon cross here stirs new thoughts. When the first church was built, did part of the shaft become its threshold, so that every parishioner who came or left would touch it?

7–8 December 1990

High pressure over the UK begins to slip westward; a cold front arrives from the north-west; Arctic air follows; pressure falls; during the night there is heavy snowfall, at times over two and half inches an hour. Next day, a Saturday, nothing can be done outside until the snow melts.

Friday 14 December 1990

Misty, cold, calm. Lighting-up time, 3.38 pm. On these shortening days, there is not enough natural light to dig by in late afternoon, so the outdoor excavators are beginning to wrap up. Paul, a friend, arrives from Leeds. He's heard me talk about the work but has not so far seen it. We do the tour. By the time we finish, it is quite dark. We stand on a scaffold platform outside the east end and look down on a row of graves under excavation. Among them are three skeletons of children. Their skulls are like large ostrich eggs, and glitter in the frost. Cutting light from a nearby floodlamp deepens the shadows in the eye cavities. Each orbit is an inky pool. Paul follows their gaze upward. Upon what are they fixed? Polaris.

Back home, I look up Polaris; astronomers say that its light set forth some four hundred years ago, around the time the youngsters died.

Saturday 15 December 1990

Dismantling of the tower begins. Each stone is individually numbered and recorded, in due course yielding discoveries: of moulded stones reused, masons' marks, graffiti, settings which indicate where the original floor stages were. The tower is taken down a course at a time, the stones being carefully laid on wooden pallets, packed with straw, lowered to the ground by crane, and carried to the compound where the pallets are laid in rows and covered with tarpaulins. This work will continue until Easter 1991.

Monday 24 December 1990

As the vans pull away, I reflect on what we have found. The underground room was a surprise. So was the carved and not-yet-dated Anglo-Saxon stone under the threshold, not to mention the north-pointing grave under the disturbed cairn. An earlier, smaller church inside the present one, like Russian dolls, was to be expected, but the stone rectangle under the nave is a puzzle, as are the signs that it was laid out in an existing graveyard. And what about the white quartz pebbles? There is a clue in verse seventeen of the second chapter of Revelation:

> He that hath an ear, let him hear what the Spirit sayeth unto the churches; To him that overcometh will I give to eat of the hidden manna, and will give him a white stone, and in the stone a new name written, which no man knoweth saving he that receiveth it.

Death is rebirth, and with it comes a new baptism.

Two o'clock – still no sign of the guard. I'd like to go home. I want to ring the office of the security firm to find out where the guard has got to, but the portable phone (a great chunky thing about the size of a brick and every bit as heavy) has gone back to York with the crew. I drive into the village and call from a telephone box. Ah, yes, they say, sorry, he'll be with you in about an hour. (We find out later that the guard had been moonlighting on a second job and had fallen asleep.)

Back on site, I look into the finds hut. I have spent hardly any time here since we started; excavated objects are safe, so if you are in a hurry, you look at them later. The climate in this hut differs from the others. There is a humidifier and permanent heating, and it feels warm and moist. Everything is orderly. On the fitted counter are hard-back notebooks with lists of contexts and finds numbers; indelible inks and varnish for marking pottery; at the far end are stacks of labelled bone boxes – there are hundreds of people in here. Shelves on the walls bear clear plastic boxes containing metalwork, samples, pottery. I reach for a box, open it, and with a stab of surprise realise that it contains Anglo-Saxon pottery. How much of this have we been finding? From whereabouts has it been coming?

Attention turns to a small cubical box. Its lid is half off, revealing a small bell nestling on a bed of acid-free paper within. I look more closely. It is of copper alloy; the upper half is hemispherical, the lower part openwork, the clapper still there. Carefully, I lift it. For a fleeting moment, I recall the bonfire at Blackwell and M. R. James's story about the whistle, which come to think of it was found on the site of a preceptory of the Knights Templar. Does it still sound? Even more gently, I let it swing. It has a high, silvery voice. As it speaks, the door swings open. I turn to welcome the security man, but no one is there.

Wednesday 26 December 1990

We are all very tired. Driving home after a visit to a relative, I doze off and lose control of the car. The vehicle spins round and comes to rest halfway through a drystone wall. None of us is hurt. We coax the car home, but next day the garage pronounces it a write-off.

Saturday 30 December 1990

The year's last days are blustery, cold, often wet. A gale blows on the night of the thirtieth. The excavation is now close to its full extent, and on the south side it has revealed the entire length of the substructure upon which the south wall stands. It dawns on me that the footing of cobbles on which the wall stands is a bit like a ribbon of ball-bearings – safe enough if the ball-bearings lie tight-packed in the ground, but becoming unstable if the ground is removed. Which is what we have done. As the roof groans and heaves in the gale, I wonder if they will squirt out sideways under the pressures of the live load.

Sunday 31 December 1990

One of the last discoveries is of a small rectangular structure made of posts in the south-east corner of the original chancel. It's about the size of a thin garden shed, and it looks as though it was there when the chancel was laid out around it. If it was a little mortuary house, the acid sands have eaten the bones of its occupant. Was this a founder, or a member of the founder's family? Someone like Baret?

Monday 1 January 1991

We have completed what we believe to be the fullest excavation of a parish church in use ever undertaken in England. We are on site to hand it over to the contractor. But of course, New Year's Day is a contractor's holiday, and we have the site to ourselves for a day or two more. I take some photographs. Kellington was one of the first churches I photographed with the Yashica 35. It is also the last: sand from the excavation has jammed the mechanism.

September 1991

I move to a new job. Responsibility for overseeing analysis and substantive publication of results passes to a colleague.

Sunday 3 May 1992

The church reopens for worship with a service of rededication led by the Bishop of Wakefield. Since January 1991, an entirely new substructure has been inserted, the tower has been dismantled and rebuilt, the furnishings and organ are returned, the gravestones are back where they were. Andy Jacobs walks over after the service and asks, quietly, if I have heard the news? I shake my head. In an even lower voice: the word on Big K's street is that an unexpected geological problem caused the abandonment of the original plan for the face. The subsidence never came.

Tuesday 19 July 1994

The Coal Industry Act 1994 receives royal assent. What little remains of British Coal is privatised. Kellingley is one of the seventeen deep pits bought by RJB Mining, which according to Malcolm Webb feels no obligation to honour the undertaking given by its predecessor further to support the writing up or publication of the excavation.

Wednesday 1 August 2012

A metal detectorist searching in a field near the church finds part of a nocturnal – an astronomical instrument for telling the time at night.

A nocturnal has several graduated dials, a movable arm, and a sighting hole. They entered widespread use for navigation in the sixteenth century, but there are written references from before 1200. This one is of copper alloy, and a fragment: someone cut it down to a quarter circle. The letter forms suggest it was made between 1550 and 1700. The way it works is that the outer edge is marked off in months and days. An index pointer on the inner dial is set to the current date on the outer dial. There is a central sighting hole for the main star and a movable arm that is then aligned to a reference star, allowing the time to be read off from a graduated scale. The main star? Polaris.

Friday 18 December 2015

Kellingley Colliery closes. Deep mining for coal in the UK comes to an end.

Austin plant, 1935. Longbridge Lane traced by double row of trees upper left, site of future church in adjoining field. Water pumping station lower right.

Artist's impression of new church of St John and vicarage at Longbridge, 1956

Ascensiontide at Longbridge, 1958

Sanderstead rectory, 1964

Medieval graffiti on reredos at Beverley Minster, near former shrine of St John of Beverley. Ships symbolised journeys; graffiti made an enduring link between pilgrims and places they visited.

Battersea church of St Mary and bridge c.1796, by J.M.W. Turner

Ringers' rhyme board
and bell ropes in tower
of St Brevita's church,
Lanlivery, Cornwall

Church of St Edmund, Kellington, North Yorkshire, under repair by
contractor following archaeological excavation, May 1991

Shrine of St Melangell c.1150-60, reassembled from fragments, Pennant Melangell, Powys.

Underside of soundboard of sixteenth-century organ, found reused as door at Wetheringsett, Suffolk.

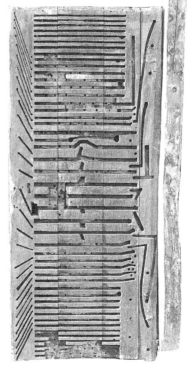

Europe's oldest intact book: Gospel of St John, produced at Wearmouth–Jarrow early in the eighth century, later placed in coffin of St Cuthbert.

Bede's workplace: St Peter, Wearmouth, by 1946 surrounded by shipyards, workers' housing and wartime prefabs.

Migratory cranes, carved on the west entrance of St Peter's church, Monkwearmouth, c.675-700, symbolise timekeeping (Jeremiah 8:7, Isaiah 1:3) and hence monastic discipline.

Monastic church of St Paul, Jarrow, established AD 685, now in post-industrial surroundings. The eastern part of the church, formerly a freestanding chapel, dates from Bede's lifetime.

The navigator of a 60 Sqn Mosquito back from a sortie, April 1945, is met by ground crew, intelligence officer, and camera fitters. The Gargano hills rise beyond.

Penitents of the Confraternity of Help, San Severo, Good Friday 1945

Westcott House and All Saints, Jesus Lane (foreground), Jesus College on site of former nunnery of St Radegund beyond

Scene from *Androcles and the Lion*, Westcott House, 1949, directed by Simon Phipps. Androcles is played by Bill Vanstone, his wife by Elsie Morris.

June 1952: Martin Cooper, rector of St George's Hockley (on bonnet), and his curate, John Morris, publicise the forthcoming fundraising carnival and attract criticism from fellow clerics.

Carnival newspaper,
June 1952

9

ANGLICANS, CELTS, COINCIDENCES

MAISCOGGABATAUXELODUNUMCAMMOGLANNA
RIGOREVALIAELIUSDRACO

On the last Sunday of June 2003, a metal detectorist working near
Ilam in the Derbyshire White Peak came upon a copper-alloy
bowl. Imagine yourself the finder: at first sight, the object is not much
to look at – a bit like a metal doorknob cut in half, small enough to
lay on the palm of your hand, grubby. A closer look reveals exquisite
decoration: coloured enamel inlay of reds, turquoise, yellow, and blue
arranged in an asymmetric pattern of swirls, lobes, and roundels of
the kind people call 'Celtic'. A smudge of solder hints at a lost handle.
Above the decoration, running around the bowl's circumference, are the
fifty-five letters above.

The letters are in an unbroken sequence, but if you split the words
out, you get the Roman names of four forts along the western portion of Hadrian's Wall: MAIS (Bowness today), COGGOBATA (now
Drumburgh), UXELODUNUM (Stanwix), and CAMMOGLANNA
(Castlesteads). The remaining letters give you RIGORE VALI AELI
(probably 'On the line of the vallum of Aelius') and DRACO (a personal name). Aelius was Hadrian's family name; '*Vallum Aelium*' was
what Romans called the Wall. Draco may have been the owner or the
maker of the pan; if he was the owner, perhaps he had been a member
of the Wall garrison, and maybe the vessel (which is of a type known as
a *trulla*) was a souvenir of his tour of duty.

Enamelled *trullae* are rare, but two more are known which list
forts along the Wall. On one, found near Froxfield in Wiltshire in
the 1720s, a stylised depiction of the crenelated Wall runs round the
bowl surmounted by the names of five forts. As on the Ilam *trulla*,
they run from west to east: A MAIS, ABALLAVA (Burgh-by-Sands),

VXELODUM, CAMBOGLANS, BANNA (Birdoswald). In this list, the fort at Drumburgh mentioned on the Ilam bowl was left out (it was smaller than the others), and BANNA, the next fort east from Castlesteads, was added. A third *trulla* (found at Amiens) names the forts at Bowness, Burgh-by-Sands, Stanwix, Castlesteads, Birdoswald, plus ESCIA, today's Great Chesters.

We shall return to the lists, but consider now a declaration written by Patrick, the apostle of Ireland. The earliest manuscript we have was copied in the early ninth century, but there is wide agreement that the original was written in the fifth and that Patrick himself was the author. This is how it starts:

> *Ego Patricius, peccator rusticissimus et minimis omnium fidelium et con-*
> *temptibilissimus apud plurimos, patrem habui Calpornium diaconum,*
> *filium quondam Poiti presbyteri, qui fuit vico Bannavem Taburniae;*
> *villulam enim prope habuit, ubi ego capturam dedi. Annorum eram tunc*
> *fere sedecim. Deum enim uerum ignorabam et Hiberione in captivitate,*
> *adductus sum cum tot milia hominum . . .*

In translation:

> My name is Patrick. I am a sinner, a simple country person, and the least of all believers. I am looked down upon by many. My father was Calpornius. He was a deacon; his father was Potitus, a priest, who lived at Bannavem Taburniae. His home was near there, and that is where I was taken prisoner. I was about sixteen at the time. At that time, I did not know the true God. I was taken into captivity in Ireland, along with thousands of others . . .

The search for Bannavem Taburniae has been to no avail, and the two words do not look likely in the languages of late Roman Britain. However, if we go back a step, a ready solution emerges. The historian Diarmaid MacCulloch points out that Patrick or his secretary would have written in *scripta continua*, a form with no spaces or punctuation between words or sentences – like the list of forts on the Ilam *trulla*. Spacing came in later, in seventh- and eighth-century ecclesiastical writings. The copyist of Patrick's text would thus have had to use his judgement about where breaks between words should come. MacCulloch goes on:

> Provide a different spacing for the words: separate out 'Banna' (as in Birdoswald); transform 'vem ta' into the word 'Venta', a common

Romano-British placename usage for a market centre; add a word describing the local catchment area of the market as is customary with these 'Venta' names, and you have a plausible 'Banna Venta Burniae' pretty well nailed down at Birdoswald.

'*Banna*' means peak or crest, which exactly describes Birdoswald's position atop a lofty bluff overlooking the River Irthing. Its proximity to the Roman regional centre of Luguvalium, today's Carlisle, provides a context for the local government office we are told was held by Patrick's father; Birdoswald is just seventeen miles from the eastern shore of the Solway, handy for slave ships; and excavations have found substantial evidence for life continuing in the fort through the fifth century and into the sixth. It all fits.

The evidence for Birdoswald's continued use through Late Antiquity reminds us that when Roman provincial government ended, frontier units in forts along the Wall stayed where they were. These formations were cosmopolitan in origin – Birdoswald's garrison was originally raised in what is now Romania – but by 400 they were being maintained through local enlistment and hereditary service. They were thus well placed to provide leaders of local dynasties, which in due course came together through marriage or war to form larger polities. It is noteworthy that all the monarchies that eventually combined to form the English kingdom of Northumbria bore British names.

Aback of both the church in Ireland and the kingdom of Northumbria, then, we have a Roman Briton whose family lived close to Banna (Birdoswald), who was in his teens early in the fifth century, was kidnapped, escaped, gained experience of monastic life in Gaul, and later returned to Ireland to evangelise.

Many Anglicans feel a special affinity for early Christianity in Celtic-speaking areas. The Church of England's own website says that Anglican roots 'go back to the time of the Roman Empire when a Christian church came into existence in what was then the Roman province of Britain'. And in the next paragraph, 'The British church was a missionary church with figures such as St Illtud, St Ninian and St Patrick evangelising in Wales, Scotland and Ireland.'

It might be thought that the pinpointing of Patrick's birthplace, in England, would stir some interest. In practice, Anglican enthusiasm for the early Church usually has less to do with current research than with what the early Church is imagined to have been. Imagination has operated in a long succession of revivalist movements, from the later Middle

Ages through the rise of nationalism to Californian New Age. At each step, ideas of a 'Celtic Church' have been used to suit changing ends. The idea of a 'missionary church', for instance, recalls Britain's position as a colonial power, when collection boxes for the Church Missionary Society (founded 1799) were at the back of the church, and down to the 1960s bishops and deans were being consecrated to dioceses and cathedrals in faraway places. Indeed, if we go back to the Church of England's website, we can see reimagining at work right now in its claim that what became known as the Church of England was the result of a confluence of three streams of tradition: the Roman tradition introduced by the mission of St Augustine, vestiges 'of the old Romano-British church', and Celtic practice 'coming down from Scotland', identified with figures like Cuthbert and Aidan. There never was a Celtic Church, but the fact that most historians have stopped speaking of one has done nothing to hinder a notion of 'Celtic worship', and with it a yearning for supposed Celtic mystical values: closeness to nature, ancient wisdom, divinity in all things, silence and solitude, holiness of the senses, and the numinosity of boundaries and edges. This conception of Celtic spirituality holds a freshness and sense of authenticity for both independent groups and members of established congregations. Among the independent groups there is even a self-proclaimed Celtic Orthodox Church which describes itself as the 'original Church of the British Isles' founded in AD 37 by Joseph of Arimathea.

According to the Gospels, it was Joseph who buried the body of Christ in his tomb after the crucifixion. There is not a speck of historical evidence to connect him with Britain, and if there was, his arrival in AD 37 would be good going – this was six years before the Roman invasion of Britain, and Paul himself did not reach Rome until c.AD 60. The connection between Joseph, Britain, and Glastonbury was invented over a thousand years later in a cycle of Arthurian romance literature. However, the religious community at Glastonbury did indeed have an illustrious history, and thanks to recent work we now know that some sort of community was there for several centuries before the English took over, while its position in the south-west, closeness to Wales, and connectivity with Ireland made it a ready candidate for an origin myth for the entire British Church. This foundational story took hold towards the end of the twelfth century, when Glastonbury's Benedictine monks happened upon the purported graves of Arthur and Guinevere, and their discovery was publicised by Gerald of Wales. Thereafter, the abbey promoted Glastonbury as Avalon, encouraged Joseph's cult, and declared itself to be the oldest religious house in Britain. As is often the way with fake history, the more time elapsed between the story's telling and the events it described, the more detailed it became. By the fifteenth century, Joseph had become a full member of Glastonbury's pantheon, and when Sir Thomas Malory (c.1415–1471) wrote *Le Morte d'Arthur*, Joseph, Arthur, and Glastonbury were in it. The abbey prospered accordingly: by the time Henry VIII closed it in 1539, it was the largest monastic landholder in Britain.

Glastonbury Abbey was now suppressed, but the origin stories were not forgotten and would not lie down. By the end of the nineteenth century, the abbey ruins were attracting ten thousand visitors a year. In 1907, after three and a half centuries in private hands, the site was offered for sale. The auction was national news. The purchaser, Ernest Jardine, a maker of textile machinery in Nottingham and Liberal Unionist politician, said that his purpose in buying the ruins was to keep them out of unsuitable hands. He offered the abbey to the Church of England, at cost price, and on 8 June 1907 the Bishop of Bath and Wells wrote to tell readers of *The Times* that he had made himself responsible for raising the necessary funds to do so. The bishop went on, 'it would be a matter of very deep regret to many members of the Church of England if the Abbey were to pass into the possession of any other communion'. Given the role of Henry VIII in the abbey's closure, and of his son and daughter in the suppression of Catholicism, this was a strange thing to say, and it duly drew a reproachful letter from the abbot of the nearby Benedictine community at Downside. There was something odd, too, about celebrating an institution which had gained so much of its standing through falsehood. But as we have seen, when it comes to the early Church, fact and logic are usually trumped by feeling and sentiment. The bishop accordingly summed up his appeal by quoting Edward Freeman (1824–1892), a former Regius Professor of History at Oxford, who had described Glastonbury as 'the one great religious foundation which lived through the storm of the English conquest, and in which Briton and Englishman have an equal share'. Glastonbury was being visualised as a kind of conductive medium, a flow from the British Church, through early England, across the Reformation, into the present, and back.

In June 1909, a service of thanksgiving was held to mark the site's acquisition by Anglican trustees. The Prince and Princess of Wales, the Archbishop of Canterbury, and thirty bishops were among those present, and the *Daily Mail* saw no incongruity in describing the occasion as the 'restoration' of the abbey to 'the English Church'. There seems to be no sense of irony or inaptness, either, in the self-description of the Anglican charity that now cares for the site as being 'to advance religion in accordance with the doctrines of the Church of England'.

Glastonbury's pre-eminence in faith and fraud continues to influence perceptions of early Christianity in Britain. Leaving aside the question of Arthur's historicity (more on that later), one overriding effect has been to reinforce his associations with south-west England. Another has been for the exposure of the frauds to distract attention from the possibility that followers of Christ actually did visit Britain in the first century. There is no direct evidence for this one way or the other, but archaeological evidence for long-distance seaborne trade between western Europe and the eastern Mediterranean grows by the year, and if tin, glass ingots, or wine were travelling, there is no reason why ideas and believers should not have moved with them. Of course, such transient contact would not have led to Christian communities, let alone the founding of an 'original Church', and in any case it was not until the second century that believers themselves began to work out whether being Christian was (as Robert Markus put it) a way of being Jewish or whether it was something else. Nonetheless, the subject of the first Christians in Britain, as distinct from Britain's first Christians, is richer than the scam busters have made it seem.

A third effect has been to intensify guardedness about the historicity of the early Church in general. All those romantic names that attach to churches, chapels, rocks, and wells in the south-west and Wales – names like Maelog, Carantoc, Teilo, Endellienta, Trillo, Non, and Winwalloe. Can we believe in them? Was there really an 'Age of the Saints' in the fifth and sixth centuries when holy men and women sailed between western Britain, Ireland, and Gaul, spreading the Word and founding religious houses? When we reflect on the 'Cornish Celtic Way' (a pilgrimage route established in 2017, 125 miles, from St Germans to St Michael's Mount, 'to aid people of all ages who are interested in spirituality to explore faith in a different way'), is there anything sure to be said about any of the saints along its route? Was St Piran really from Ireland and born in the fourth century? Was there one person called Mawgan or two? By the 1980s, it was possible for a Celticist to say that most early Welsh and Irish saints never existed as real people.

Scepticism arises because next to nothing that was written down about these people survives from before the eleventh century. In some cases, the source is later still. In tradition, for instance, St Melangell, patroness of hares, was a sixth-century Irish princess who retreated into a life of prayer in a remote valley in Mid Wales. The story goes that hounds in pursuit of a hare recoiled when the hunted animal took refuge under her robe. The hunter, a prince, was moved by her stand and gave her the valley as the site for a religious community. The story was clearly current in the later Middle Ages: in the church at Pennant Melangell, there are hares on the fifteenth-century oak screen, hares carved beside the effigy of a fourteenth-century lady, and the astonishing twelfth-century shrine of Melangell herself, reassembled from fragments thrown out by reformers in the 1560s. But the earliest full account her life was written down no earlier than around 1500. What can we believe? Whether or not Melangell existed, her protection for hunted animals does not extend to the tens of thousands of pheasants which are reared on nearby estates for the pleasure of those who between October and February visit to shoot them.

A medieval saint's cult was normally established by a *vita* ('life'), a specialised kind of biography which gave an account of the saint's life and described miracles and signs of holiness. *Vitae* were idealised biographies in which authors often drew upon stock motifs. It is not always easy to distinguish between such conventions and events that could have been real, and the tendency of later authors to add details increases the challenge of using *vitae* for primary historical purposes. This is notably true of the lives of Welsh saints, nearly all of which were composed after the Norman Conquest, and most of which survive only in still-later manuscripts, in some of which details may have been added or changed. Of course, it is possible that some of these drew on earlier texts, and in places there are signs that they did. The eleventh-century *Life* of St David, for instance, met in the prologue, contains a passage describing David's monastic way of living which from its content and pattern looks six centuries older. We can also take bearings on some figures through other sources. For instance, the altar of St Teilo is mentioned in the first of a series of marginal inscriptions in the early eighth-century gospel book kept in the chapter house of Lichfield Cathedral. Several of the subsequent inscriptions mention lands in the vicinity of Llandeilo (a place name that translates as 'the (ecclesiastical) enclosure of Teilo'), and while the reference in the gospel book does not confirm that Teilo was a bishop who worked in the sixth century, it brings us a lot nearer to his time than a twelfth-century *vita*.

A handful of writings takes us yet closer. One of the most vivid, yet strange, is the *Life* of St Samson, written by a Breton monk early in the seventh century about the career of a man born in what is now south-west Wales at the end of the fifth. Samson's biographer gives glimpses into a world of elite high learning, disputes over hereditary monasteries, woodland witches, vicious jealousies, attempts at assassination, Irish noblemen on their way home from Rome, apostate Christians wor-shipping an idol, and a drunken abbot who dies after falling down a well – yet is revered as a saint. Samson is portrayed in the tradition of third-century ascetic monks in Egypt's Nitrian desert – a harsh life of near-sleepless self-denial, since imitated on the islands of Lérins off the French Riviera and spread from there to other places in north-west Europe, like St Ismaels. On the other hand, Samson's monastic brothers eat and drink well. In relation to sixth-century norms, Samson is an outlier, happy to be on the move and live in a cave – which presumably is why he is remembered as a saint. Contemporaries like Bishop Dubri-cius and Illtud the master come and go, encouraging confidence in their reality.

There is little sign here of the kind of spirituality imagined in Angli-can 'Celtic worship', or evidence to support the Church of England's claim that its Celtic ancestor was 'a missionary church'. Illtud, Samson's mentor, is described as 'famous master of the Britons', accomplished in the scriptures, widely read in rhetoric, grammar, mathematics, geom-etry, and natural philosophy. Illtud is an illustrious priest who trains his protégé in fasts, vigils, and mastering the psalms from memory. He does not tramp the countryside preaching to peasants. What does stand out from the *Life* is the rising popularity of monasticism in later fifth- and early sixth-century Britain, and very extensive interaction with Gaul. Members of these communities (like Samson himself) are typically of noble birth, and some at least of the monasteries are family concerns. There are journeys to and from the continent. And to Rome. The Anglican claim that British Christianity was led into the Church of the west and brought under papal authority as a result of the mis-sion led by Augustine at the end of the sixth century is tosh. It was already there.

Attempts to use the geography of churches themselves to achieve independence of literary sources can bring problems of their own. The doyen of this approach, Emrys George Bowen (1900–1983), was a geographer who reasoned that if we accept that churches and toponymy bearing the names of Celtic saints relate in some way to the saints in question, then by mapping the distribution of churches bearing particu-lar dedications we give ourselves the means both to ascertain the extent of a saint's influence and to examine his or her relationship to physical and cultural surroundings.

Bowen introduced these ideas in an essay in 1945, and developed them in three influential books: *The Settlements of the Celtic Saints in Wales* (1954); *Saints, Seaways, and Settlements* (1969); and *Britain and the Western Seaways* (1972). In many respects, he was right about the seaways. Seaborne travel is a constant theme, and the dedications to Welsh, Cornish, and Irish saints that dot western France and turn up in coastal places as far south as Galicia reflect it. However, Bowen's methodology contained two flaws. The first is that architecturally the churches we see today are seldom older than the eleventh century, and without excavation or special contextual work there is usually no way of telling whether they had an earlier predecessor. The second is that even if they did, people who became saints did not dedicate churches to themselves. It is a modern assumption that a church bearing the name of a Celtic saint in the later Middle Ages would have borne it when it was new, or anytime soon afterwards. A church dedication needs a saint, a saint means a cult, a cult needs a *vita*, and the *vita* needs an established audience and patrons to promote it. Such a sequence must occupy a term of years, and if the biographies date from the later Middle Ages, the dedications are unlikely to precede them. It is no surprise, then, that in the handful of cases where we do know the names of saints to whom early Welsh churches were dedicated, they were the same core group as is found across the rest of western Europe: Mary, Peter, John, Andrew, Martin, Michael. In summary, distribution mapping alone cannot differentiate between dedications that are genuinely early and those that resulted from later waves of enthusiasm; it thus runs into the very problem Bowen was trying to avoid: the influence of later hagiographers, whose writings both reflected and boosted the popularity of Celtic saints in the eyes of bishops and patrons in the eleventh and twelfth centuries.

Bowen dealt with all this disarmingly, first by conceding the basic argument and then by saying that it missed the point. For a geographer or anthropologist, he said, time was not the prime concern: a 'cultural area' possessing 'cultural unity' was something that existed across time rather than just at particular dates. He believed in an 'Outer Britain' where 'continuity of tradition' caused cultural patterns to recur and renew themselves over millennia. The fact that a cluster of church dedications to, say, Illtud, might be no older than the twelfth century did not deprive it of meaning in relation to events half a millennium before.

Here we meet the paradox that most of the architectural memorials to 'Celtic Christianity' were built at least half a millennium after its time. There are several reasons for this, but the main one runs like this: many of the first saints of the English church (figures like Cuthbert, Hild, Chad, Oswald) were educated under Irish monastic influence. Their relics and resting places were looked upon as stores of power. Hence, after the Norman Conquest one of the first steps taken by the new rulers was to find out who they were and provide them with new shrines and churches to win their favour. Vast Romanesque buildings like the cathedrals at Durham and Ely were the result. This is why it is in smaller, off-the-beaten-track places and churches that the most vivid encounters are likely to be had. Typically, they escaped later rebuilding or retain earlier evidence because for one reason or another attention later shifted away from them. Here are two examples.

Attention deserted the tiny church at Caherlehillan, in the far south-west of Ireland, very early indeed. It was out of use by the start of the ninth century, and there is no record or tradition of a patron or founder. Until archaeologists from the University of Cork began to examine it in 1992, there was little to see beyond a low bank forming a sub-circular enclosure, the remains of an early medieval shrine, and two cross-inscribed stones. Excavation revealed traces of a tiny wooden church with traces of a wooden altar and a sacrarium; an adjoining domestic area; and some eighteen graves, one of the oldest being under the later shrine, covered by a stone lintel which had been worn smooth. This special grave was presumably the resting place of the holy recluse who founded the site; the stone over his grave was polished by the knees and hands of people who came to venerate it. We are in the presence of someone looked upon as a saint. The date? Radiocarbon determinations show that the site was laid out soon after AD 450, making this possibly the earliest church so far found in Ireland.

Some of the pottery recovered from Caherlehillan is of a highly distinctive kind known to have been made in the later fifth and early sixth centuries in a city on the Aegean coast. Studies of the distribution of this pottery, and correlation with distributions of other kinds of material, point to long-distance traffic in which cargoes of Syrian wine were loaded onto large galleys in the eastern Mediterranean, shipped westward via calls in north Africa to collect subsidiary cargoes, then on through the Straits of Gibraltar to ports on the Atlantic coast, where cargoes were split and transferred to smaller local vessels for onward distribution. The existence of long-distance traffic in bulk goods in Late

Antiquity has been detected with other commodities, like olive oil and raw glass. Such trade provides a context for otherwise perplexing finds, such as the sixth-century Egyptian clay pilgrim flask bearing a depiction of St Menas between two camels, found on the north Wirral shore – a former beach harbour. It may also have a bearing on two carvings to be seen on one of the Caherlehillan cross slabs. One depicts a kind of ritual fan used to drive insects away from the consecrated body and blood of Jesus during the Eucharist; the other is a peacock, symbol of immortality; both are characteristic of the Mediterranean world. Above all, it illuminates the formative period of Christianisation in Ireland and western Britain.* The scale and layout of Caherlehillan evokes the world of separately living ascetic master–pupil monks and small communities in parts of Egypt, Judea, and Syria, and their counterparts in fifth-century Gaul. If wine, oil, and glass could reach fifth-century Ireland, Wales, and south-west England from the eastern Mediterranean, so could people, books, and ideas; and when the big galleys returned, no doubt bearing cargoes of commodities such as British tin, pilgrims could travel with them.

Here, then, we have it: the Age of the Saints is real, and every bit as ancient as tradition said it was all along. And although its priests, bishops, solitaries, and teachers were on Christendom's edge, they were in full, living contact with its mainstream. The 'Celtic Church' was not remote or insular: it was international. Two later books epitomise this connectedness. The decoration of the Lindisfarne Gospels, produced c.700–720, is often said to typify 'Celtic art' which evokes a contrast between the insular Church and the tightening clasp from Rome. What it actually celebrates is ecumenism: every form of cross then known is carefully woven into its pages, epitomising engagement with the entire Christian world. The other is Europe's earliest intact book: a tiny hand-written copy of the Gospel of St John, written probably between 710 and 730, which was placed in the coffin of Cuthbert. The book was in the genre of Irish pocket gospels, but its binding is sewn in a Coptic style, it is bound in goatskin leather akin to that used in sub-Saharan Africa, and it is decorated with imagery from the eastern Mediterranean, a stylised vine springing from a chalice (recalling a verse from the Gospel:

---

* The story with which my father grew up (*Marten and Carter's Histories* Book 1) was that Ireland became a place of asylum: 'During the Barbarian invasions, many priests and learned men had to fly from the Roman Empire and took refuge in Ireland and preached the Gospel there.'

'I am the vine, you are the branches'). The gospel is an essence of the eighth-century Christian world; in several ways, it links with a second example, the church of St Mary at Lastingham on the flank of the North York Moors.

St Mary's is a fragment of a Benedictine priory which was begun in the 1080s but soon abandoned in favour of another site. Norman leaders were drawn to the place by its reputation as the site of a religious community established in the mid seventh century under royal patronage by Northumbrian saints. Two of them are well known: Cedd (d.664), who evangelised among the East Saxons, and best of all his brother Chad (d.672), who went on to become the first bishop of the Mercians at Lichfield. Both were trained at Lindisfarne and had spent time in Ireland. Cedd was buried at Lastingham.

The site slopes, and the builders in the 1080s used the downward slant of the ground to put a crypt under the east end of the church. The crypt survives intact. Physically, it is impressive: roofed by a groin vault supported by thickset columns. As you enter, it is unexpected, shadowy, quiet; a place for thought; also, a place where time and distance are condensed: a door in the north wall takes you into a blind corridor which was once said by locals to emerge among a group of prehistoric barrows several miles away up on Spaunton Moor. If you look at the crypt vault, you can see impressions of the planked shuttering used by the people who made it nine and a half centuries ago. The walls keep secrets and litanies. In their cracks and chases, you can feel quartz pebbles, beads, and shells put into them by modern pilgrims praying for and to who-knows-whom. And from where did the Norman builders take Roman building material that they used in the walls?

Spaces like Lastingham crypt are fragile as well as numinous, and down the years some chancy things have been done in the name of maintenance and improvement. Was it a local jobbing builder who hacked a channel through the ancient shuttering imprints and patched it with cement? No faculty sought for that job, one guesses. When it was decided to use the crypt to display some of the church's collection of Anglo-Saxon sculpture, it was wise to secure the items to the floor – such pieces are vulnerable to theft – but who directed that the eighth-century piece bearing finely carved bunches of grapes be erected upside down, so that the grapes (symbolising the true vine and the blood of Christ) hang upwards, like helium-filled balloons? And who was it who dumped the most astonishing pieces of all in a pile of rubble in the magic corridor that takes you to Spaunton Moor?

The unheeded pieces were presumably put aside because no one knew what they were. Recent study recognises them as parts of a saint's shrine. They fit with several of the pieces on display in the crypt to indicate that it was a rectangular box composed of carved stone panels supported at the corners by upright carved stone posts. Set in one side was a vesica-shaped embrasure, fitted with shutters, through which pilgrims could be granted a view of relics within. The vesica has connotations of Christ in Majesty, Revelation, and the End of Time; the shutters imply that viewing was granted on special occasions. On style grounds, the shrine is likely to have been created around or after c.750. We do not know the occupant. The obvious candidate is Cedd, but according to Bede (who knew a lot about Lastingham, having been taught by one of its brothers), Cedd was already housed in a shrine beside the high altar. Moreover, several nearby churches contain pieces of eighth-century shrines which point to an entire generation of otherwise unknown subregional saints, so it is possible that someone other than Cedd was being venerated.

At some point between the eighth century and the eleventh, Cedd's remains were moved to join those of his brother at Lichfield. We do not know when this was, but he and an otherwise unknown saint, Ceatta, are both put at Lichfield in a list of saints' resting places written down c.1030. In Chad's day and for some time afterwards, there was cross-membership between the communities of Lastingham and Lichfield, so that, in effect, they formed one brotherhood; hence, the translation might have been viewed at the time as akin to moving Cedd between rooms in a single house. The occasion might have been the transfer in 787 of part of the province of Canterbury to a new archdiocese centred at Lichfield. The impetus for the reshaping came from Offa, powerful king of the Mercians (d.796), and it may have been under his influence that the brothers were reunited.

They may still be together now. Motorists inbound to Birmingham on that strange stretch of the A38 that passes into a tunnel near the Holiday Inn Express Hotel may not register the presence of a large church across the road; if they do, they may wonder why it looks like a building from the German Rhineland. The answer is that it was the first Catholic cathedral to be built in England since the Reformation, and that its architect, Augustus Pugin (1812–1852), was making a point about Catholic universality in contrast to English exceptionalism.

Consecration of the church in 1841 followed a series of steps taken since the 1770s to enable Roman Catholics to own property, practise their faith without reprisal, and participate in public life. The saint to

whom the cathedral is dedicated is St Chad, and the whole neighbourhood is dotted with references to him – St Chad's Queensway, Shadwell
Street, St Chad's Sanctuary, Little Shadwell Street. What brought Chad
into nineteenth-century Birmingham?

We have already seen that in 1538 royal injunctions ordered clergy
to remove images that were the focus of superstitious behaviour and
to preach against pilgrimages to shrines. There were several shrines to
Chad in different parts of Lichfield Cathedral. One, a chapel centred
on a cult of his head, was neutralised by confiscating the skull, while
the principal shrine with its reliquary was destroyed. However, a box
of bones, reputedly including some of Chad, was smuggled away by
a member of the cathedral clergy and put into the hands of relatives,
who in turn passed it to two brothers. On their deaths, the bones came
into the keeping of a Jesuit priest, and thence to Basil Herbert of
Swynnerton Hall near Stoke-on-Trent, together with a written account
documenting the successive keepers and circumstances. When Fitz-
herbert died in 1797, his widow moved to Aston Hall by Stone, where
the bones were placed in a family chapel. In due course, the family
moved back to Swynnerton, and the chapel at Aston was closed. However, in 1839 the chapel reopened, and from it a box containing six bones
wrapped in silk was retrieved. The bones were passed to the authorities
of the new cathedral then a-building. Pugin designed a shrine to house
them.

One of those present on the day of consecration was John Hardman,
a Birmingham craftsman much favoured by Pugin who had contributed
fittings, metalwork, textiles, and ornaments to the project. Early in the
proceedings, Hardman stepped forward at the head of a body of gentlemen, faced the bishop, and read aloud from an illuminated parchment:

> We, the Catholics of Birmingham, mindful of God's mercy towards
> us, and trusting to share his bounty for the time to come, do, by these
> presents, make a free and voluntary surrender of all that we have
> given towards the building and adorning of the cathedral church
> about to be consecrated on this day to the worship of the only true
> God, under the invocation of holy patron, St Chad; and we likewise
> do promise, with God's help, to make good all payments now due for
> the same – our several and joint offering thus being to the amount
> of about seven thousand five hundred pounds. In token whereof, we
> now prostrate ourselves humbly at your lordship's feet, and suppli-
> antly implore your apostolic benediction. Given this twenty-first day

of June, in the year of our Lord God 1841. Signed on behalf of the Catholics of Birmingham, JOHN HARDMAN &c.

The bishop made a 'short and feeling' reply. The great west doors of the cathedral were then thrown open, and to the sound of the choir and of the bell ('which then for the first time sent forth its deep voice to invite the faithful to the house of God') four priests carried the relics down the nave, followed by hundreds, 'nay ... thousands' in procession. The ceremony of consecration continued with a high mass, sung with Gregorian chant.

Britain in 1841 ran a large part of the world, and the event was widely reported. The *Dublin Morning Register* noted that the ceremonial had been 'long and anxiously looked forward to by the Catholics of the British empire'. Nothing like it had been seen in England since the days of Henry VIII, whose officials had done their best to do away with the six bones now enshrined near the high altar. Whence sprang the congregation's confidence in the authenticity of these remains? Did hard-headed Birmingham ironmasters, brickmakers, plumbers, and glaziers really believe them to be from a seventh-century Northumbrian who had been educated at Lindisfarne and in Ireland?

At several points in this book – at St Davids, Birdoswald, Glastonbury, Caherlehillan – archaeological science has corroborated aspects of a medieval narrative involving holy men and women who were active between the fourth century and the seventh. In 1995, science spoke again, when the Archbishop of Birmingham arranged for a scientific study of the bones. The examination found two of the bones to be left femurs, so from different people, while radiocarbon assay showed five of them to date from the seventh century, and the sixth from the eighth. We are thus looking at parts of three individuals. Press reports said that the bones had become 'jumbled'. A more satisfying hypothesis emerges when we compare the radiocarbon results with what was said in the early eleventh-century list of saints' resting places: that there were three saints resting at Lichfield, two of whom were brothers who died in the seventh century (Cedd and Chad), with the third (Ceatta) otherwise unheard of. The simplest explanation is that one of the femurs belonged to Chad, the other to Cedd, and that the later bone derived from Ceatta. Here it is worth noting clear signs that although the eleventh-century list was a compilation of several catalogues, the section in which the three saints are named was a good deal older than the compilation itself, and that nearly all the saints and relics named in this early section were translated before AD 900. Bearing in mind the eighth-century shrine recognised at Lastingham, we might thus go further and speculate that Ceatta was another member of the Lastingham–Lichfield connection, perhaps a later abbot, and that he and Cedd were translated together. In sum, whether or not bones of Cedd and Chad rest in St Chad's Cathedral in Birmingham, scientific measurement confirms that the cathedral cherishes bones of St Chad's day.

Science also now throws light on the greatest of all puzzles in the years between Patrick and Augustine: the life of the only contemporary churchman whose writing about them has survived – Gildas. Gildas is remembered for the tract *De excidio et conquestu Britanniae* ('On the ruin and conquest of Britain'), which warns of divine punishment, criticises contemporary British rulers, fulminates against ecclesiastical backsliding, and attributes takeover by the English to British moral failings. Bede, whom we meet in the next chapter, knew his work and made use of it.

Gildas witnesses the high standard of Latin culture and education that still existed in Britain c.500. But nothing about him is clear. Later accounts of his upbringing and education are in mutual conflict, placing him at different times with Illtud, in Ireland, at Rome and Ravenna, and eventually in Brittany, but we know nothing about his family or where he studied the Latin writings of late-fifth-century Gaul. As history, *De excidio* itself is exasperatingly circuitous; as Latin literature, it is laced with stylistic and formal puzzles, and the one clear pointer to when it was written – a battle at a place he calls Badonici montis ('Badon hill') – is an event about which historians have argued themselves to a standstill. Gildas tells us that the battle was fought in the year of his birth, and that he was writing one month into his forty-fourth year (DEB 26.1).

With all this uncertainty conceded, there are three aspects around which most historians would rally: that the *De excidio* is one integral work; that it is the authentic product of a British churchman; and that it was probably written within a few years of 540. Until recently, this was about the limit of what could be said, but the picture is now changed by two advances in different disciplines, which when taken together enable us to pinpoint when, and conceivably why, *De excidio* was written.

One of the articles appeared in the *Journal of Theological Studies* in 2010, where the Irish classical historian David Woods drew attention to an apparent allusion in *De excidio* (DEB 93.3) to a mysterious cloud which obscured the sun and moon for a year or more. Wood suggested that it might well have been this phenomenon that moved Gildas to make his call to repentance, and pointed to other contemporary writers who described it. Among them were the Byzantine historian Procopius (c.500–570), the praetorian prefect of Italy, Cassiodorus (c.485–c.585), John Lydos, writing in Constantinople in the 540s, and several Syriac authors. Their accounts of a dark foggy veil that dimmed the sun and turned it blue date the event to AD 536–537.

The second advance has been in the field of quaternary science. Scholars were once open to the possibility that the cloud witnessed by sixth-century observers was caused by remains of a comet or asteroid, but modern data from stable carbon isotope records, tree rings, and ice cores from Switzerland, Greenland, and Antarctica confirm the event as volcanic: two colossal eruptions some four years apart. Ice cores which entomb fallout from volcanic activity and pollution show the first to have been in the northern hemisphere, perhaps in Iceland or North America. The second, in 539 or 540, has been traced to Ilopango in modern El Salvador. The two together injected several million tons of sulphates, sulphur gases, and dust into the atmosphere. The debris reflected sunlight away from the earth. The result was a volcanic winter, the coldest decade for two thousand years, crop failure, and famine.

In his 2010 paper, David Woods noted, 'The gospels specifically report that the sun will grow dark and that the moon will no longer shine at the coming of the Son of Man (Matt. 24:29; Mark 13:24; Luke 21:25), and strange celestial phenomena had sparked religious panic during earlier centuries.' Woods further observed that in his criticism of contemporary kings, Gildas

> quotes Isaiah 24:23 on the day of judgement, where he describes how the moon will grow red and the sun will be confounded (DEB 45.2). He also quotes Zephaniah 1:14, where he describes the same day as a day of cloud and fog (*dies nubis et nebulae*) (DEB 55). It is a strong possibility, therefore, that Gildas regarded the mysterious cloud that so dimmed the moon and confounded the sun in 536–7 as a sign that the end of time was near, a suitable time at which to throw off his fear and doubt and to call the powerful to repentance.

The intersection between science and the writing of a sixth-century prophet is a key that turns in other locks. Gildas's birth and the British victory at Mount Badon can now be put in 493. The independent scientific dating of the catastrophe also provides a crosscheck on annals that purport to record events in early medieval Wales and Ireland. The annals exist only in later copies, their historicity has been compromised by later interpolations, and historians are understandably wary of them. But Irish annals speak of a 'failure of bread' in 536, and the Welsh annals record a *mortalitas* (presumably a famine) in 537. Given the firm date now provided for Gildas's birth, the annals' record of AD 570 for his death becomes credible.

Perhaps most remarkable of all, the annals give a glimpse of an Arthur: a warrior who falls in a battle fought in 537 – that is, during the *mortalitas* in the first year of the volcanic winter. In a series of essays, the philologist Andrew Breeze has pointed out that this and a ninth-century list of Arthur's other battles give a context for who he was and what he was doing. He was not a king; he was not the sub-Roman cavalry general pictured by R. G. Collingwood who rode around Britain to fight off the English; he was not the illusory or folkloric figure against whom since the 1970s we have been warned by a generation of historians and toponymists; he was not involved at Badon, and he had nothing to do with Glastonbury. He was a North Briton, very likely a dynastic leader from the Strathclyde area, who fought against other North British dynasties. In 537, he was presumably fighting over diminishing resources of food and livestock. His name was carried to Wales from northern sources, whence he became the universal British hero, diffusing to Cumbria, Cornwall, and Britanny. By the ninth century, when the British and English had come to see themselves as cohesive peoples and customary enemies, he was being evoked as a champion of British resistance.

The Welsh annals say where Arthur died:

537 *Gueith cam lann inqua arthur & medraut corruerunt et mortalitas in brittannia et in hibernia fuit*
537 the fight of Camlann in which Arthur and Medraud fell and there was death in Britain and Ireland

Camlann identifies as Cammoglanna, the fort at Castlesteads on Hadrian's Wall, third in the list we met at the start. The next fort along is Banna, St Patrick's birthplace. Arthur and Patrick side by side – what could be the chances?

MAISCOGGABATAUXELODUNUMCAMMOGLANNA
RIGOREVALIAELIUSDRACO

10

JARROW CRUSADES

What is it about early medieval names that appeals to business? In the 1970s and 1980s, archaeology raised awareness of Viking-age York; visitors today will spot vans bearing such names as Jorvik Heating, Yorvik Electrical Contractors, or the Jorvik Elite Low Step Through Electric Folding Tricycle. Eighty miles north, the Metro station serving the town of Jarrow in South Tyneside is called Bede, the monk, historian, and theologian whose reputation has lasted from his day (672/3–735) to ours. Nearby is a Bede Trading Estate; in Jarrow itself are the Bede Motor Company, an office-rental agency at Bede's Chambers, and the Bede Burn Store supermarket. Upriver in Newcastle can be found a more mysterious connection: Bede Gaming, makers of online gambling software.

Bede's best-known work, *The Ecclesiastical History of the English People*, was completed at Jarrow c.731. It has a strangely elegiac finish in which he tells us that he was born nearby, and that at the age of seven his relatives placed him in the care of abbot Benedict Biscop (c.628–690), head of the religious house of Wearmouth–Jarrow, for his education. Bede was about eighteen when Biscop died, and he formed a close relationship with his successor, Ceolfrith. 'Since then,' says Bede, 'I have lived all my life in this monastery; I have devoted myself to the study of scriptures; alongside keeping the discipline of the Rule, and daily singing in church, it has been my delight to learn, to teach and to write.' He goes on to list what he had written: around forty works on computation, chronology, grammar, and language; biography, hagiography, poetry, hymns, homilies, and biblical commentaries. Bede took a keen interest in natural philosophy, what we would call science, and from his Tyneside scriptorium he established that tidal motion is influenced by the moon. It was Bede who popularised the calendrical system of dates we use today.*

Demand for Bede's works was strong from the start. The survival of manuscripts of his works is in itself a sign of his fame and lasting effect. Some 150 medieval manuscripts of the *Ecclesiastical History* alone have come down to us, including one that was copied by colleagues who may have known him. No historian of the origins of the English can avoid this book. This is partly because it is the channel through which so much of our information on the subject comes. It is also because Bede's perception of the *gens Anglorum* as a grouping of shared descent with a common destiny before God has carried into general understanding. In key ways, such as its pantheon of saints drawn from different parts of the country, *The Ecclesiastical History of the English People* prefigures the history of the English Church.

Bede's workplace was a religious community split between two sites: Uiuraemuda (Wearmouth) and Ingyruum (Jarrow). Each stood on the terrace of a tidal river: Wearmouth, the first-established, beside the Wear, Jarrow in a strange space framed by the waters of the Don, Tyne, and a sweep of inter-tidal mudflats known now as Jarrow Slake, and then as Portus Ecfridi – Ecgfrith (c.645–685) being the Northumbrian king who endowed the two houses with land. Jarrow Slake was a royal beach harbour, functionally akin to the Portus Magnus we met at St Davids. It put Bede's Jarrow at the hub of a communications nexus that reached far inland via the Tyne valley, took in Britain's east coast from eastern Scotland to Canterbury, and looked abroad to Frisia and Frankia. Bede's world was a big place. On his deathbed, he gave small gifts to friends. Among them was some pepper, which James Campbell pointed out can hardly have come from anywhere closer than India.

The sister houses embodied the vision of Wearmouth's founder and Bede's first mentor, Benedict Biscop, a Northumbrian nobleman who very likely had royal connections. Biscop made repeated visits to continental Europe and Rome, in the course of which he visited religious communities and studied their rules of life, and from which he returned, inspired, with books, music, and in due course specialist craftsmen who oversaw the building of churches, chapels, and living quarters for the several hundred young and aristocratic followers who by the end of the seventh century made up Wearmouth–Jarrow's community.

---

* In the Roman Empire, years had been numbered in various ways, including the names of consuls in office, and the year of an emperor's reign.

This much we can gauge from Bede's writings, but until the later twentieth century no one knew what the monasteries were actually like. Remarkably, movingly, parts of both churches survive, each since passed into parish use and mated with Victorian rebuilding. From Bede's writing, we can discern the contents of the library. However, nothing was known of the monastic settlements themselves, or the kind of lives lived within them. The unknowing was compounded by changed surroundings: by 1950, the church at Wearmouth was hemmed in by dense workers' housing, bordered by Sunderland's shipyards, while at Jarrow the edge of the Slake had been industrialised, the River Don had been canalised, and an oil depot stood north of the church.

Rosemary Cramp at Monkwearmouth, 1963. Cramp's excavations at Wearmouth–Jarrow helped to contextualise the production of such works as the Cuthbert Gospel, Bede's Ecclesiastical History *and the Codex Amiatinus, the world's oldest complete surviving Latin Bible.*

So things stood in 1955, when Rosemary Cramp, a twenty-six-year-old English don, took up a post in Durham that combined teaching Old English with archaeology. Rosemary came from a farming family at Glooston in Leicestershire. Her enthusiasm for archaeology had started young:

When I was about 12, I became an archaeologist – or I thought I did – because we found a Roman villa on our land. To be strictly truthful, my sister said she had found some nice things for the floor of the little house which we were building, as children do in the country. She had found the *pilae* tiles of a Roman building. At least I thought it ought to be Roman. I only had a children's encyclopaedia, and I looked it up there. Then I went to see the rector, as the most learned person in the village. Like most rectors, he took away part of the Roman things and put them in his garden.

In 1947, Cramp arrived in Oxford:

I hadn't known whether to read History or English . . . – I liked both – and in the end had plumped for English. At the end of my first year, I was taught by Dorothy Whitelock. She told me I should specialise in 'Course II', which ranged from primitive Germanic to Spenser. And when I was 21, I turned from being a disorganised undergraduate to being a disorganised young don, teaching Anglo-Saxon at St Anne's College, Oxford.

At St Anne's, Cramp became good friends with another up-and-coming don, Iris Murdoch:[*]

I realised that my interest in archaeology and my interest in Anglo-Saxon were coming together. I taught my students a lot about the historical background and the archaeological evidence. In those days, there weren't many people bringing those two together.

In 1963:

At Monkwearmouth, they were doing a development and were going to pull down houses near to the church. Somebody said that perhaps we ought to see if there was anything left of the monastery of the Venerable Bede. When I worked on the south side of the church, the houses were still occupied, and I was digging in people's backyards; it was sometimes difficult to get access to them, but eventually you were nobody unless you had a trench in your yard. We recruited small children to look after the trenches at night. As a reward they were allowed to trowel through the barrows of excavated soil to see if any bit of pot had been missed and tipped in with it;

---

[*] Murdoch's Booker prize-winning novel *The Sea, the Sea* (1978) is dedicated to Rosemary Cramp. The dedication embodies a small joke: Murdoch pointed out that Glooston is about as landlocked in England as you can get.

sometimes they found them. And when they had done three years of that, I had a special trench in which they could learn how to trowel properly. I have always involved the local communities in my digs.

And in the following year:

> At Jarrow, the Ministry of Works had restored the existing buildings and made them safe, and then wanted to date them. That was all I was asked to do. I started with a couple of trial trenches. And then the next year – in 1965 – I dug inside a building and found, underneath the walls, another stone structure and one with an *opus signinum* floor,* which I knew would be Anglo-Saxon. Nothing stopped me after that. I dropped the idea of just dating the standing buildings, and went for trying to find the plan of the monastery.

Over the next twenty years, Cramp and her team brought the two monasteries into focus: their workshops, communal buildings, cemeteries, devotional geographies. Her publication of what they found is a many-stranded story, of churches agleam with richly coloured glass, of systematically organised buildings, panels of coloured Italian porphyry. Wearmouth–Jarrow was not the origin of the cloister plan that became the monastic standard across medieval Europe, but it was on that idea's threshold, a link between late antiquity and the future.

Towards the end of Cramp's campaign at Jarrow, I got lucky once more: she became chair of the Churches Committee for which I worked. I admired her style, persuasive mingling of humour, strategic thought, and eye for the pith of an issue. If you backslid, she could be fierce, but admonition was followed by a smile like a sunrise, and you were encouraged to start again. Our first collaboration was in the preparation and presentation of evidence to a Commission on Faculty Jurisdiction set up in 1980 to review the way in which churches are cared for. In our written submission, we made a case for the mandatory provision of archaeological expertise in every diocese and cathedral. On the day we arrived to give evidence in person, we found a table-tennis table in the corridor outside the room in which the Commission sat. We were early, and accordingly picked up bats and began to play. After ten minutes, the Commission's secretary arrived and found us out of breath, giggling because of the incongruity. Since any pre-meeting adrenalin had been burned off, we went in calm and made the clearest case we

---

* A material in which crushed tile and mortar are combined.

could. When the Commission reported in 1984, it recommended new legislation which among other things would embed responsibility for archaeological oversight across the Church of England's estate. When this was enacted, it completed the task I had been given in 1975.

In Jarrow Hall, meanwhile, an attractive building overlooking the church, built around 1775 by a local businessman, Rosemary had established a small museum to display objects that had been found. Out of this grew the idea of a purpose-built museum to tell the story of the excavations, share their results, and reconstruct a landscape to illustrate the kind of surroundings and economy in which the monasteries had stood. Since upwards of five hundred calves needed to die to provide the skins for one large Bible, Wearmouth–Jarrow's economy was no mere footnote.

The petrol-storage depot north of Jarrow Hall was being dismantled. Its heavily polluted land became available. Step by step, a new landscape was shaped, planted, and peopled – not a stage set, but a living experiment to explore what might once have been. Gradually, funds were found for the museum. Its red brick and tile, forecourt, and atrium evoked the Mediterranean south and the journeys of Benedict Biscop.* On sunny days, the atrium – a pool at its heart, open to the sky – dazzled with blue heavens against its white walls. The galleries around a central square recollected the layout of a priory. So it was that in the midst of a post-industrial landscape, bracketed by a timber yard and petrol storage, over-slung by electricity cables, a complex took shape. In its concept and offering to mind, body, and spirit, it invited comparison with a small national park. It was called Bede's World.

Bede's World was formally opened by Her Majesty the Queen in December 2000. A few weeks later, I received a telephone call from Peter Fowler. You may recall Peter from 1975, when he was working in adult education in Somerset, and I was touring England's dioceses to recruit archaeological advisers. Half a lifetime later, Peter was professor of archaeology at the University of Newcastle upon Tyne. He had had a large hand in developing the farm, and following Rosemary's initial impetus he had chaired the board of trustees that had brought Bede's World to birth. He asked if I would consider succeeding him.

I was told the board met around four times a year. There would be occasional one-off events and meetings, and since the trustees had

---

* The museum was designed by the partnership of Eldred Evans and David Shalev.

worked hard during the set-up, a number of them felt that they had done their bit. Reasonably enough, some wished to step down. Nonetheless, the overall commitment looked modest – and of course there was a very capable staff, and funds were still arriving from grant-giving bodies. Moreover, one of the trustees' many achievements had been to secure an undertaking from South Tyneside Council to make an annual contribution to Bede's World's revenue. There was no guarantee about the figure, but South Tyneside's assurance of continuing support was one of the factors that persuaded the Heritage Lottery Fund to finance completion of the museum. As projects went, then, it all looked very appealing. I felt rather flattered, accepted, and soon found that sharing the results of original historical research with the public is the hardest kind of work.

The first problem hit us within a month: in February 2001, the outbreak of foot and mouth disease forced closure of the farm to visitors. Since the farm and its animals formed a key attraction for families, and drew repeat visits at different seasons, this hit us hard. A suggestion by South Tyneside's head of Leisure Services that we slaughter the animals to enable reopening rested on an incomplete understanding of why the farm was so popular. Vaccination seemed a better bet. This was not national policy, but our circumstances were special, and since the legacy of polluted land meant that none of the animals could enter the food chain, it at least seemed worthwhile to ask. After some weeks, a template reply from the Minister for Agriculture arrived which ignored our question but said that Britain's countryside was 'open for business' – which manifestly it was not.* In the event, the farm was closed for seven months, and we lost the best part of a season's business. By then we had also lost two of the three senior managers, who decided to move to other work.

On the upside, we had recruited a new director, Keith Merrin: young, personable, talented, committed to Jarrow and its people, whose only drawback was a likelihood that before long others with greater tasks and resources than ourselves would wish to have him in their service. In the event, Keith was with us for six years. At his elbow was Laura Sole, the museum's archaeological curator, who had survived the stresses and strains of the fit-out and had a good grasp and care for the collection. Laura and Keith knew what Bede's World was about.

---

* Most of Britain's countryside was then in quarantine. Footpaths, historical monuments, woodlands, even some parks were off limits to the public.

I loved the building. It had a mood, a serene spirit; whenever I passed through, I came out feeling better for having done so. In its textures and spaces, there was a sense of recognition and respect for Bede's genius. Phrases and fragments from his writing were inscribed on its paving and walls. As you moved through the galleries, it was as if he was beside you. At one point, if you stood in a certain place a wall began to speak to you in a Geordie voice.

But there were problems. All new projects pass through a desnagging phase, but as time passed our problems seemed to mount rather than lessen. For a start, part of the roof leaked; efforts to deal with it went on for years and were disruptive. The gentlemen's lavatories were impressively finished, yet an odd smell hung near them; eventually, we found that the urinals had never been properly connected to the drainage system. Yet a tidy sum had been spent on them, and there had been a professional project manager, who presumably had signed these things off. After several years, the wonderful tiles in the courtyard began to spall, in some cases so badly that dangerous hollows formed against which visitors had to be warned with tapes and barriers. There were no funds to put these things right. Meanwhile, the raised beds to either side, which had been carefully and imaginatively stocked with plants that related to the early monastic world, became partly overgrown. There was no one on the staff whose job it was to keep the beds tended, and when the work was taken up by volunteers, there was usually no one available who knew the significance of the original planting to guide them. Out on the farm, a similar problem arose with the monitoring of reconstructed buildings.

There were things outside our control that provoked ill-feeling. For instance, one of the brown signs to guide motorists to us had been positioned in such a way that most drivers never saw it, while another lured drivers into the wrong lane. The cumulative effect was a succession of enraged visitors.

The business plan assumed there would be income from use of our central hall for conferencing. But here too there was difficulty. For one thing, financial strains meant that there was next to no marketing budget. For another, although the room was gorgeous its acoustic was poor, and the elaborate audio-visual equipment that was meant to make us the go-to place never actually worked. We were told that the installers had gone bust before the work was finished, and the people brought in to complete it seem not fully to have understood what they were doing.

One thing that did work, and did so well, was a five-minute video that visitors saw when they left the museum's galleries. The film was mounted on a special overhead screen. It was striking for several reasons. For one thing, it set the exhibition in a global context; for another, its commentary was in Latin, with English subtitles – a spine-tingling stroke: spoken Latin has a special sound, a firm authority. However, the day came when it failed. On investigation, we found that the installation should have been serviced every two years, but with cashflow always tight, finding the four-figure sum to do this was not always possible. There were months at a time when the screen was dark.

Out in the world of heritage professionals, there were critics. Some asked why the Lottery was funding so many new museums when the ones we already had were structurally underfunded and overstretched. A five-year scheme introduced by New Labour to tackle this then channelled funds to local authority museums – which were free to enter – but not to independents like ourselves, which meant that in effect we were facing state-subsidised competition.

The exhibition was criticised. Some said there were too many reproduction items and not enough original objects. At first sight, some of the original objects were indeed not much to look at. But if you looked again, they were. The simplest things were charged with meaning: oyster shells that had been used as palettes for the mixing of ink or pigments in the production of manuscripts; styluses, through which words had flowed thirteen centuries before; whetstones for sharpening knives with which to cut goose feathers for pens, with which to write an ecclesiastical history.

We were hampered by health-and-safety paranoia. Some of the reproduction Anglo-Saxon weapons looked so realistic that we had to review their display, lest a visitor be moved to seize one off the wall and run amok. One of the first areas on the farm to flourish was the margin of its stream and small lake, which was soon fringed by golden flags and colonised by toads and frogs. The water was only a few inches deep, but Environmental Health insisted upon garish lifebelts and roped barriers, and their refusal to countenance the addition of dung or urine to the daub mix did not assist the walling of the great Anglo-Saxon hall.

The farm was one of Bede's World's happiest areas. The great hall was of the kind Bede imagined when he likened human life to a sparrow flying out of a winter storm into light and warmth and back out again into the dark. On some winter evenings, Laura Sole organised storytelling events around its hearth. Out on the farm's northern edge, overlooking the ballast hills by the Tyne, I recall the thrill of finding knapweed and bird's-foot trefoil recolonising the ground, and a colony of Burnet moths – day-fliers, rather snazzy, with dark green iridescent wings splashed with scarlet. But like the rest of the Bede's World experience, the farm covered so much, in so many ways, that some visitors found it baffling. For instance, all the love and expertise that had gone into the experimental building reconstructions counted for little in the eyes of those who did not know what historical puzzles they were meant to solve. In such eyes, the buildings were more like film sets than laboratories. How many knew about black thatch, or the controversy over the function and structure of *grubenhäuser*? Who was to tell them that the herb garden and goose house were modelled on prototypes in the ninth-century plan of St Gall? Did anyone notice how the ground surface had been modelled to embody a palimpsest landscape, or how the two Dexters had been trained to plough on command? Imaginative touches in the dramaturgy of the exhibition went unnoticed. For instance, when visitors emerged from the museum's galleries, they were faced with a great wall-painting, scaled up from a drawing in the eleventh-century Harley Psalter (which is a copy of the Carolingian Utrecht Psalter) that depicts rural scenes. Its purpose is to prepare the visitor for the next stage in the experience – their tour of the farm – but unless the visitor knew this, its purpose was a mystery. After several years, we mustered the funds to publish a booklet by Laura Sole which explained a lot of this, and with a generous financial gift from Ian Wood, now Professor of Early Medieval History at Leeds, we started a publication series to explore different aspects of the place and its history – but tourists do not expect to have to go on a course to know what it is they might enjoy.

The presence of so much that went unrecognised brought a paradox whereby many visitors came away with a sense that there was not much there. However, this was readily disproved by one of the things of which we were most proud: the programme we ran for schools. On most weekdays an entire class would visit for half a day, to be met by an education team that guided them through different aspects of the exhibition, encouraged them to try monastic things for themselves (like an orrery, to forecast the movement of stars and planets, or sign language, to communicate without speech), and explore the farm. Around twenty thousand young people visited each year. Their enthusiasm encouraged our hunch that as a new kind of heritage attraction, what Bede's World really needed was a new kind of visitor – people willing to immerse themselves in its different aspects and put the time in to do so: reflect in the church, walk the land, explore the exhibition, experience the farm, eat and drink at Jarrow Hall. We did welcome such people, but not in numbers. Across the road, the area that had been optimistically laid out as a coach park was increasingly fringed by buddleia and weeds.

A good way to attract repeat visitors is to run special events and negotiate loans of objects with star quality. We did this. Laura Sole organised a brilliant temporary exhibition about the life and work of Brian Hope-Taylor, whose work at Yeavering in the 1950s had transformed perceptions and understanding of seventh-century royal power. Hope-Taylor found Yeavering to be a place with a long history of assembly. The mass baptisms made there in the River Glen in the 620s said less about the charisma of the Roman bishop Paulinus than the fact that at certain times of the year large numbers of Northumbrians had gathered there anyway. Another series of events centred on the loan of a facsimile of the Lindisfarne Gospels, which Michelle Brown, Curator of Illuminated Manuscripts at the British Library, introduced in a talk that no one in the packed audience that heard it will have forgotten.

The museum was provided with a reinforced high-security room which could be used to display valuable items. Discussions with the British Library and British Museum showed that they were very ready to consider the loan of relevant manuscripts and objects. The only problem was that in the course of the fit-out, the environmentally controlled display cabinet needed to contain them had either been forgotten or was perhaps overlooked in some value-engineering exercise. Hence, for most of the time the room was no more than a cleaners' cupboard. One of the few objects we ever did exhibit in it was the banner that had been carried at the head of the Jarrow Crusade in 1936, when two hundred marchers (selected from around twelve hundred volunteers) walked the 291 miles to Westminster to present a petition urging action to re-establish industry and employment in the town. One of the banners was displayed at Bede's World pending its incorporation in a new exhibition. As with many things to do with Jarrow, its earlier keeping had been attended by a kind of tragedy. The 1936 lettering had suffered from wear and tear; someone well-intended had cut out the original letters and stitched in new ones.

The context for the Jarrow Crusade was the closure of Palmer's shipyard, mass unemployment in a town of forty thousand people, and the subsequent failure of a plan to bring new employment to the town through establishment of a steelworks. The Crusaders were widely admired, but their petition ultimately ran into the sand of political indifference. Seventy years later, the economist Peter Jay visited Bede's World in the course of taking regional economic soundings on behalf of the Bank of England. It was the only time he and I ever met, but since his father, Douglas Jay, had known my father back in Battersea days, and indeed my father had given the address at Douglas Jay's funeral, we naturally fell to talking about wider things. One of them was the destruction of Jarrow Slake's 230 muddy acres, where one of England's greatest habitats for migrating birds and an Anglo-Saxon royal harbour now lay buried beneath the Port of Tyne's car terminal, grain elevators, concrete plant, container bays, and a scrap-metal concern. Peter Jay replied that his father regarded the industrialisation of Jarrow Slake as one of his greatest achievements. Following his appointment in 1947 as Financial Secretary to the Treasury in Attlee's government, Jay was determined to spread the economy away from London. Industrial development beside Jarrow Slake was one of the results – and whereas politicians had failed Jarrow in the 1930s, on this occasion they followed through. We agreed that the Port of Tyne was but a continuation of the spirit of Portus Ecfridi.

The Jarrow Crusaders were blessed by the Bishop of Jarrow on the morning of their departure in October 1936, and it was the Bishop of Jarrow who headed another campaign seven decades later, for the inscription of Wearmouth–Jarrow as a World Heritage Site. World Heritage was a concept launched by the 1972 UNESCO Convention Concerning the Protection of Cultural and Natural Heritage. In essence, it is a system to enable international cooperation to identify, cherish, and pass on to posterity places which are of Outstanding Universal Value (OUV). UNESCO defines OUV as cultural or natural significance so extraordinary that it transcends national boundaries and is of common importance for all the people of the world. In time, one interesting effect of this definition was to break the hitherto dominant identification of heritage with European culture and Judaeo-Christian civilisation.

World Heritage Sites can only be nominated by a national government, and only UNESCO's World Heritage Committee can decide whether to accept them. The Committee consists of representatives of twenty-one states. It meets once a year, and since it cannot be expert on everything, it receives specialist evaluations from two international organisations: the International Council on Monuments and Sites (ICOMOS) (for cultural sites) and the International Union for Conservation of Nature (for sites that are natural). The World Heritage Committee has agreed ten criteria by which OUV can be assessed and will consider a site as possessing OUV if it meets one or more of them. In addition, World Heritage properties must have integrity and, if they are cultural, authenticity, as well as appropriate legal protection and a regime of care to protect their OUV.

Already we see a tension between a scheme which is altruistic in intent but bureaucratic in personality, with its own jargon, definitions, and systems. Moreover, in the membership structure of the World Heritage Committee lie seeds of inappropriate practice. While some governments adhere to the Convention's rules and processes with scrupulous care, there are others which fall short, either by failure to maintain standards, or by trading votes in pursuit of other agendas – such as, for instance, those that followed the Iraq War. The UK's record is mixed. While its government has followed rules governing the presentation of nominations, neither it nor the English planning system have gripped the kinds of spatial planning issues that have arisen at World Heritage properties such as Stonehenge and Liverpool.

To be eligible for nomination a site must first be on a nation's Tentative List: that is, a list of places which a government considers that it might nominate in coming years. Each Tentative List must be correctly submitted to UNESCO, and UNESCO expects Tentative Lists to be reviewed about once a decade. In 1999, the UK government put the twin monasteries at Wearmouth and Jarrow on its Tentative List, on the grounds that their combination of rare early medieval standing fabric with one of the most lastingly influential figures of contemporary culture made them a site of world importance.

The government suggested that Wearmouth–Jarrow possessed OUV in relation to three of the World Heritage Committee's ten criteria: it bore 'a unique or at least exceptional testimony to a cultural tradition'; it was 'an outstanding example of a type of building, architectural or technological ensemble which illustrates a significant stage in human history'; and it was 'directly or tangibly associated with events or living traditions, with ideas, or with beliefs, with artistic and literary works of outstanding universal significance'. The last criterion seemed particularly apposite: the works of Bede – Doctor of the Church – are still in use the world over; if they are not of universal significance, what would be? And in case anyone asked that question, there was a back-up answer: Ceolfrith had organised the making of three giant Bibles, using Jerome's (d.420) Vulgate translation, one apiece for Wearmouth and Jarrow, the third as a gift to St Peter in Rome. The Roman volume survives. It is the earliest complete Latin Bible in the world. UNESCO fairly advises that OUV must lie primarily in sites, not associations. But Rosemary Cramp's excavations had uncovered and contextualised the place of this great book's making.

The UK's approach to World Heritage nomination is to leave the main work in local hands. Often, this is the local authority or site owner, to whom it falls to prepare, and pay for, the nomination document and a management plan, each of which must follow a precisely specified format and will run to several hundred pages. Historic England (then, English Heritage) has a Head of International Advice who will guide the nominators through the process, and advice is also available from the UK branch of ICOMOS whose members and secretariat like to play a leading role in implementing the World Heritage Convention in the UK. But the main work is done and paid for locally. It takes years. When the UK government is satisfied that the proposal is fully documented and in a form that will meet the World Heritage Committee's tests, formal nomination may follow – but since the UK makes no more than one nomination each year, and spreads its proposals not just across the four home countries but also Britain's overseas territories, more years may pass before it is submitted.

For Wearmouth–Jarrow, there were more challenges. Most basic was the fact that behind the site's two parts lay fragmented responsibilities. They were in different local authority areas, under two Church of England parishes, in Jarrow's case split between the church (the parish) and English Heritage (display of the remains outside); and interpretation was spread between the churches and two museums. Nonetheless, in 2002, under Keith Merrin's initiative, later much supported and led by Laura Sole, a formal partnership was formed which brought all these participants together under the chairmanship of the Bishop of Jarrow.

World Heritage operational guidelines are lengthy, demanding, and head-achingly particularistic. Gradually, the Wearmouth–Jarrow Partnership worked through the tasks. For instance, the sites' original boundaries had been lost; how could the nomination document answer UNESCO's questions about where their edges lay? 'Buffer zone' has precise meaning in the diction of World Heritage – in post-industrial surroundings, what should it be? The planning policies of Sunderland and South Tyneside had to be harmonised to meet the necessary tests. The nomination document had to contain a comparative analysis which explained why the site was outstanding and showed that it was not paralleled elsewhere. Since monasticism is not confined to Christianity, this had to begin with a review of monasticism and monastic archaeology worldwide.

The 'Statement of Significance' explained why the remains at Wearmouth–Jarrow are exceptional, both architecturally and archaeologically: they preserve incomparable evidence of the renewal of Roman tradition and the early, experimental, stages towards the development of the claustral layout that would later dominate European society. And, of course, they are intrinsically associated with the development of ideas and literary works of outstanding significance, through the work of Bede.

It took eight years to bring the nomination to the point of submission. The two local authorities, the parishes, the diocese, and local communities sank their hearts into it. So did English Heritage. Elsewhere, there was scepticism. ICOMOS-UK repeatedly asked, 'Where's the OUV?' Colleagues who ran courses on heritage management found it difficult to reconcile the needy, messy, surroundings of two rather drab-looking and partly Victorian churches with their conception of World Heritage. Members of the public, repeatedly told by the BBC and local newspapers that World Heritage designation would put Wearmouth–Jarrow on a par with the Taj Mahal and the Great Wall of China, were disillusioned with what they found when they came to look. Somewhere along the way, the idea of 'heritage' as being that which enhances lives, is worth cherishing, and bears knowledge not otherwise accessible had been traded for an expectation that 'heritage' must be visually arresting, physically imposing, and instantly comprehensible. The logic of this is that if you do not recognise OUV when you meet it, then it is not there.

And so it proved. While English Heritage said that the comparative analysis was one of the best they had seen, the ICOMOS evaluation released in May 2012 said that it was weak. ICOMOS's reviewers said that Wearmouth–Jarrow was not exceptional because comparable properties existed elsewhere – although none of the ones they mentioned met the tests given in the analysis. They said that the UK was making inflated claims, misrepresented the case that was actually being made, and managed in some respects to be in conflict with ICOMOS's own assessments elsewhere.* It was as if the comparative analysis had been skimmed, not read. The UK Government takes up the story:

> On receipt of the ICOMOS evaluation report, the UK considered carefully the seriousness of the factual errors, referenced repeatedly and on which flawed judgements and the consequent recommendation not to inscribe appeared to be built. It assessed the recommendation not to inscribe, and its consequential risk that renomination would be disallowed. It also considered the seriousness of the other points raised in this report relating to inconsistencies, flawed process and lack of transparency.
>
> This led the UK to the view that there was not time available between the receipt of the report on 11 May and commencement of the World Heritage Committee on 24 June to allow for the in-depth discussion necessary to address all of the issues raised through the process of highlighting factual inaccuracies.†

Rather than face the near certainty of a rejection (which would preclude resubmission), the nomination was withdrawn.

In September 2012, the UK Government sent a twenty-three-page memorandum to the World Heritage Centre in which factual errors and inconsistencies were documented, flawed elements of the evaluation were pointed out, and a response from ICOMOS was requested. One big factual error was referenced throughout the report, and appeared to have been a major factor leading to the recommendation not to inscribe. The UK told ICOMOS that this error risked 'undermining the credibility of ICOMOS as expert advisory body'. ICOMOS's reply was unblushing. It declined to identify the 'expert' assessors and brushed the Government's protests aside.

So there it was: another failed crusade. It was not the conceit of

---

* An example was the evaluation's citation of written evidence for the early history of Lindisfarne and Whitby as justification for their potential greater significance as UK sites representing this key stage in early monasticism, when it was understood from UNESCO itself that the World Heritage convention is a site-based convention, and documentary evidence alone is not sufficient to justify World Heritage status.

† The World Heritage Committee met that year in St Petersburg. Its members on that occasion included representatives from Algeria, Cambodia, Estonia, Ethiopia, France, Germany, India, Iraq, Japan, Malaysia, Mali, Mexico, Qatar, the Russian Federation (which held the Chair), Senegal, Serbia, South Africa, Switzerland, Thailand, and the United Arab Emirates.

ICOMOS or the shortcomings of its supposedly specialist advisers that left me depressed, but the realisation that once again Jarrow had put an important case, and once again authority had failed.

Early in 2016, Bede's World ran out of funds. South Tyneside Council said that despite having provided substantial support, it was 'not currently financially viable'. The Council had indeed provided very substantial support. However, its spokesman omitted to say, or had perhaps forgotten, that since 2002 its annual contributions had always been below the level recommended by the independent consultant from whom it had sought advice on viability. The collapse came six years after I stepped down, in circumstances I do not know. I do know that in my day there had been of an ever-widening gap between what was needed to achieve viability and what could actually be done. From where I stood, Bede's World had always been running to catch up, increasingly breathless, and eventually sank to its knees.

Heritage lottery-funded projects are not often allowed to fail, and later in 2016 the site was reopened under new management, and with a new name: Jarrow Hall. The name change said a lot: behind the crusades and crises, and despite the founders' values of scholarship and innovation, the truth was that too few heritage decision-makers believed in their bones that there was a significant audience for the world of Bede as an idea in itself. For some of us, the story of this man who spent his entire life in the compass of a few square miles, yet shaped a nation and spanned the world in his thought, was as great as any that could be told. But behind all the heritage talk of widened access, inclusion, new audiences, and public engagement, there was a loss of nerve: it was all too esoteric – a pill to be sweetened rather than something to be tasted for itself.

Bede died on Ascension Eve, 735, and was buried at Jarrow. A cult developed. In the eleventh century, his bones were moved to Durham, where they were placed first with those of Cuthbert, whose life story he had written, and later translated into a shrine on the south side of the Galilee chapel at the cathedral's west end. In 1542, the shrine was destroyed, but the bones were placed in a coffin under an unassuming tomb chest. It is still there, and beside it is a prayer written by Bede thirteen centuries ago:

> Christ is the morning star
> who when the night of this world is past
> brings to his saints the promise of the light of life
> and opens everlasting day.

In 1831, on the anniversary of Bede's death and amid some theatre, the tomb was opened by the clergyman-antiquary James Raine (1791–1858). Within, Raine found the upper part of a skull, the lower jaw, heads of a number of long bones, and parts of the feet.

Raine published an account of his discoveries and organised the making of three plaster casts of the skull before the bones were reinterred. One of the casts later came into the hands of Dr John Thurnam (1810–1873), a physician, proto-psychiatrist, antiquary, and ethnologist who was a student of racial typology. All the casts were since believed lost, but Thurnham's has recently been found in the Duckworth Laboratory collection at the University of Cambridge.* Its finder, Professor Jo Storey of the University of Leicester (which is gaining a notable strike rate in finds of famous medieval people), has since joined with Professor Richard Bailey (formerly Professor of Anglo-Saxon Civilisation at the University of Newcastle upon Tyne) in a study that traces the transfer and authentication of the bones through successive resting places. While certainty is not possible, they conclude that the skull is likely to have been among the bones brought from Jarrow that were believed to be those of Bede.

John Thurnham worked with the doctor Joseph Barnard Davis to publish *Crania Britannica*, a study which argued that the racial origins, social standing, intellectual endowment, and abilities of men and women by whom Britain was peopled can be read from the forms and measurements of their skulls. We recall from Brian Hope-Taylor's work at Sanderstead in 1948 that even in the aftermath of the Holocaust it was widely assumed that people of different historical background could be told apart through the shapes of their heads. This is why Thurnham had his doubts about the identity of Raine's plaster cast: in Thurnham's view, the shape of the skull did not correspond with someone of Bede's intellectual stature.

---

* The Duckworth Collection is held by the Leverhulme Centre for Human Evolutionary Studies.

11

QUIRES AND PLACES WHERE THEY SING

In 1977, the renovators of a sixteenth-century house at Wethering-sett, near Stowmarket in Suffolk, came upon a door made of reused planks. It had been hidden behind a partition and was put to one side because it bore intriguing features: on one side, rows of holes; on the other, grooves. For some years, this strange structure was in the hands of Timothy Easton, a historian of vernacular buildings who in due course brought it to the attention of Stephen Bicknell (1957–2007), an expert in organ history. Bicknell saw that the holes and channels were for the supply of air to pipes, and that the board was the wooden table upon which the pipes of an early organ had stood. It was made of four pieces of imported Baltic oak, a timber favoured for this kind of work because it was straight grown and even-grained. It was not the only soundboard in the area. Nine miles away at Wingfield another was found in 1995, amid lumber in the churchyard coffin-house. This was a rediscovery: it had been described on several occasions since 1799, but lost track of since the 1950s. The Wingfield board was fashioned from a single piece of walnut or chestnut.

Analysis of the soundboards was published in 1995. The organs whence they came were thought to have been made in the 1530s: at any rate, tree-ring dating showed that the trees which provided the Wetheringsett boards were still growing in 1525. Until then, the only clues to what pre-Reformation organs were like had been signs of their fixings on some church walls, a few of which gave indications of scale, and two contracts: one for an organ provided for All Hallows by the Tower in 1519, the other for Holy Trinity, Coventry, in 1526.

Correlation of details in the contracts with the evidence of the boards led to new understanding of what the instruments were capable of and how they were played. The soundboards indicated the number of stops and the character of their voices. Overall size gave the organs' plans. Holes for the front pipes gave an idea of what the organs looked like.

From shape and distribution of the holes it was possible to determine which pipes were made of metal and which of wood and from this their different tonal qualities. The soundboards showed the compass of each instrument, which in turn helped to determine the kinds of music of which they were capable, their relationship with contemporary repertory, tuning, and pitch. Wetheringsett had a fully chromatic compass of forty-six keys, choruses of pipes of the same scale and style, including a nineteen-note rank of ten-foot bass pipes sounding an octave below.

The logical next step was to reconstruct the instruments. This was done in 2000–2001 by the organ builders and restorers Martin Goertz and Dominic Gwynn. In 2005, the Royal College of Organists took ownership of them. The College has since overseen the Early English Organs Project, which tours the organs to different buildings across the country to enable players, listeners, singers, and students to re-enter the sound world of the later Middle Ages.

In 2007, the Wetheringsett organ was in residence at Durham Cathedral. By then, I was back at the University of Leeds with its Institute for Medieval Studies, which ran a course centred on parish worship. Bill Flynn, the Institute's Latinist, is also a musician, and he arranged for us to take a minibus full of students to re-enact a pre-Reformation service. The organ was in the Galilee chapel, close to Bede's tomb. Jane Flynn, his wife, played. We used music in notation of around 1500. One of our postgrads who claimed to be tone-deaf worked the two weighted bellows: a mesmeric process in which each is raised alternately with a polished wooden handle, released, left to subside, its neighbour being operated towards the end of the fall to ensure continuity of supply. The configuration of wind supply and use explains why an organ in fifteenth- and sixteenth-century sources is always described as 'a pair of organs': like a pair of scissors, it is in two halves, each indispensable to the other.

Next to a clock, it has been said, an organ was probably the most sophisticated and complicated mechanism in later medieval England, and the organs project raised questions. How many churches had them? Were they restricted to larger or specialised institutions, or widespread? If parish churches had them, where were they put? Who played them, and how were they trained? In what ways did organs contribute to worship? If organs were common before the Reformation, what happened to them afterwards? And why had little attention been given to these questions before?

A project to answer such questions came into being. Sounds Medieval is led by the singer, historian, and organ builder Martin Renshaw,

whose 2012 lecture on the archaeology of the late medieval organ sets
the scene: 'Medieval churches were built primarily for singing in, and
not for speaking. Spoiling the acoustic with loads of carpets or pews
or other obstructions was a 19th-century habit, not usually a 15th or
16th-century one.' Renshaw reminds us that while we already knew the
medieval church to be 'an arena for a full-on sensory experience of light,
colour and smells and for social interaction, meetings and contempla-
tion', when this environment is revoiced, a church becomes 'in every
sense a living and breathing building'. Put another way, while architectural historians study churches by looking, Renshaw and his colleagues
also explore them by listening. Their business is the soundscape of early
modern England.

Answers have come thick and fast. By the fifteenth century, nearly
all cathedrals and religious houses had organs; fieldwork and written
records studied for a sample of parish churches make it safe to think that
some thousands of them, too, with their choirs and guilds, maintained
an organ. Some had several, and since poor churches were among them
it is likely that parish church organs were widespread. The placing of
parish organs depended on their size, and on the layout of the churches
which installed them. The ideal was to put an instrument as close to the
singers as possible. If a chancel had an aisle or aisles with open arcades,
then there might be room there. If not, it was sometimes possible to
put the keyboard and pipework in the chancel and the bellows in an
adjoining room or chapel. A number of churches, like Stoke-by-Clare
in Suffolk, have remnants of an upper gallery propped out from a wall,
with a door cut through for access, reached either by a ladder or stair-
way. In a few cases, the gallery itself survives, either in situ or relocated.
A fourth solution was to perch the organ on a screen.

Choirs were the nurseries of organists, and the numerousness of
organs in the early sixteenth century reflects the scale and quality of the
choral tradition in late Plantagenet and early Tudor England. Much of
the rationale for this tradition, we have seen, revolved around prayers
for the dead. By the fifteenth century, organ tuition was part of a young
chorister's training. At first, this was provided in larger religious houses,
later in collegiate and greater parish churches. Keyboard skills were
reinforced by practice on a clavichord. Organ training mirrored singing,
which encouraged the embellishment of memorised plainchant with
improvised polyphony.

Organs were used on higher-ranking feast days, during certain
votive masses, at times of popular celebration, and in greater churches

and magnate chapels to add solemnity and colour to formal moments. In canticles such as the '*Te Deum*', it was the custom to alternate sung verses with passages for organ alone. Selective use of organs on high days and holidays made it possible for parishes of slender means to hire a player by the day, or even the hour, in some cases with a small instrument itself.

These findings have large implications for the ways in which we understand churches today. Renshaw notes that they explain, for instance, why a parish church chancel is so often a double, sometimes triple, cube – volumes that foster a good acoustic. Renshaw points out that most of the words we use to describe churches, like 'piscina' or 'aumbry' (the kinds of terms savoured by John Betjeman), were not original but selected or invented from the 1830s onward by ecclesiologists who needed a vocabulary with which to name or discuss them. 'Nave' came into use only from the seventeenth century. Before that, what we call the nave was usually either '*populus*' ('the people') or simply 'church' (or '*ecclesia*'), whence come the people's representatives, the *church*wardens. The people were firmly divided from the priestly, musical area to the east by a screen.

Renshaw further points out that a *chaunsell* (which goes with chantry, and chanting) was not a single space, but had an intricate geography of quire (the place of the singers), a gathering place (between the quire and sanctuary step), and the sanctuary. Archaeological excavation shows how these differentiated spaces evolved from eastern chambers in the tenth and eleventh centuries that were often little more than alcoves for a priest, through eastward extension that begins in the later twelfth century, to the enlarged spaces of the later Middle Ages. Significantly, while many large *chaunsells* date from the fourteenth and fifteenth centuries, a good many date from the age of Henry III; the music-adapted *chaunsell* originates in the thirteenth century. Towards its south-west corner, often, is an extra window, lower than the others, typically with signs that it was originally shuttered. Antiquaries have devoted years of toil and theorising to attempts to explain these features, which can now be understood as means to admit light to read books and music for matins in poor or early daylight. The shutters were for security: such windows were low enough for a thief to climb in.

Renshaw explains that the so-called 'priest's door' on the south side of a *chaunsell* was in reality a point of access for use at times when the screen dividing the people from the quire was locked. In a larger church in the late Middle Ages, such users, in addition to the parson himself, might include one or several chantry priests, choral singers, an organist, and sacristan, who would come and go for offices said and sung over several hours each day. On weekdays the *chaunsell* was a busy place, with hours of daily offices, masses for different clienteles and commemorative prayer. The range of its sustained activity helps us to see why responsibility for the upkeep and development of a church east of the screen, and with that for liturgy, ritual, and music, came to rest with the rector, while accountability for the *populus*, and for the screen, lay with the parishioners. For churchgoers, one of the shocking effects of Edwardian and Elizabethan reform was that these spaces became visually combined.

Architectural historians seldom talk about the subsidiary structures that adjoin church exteriors – the boiler houses, Victorian organ chambers, vestries. Often, this is because they seldom get into them; such rooms are generally kept locked, and during a visit lasting an hour or two the time needed to trace the keyholder may not be available. As a result of Renshaw's surveys we can now see that some of these structures either replace or have been adapted from rooms that were originally added to house organ bellows. A number of north-side two-storey 'vestries' found in areas like the Cotswolds, eastern Midlands and parts of East Anglia turn out from study of their original access arrangements to be conversions of chapels, sacristies, and organ rooms; even the position of a wind trunk is occasionally indicated by a still-existing channel through an intervening wall. Meanwhile, close study of wall surfaces themselves has begun to produce a body of extraordinary evidence that earlier historians missed: a micro-archaeology of inscribed musical notation, often at eye level, beside doors, on pillars, below shrines, to provide prompts where a procession paused once or twice a year, or as teaching aids for choristers.

Anglican liturgy made little explicit provision for music or choirs, and none for organs. Hence, while the 1549 Prayer Book borrowed much from the Use of Sarum, the formal abolition of the Use removed the need for organs, while the dissolution of chantries cut off funds hitherto earmarked for the payment of musicians. The Reformation thus eroded the role of the Church as a patron of new music and training, and stirred demand for and interest in secular musical forms. The recent find of part of an organ at Kirby Hall, Northamptonshire, also reminds us that while Elizabethan and Jacobean music-making moved into houses of the aristocracy, the later sixteenth century was in general a time when church choirs were disbanded and many organs were dismantled; in places you can glimpse the selling off of their bits and galleries in parish accounts. But the episodes of rapid change put composers on their mettle, and the brief revival of demand for elaborate music and organ-mending during Mary's reign provided a bridge of performance tradition to the age of Elizabeth, who liked ceremonial, and used her influence to encourage the dissemination of psalmody in parish churches, where parson and people now sang together in each other's sight. Evangelicals wanted textual meaning rather than complexity and melisma; in the new Anglican service music of Tallis, Byrd, and Morley, simple syllabic writing came to the fore.

The Reformation, then, was a watershed but not a final crisis. That came with Parliamentary victory in 1645 and the Commonwealth that followed. It was then that the organ in Worcester Cathedral upon which Thomas Tomkins played was trashed. With it, as far as we know, went the breaking of every other organ in the country that had survived thus far.

Our ability to re-enter the world that Puritanism muffled and blinded enables us to see that the outpouring of music during England's renaissance was not some spontaneous starburst. Composers from the 'nest of singing birds' – artists like Fayrfax, Ludford, Taverner, Tallis, Sheppard, Byrd, Morley, Tomkins, Farmer, Gibbons – were fledging from the days of Henry VI through to James I; they did so because aback of them were at least two centuries of practice, experience, and training. Angel musicians in medieval stained glass, hovering below church ceilings, carved on walls, poised to play their harps, gitterns, rebecs, trumpets, tabors, and organs in a sinfonia at the end of time, remind us that this was so.

12

INTENSIVE CARE

The end of time for Dad came without warning. *Plane Crazy*, the first Mickey Mouse cartoon, was premiered on 15 May. That day's other anniversaries include Anne Boleyn's trial for treason and adultery; the feast day of St Denise, the patron saint of headaches; and his death, which was heralded by a headache. And come to think of it, my childhood nickname for him was Mickey.

His passing in 2000 illustrated the medieval proverb we noted in the Prologue, that nothing is more certain than death, and nothing more uncertain than its hour. Dad was seventy-six, fit for his age. Indeed, for reasons to which we shall come, he had kept himself fit all his life. He walked a lot, laboured in his garden, and watched his diet. If he drank a glass of wine, it was, literally, just the one, and he gave up his pipe years before. He played in chess matches and kept up with the latest theological writing. And in April 2000, there was a spring in his step: there was an interregnum at All Saints Bramham, a church in West Yorkshire, and he had been asked to help out. For the next few months, he would be back where he was happiest: in a parish.

The Sunday after Easter he came for lunch. He was subdued, ate little, and afterwards went for a rest instead of the usual walk with the dog. Two days later, he visited his GP, who sent him away with some antibiotics. By Friday, he was becoming jaundiced. A neighbour took him to the York Hospital, where he was diagnosed with pneumonia.

I drove over to see him with my daughter. He was in a side ward and smiled as we walked in. He was lucid and apologetic at having dragged us so far. I was startled by the mound under the sheet where his normally flat stomach would be: his liver was swollen. A nurse said that there were different kinds of pneumonia; they were running tests to identify the type.

We went back again next morning. He was confused, being grappled by a nurse who tried to stop him thrashing himself out of bed. Sedation followed, then transfer to the intensive care unit, and a ventilator. For the next eight days, he lay unconscious, watched over by shifts of nurses who graphed his functions on a drawing board at the foot of his bed. Beside him were machines and bags to which various parts of him were connected by a web of lines and tubes. There were fluids in the bags, one of which took on the colour of stewed tea. Every now and then the nurse reacted to a flashing light or a beep.

He became our routine. We set off after breakfast and sat with him in relays through the day. The journeys back and forth took us between roadside drifts of spring flowers.

We talked to him quietly, passed on news, sometimes stroked his hand. Rarely, very rarely, he made some sound or faint movement which made us wonder if he was aware of us – or more probably made us hope that it might be so.

On Thursday, the test results arrived. The infection was *Legionella* – a bacterium that occurs naturally in water and is often spread by the inhalation of vapour. It can cause an aggressive pneumonia, as it had here. We were told to expect a review on the following Monday. When the time came, we were shown into a side room that was set out with easy chairs and old magazines. The consultant seemed ill at ease. Rather abruptly he told us there was multi-organ failure and that sepsis had set in. He was not going to recover. In our bones, we already knew this, but the consultant seemed braced for argument when he told us that the moment had come to withdraw the life support.

We were given a little time to collect ourselves. The ventilator was switched off around noon. A curtain was drawn around the bed. A hospital chaplain arrived from somewhere and prayed. The dying was an ebbing rather than a moment, a gradual flowing away that took maybe twenty minutes. As his breathing subsided, bubbles of foam formed on his lips. During his fifty years' ministry, he had sat with many people as they died. Hearing, he once told me, is the last sense to go. When he was with unconscious parishioners in their last hours, he had always spoken accordingly. So now did the chaplain, who addressed him directly. 'You who have ministered in faith,' he said, 'now die in faith.' Wherever he was, did he hear that?

We returned to the room with the magazines and composed ourselves while waiting for a doctor to bring the death certificate. Before we left, the nurse invited us back to his bedside. She had combed his hair, washed his face and taken away the paraphernalia. Half an hour before he had still seemed present; now he was clearly dead.

We drove to his house. On the kitchen table was a pencilled to-do list – water runner beans, some items of shopping, the name of a wine recommend by Jane MacQuitty, a just-opened letter from Bob Runcie. His diary: car insurance to pay, upcoming services at Bramham, various committees, a flight to Ibiza on the twenty-fourth to spend a week with Nick Stacey. Nearby, a chessboard set with pieces in midgame – perhaps a problem he had been working through. I remembered his first chess computer at Battersea, which made a pinging sound when it made a move. After a while, he found its measure and bought a more powerful opponent. This happened several times.

Next to the chessboard was a book, David Brown's *Tradition and Imagination: Revelation and Change*, published the year before. It was open at page twenty-six. Here probably were the last words he had read. Near the top of that page: 'For most of Christian history biblical revelation has been conceived of as something like a thunderbolt from heaven, as a message from beyond our own world that spoke of eternal verities and so, though applicable to its immediate context, it carried none of the transience that marked it as the product of its age.' Lower down: 'Yet at least since the Renaissance, and particularly with the advent of the Romantic movement, the artist has commonly been seen, on the model of the prophet, as an inspired figure who stands against the currents of the time to draw out daring and new insights from which we can all learn.' Folded into the book was a sheet of paper. He had been making notes. From page twenty-eight: 'The imagination is there to challenge, not to reinforce conformity, however valuable or true we may think our present assumptions to be.' And from page twenty-nine: 'Dynamic interaction with the inheritance of the past remains constant, however apparently new particular ideas or practices may at first appear to be.'

In the following days, we cleared the house, finding notes he had made as a student; furniture husbanded from one vicarage to the next; the filing cabinet still with a faint smell in the drawer where he had kept the tobacco jar; a jotted note of Bede's prayer:

Christ is the morning star
who when the night of this world is past
brings to his saints the promise of the light of life
and opens everlasting day

There were photographs: of fundraising capers at Hockley; laying the foundation stone at Longbridge; parishioners about whom I had forgotten; the dog. There were books by or about his friends, and group photographs at Wescott which showed how many of them went back to 1948. I was struck by the ceremonial of the Church: the vellum for his collation to the benefice and licence to officiate at Longbridge, Leonard Wilson's signature across the seal.

There was an obituary. Ironically, for one who had spent his life on the Left, it was in the *Daily Telegraph*. It described him as 'one of the Church of England's most able parish priests' and said he had succeeded 'in combining active political work with a strong pastoral concern, and this won the support of those who did not share his Left-of-centre convictions'. The obituary was unsigned, but its author was Trevor Beeson, the recently retired Dean of Winchester, whose colourful volume of collected clerical obituaries marks him as the Church of England's Yashica 35.

And then there were the letters, about which we had heard but not before seen. They were written between my mother and father during their engagement, and bridged the Atlantic from the day he left Canada in May 1944 to the day in April 1946 when she boarded the SS *Argentina* to return to England. The letters were numbered against the chance that they would arrive out of order or a ship be torpedoed. They were in two boxes. One was quite large, of stout cardboard, flattish and rectangular. The other was blue, smaller but deeper, cubical, with a lid hinged by ribbons. If you lifted the lid, there was a smell of soap: a Christmas present in 1945.

It took several weeks to read the letters, and several years to grasp what had happened, and how it fitted with all that followed.

Part Three

MICHAEL IN THE WINDS: 1940–1950

13

AMPHLETTS AND ITINERARIES

John Morris, twelve, met Maurice Cohen, thirteen, in the summer of 1935 on Highbury Fields. Maurice was riding his new bicycle; John was flying his new glider, courtesy of Quaker Oats. By the end of the afternoon, Maurice was flying the glider and John had ridden the bicycle. Friendship grew. They spent their free time doing battle on the tennis court, the boating lake, the chess board, or went to see the latest films at the Finsbury Park Astoria. Occasionally, they fell out, but always there was reconciliation.

Maurice Cohen, drawn by his friend John Morris, 1942.

In September 1939, they were both evacuated with their respective schools, John to St Neots, Maurice to Kimbolton – sufficiently close for them to keep in touch. In any case, after a few weeks they both left school and returned to London. John's main talent lay in drawing, and when things got back to normal, it seemed likely he would go to art college. Meanwhile, he became a temporary civil servant in the Air Ministry, where he joined the Home Guard when he turned seventeen. Maurice enrolled as a student at Birkbeck College and continued his piano studies at the Royal College of Music. In the evenings, they compared notes about their respective worlds and the people who belonged in them. They went on walks together, relaying experiences, discussing books, art, music, philosophy, and religion. From September 1940, as the bombing began, their long walks through central London and suburbs were lit by searchlights, fires, and flaring gas mains.

When Dad spoke at Maurice's funeral a lifetime later, he thought their association had been unusually intense: 'It was not exclusive of other relationships, but it did have a marked priority.' There were some who thought Maurice's influence was too dominant, which may have been true, but Dad believed then and never doubted afterwards that he owed a great deal to him. Maurice's fervent enthusiasms swept him into areas of thinking and feeling which might not otherwise have been entered. His love of music, for instance, was sparked by Maurice practising Beethoven's late piano sonatas and playing the organ in a local church. Maurice's feeling for the power of words led Dad to ask where his own creative aptitudes might lie.

They were separated by the progress of the war. In 1941, Maurice volunteered for the RAF and left the scene to train as a pilot. In due course, Dad followed in his footsteps, and on Monday 2 June 1942 reported to the Aircrew Reception Centre at St John's Wood. With him in that week's intake were 1,700 others. Each was issued with kit, bedding, uniform, and boots, and marched to billets in nearby requisitioned flats. In Dad's kitbag was a knife, fork and spoon ('irons'), an enamel mug, greatcoat, gloves, steel helmet, anti-gas cape, jersey, bedding, webbing kit, a canvas roll with needles, wool, thread and buttons known as a 'hussif' (housewife), polishing brushes and boot blacking, clothing for physical training (canvas shoes known as 'daps', shorts, vest), a side pack, and gas mask. In the following days, they were shorn with electric clippers, given a dental check, inoculated against smallpox and diphtheria, and marched to the Odeon Swiss Cottage to watch a famously explicit film, shot in colour, to encourage them to avoid venereal disease. For the next three weeks, they were drilled, sent on route marches, lectured on first aid, hygiene, and service law, sent swimming, and given aptitude tests and preliminary instruction on small arms. They were also watched for leadership potential and abilities. New trainees held the rank of Aircraftman Second Class (AC2), the lowest form of RAF life – but their status as cadet aircrew was indicated by a white flash on the forage cap.

It took over a year to train a pilot or navigator. Since this set the amount of notice needed to make any change in future manning levels, keeping a balance between recruitment, and forecast and actual need was a high-wire act. As trainees proceeded through a series of fixed-length courses, there were accordingly times when changes in the volume of the pipeline meant that progress from one stage to the next was slowed, and those following were diverted into holding camps.

This is what now happened, when on 18 July AC2 Morris (164121) was sent to the Air Crew Camp just outside Ludlow. Ludlow was an overspill site for cadets waiting to join an Initial Training Wing. It had opened only two months before, and its facilities were modest. Several thousand cadets lived under canvas, and washed and shaved in a stream at the bottom of the field; their regime of 'organized activities in a healthy outdoor environment' involved digging ditches, labouring for nearby farmers, cross-country runs, and swimming in the River Teme.

There were three intakes of cadets at Ludlow at any one time. Two weeks ahead of John Morris and in another part of the camp was Stuart Blanch, who was several years older than most of those around him. Stuart had enlisted back in 1940, and for two years had served in the RAF Police, where his gentle ability to exert 'authority without being authoritarian' had served him well in the enforcement of discipline, arrest of leave breakers, and occasional breaking-up of fights. At the end of 1941, now a corporal, Stuart had volunteered for aircrew duty and was on the same path as John Morris, but a few weeks ahead. A fortnight before, he had attended evensong in Ludlow's parish church, when one of the hymns was 'Lead Kindly Light'. He wrote to his girl-friend, Brenda Coyte, and described the 'strange tug at the throat' as they sang it.

Their next step was to an Initial Training Wing (ITW) which provided an eight-week foundation course for potential pilots and navigators. ITWs were typically accommodated in seaside towns. No. 12 was at St Andrews in Fife, and it was here that AC2 Morris presented himself early in August.

An ITW course was intensive, and anyone who failed it would be washed out and reallocated to another role. The syllabus was divided into 446 periods which varied in length according to subject. Straight lectures on subjects such as navigation, principles of flight, and meteorology (fifty-six, twenty-eight, and twenty-two periods, respectively) were of forty-five to fifty minutes. Send-and-receive skills in Morse using buzzer, lamp, and phonetic alphabet, initially up to five words per minute, were fostered through brief twice-daily exercises. The working week consisted of six eight-hour days, each comprising four hours of lectures, two hours of practical (signals, first aid, aircraft recognition, armament work and firing on the range, routine parades), and two hours of physical exercise.

Six periods were allocated to discussions and debates, in which groups of up to twenty-five cadets were encouraged to practise self-expression, weigh up arguments, and reach decisions. On the fringe of this was what was called the Padre's Hour, at which Squadron Leader Desmond Dean, the Anglican chaplain, provocatively trailed his coat with a short evangelical address followed by an invitation to ask questions and make comments, to which cadets usually responded with a mixture of ridicule and mainly hostile questions. Dad was struck by the way in which Dean stood his ground and warmly commended his belief. John Morris began to ask himself whose side he was on and enrolled as a trainee believer.

The Padre and his wife held open house one evening a week to which any airman was welcome. There was some discussion, the Padre led vigorous hymn singing from the piano, and supper followed, which hungry airmen would attack with evangelical fervour. Returning after hours from one of these visits, he was put on a charge and awarded three days 'jankers' by the Commanding Officer.* When the Padre got to hear of this, he protested to the CO, who revoked the punishment, saying that he should have explained where he had been: 'This gave me, and the rest of the Flight, food for thought on the Church's power of intercession.'

On one of these evenings, he found himself next to Stuart Blanch:

I was conscious of the difference in rank but Stuart's friendly manner bridged any uneasiness I felt at being very new in the service of King George VI and even newer in the service of the Lord. And so it was to be throughout our subsequent relationship, for while I recognized

---

* Jankers – service slang for punishment involving confinement to barracks, and parading after hours in full kit and fatigues.

in him a superiority of intellect along with a deeper, surer grasp of what it meant to be a Christian, his manner to me, as it was to everyone, was of outgoing brotherly affection, not embarrassingly hearty, but evenly good-humoured, gentle and considerate.

Stuart's infancy was passed on a farm in the Forest of Dean, where he remembered days on warm flagstones, the smell of hay, and animals in the byre. On the last day of August 1922, his father, William, a former collier, left the house early, apparently to shoot rabbits. When by lunchtime he had not returned, Stuart's elder brothers, Will and Ron, set off in search of him. Stuart tagged along and was the first to come upon his father's body. It was in a ditch, ripped open. The gun lay in a gap in a nearby hedge. The weapon was faulty, and the theory advanced at the inquest was that it had gone off as William was passing through the hedge. The coroner nonetheless noted that William had just sold the farm, and that 31 August was in law their last day of occupancy.

William's widow moved the family to London, where in due course the eldest son entered the Inland Revenue and Ron joined Lloyds.* By 1939, Stuart was working in an insurance office in Chancery Lane, overlooked by a large oil painting of the first chairman and a chiming clock. He was toying with a career in journalism, but then came war, and enlistment.

Christmas 1942 found him rostered for guard duty at the Aircrew Distribution Centre at Heaton Park. Since almost everyone had gone home, he used the days in the near-empty camp to study the Gospels and re-read a letter from Desmond Dean in which he described his own calling two decades before – 'not wrought by any of my own doing' (Titus 3.5). Dean urged Stuart to examine his own heart and life to see what God might have in store for him.

Dad, meanwhile, had moved on to No. 11 Elementary Flying Training School at Perth, where cadets were introduced to the basics of flying through a series of exercises – familiarity with controls, taxying, turns, stalls, and so on – in ageing Tiger Moths. There was a breakpoint during the course whereafter cadets considered to have greatest aptitude carried on as pilots, while others were reassigned.† In early December, Dad was

---

* William ended his career as a Senior Inspector of Taxes; Ronald rose to become Assistant Chief General Manager of Lloyds.
† The decision on which path a cadet should take was not entirely governed by natural flying aptitude; the more advanced courses were of fixed hours, and part of the judgement was about cadets' ability to complete them within their lengths.

restreamed as a navigator. He maintained that the main reason for this was that the open cockpit of a Tiger Moth was so noisy that he could never hear anything the instructor said.

By this stage in the war, there were five different categories of navigator, each with its own training pathway that led to a different kind of operational crew. Dad was designated as a Navigator/W, a role combining navigation and wireless operation which made it likely that his future would lie in a crew of two in a machine such as the Mosquito.* The training of a Nav/W began with a twenty-four-week course in wireless telegraphy, followed by a twenty-week flying course in air navigation. The wireless course was provided by No. 1 Radio School at Cranwell.

Cranwell is on a plateau that tilts east from south Lincolnshire's limestone scarp towards the fens. It is in an open land with wide views, amid fields edged by sandy-fawn stone walls, straight roads with broad verges, and churches stranded at lane ends. There is a deep sense of past here. Roman Ermine Street runs just to the west, ghosted in lengths of minor road and green lane. To the north are remains of the Templars' preceptory at Temple Bruer, where William de la More, Preceptor and Grand Prior of all England, ultimate overlord of Kellington's church, was arrested in January 1308 and taken with other knights for trial.

Stuart Blanch was on the same course as my father. They were in different Flights but saw each other often at the station church. One of the Anglican chaplains was Richard Amphlett, patrician, slightly odd in manner, enthusiastic and infectious in his love for God and devotion to the Church of England. Amphlett came from a prominent landed family in north Worcestershire. Since the 1820s, the seat of his branch of the family had been at Wychbold,† near Droitwich, whence his ancestors had followed distinguished careers as barristers, judges, surgeons, and rectors. His father, Richard Ferrand Amphlett, had been killed in the Great War when Richard junior was four, leaving him and his two sisters in the hands of their American-born mother and his grandparents.

Wychbold Hall was then running into difficulty. The pumping out of brine from salt-workings at Droitwich led to episodes of subsidence, one of which was so severe that when Amphlett's grandfather awoke

---

* Mosquito roles for a Nav/W were intruder, fighter-bomber, or photo reconnaissance. Another type calling for the Nav/W was the Beaufighter torpedo fighter.

† Before this at Hadzor Hall, which was sold in 1821.

one morning a joiner had to be summoned to free off his bedroom door. On the death of Amphlett's grandmother, the house passed to Richard, who was now twenty-three. Considering the house to be a liability, he built a new hall in Queen Anne style, and demolished the old one. Amphlett was ordained priest in 1939 and joined the RAF as an emergency chaplain in November 1942. By 1943, the upkeep of the new hall was already becoming a strain.

Dad was preparing for confirmation; Amphlett was an energetic talker. On some evenings their debates ran into the early hours. After Sunday services, Amphlett held discussions on faith and ethics, war and peace, social and personal morality. A recurrent theme was whether the German people formed the enemy and should be so treated when the war was over, or whether their opponents were more narrowly defined. This question became more acute when news arrived from Maurice Cohen, who had completed his flying training and was on the point of joining a frontline squadron when he'd told his commanding officer that he was unwilling to take human life. Maurice was thrown out of the RAF and imprisoned for his refusal to take further part in the war. The situational irony was not lost on either of them: Maurice had become a conscientious objector and was abandoning any commitment to institutional Christianity, while Dad, who had left school virtually faithless, was becoming a Christian and on his way to war.

Stuart's contributions to the late-night Cranwell discussions 'were usually biblically-based in a thoughtful, traditional but not fundamentalist style'. Amphlett had a special admiration for him, confiding on one occasion that 'Stuart was a man of prayer'. He noticed that Stuart was not only a regular at services but spent off-duty time in the station church when no one else was around. Amphlett encouraged them to read widely, introducing them to William Temple, Jacques Maritain, and Evelyn Underhill. For those willing to have a stab at serious Bible study, he had a standing order with Thornton's of Oxford for second-hand copies of the Gore, Goudge, and Guillaume *New Commentary on Holy Scripture*. Such volumes were heavy in an airman's kitbag yet were faithfully toted from posting to posting. Chaplains in Canada became intrigued by the succession of cadets emanating from Cranwell with their *New Commentaries*. And it was to Canada that Dad and Stuart were now sent.

Aircrew were trained in Canadian skies because they were wide, safe from attack, and enjoyed predictable weather. When Dad passed out from the radio course in August, he was given a fortnight's embarkation leave, then with four thousand others boarded the RMS *Queen Mary* at Gourock on the Clyde for the Atlantic crossing. Fast liners working as troopships usually voyaged alone, relying on speed and zigzagging to evade U-boats. *Queen Mary* duly docked at New York five days later, and on 17 September John Morris joined No. 33 Air Navigation School at Mount Hope, Ontario.

Many RCAF training stations were remote, but Mount Hope was in a well-farmed area, just a bus-ride away from the port city of Hamilton at the western end of Lake Ontario. It was thus a popular posting, and for the newly arrived trainees all the more so for the variety and abundance of its food. After nearly four years, they tasted fresh eggs, steaks, and many kinds of fruit.

Training began with refresher work in the classroom – chart-plotting, meteorology, signalling. This soon gave way to a series of air exercises in which students studied a point of navigation on the ground and then went aloft to perform it in practice. The aircraft were Avro Ansons, slow, docile machines of pre-war design which carried a crew of up to six – normally a staff pilot and trainees who took it in turns to serve as first or second navigator, wireless operator, or perform dogsbody tasks like the 144 turns of the crank that were needed to retract or lower the undercarriage. Aerial navigation exercises were exacting, the ever-moving position of the aircraft being calculated according to its speed, heading, the direction and strength of wind, and time. On return, the logs of data kept by each student were examined by an instructor, and the aircraft's intended path and turning points during a flight of perhaps three or four hours were compared with what had actually happened.

Dad made himself known to the station chaplain, Sqn Ldr Howells, took part in the Tuesday evening discussion groups, played badminton in one of the hangars, and joined The Mount Hope Players, an am-dram group led by Guy Saint Vincent Radcliffe Thackeray, a former headmaster in his early forties. By day, he was a temporary instructor in astro-navigation; off duty, he was a veteran of the Oxford University Dramatic Society, a descendant of William Makepeace Thackeray, and in October 1943 he decided to organise a production of A. A. Milne's detective play, *The Fourth Wall*.

Auditions followed. Dad was allocated the part of Jimmy Ludgrove. Since there were no female actors on the station, Thackeray made contact with drama groups in Hamilton, who found four volunteers for the first read-through. Because there were only three women's parts, Elsie Wearne, who did not read any of them, decided at the end of the evening that this was not for her. However, the following Sunday, she returned from a long walk to find an RAF station wagon outside her house with two of the three other girls beside it. The third had dropped out, which meant someone was urgently needed to read her part – would Elsie do it?

Up at Mount Hope, Guy Thackeray got to work on Act 1, with Elsie cast as Susan, who is the girlfriend of Jimmy. During a break, Jimmy came over and asked politely whether if Thackeray asked her to take the part, she would agree. Several other members of the cast, professional actors in civilian life, thought this would be a good idea; encouraged, she agreed.

During a break at the next rehearsal, over cups of tea in the canteen, they exchanged their real names – Elsie, John. She was thirty-five, he twenty. Elsie explained that she had been born and grown up in north-east Yorkshire. In 1926, the family had emigrated. Since then, she had worked as a teacher, latterly specialising in drama and speech. During that first tea break she probably did not tell him that her acting had taken her to the boundary between hobby and career, that there had been overtures from a film company, or that her engagement to a man in the theatre world had eventually been broken because of his prevailing affection for his mother.

John asked if she ever wanted to go back to England. Yes, she said; yes, she did. Every spring. There is no real spring in Ontario; one day in April it is winter, the next the temperature is in the eighties and it is summer. She missed the hawthorn blossom and the primroses.

For the next few weeks, two or three times a week, the three girls were picked up promptly in the station wagon and whisked up the hill to Mount Hope. Years later, Elsie recalled: 'Everyone was polite and kind and very, very British.' The other girls in the cast were impressed by 'Jimmy's' thick, black, wavy hair and emphatic nose. They supposed he was Jewish, and in Canada Morris was usually a Jewish name. Elsie asked for the name of the friend about whom he often spoke; he said Cohen, which seemed to settle it. But they were wrong.

The play opened on 6 December. It went well. The Works and Buildings Department's conversion of the station recreation hall into a theatre impressed everyone. So did the sophisticated sets, augmented by furniture loaned from the Officers' Mess. The *Mount Hope Meteor* said the show was 'probably the best' that the camp had seen. The cast party after the last performance was held in the Officers' Mess, which meant that Jimmy and other non-commissioned airmen were not invited.

Elsie slipped out and joined them in the Sergeants' Mess for ham, eggs, chips, and tea.

Curtain call after performance of The Fourth Wall, *RAF Mount Hope, Ontario, 6 December 1943. Elsie Wearne is fourth from left.*

After the weeks of concentration came anticlimax, and magic. On nights when heavy snowfall prevented flying, John visited Elsie at her digs in Herkimer Street. They went to the ballet, to church, for walks, to look at Niagara Falls. The read to one another, beginning with Henry Williamson's *Tarka the Otter.* A year later, Dad recalled:

> Buses were celestial, and life was a fever of impatience between visits … I seemed to be variably in two states: either I was coming to you or staying (forcibly) away. I used to watch the lights of Hamilton so wistfully from the plane at night or approach them in the bus so gladly. Is there anywhere at all a corner of our experience that is unlighted by our love. Trains, journeys, jobs, people – they are so easily linked.

A few days before Christmas, they went to a carol service at McMaster University, which began with the suggestion that Christianity rests on a manger mysteriously filled, and a tomb mysteriously emptied. Somewhere on the way back, Elsie put her hand in his.

Christmas came. Elsie went home to her parents in Windsor. John went to friends in Chicago. Before they parted, he gave her recordings of Brahms's Second Piano Concerto and Sibelius's Second Symphony, and she gave him a copy of Kahlil Gibran's *The Prophet*. Between New Year and Dad's completion of the course on 25 February, they listened to the Brahms incessantly, and became engaged.

He passed out top in the end-of-course examinations, was immediately commissioned, and joined the officers' mess as a Pilot Officer. There was a very large mathematical component in the course, and he was no mathematician; twenty years later, during a summer evening walk, he told me that he had drilled himself to become absolutely proficient in the different skills that were needed. Until the end of his life, he usually wore his wristwatch with the dial under the wrist – the position that enables a navigator to read the time to the second when holding up an astro-sextant to take angular measurements.

The end of the course meant parting. In March, Dad was sent to the school of General Reconnaissance at Summerside, on Prince Edward Island. Before he left, Elsie introduced him to her parents, sisters, and brother, who lived in and around the town of Windsor, on the south bank of the Detroit River.

Summerside is the best part of a thousand miles from Hamilton. The course ran for nine weeks, during which they managed to meet once. On the return, moving along the train corridor, Dad ran into Stuart Blanch. They would not meet again for two years.

One letter of Dad's that survives from Summerside reveals him in a kind of ecstasy of inquiry, exploring relationships between science, religion, and literature. He had been reading Arthur Eddington's *The Nature of the Physical World* (1928), which was written immediately after the discovery of quantum mechanics, and ends with a chapter entitled 'Science and Mysticism'. When not flying or in training, his main pursuit was reading. It was as if he was cramming himself with words, ideas, and experiences. Amid the excitement of a return to the 'acknowledgement of the unsearchable depths in nature', he had come across a copy of Mary Webb's *The Golden Arrow* in the station library. Elsie already knew it and had mentioned it to him. In it he found Revelation imagery, seasons, Shropshire, and a 'wedding of generosity and penury': 'How much is personally and immediately relevant to us!'

On 3 June, Dad arrived in Halifax, Nova Scotia, to join the RMS *Andes* to return to England. Six days later, he was among five thousand soldiers and airmen who disembarked at Liverpool. His talks with Elsie during the Canadian winter had transfigured the way in which he now looked at England. He told her, 'And now England once more and you are closer still ... The countryside is as fresh, as green, and as breathtaking as we imagined it.' The first letter was numbered 'JE 1'; her first 'EJ 1'. Thus would they know whether a newly arrived letter was in or out of sequence, or indeed whether the sequence had been broken.

His new posting was to the RAF's Personnel Reception Centre at Harrogate, which at any one time held several thousand aircrew who had just returned from overseas. A week later, he was given leave and travelled to see his parents:

> Yesterday afternoon I arrived in Birmingham and Father who had met every possible train that day collided with me as I was drifting absent mindedly down the platform. After we had exchanged exuberant greetings and clapped one another on the back (during which, inadvertently, I almost knocked Father, who is not very large, under the London Express – or something –) absolutely boiling over with secret triumph and gloating considerably he announced mysteriously that he had received a letter from Canada.

Elsie and John had talked a lot about how to break news of the engagement to John's parents. The resulting plan rested on preparatory letters from each of them, but Dad quickly sensed that his parents had worked it out for themselves. This came as a relief; he had been anxious. When he produced a photograph, gleefully, 'They seemed *prejudiced* on your behalf. I do believe that had I shown them a picture of Frankenstein they would have been as nice.'

Amphlett was positive, pointing to ways in which marriages can draw strength from dissimilarity as well as likeness. Amphlett was in his early thirties, and the precocity of this twenty-one-year-old's letters hints at his need for older mentors who could pace, if not outpace, him. The wisdom, judgement, and intuition he found in Elsie's letters was influential. Although later he often appeared to be the stronger influence, this was only because she allowed it to seem so. The balance here at the outset is an equilibrium, as much or more passing from her to him.

While John's parents welcomed the proposed marriage, Maurice Cohen opposed it vehemently. In a succession of hard-hitting letters, he warned that it was idealism running ahead of experience. He told John that his motive for wishing to marry was 'a sense of duty and a false "ascetic bias", not from sound motives which would stand the test of years'. He thought the marriage would 'necessarily' be childless, and that knowing this it would be wrong to enter it. However ideal it seemed now, he wrote, time would turn it to ashes of remorse. Maurice's father called it 'a tragedy indeed'. Dad worked hard to suppress his annoyance and respond with a conciliatory but firm and closely argued reply. Nonetheless, he was unsettled and turned to Amphlett for further advice.

In July, Dad was sent on the course for newly commissioned officers at the Aircrew Officers' School at Credenhill, Herefordshire, where Thomas Traherne (1637–1673), the last Anglican mystical poet, served as rector between 1657 and 1667:

> In all Things, all Things service do to all;
> And thus a Sand is endless, though most Small.
>   And everything is truly infinite
>   In its Relation deep and exquisite.

The Officers' School itself was an ugly rectangular grid of Nissen huts dropped into the countryside, where he was introduced to dress and saluting, airmen's conditions of service, procedures for arrest and custody, pay and accounts, courts of inquiry, and official communications. Interspersed with the classes were exercises in the course of which burly RAF Regiment teams were given practice in the interception of young men turned out in the middle of nowhere with orders to find their way back across country. On at least one of these, Dad and a colleague succeeded by the expedient of catching a bus that stopped by the main gate. Course completed, he returned to Harrogate to await events.

He made himself known to Canon Gascoigne Clare, vicar of the church of St Peter in the town centre, where he began to attend services. Marking time, he managed to attach himself to a Group Captain chaplain-in-chief to help run his office. Having questioned Dad closely, the Group Captain put him in touch with the Director of Service Ordinands, who sent a form to be filled out. Ominously, several of the questions were about relationships and marriage. Theological colleges liked their students single. Did he have a fiancée?

Letters travelled back and forth at the rate of two or three a week. As the summer warmed, he liked to write outdoors, where the gardens of the hotel in which he was billeted, four to a room, were thick with thousands of dig-for-victory cabbages, interspersed with scented wildflowers that had taken hold. The letters tell of books being read, war's poignancies, impressions of new places. Themes which would dominate Dad's ministry were forming. From the trains which took him between postings and on leave to Birmingham, he saw the squalor, social injustice, and poverty of industrial England. He protected himself from the casual brutalism and profanities of Service life with what he called a 'provisional isolationism', but it was already clear that 'When peace comes I must not be content to be an isolationist tolerably free and oblivious of the misery and ignorance and pain that will still exist.' Since the Church seemed poorly equipped for this momentous task, there was work ahead.

Little was said directly about the war but much about its moral dilemmas and propagandistic evils. The letters are sometimes funny, more often serious. Their underlying temper has a sweet and searching gravity. Many of them, in both directions, reflected on ways in which what they were reading connected with things spoken and felt during the sixteen weeks when they had been together. Above all, they talked about faith, which was inextricably linked with their relationship: 'I am certain our love does not exist apart from Christ.'

More steps were taken towards ordination. At the end of the officers' course, he wrote to Amphlett for guidance. Amphlett was now chaplain at Cranfield, where night-fighter crews trained, and invited him to visit: 'Come in an apostolic spirit; it's a long walk from the station.'

Amphlett suggested five tests. He must be sure that he was being called by God; be prepared, without reservation, to dedicate his life to God; be ready to keep himself mentally and physically fit; be able to work hard unceasingly; and be willing to spend a lot of time doing boring things. Ordination would call for a degree in theology: 'He is quite clear that I shall go to Oxford (perhaps Cambridge).' Amphlett had studied at Oriel College, Oxford, where he would make inquiries.

'Seeing Amphlett was marvellous!' he told Elsie. He was steadied by Amphlett's advice about the tensions with Maurice, which recently had been complicated by an argument over the intellectual foundations of Maurice's pacifism. On the way back to Harrogate, he bought copies of Gore's *Jesus of Nazareth*, *Midnight Hour* by 'Nicodemus' – 'the confession of inner religious experience under the stress of public and private events' – and the *Complete Works of St John of the Cross*. As Elsie's birthday approached, he sent his copy of *Midnight Hour* to her.

As August turned to September, before the disaster of Arnhem, the swiftness of Allied progress through France towards Germany raised talk about an early end to the European war. If that happened, he asked, would she be able to come to England as soon as civilian travel resumed? His parents were going to move from their bungalow to a larger house on the south side of Birmingham; if she wished, she could live with them until they were married. In asking this, there is no sign that it crossed his mind that a woman fifteen years his senior might have second thoughts about giving up her well-paid career in a prosperous country for the spare bedroom of a family she had never met, in austerity Britain, as the prelude to marriage to a penniless student.

Maurice Cohen, meanwhile, remembering that Dad was in Harrogate, wrote a placatory letter which ended with breezy advice:

> Oh yes! And you must get to Fountains Abbey. It is best to get on a bus to Ripon and get off it at some point along the road to Ripon (about five miles out of Harrogate) and then go straight through fields, woods and all obstacles in a due easterly or westerly direction (can't remember which) until you come to Fountains . . . I hope you are very well and not within a hundred miles of an aeroplane.

By the time Dad read this, he was very close indeed to an aeroplane. On 10 September 1944, the fourteenth Sunday after Trinity, just promoted to Flying Officer, he wrote, 'Rather unexpectedly I have been posted here to resume training.' 'Here' was Haverfordwest, in Pembrokeshire, the home of No. 4 Flying Refresher Unit. He was being fast-tracked into the war.

In 1944, the Allies had an aircrew surplus which was growing by the month. In crude terms, training output exceeded attrition, and because of this many airmen kicked their heels for months before being called forward for final operational training and entry to active service. In Dad's case:

> The circumstance of the posting is a bit intricate to explain – and not worth it – but I am quite a way ahead of my turn, I believe. As a result of a split-second decision I made on Friday afternoon, on Friday evening I was on my way here. It is most probable now that within five months I shall be posted to a Squadron either here or overseas . . .

What had happened was that a South African reconnaissance unit in Italy which flew the Mosquito, a high-performance type with a crew of two, had asked for the secondment of several navigators from Britain. The Mosquito PR XIV called for a Navigator/W. A call had gone out for volunteers: 'If I had said no, I need not have gone, but I knew I was meant to go, and said yes.'

Pembrokeshire in autumn stirred memories of September the year before. After two years of billets and huts, 'For the first time in my RAF career I have a room of my own in which to sleep and read and pray and write to you.' On the first Sunday, he walked to evensong in the nearby church of St David, in the village of Prendergast. He was uplifted: 'The home of the CoE is in Wales! The singing was beautiful. These people have a sense of music and poetry. They are a race apart from the English, walking, speaking and living differently. They possess great dignity . . .'

The rector, Christopher Lewis, invited him to supper, at which they were joined by his daughter – the kind of girl, he told Elsie, whom Maurice would wish him to get to know.*

After six days of navigation exercises flown in the Unit's Wellingtons:

Yesterday was my day off and I went with a friend to St Davids, the birthplace of the Patron of Wales. The Cathedral there was founded in 570 and it is full of age and ghosts. The ceilings, altars, carvings and chapels were especially beautiful: I made up my mind to go there again; that visit may be years hence but then, please God, you will be with me.

He drew the cathedral in the middle of the letter.

St Davids cathedral, 'full of age and ghosts', sketched in the middle of a letter to Elsie Wearne, September 1944.

---

* Lewis was rector of Prendergast from 1941 to 1963, and was concurrently the Archdeacon of.

In October, he moved on to the School of General Reconnaissance at Blackpool. While he was there, Amphlett brokered a meeting with Wilfred Askwith, the Bishop of Blackburn, for provisional assessment of his suitability for ordination.

On 11 November, Dad took the train north to join No. 8 Operational Training Unit at Dyce, near Aberdeen, the last step in training, where crews of photo-reconnaissance Mosquitoes and Spitfire pilots were prepared for war. Here he met Captain Leslie Byrne, his South African pilot, and began eight weeks of operational practice. During the course, the Navigator/W did forty hours in the air. Training included practice in flying up to 38,000 feet, navigation in winds up to one hundred miles per hour, cloud flying, and photography of fixed points. The Mosquito was fast, and demanding – the aircraft could cover a dozen miles in the time it took to make a single calculation. Maps bearing pencilled tracks and prick marks from his dividers tell of their long winter sorties out towards Rockall and the Faroes, and precision exercises, flying straight for maybe thirty miles to take a succession of overlapping photographs, and then turn back to photograph an exactly adjoining and parallel strip, which would be spoiled if the aircraft crabbed or drifted. Since most of the flying was at high altitude, oxygen was used throughout. Dad said that the tubes gave out a slightly fishy smell, like sardines.

At December's end, he wrote his last letters from Dyce, in bed, on freezing nights. To his annoyance, the last three weeks of the course were transferred to Haverfordwest – a change which unsettled him because he had set his heart on not going there again until Elsie was with him.

Late in January, he was sent on ten days' embarkation leave. He told Elsie that he expected to be away for a year. While at home, he took the bus south from Birmingham to Wychbold, to take his leave of Amphlett. Dad was surprised by Wychbold Hall: 'I had not realized I had a friend in the landed gentry.' Amphlett's piety, intellectual discipline, and blazing pastoral concern give pause for thought about the generations of gentry sons who are held to have entered the Church simply out of custom.

On 8 February, he said goodbye to his parents and joined Leslie Byrne at Benson, the Oxfordshire aerodrome that was home to RAF photo-reconnaissance. Here they were allocated a Mosquito and briefed for departure. They were to join No. 60 Squadron of the South African Air Force, which formed part of the Mediterranean Allied Photo Reconnaissance Wing, stationed at San Severo in Italy's southern region of Puglia. Their voyage would be in two stages: a short trip to

Portreath, on the north-west tip of Cornwall, whence they would make the 1,200-mile journey to San Severo in a single flight, along a route that would take them to the French Riviera, then south-eastward over Corsica, and finally east past Rome and on to the Foggia plain. The pause in Cornwall was to enable topping up of fuel, final inspection of their aircraft, a weather check, and briefing on signals protocols and diversion airfields along the route. Such send-off services were provided by an Overseas Dispatch Unit which assisted the departure of Allied aircraft to faraway places.

A succession of delays now ensued. First, Byrne fell ill with flu. Dad was sent home, and when Byrne recovered, he said goodbye to his parents for a second time. Poor weather followed, and when this lifted the ground crew found a mechanical problem with the aircraft. On 19 February:

> We are still held here for a day or so. I managed to return home for another day; I enjoyed it and Mother and Father were very pleased. Saying 'Goodbye' was becoming so frequent an occurrence that we were saying it quite perfunctorily at the last in the 'taken for granted' fashion which was just as well because such occasions are very sad ones for Mother. Mother always takes my departures very well on the surface but very sadly within and this time she is, I believe, sadder than before.

On Friday 23 February, their aircraft still unserviceable, Byrne and Dad took a train to London for the afternoon – Byrne to look up an old girlfriend; Dad to take his leave of Maurice Cohen. He found Maurice in a park close to his home. Peace was made. They talked about 'materialistic and ignorant Britain', and a Church of England that in many respects was likewise.

Byrne and Dad flew to Portreath three days later. Until the previous autumn, the airfield had been busy, but since the retaking of France it had become a backwater. The Cornish spring was under way: 'hedgerows and lanes a delicious exciting tangle'. Dad knew this was Wearne heartland: although Elsie had grown up in Yorkshire, her father was a tin miner who had been born nearby. There were Wearnes in the phone book. Moreover, Mary Webb's *Precious Bane* was in the mess library. It recalled his reading of *The Golden Arrow* at Summerside, and thereby revivified the entire experience of the previous spring. It was becoming obvious, he told her, that if he came home, their honeymoon would have to be in Cornwall.

But to return, they first had to leave. On 28 February, he wrote another letter from Portreath. He had begun to read Henry Williamson's novel *The Pathway*; his wish that he could finish it was granted when he fell ill and was moved to the station sick quarters. Having reached the end of its tale of a penniless visionary idealistic in love and in search of Christ, he opened the window. Right beneath it, he told her, were primroses. The constellations of pale buttermilk flowers, each with a darker, antique gold centre, swept him back to their talk during the tea break in the second rehearsal of *The Fourth Wall*.

On 2 March: 'Yet another letter from Cornwall? Yes, why not: I like it here.' This time, a storm had stopped their going. He had been for a long walk along the cliffs, where woodland was thronged with birds and there were spring flowers he did not recognise. A small black-and-white dog had bounded up – a relationship he encouraged, 'not remembering until it was too late that I was storing up for myself the unpleasant and perhaps unkind duty of getting rid of him later in the day'. He sketched the dog. Perhaps one day they would have a dog like it. Luckily, the dog transferred its affections to a passing group of WAAFs. He walked down to the beach. 'The sea seemed to be asleep,' he wrote, 'sighing a little as it dreamed.'

Then they did go. As Byrne ran up the engines at the end of the runway, Dad turned in the cockpit and looked out sideways; his last sight of England, and of Cornwall, was a flock of goldfinches.

14

ITALY AND THE TESTING OF HEARTS

S t Michael travels well. This is partly because travel is what angels do: being pure energy, they can whoosh across the cosmos in an instant. It is also because angels leave no relics, and being attached to nowhere are adoptable anywhere. St Mary, likewise, having been taken into heaven, is linked to no one place. Mary and Michael go together through association with birth and death, the two certainties of human being, and in the Catholic litany of the saints. Looking out of the cockpit as Byrne let the Mosquito down on its final approach, there they were: the cathedral of the Assumption of the Virgin Mary in San Severo to the west, and the sanctuary of Saint Michael, Europe's oldest shrine to the archangel, high on the crest of the Gargano hills to the east.

Dad was at first quartered in a requisitioned house in the town. His room had an ornamental plaster ceiling and coloured frescos. With it came a batman, Bruno, who liked to murmur the names of Italian artists like Dante and Brunelleschi as he went about his tasks.

Portreath's goldfinches were still in his mind as he sat down to write his first impressions. There were 'very few birds' in San Severo. They were being eaten. The poverty shook him. Streets in the town were full of 'broken and despairing old people in rags and filth'. Few children wore shoes. Everyone was hungry. Much of the town had been rebuilt in Baroque idiom in the eighteenth century. Its walls were 'covered with "Vivas" – "Viva Stalin", "Viva Republica"'. The townspeople seemed friendly, and he developed an affection for farming families, but there were score-settling tensions between communists and residual fascist elements 'whose reactionary ideas make it definitely unsafe for Allied troops to move about alone at night'. Members of the Squadron made him welcome. They struck him as 'a magnificent crowd'. A friend from Mount Hope was among them.

During the winter, the Squadron had been accommodated in the town. The drive out to the airfield took them past bombed houses, old women with vast bundles balanced on their heads, shoeless beggars crouched on doorsteps; then, into sunlit countryside aglow with pink-and-white almond blossom. Overlooking all was the two-thousand-foot scarp of the Gargano massif: 'Although it is only March the weather is already warm and we shall soon be in tropical kit. The life here soothes [sic] and contents me in a way that I had not expected; I think I shall continue to be very happy here; very much in love with life; very much in love with you.'

San Severo was home to the Mediterranean Allied Photo Reconnaissance Wing: the reconnaissance and intelligence arm of the Mediterranean Allied Air Forces which processed and analysed aerial imagery across Austria, southern and central Germany, Czechoslovakia, and the Balkans. In and around the town, working from requisitioned buildings and trailers, were mainly British and American photo laboratories and teams of interpreters and intelligence analysts. To meet the demands of the US Fifth Army and Britain's Eighth Army, a Photographic Technical Squadron was co-located with MAPRW with capacity to produce half a million prints per month.

The airfield had been laid out two years before by American engineers. Everything about it was makeshift: the runway and dispersal hardstandings were surfaced with pierced steel planking, accommodation was in tents, buildings were improvised from packing cases. In winter, the airfield turned to mud; in summer, to dust. It was but one in a complex of some thirty airfields in close proximity on the semi-desert Foggia plain from which the US Twelfth Air Force, Fifteenth Air Force, and RAF bombarded northern Italy, Germany, and parts of Europe at extreme range from the UK.* Joseph Heller did not set *Catch-22* on the Foggia plain, but those who flew from it recognise *Catch-22*.

Leslie Byrne and John Morris flew their first operation on 14 March, to photograph ports along the north Adriatic coast, in preparation for the Allied attack into the Lombard plain that was planned to begin three weeks later. The sortie was successful, and, apart from the approach of two unidentified aircraft near Grado, uneventful. As operational flying

---

* In addition to 60 Squadron, San Severo accommodated the 90th Reconnaissance Wing of the USAAF (departed for the USA in April 1945), and two RAF units: No. 683 Squadron, which was equipped with PR IX Spitfires, and a detachment of No. 680 Squadron, which like themselves operated with Mosquitos. From time to time, San Severo was also used as a stopover by aircraft from the UK, which could increase their range by pausing to rest and refuel on return from missions deep into central and south-east Europe.

went, aerial reconnaissance was at the safer end of the scale. PR Mosquitos flew high and fast, and until later 1944 it was rare for one to be successfully intercepted. The most hazardous phase of a sortie was over and near the objective. The aim was to bring back a run of overlapping photographs across a briefed target, which called for straight and level flying in the approach and overflight. Steady flight could make the aircraft susceptible to interception. When in enemy airspace, the navigator accordingly spent much of his time looking backwards. When he left his seat to go down into the glazed nose to line up the pilot on the target, the pilot became responsible for lookout over the tail using mirrors.

Risk increased if an aircraft drew attention to itself by leaving a condensation trail. Such trails began to form when the air temperature fell below $-37^{\circ}C$, the trail height being lower in winter and lifting in spring. In theory, the trail-forming layer had a finite thickness above which a crew should have been able to climb, but Dad and his colleagues found that this was seldom the case. Their normal tactic was thus to fly a touch below the trail level,* so that an intercepting fighter climbing to attack from behind would give itself away by leaving a trail of its own.

There were other hazards. One was mechanical failure. Another was what to do if an objective was obscured by cloud; if a crew elected to go lower to obtain photographs, it would come within range of flak and become more vulnerable to fighters. A third was attack by other Allied aircraft. In the last months of the war, the presence of large numbers of US fighters in a shrinking area made this likely. In an effort to avoid it, 60 Squadron and 680 Squadron Mosquitos were decorated with black-and-white invasion-type stripes painted on their wings and fuselage, and conspicuous red-and-white diagonal 'barber's pole' stripes on the fin and rudder.

Enemy aircraft regarded as dangerous included the Focke-Wulf Fw 190 and the Messerschmitt 410, but their supreme foe was the Me 262 jet fighter, which had entered service in August 1944 and outpaced the Mosquito by a wide margin. A number of the Squadron's aircraft had been attacked by them, in several cases with fatal or damaging results. They operated chiefly in a triangle between Vienna, Munich, and Prague, which accordingly was known as the 'jet area'. When a 60 Squadron Mosquito went into the jet area, it was normally escorted by half a dozen P-51 long-range fighters which were briefed to disrupt an interception should one develop. In March 1945, the jets were withdrawn

---

* In March 1945, this was usually around 27,000 feet.

to Prague-Ruzyne, and fuel shortages increasingly kept them on the ground, but the threat persisted until the end.

The lessening of opposition during the last months of the European war was offset by an increase in the difficulty of the targets they were sent to examine. In place of large, spread-out objectives like marshalling yards and airfields, February found them being sent more to isolated sites like entrances to underground factories, radar installations, bridges, and highway intersections. In terms of photography, such targets called for only a few exposures, but precise navigation and skilful map reading was needed to find them and aim the cameras.

In parallel, Allied concern that German forces would make their last stand in Austria brought a request for aerial survey of the entire country to enable its up-to-date mapping. A mapping mission usually entailed flying up to seven parallel strips, each between three and five miles apart and thirty to forty miles long. Finding the precise position and track for each run called for close concentration, and it was in the course of such work near Linz on 20 March that tragedy brushed them. While lining up for the final run, several fighters escorting a passing formation of USAAF bombers mistook them for a German aircraft and began an interception.* Persistent attacks ensued. At one point, Dad attributed their survival to his call to Byrne to 'Break left!' when in fact he meant right; the error (which arose because he was facing backwards) coming as much of a surprise to their assailant as it did to themselves. After fifteen minutes of violent evasive action, Byrne managed to escape into cloud. This was not the only incident of its kind that week, and a conference with representatives of the unit concerned ensued.

Dad told Elsie that he was doing a 'comparatively safe job': 'Our narrowest escape was from American fighters (who are notorious for shooting down people on their own side: their aircraft recognition is even worse than mine.)' Behind this was a fatalism: 'Whether by fate, by Providence, by destiny or by any other name – there is a ruling power which decrees when we shall die, when we shall fall, whom we shall meet and when – physical life, "danger" loses its significance. With regard to spiritual life that is another matter.' And behind that: 'Even if we never met here again, there was reason for us to be the happiest people in the world.'

---

* In some respects, the Mosquito resembled the Me 410. The assailants were P-38 Lightnings, apparently from the 1st Fighter Group, then stationed at Lesina a few miles north of San Severo.

He went on:

> There is a deep reason for saying things over again to someone; it
> is that in the reiteration things may be known and understood all
> over again ... It is the deep secret of rebirth; it is why music can be
> enjoyed twice over; it is why there is no end to love and no end to
> life. I believe too that we shall meet again and marry. I believe it very
> strongly, so strongly that if we do not it will not matter – a strange
> paradox, but one that you understand.

The 24th of March found them back over Austria and Czechoslovakia
during a sortie that lasted six and a half hours. The next, photograph-
ing stretches of the Milan–Turin railway, took over five hours. After a
long sortie, flown on oxygen, in extreme cold, at high altitude, he lay on
his bed in relief.

Weather permitting, they flew an operation roughly every four days.
There was a good deal of free time between. He loved the sincerity and
simplicity of the Squadron's chapel: a small room with a table, across
which met a slightly scruffy group of servicemen of all ranks – in marked
contrast to 'respectable assemblies in England'. The chaplain gave lessons on the rudiments of Greek and the historical development of the
Bible. The Squadron's Operations Officer turned out to be a Latinist but
was usually too busy to share his skills.

In late March, Dad went to the Gargano with two colleagues to trade
cigarettes for eggs. In their jeep, they climbed up the dizzying limestone
scarp, hairpin after hairpin, into cooler air that rang with cow bells. New
grass dotted with silvery daisies and blue anemones grew by the roadside. To the west, beyond the Foggia plain, the Apennines shimmered.
'Spring is wonderful here,' he told Elsie. Insect life was 'triumphant'.
Lizards on the airfield were 'lovely green and yellow creatures'.

He watched ceremonies. The funeral procession of a prominent communist impressed him by the dignity of its poorly dressed but composed
members, and the artistry and boldness with which the band played
their battered instruments. On Good Friday, there was a procession in
the town that started at dawn from three different places. One section
set forth from the Church of the Pieta bearing a statue of Our Lady of
Sorrows. A second, from the Trinity Church, carried a wooden effigy of
Christ tied to a column. The third was a procession of hooded penitents
who bore the heavy cross of Simon of Cyrene. The three groups met in
the Piazza de Castello, where an intended embrace between the statues
of the mother and her son was barred by the cross that arose between

them. A month later, he watched the Festa del Soccorso at which San Severo's Black Madonna was paraded through the town with fire crackers and games, the better to banish evil and revel in life.

By then, the Squadron had moved out into tents on the airfield for the summer. Officers were accommodated four to a large square tent: 'One wit, summing up the contents . . . remarked "H'mm, two drunks, one bitcher and a bishop."' Their tent became known as 'The Bishop's Palace'. His camp bed was so narrow that to sleep on it without falling off he had to truss himself in a kind of chrysalis. He made a writing table with wood 'pillaged from the Americans who have everything'. With the flap up, he could see the Gargano hills.

He had been there for five weeks. After the first days when all was new, ordination and Elsie were back in his foreground. Correspondence with Amphlett led him to make a provisional application to Oriel. Amphlett provided an elegantly drafted template letter to the college's provost, the philosopher Sir David Ross (1877–1971); he advised that parts of the entrance exam might be waived; but if not, he would be examined in modern history, Latin, and French. The distance from Elsie was beginning to weigh. On 5 March, he had told her, 'Although this journey seems in the wrong direction, I regard it as a step towards you.' On 12 April, 'I wish I knew how long it is to be before I see you again; how long we have to wait.' And there were frustrations: 'Letter E95 turned up after travelling to many quite unnecessary places including India.'

His circle widened. The photographic interpreters at San Severo included a strange mix of aristocrats, academics, and archaeologists. Among the aristocrats was Lady Dorothy Lygon, youngest daughter of the 7th Earl Beauchamp, whose Worcestershire family and home at Madresfield Court – Amphlett country – and friendship with Evelyn Waugh had fed into a novel that was to appear the following month: *Brideshead Revisited.** Among the academics was Arnold Taylor, a regular member of the Anglican congregation, who came from a family of Battersea schoolmasters and was making a name for himself in the study of Welsh castles. In civil life, he told Dad, he was an Inspector of Ancient Monuments: 'What a glorious thing to be!'

Cyril Garbutt, the Archbishop of York, visited the camp for an evensong and confirmation. Dad thought him a 'lovely old bird' – at once old and frail yet strong and impressive. Surveying the room beforehand, Dad reflected, 'There is something exciting about an empty hall filled

---

* Dorothy Lygon is regarded as the model for Cordelia Flyte.

with empty seats, ready for a performance of a play or the holding of a
meeting or a religious ceremony. "Give me a village hall and some chairs" I
thought, "and I shall be perfectly happy." Think of the things we could do!'

In the evenings, he went into the town for Greek lessons with the
padre's batman (who it turned out was also an ordinand, and handily
fluent in Italian). The chaplains from different denominations sometimes
had dinner together. On one evening, Dad listened approvingly to an
Irish Roman Catholic padre who defended 'the Germans' from 'typical
hate' fostered by the 'hideous propaganda machine' which painted them
all as evil. After listening to Rachmaninov's Second Piano Concerto on
a wind-up gramophone, he hitched a ride with a group of well-oiled
airmen returning from a night out in the back of a truck. The roisterers
turned out to be his own ground crew, who became 'very affectionate
and friendly' when they recognised him.

The last operation in April, and, as it turned out, their last of the war,
was flown on 25 April. It was to Venice and included an encounter with
an Me 410, which waggled its wings and turned away, as if the pilot was
signalling the futility of more fighting. Situation maps in the Operations Room showed the progress of the ground offensives in northern
Italy and inside Germany, where in places Russian and US forces were
now in contact. At the end of the month, he told Elsie that there was
'very little enemy territory left to operate over'; by the time his letter
arrived, Germany might be defeated. But that might not be the signal
for his return home: 'I have a fair idea where I am going and it isn't
towards England.'*

In the event, when the surrender came, he was on leave. The pattern
consisted of short leaves every three weeks or so, with longer rests after
a given number of operations. During the first short break, they went
to Bari, where a hotel was kept for officers, and saw a performance of
La Bohème:†

> The journey by road to Bari was for me . . . delightful. The Italian
> people seem to be excellent agriculturalists, and have their fields
> planted out so ably . . . almost artistically, in fact, and I love to look

---

* As a Navigator/W with experience in the Mosquito PR XVI, a likely next posting would have been to No. 684 Squadron which was then flying reconnaissance
over Japanese-held Burma.

† There was occasional opera in San Severo itself, where the town's opera house
had been turned into the Officers' Club but occasionally reverted to its original
purpose when a touring company came to town.

at them. At this time of year when there are flowers and blossom and so much new green the orchards and groves of trees beckon very invitingly and I was waiting all the time to stop this car and get out and go exploring.

On 3 May, having completed seven operations, Byrne, Dad and another navigator, Jolf, were given ten days' leave and the loan of a jeep in which to travel.

They went first to Rome, where Dad reflected on the rich opulence of St Peter's and 'the poor and wretched in the streets, begging and scavenging; their misery plain to all the world, and all the world passes by'. He went to the Anglican church of All Saints for communion, and 'could have shot the priest' for the way in which he took the service. A performance of Petrushka left him stunned. Gigli's resemblance to Mussolini in *The Force of Destiny* brought 'the heaviest odds against him looking dignified'. In Naples, two evenings later, the soprano playing Tosca was 'at least 200lbs' and the audience was accordingly intrigued as the point approached when Scarpia flings her on the couch.

They drove on to Sorrento, where the Hotel Minerva, an attractive clifftop hotel converted from a nineteenth-century villa, was used by the RAF as a rest centre for aircrew. The Minerva looked out over the Gulf of Naples. For the next four days, they swam from a boat and sunbathed. After the idyll, back at San Severo, Dad realised that until then he had not allowed himself to think beyond the end of war, and 'must have hoped for more than I had known'.

John Morris on leave at Sorrento, May 1945

They returned to an intensive flying programme. Some of the South Africans had been with the Squadron since 1943, and were thrilled with the prospect of imminent release and return home. However, there was more for them to do before they left. During later May, 60 Squadron was put to work on mapping surveys of Corsica, Crete, and the Aegean Islands. Crews flew sorties on alternate days, in some cases landing away, stopping overnight, and flying a second sortie on return. Each mission lasted five or six hours. A 30 per cent overlap was needed between each strip, and aside from the navigational precision this called for, for the pilot it limited the amount of permitted 'wander, tilt or crab'. The Squadron's CO considered the work to be a greater source of strain than some of the operational PR in the last months of the war.

On 29 May, Dad was told that he was about to be posted away. He reflected on his relationship with Leslie Byrne. They had been flying together for six months and had been through some exacting times. They had not become close friends; on the ground, Byrne was a married gentleman 'in the English public-school sense' but 'a wolf' where other women were concerned. In the air, on the other hand, they understood each other. They had developed a 'high sense of communion' at difficult moments: 'Interesting.'

Two days later, he was told that he was to stay with the Squadron after all. There was more flying ahead: their survey was to be extended to Sardinia, all of Greece, Sicily, Albania, and Italy south of the forty-fourth parallel. By the end of July, 60 Squadron had surveyed the best part of three hundred thousand square miles.

Maurice Cohen wrote with news of an old mutual friend: Patricia Gilder, a girl of Dad's age they had known in their teens, now an actor, who had just achieved success in a play in the West End. Maurice passed on her address and suggested that Dad get in touch. Rather loftily, Dad dismissed this as another of Maurice's stratagems. But just as one can walk into an obstacle while turning away in self-congratulation following avoidance of another, a real test now ensued.

In mid June, there was another long leave at the Minerva in Sorrento. He loved the town and the climate, and he was with friends from the Squadron. There was a convivial dinner on the first evening, with wine and whiskey. Next morning, in a letter to Elsie he mentioned two chambermaids who were much admired: Gloria, small, pretty, unpredictable; and another, taller and darker: Maria. A week later:

I tell you of my experiences because they seem important to us. Some I never speak of, either because they are less important or because they are not suitable to write about. This experience deserves description because it is 'important'. It is tremendously difficult to describe in writing and what is told here will one day be amplified in spoken words. But there is another reason for writing about it, in spite of the difficulty. In my last letter I wrote of honesty and shared experience and in the light of such principles this story must be told because it concerns another woman and my feelings for her. It is about Maria.

He reminded Elsie of the two woman-servants mentioned in the previous letter; their efficiency, attractiveness, and respectability were an asset to the hotel. Dad shared a room with a man called Scott, who he considered 'out of the ordinary grade, with thinking power and a sober self-control and self-criticism':

> Gloria was careful to be very nice to both of us in fact she definitely set herself to watch another couple of enthusiastic admirers. In Scotty she had one already, in me she soon found another. I admired her verve, charm, impudence and unpredictability. At first, she showed more attention to me and I was flattered. Moreover, I began to succumb to the extent that I began to welcome chance encounters with her and hoped that she would catch us in passing or something of that sort. I find no condemnation in myself for being thus attracted: she was, most definitely, a most attractive creature and what I felt was perfectly natural; *BUT* I was dangerously near losing self-control; perhaps, indeed, in principle, in my heart, I did lose it many times. There I was a failure to God, to you, to myself, and in a sense even to Gloria. Thank God I was never demonstrative one way or another . . . Truly I never encouraged her, except of course by failing to *dis*courage her . . .

This attraction soon died away: 'No credit to me for that . . . I suspect that the madness gave place to a subtler feeling engendered by the gentle and shy Maria.'

In following days, it became clear to Scotty and Dad that they were being singled out by Gloria and Maria for special attention. Extra things were done for them. If they were in their room during the afternoon, tea would be brought; they began to make a point of staying in their room in the afternoon. An open conspiracy began, a tacit understanding that they would organise their days to engineer encounters on all possible occasions:

> Now I must tell you how Maria gradually attracted my attention ... From the first I thought her beautiful, but I wasn't interested and I passed her by as we can pass by a lovely flower or a beautiful picture without stopping to see and worship. But as I saw her more often the spell began to develop and I was an enchanted man. When I looked at her, she would smile and drop her eyes. In feature she was extremely like Ingrid Bergman except that she was dark. Her hair was black, her eyes deep brown and her teeth white and even. One evening about halfway through the week the following incident occurred. After dinner I had left all my friends, including Scotty, downstairs propping up the bar ... I went upstairs to write to you ... My room opened out onto a flat roof and I walked out on to this to watch the sunset and listen to the strains of Traviata. As I reached the parapet and looked over and down into the garden below, my eye fell ... on another rooftop lower down and there just appearing on it was Maria. I was surprised because Gloria and Maria usually left the hotel for the night at about 7.30 ... I watched curiously. She was not aware of being watched and ran to the parapet and fell half over it. She hung motionless over the edge, one arm pressed half over it ... palm inmost against the wall. Her cheek lay against the wall ... She was listening to the music. Soon the music ended and she looked up and saw me ... and smiled. Again that smile – dazzling even at that distance.

Dad went in and tried to resume his letter but found it difficult to write about anything other than what he had just seen.

By day, Maria wore a nondescript dark skirt and dark jumper: 'I would look down at her feet encased in shabby and well-worn sandals and my heart would melt. As the days went by my faith in her, my love for her was reborn and each encounter strengthened a belief forming in my heart: that I would trust and believe in her till the end of the world':

> One night towards the end of the week, Scotty and I were going down the stairs for dinner. In the mirror at the end of one flight I saw a swirl of black; Maria swept round the corner and began to ascend our flight; she was running. She passed on my side and in passing turned and swayed towards me so that she brushed past me.

As her breast came against my arm I looked into her face and saw what I could not fail to recognise: the mysterious imprint of love, wild, impetuous. She was gone!

Any time after that, given the opportunity, I could easily have kissed her and made love to her . . . Certainly, I should have liked to. But the opportunity did not come . . .

But there were more close encounters. On the last morning, Gloria and Maria appeared and set about clearing their room: 'Gloria was frankly unhappy at our departure; Maria was transparently sad but she smiled still.' It was possible that they would return in a few weeks' time:

> In saying goodbye Scotty set the standard of handshaking. I took Gloria's hand. As she was saying one of her brave, silly things, her eyes *searched* mine. She was troubled and unhappy. I turned to Maria. Maria took my hand and pressed it to her. Her eyes glistened but she smiled radiantly and murmured . . . an obviously rehearsed phrase that she would not forget me. Her voice was low and musical. I looked down and saw again . . . her shoes. I said nothing but Goodbye.

As they drove out of the courtyard, he looked up through the open roof. Gloria was looking down, waving. There was no sign of Maria: 'As we drove out from Sorrento on that bright morning my heart was bleeding. "Ah, Lord God, behold I cannot speak for I am a child."'

After two days, back under the eye of Michael high on the Gargano, Dad considered himself to be almost his 'calm, slightly cynical self again'. But he was wondering about Maria, 'if she is suffering this joy and pain of love, if she is building impossible dreams – as all lovers do – and clinging hopefully to an impossible future.'

Then:

> Dearest Elsie, what will you think of all this? I have given no commentary, but have tried to describe 'history'. The thought will come to you that I am unfaithful. Do not thrust it aside: it is true; but, I beg you to forgive it. I pray God that you are not hurt by what I have said. If I had concealed it you would have been hurt more and our love would have been damaged by a lie. Somehow, I feel confident that you will know better how to deal with this situation.
>
> God bless you and keep you.
>
> I love you Elsie – John

The reply:

> Dearest John. What shall I say? You will want to know how I received your beautiful (because I do see that, too) story. As I took the letter from the envelope, my eager eyes fell upon the writing which came first to my gaze – that is, before I had opened the letter. I saw 'I thought sometimes that I would have kissed her, too; certainly I should have liked to.'
>
> I became enormously, unnaturally calm. I got up from the desk and walked over to the window and tried to pray. I came back and sat down, and read the letter through. I felt as though I was someone else reading a story which moved me to tenderness and understanding. Then I came to the end, and I was Elsie again, who loved John – who wrote this. I put the letter down and got up and walked towards my bed. I did not reach it. I dropped down to my knees and then sat back on my heels, in the middle of the room. My whole body felt strangely alive and I looked at the ceiling and said 'Dear God!' Some little time later, I realised that I had not articulated any words except – about ten times, and at intervals of about ten seconds – simply 'Dear God!' And I was smiling – that suddenly occurred to me too. It seemed strange that I should be smiling, at first. I got up and read the letter again, trying to find the clue to this reaction because the smile came from an inner glory I could not describe – a strange happiness I had never known before. Of course, there were strong underlying chords of sorrow too, but the other feeling was too strong for it.

Mum went for a long walk: 'I felt that you would want me to think carefully before I wrote any more.'

'Dear John – you have laid such a responsibility at my feet. "Somehow I feel confident that you will know better than I how to deal with this situation."'

They had a custom of praying together at the same time each day – she at 5 pm in Canada, he at 10 pm in Italy. Claiming no premonition, she told him that for the past two or three weeks her prayer 'has not been *with* you, but *for* you': 'And my forgiveness? It was yours before you asked – before you wrote – before you went to Sorrento. And now I ask you, humbly, for yours – if I have not given what you hoped. I can only look at you steadily across all these miles, and say with humility, and pride too, I love you John.'

In mid August, their mapping marathon completed, 60 Squadron prepared to fly home to South Africa, and Dad was posted to be Adjutant at the Headquarters of No. 2 Base Area in Rome. An Adjutant's job, he told Mum, was 'to know everything and be able to do anything'. He was accommodated first in a hotel, later in a palace with marble floors on the city's outskirts where the base supply officer had struck up a close relationship with an Italian princess. The base commander was well regarded, but prone to occasional spells of erratic behaviour which Dad put down to operational fatigue. The Church of England's Centre in Rome was nearby. He arranged to attend a course for prospective ordinands in early September, to be followed by a four-day selection board.

Meanwhile, he had been back to the Hotel Minerva in Sorrento to explain himself to Maria. He told her that he was engaged to be married, and he could not make love to anyone else. She accepted these and other 'little shocks':

> but my heart felt for her and for the pain I know she felt. I felt weak, humble, and helpless. There was often a strong desire to take her in my arms and comfort her springing – as far as I can honestly judge – from my compassion for her – there was something unmade between us which I could never have denied, but which I never felt called upon to deny.

When he went collect his bag to leave, she was waiting:

> I said simply 'Goodbye' and she extended both hands for me to take. I had taken one before I realised there were two; the other fell back meekly to her side. I raised her right hand to my lips and kissed it gently, placed my hand upon her head, gently brushing her temple and the dark hair. That was all.

Maria and Gloria asked him to write to them from England. He said he would write the odd line in Italian if they would reply in English.*

He described the Anglican course. Much of the discussion had been about vocation and education. Each candidate was assigned a personal chaplain, with whom long conversations ensued. Some discussion turned on the question of whether a candidate would be worthy of lengthy and expensive educational investment. Dad's chaplain was a Padre Ryecart, whom he found to be calm but serious: 'not in the Amphlett class but a

---

* My father never mentioned this episode to me, and in the letter at the time he said that he did not expect a correspondence to develop. However, nineteen years later, in conversation with a friend about his war service, he mentioned friendship with someone in Italy who was now mother to *molti bambini*.

man to whom I could speak my whole mind'. Ryecart had 'grave doubts' about the proposed marriage. Ordinarily, a candidate engaged to a girl around his own age would be expected to delay marriage until ordination training was complete. Dad returned to his room in 'tremendous depression'. Would he have to choose between ordination and Elsie? He prayed: 'It was the only thing to do.'

The course introduced him to the Anglican form of Compline: 'It's very wonderful and I use it for us both with the consciously expressed desire that we may soon use it together.' After a few days, he sent her a copy, and Compline became their office at the shared moment each evening, across four thousand miles.

'The Lord almighty grant us a quiet night and a perfect end.'

'Be sober, be vigilant; because your adversary the devil, as a roaring lion, walketh about, seeking whom he may devour; whom resist, steadfast in the faith.'

> *John:* Keep me as the apple of an eye.
> *Elsie:* Hide me under the shadow of thy wings.

After the Selection Board, Dad found himself listing likely drawbacks of his candidacy. One was immaturity – he was twenty-two. The projected marriage was certainly another: the interviewers told him flatly that 'it can't be done', if for no other reason than that he would be ineligible for necessary grants. A third was his sense of mediocrity in the eyes of experienced priests. However, a few days later, at the end of a long letter about the Roman autumn (with a paragraph about adjusting their time for Compline to accommodate the change in clocks), 'Some good news I must share with you. One of the Padres on my board . . . told me yesterday "off the record" the result of my board here in Rome. The recommendation they sent through to London for me was about the strongest possible.'

He warned my mother not to make too much of this: the real decision would be taken in London in two months' time. But it was true. In mid November, the Director of Service Ordination Candidates said that his name had been sent to the Ministry of Labour with a recommendation for immediate release from the RAF, ideally to enable him to start at Oxford in January 1946. He wrote to the Provost of Oriel to ask if this would be possible.

While he waited for a reply, life in and around the Rome headquarters ticked on. In the evenings, there were cocktail parties, trips to the opera, and amateur dramatics. During a rehearsal for *Rebecca* ('I hope to be elsewhere when it is staged'), two fashionable young ladies from the British Embassy came over to talk. They asked about his plans, and reacted with disbelief, then confusion, when he said he was going to train as a parson: 'It seems that I did not appear the normal type for a Parson. I thought it so funny! And pathetic too – that the vocation of an Anglican priest should have earned for itself – as it obviously has – this widespread contempt, amusement, suspicion and mistrust.'

On 2 December – Advent Sunday – he told his parents, 'The jolly old release came in yesterday. So far, no reply has come from Oriel, but I've decided to accept the release and ask questions afterwards. All being well then, I shall be home in a fortnight.'

The journey began in a three-ton truck which staged in Florence on the first evening. Next morning, they climbed through mountains where the snowy woodland gleamed gold in the low winter sun, on to Bologna, through rain to Piacenza; they reached Milan around midnight.

Before he left Rome, he had again been warned not to marry for the foreseeable future. He was told that the Board would not dictate – it regarded the matter as personal, and trusted him to reach the right con-clusion, but aside from technical and spiritual aspects, marriage would be unaffordable until he was ordained. Amphlett, on the other hand, foresaw no undue financial difficulty and 'very probably we could and would marry very soon. Slowly, with no hurry, I believe, darling, that the picture is taking shape.'

In Milan, he reflected on the last few years. He found it sad 'to see their joys and fears and life out of one's reach – gone and never to return. Wonderful years for me! I would not have missed them. All the personal history packed into them! – complex, enigmatic, mysterious, significant . . .' He had found a poem which seemed to catch the experience; it was 'written for you and us':

If it is true the dead return
To haunt the place they loved the most,
Then surely I'll come back to learn
If you, too, have come back, a ghost.

The next leg of the journey was in a train to the Channel coast. He shared a compartment with two other RAF officers, one of whom was middle aged and friendly; the other a young pilot (Ontario trained) who reacted to any new sight by declaring it to be 'the greatest invention since barbed wire'. At night, they rearranged the upholstery in a flat pile to sleep side by side. Dad mentioned that he was liable to thrash about in his sleep and contrived to swathe his feet in blankets for restraint. What, they asked, would happen when he was married? 'I said I would deal with the problem when it arose.'

Dad's parents had moved to a semi in Northfield, then still semi-rural, on the southern edge of Birmingham and the 144 bus route. Waiting for him was a letter from the Provost of Oriel, who told him that many old students were returning from the forces. Accordingly, entrance would be decided by competition. The next entrance exam would be in April 1946: 'This means that I can't start work at Oxford immediately, but must wait until next autumn.' It also left only three months in which to prepare: 'I doubt very much if I could reach the required standard by next April. It would take me six months at least to reach the required standard in Latin.' His parents had bought a radiogram. He had not listened to the Brahms concerto since going to war: 'The Andante, our Andante, I have not yet played, and I will not play it until I am alone and quiet – tonight perhaps.'

New Year's Eve: 'The last day of the old year; I couldn't be less interested! At the moment I'm just overwhelmed by the tremendous amount that I don't know.' He was working flat out on the subjects upon which he would be examined. He had enrolled at a tutorial college in Birmingham, where on most days he studied for four hours, working on his own for the rest of the time.

During January, the future took shape. At the end of the first week, 'I saw Amphlett this afternoon at Wychbold. It was good to hear his voice again. It was raining when I got off the bus but I spotted him waiting with an umbrella to conduct me through the myriad ways through the grounds of the house.' Amphlett agreed to visit the Provost and recommend that, given the shortness of time, the Latin requirement be waived.

Next, Dad travelled to London for a meeting with John Phillips, one of the Directors of Service Ordinands. This went well: 'I am now all set for the Oriel College Entrance with full official support.' On marriage, Phillips said 'that since I had already been into the matter thoroughly with two priests the Church authorities would not be likely to quarrel with my decision whatever it was, and the decision would of course be mine to make'. The Church would not support a family during years of training, but his government grant would include a married allowance: 'In his experience, he added, the most difficult years were not those of training but of early curacy where a married curate's average stipend was about £250–300 per annum which in these times is not much.' So, unless they were prepared to wait years, the time for marriage was now: 'He added another precedent to our collection: a friend of his who at 21 married a woman of 39 and was "supremely happy with a family of three.'"

In the middle of the month, Amphlett accompanied him to an interview with the Provost of Oriel:

He was quite charming, a little nervous and terribly businesslike. He agreed that Latin in three months was a tall order and said that if my other papers were of a high standard, deficiencies in the Latin might be overlooked. But, there were 54 entrants for the exam and he warned that the competition would be very fierce. He did not say how many successful candidates would be admitted immediately, but he spoke of many old students returning from the forces and I could see for myself how small the college was. (It is very lovable too.)

His kit arrived from Italy, 'and in the unpacking thereof I met many an old friend'. He reread some of the letters: 'On the whole I think that we have reason to be proud of our correspondence because we have been fairly successful in fulfilling its primary aim, that we should "keep in touch" (lovely phrase) with one another.'

The prospect of return was becoming real. They began to discuss things she might bring. Dad downplayed the need for presents. Something small for his mother; maybe a shirt for his father ('because they are very scarce here now'): 'China is a very good thing to bring if you can.' A 'nice tea service' was unobtainable in shops; 'the only china that had been sold in England for years now has been white utility china at extremely high prices'. He advised her to come well equipped with clothes and stockings; rationing would continue for some time, and what little was available was 'not very agreeable to good taste. The women of England just now are very badly dressed. The women of Italy put them to shame.'

After Italy's poverty, grumbling in Britain about shortages made him impatient; and in Germany, he knew, conditions were worse. On 27 February:

I have just heard about our Parliament's decision concerning food rationing in Germany: to cut the ration by one third . . . decreasing it to a comparison with our own of 1:2½. It is not surprising, but not the less damnable for that. It is the sign that we have not learnt, that we do not care for elementary principles of Christian humanity. It gives the lie to our fevered cry that we were fighting for civilization and shows only too plainly now, if ever there were any doubt, that we were fighting for our*selves*! It is the unmistakable sign that we have again chosen Barabbas and that war will come again. I cannot be surprised, but I cannot help feeling very sad and bitter. Swift was a sane man to hate mankind.

Amphlett was now with the British Air Forces of Occupation in Münster, whence he wrote, 'I am much in need of intercessory prayer, and I know of no better source to ask for it than from you. This is very urgent.' He was not personally depressed but was faced with the task of extending the Kingdom of God 'in the midst of the miles and miles of the worst possible ruins'.

The nearness of Elsie's arrival brought 'a funny feeling'. In March, he told her that it would be 'so romantic to meet you off the ship' – a telegram at the last moment 'would probably arrive in time for me to get to Liverpool or wherever it is that you will land. Other useful details of course will be the name of the ship, if you are allowed to give it, and its port of disembarkation.' He would stop writing letters when he knew her leaving date: 'Most appropriately, primroses are everywhere to be seen in the streets of the town in the baskets of the flower vendors.'

He sat the exam on 5 April, and passed. Walking along Oriel Street that evening he looked up and saw the silhouettes of a young couple in an upstairs room. Might this be them in a few months' time?

The last letter, JE213, was written on 9 April 1946. Elsie would soon board the SS *Argentina* to return to the England she had left twenty years before; the letter was timed to reach her just before she departed. He was with Maurice Cohen on a walking tour in Herefordshire and the Wye Valley. They saw hawks, and the year's first swallows:

> Above all, there is the recurring thought that soon you would be here to share this richness of countryside and England before the Spring is quite gone by.
>
> Coming across the Malvern Hills, I first thought that there you and I would come. I marked a spot high, untroubled and in deep solitude where you and I will rest after a long climb; and then that sense of being at peace and alone ... The most lovely thing is that they were wishes so wonderful, so likely to come true. I have spent time on that thought, dwelt upon it unbelievingly ... It has been a long time my darling.

In July, Richard Amphlett married them. The wedding dress from Canada was admired. The honeymoon was in Cornwall. High on the Gargano and from Herefordshire hilltops, Michael had watched it all.

15

CHURCH MILITANT

College rules for freshmen arriving at Oxford in their late teens were not easily adapted to war-hardened men in their mid twenties. One of Dad's undergraduate colleagues had commanded an entire battalion. Robert Runcie, back in October to resume his interrupted studies at Brasenose, had recently commanded a tank and won the Military Cross. Hugh Montefiore, completing his degree in theology at St John's, had risen to the rank of captain and fought at Kohima. Going in or out of college after its gates were locked in late evening posed little difficulty for soldiers practised in urban warfare or former members of special forces.

Hugh Montefiore in Burma, 1945

Oxford in 1946 was certainly not used to married students. Stepping backwards out of a telephone box having used all his change in a series of fruitless calls to landlords, Dad turned to find himself face to face with Stuart Blanch. Three years had passed since they were together at Cranwell, and two since they ran into each other in the train. Since then, Stuart had been navigating Dakotas carrying supplies from India to the Fourteenth Army in Burma.

They compared notes. Stuart was at Wycliffe Hall, overlapping his degree course with the theological college training that usually followed the degree. Stuart and Brenda Coyte had married just before he left England, and after two years apart they naturally wanted to be together. Their plan, with help from Brenda's father, was to buy a small house. This made economic sense as the interest repayments on the loan would compare favourably with the cost of rented accommodation, and an equity was being established. Brenda met Dad for the first time. Brenda and Stuart then solved his accommodation problem by proposing that he and Elsie might like to share their house.

So it was, later that year, the newlyweds joined Stuart and Brenda at 62 Wharton Road, in Headington. Here they lived during term, returning to Dad's parents in Birmingham during vacations. The arrangement meant sacrifices and strains for Stuart and Brenda, not least because they would soon be parents, but of these they showed no sign.* The kitchen was small, food rationing was still in force, the budget limited. Occasional food parcels from Canada were a cause for jubilation. Elsie was hesitant about cooking, but Stuart gave her confidence by eating anything she prepared with enthusiastic approval. He also helped Dad in his struggles with New Testament Greek. After I was born, they sometimes pushed one another's prams down to the shops; the fact that Stuart and Dad were both quite tall, dark, and spoke in similar tones occasioned some confusion among neighbours who were not sure which child belonged to which parent. Years later, Wycliffe Hall's Principal, Julian Thornton-Duesbury, observed darkly, 'I often used to wonder what went on at Wharton Road.'

What went on during term was a frenetic series of comings and goings on bicycles, and writing or typing on a large table at the front of the house where Stuart and Dad read books and prepared essays. Towards the end, they even worked during meals, when Brenda and Elsie read out 'gobbets': pieces of biblical text which candidates were required to identify, contextualise, and provide linguistic, textual, or literary comment. Stuart usually knew the answers but did not rush to give them. In a memoir for his biographer, Dad recalled, 'He would wait a bit in case I could take a rare chance to shine. Or, he would air possibilities, trailing a few clues which I might be able to use or make some kind of showing.'

---

* Susan, their first child, was born in December 1946.

What went on, in Dad's case, included politics and the foundation of Christian Action. He joined the Labour Club, became one of its officers, and was periodically deputed to greet visiting speakers. One of those who impressed him was Douglas Jay, who came to speak soon after his appointment as Economic Secretary to the Treasury:

> He arrived, looking lean, keen and rather formidable. By way of breaking the ice I essayed some airy pleasantry about something that had been recently said about the government . . . Fixing me with a piercing eye, he wanted to know instantly who had made this alleged statement, when and where and if I was relaying it correctly. It turned out that I wasn't sure about any of these things. I realised that I was meeting the experienced . . . scholar accustomed to checking the accuracy and provenance of statements, especially airy ones. His speech was not rewarded with the enthusiastic acclaim that would have been accorded, say, to Michael Foot. Nor did it score quite so highly with the undergraduate audience as young Harold Wilson, who . . . came later that term. But his acuity, his knowledge, his authority, were not in doubt.

Socialism and faith came together in the person of Oriel's dean, chaplain, and Dad's tutor: John Collins. Collins was then forty-one and was himself recently demobilised, following five years as an RAF chaplain, latterly at HQ Bomber Command, which had brought an unlikely but in fact largely companionable association between the future chairman of CND and Sir Arthur Harris. Before the war, following ordination in 1928 and a brief curacy at Whitstable in Kent, Collins had served successively as chaplain to Sidney Sussex College, Cambridge, as a minor canon of St Paul's, as vice-principal of Westcott House (1934–1937), and from 1938 as dean of Oriel College, Oxford. This itinerary brought an enduring friendship with Mervyn Stockwood, who had studied at Westcott before beginning his ministry in Bristol. Stockwood in turn brought Collins into the circle of the MP for Bristol South-East, Stafford Cripps, who by 1946 was President of the Board of Trade. Collins returned to Oriel in January that year, and with Cripps and Stockwood sought to develop the thinking of a small group they had formed to work out what a reformed Church might do to help shape the future.*

Membership of the Church Reform Group fluctuated, and since

---

* Members included Cripps's wife, Isobel, the socialist Richard Acland, George Bell (Bishop of Chichester), and Guy Mayfield (rector of St Leonards-on-Sea).

its members held strong but often differing views on priorities, there was a tendency for them to be mutually cancelling. There were other influences. One was the writing of the American theologian Reinhold Niebhur (1892–1971), whose latest book, *The Nature and Destiny of Man* (1943), came into Collins's hands towards the end of 1945. It had a large effect on Collins, and through him, his students. Another was the writer, publisher, and moral idealist Victor Gollancz (1893–1967), who before the war had opposed fascism and Nazism through foundation of the Left Book Club, had warned of the Holocaust while the war was in progress,* and now in its aftermath was organising a scheme to send food to famished Germans. In June 1946, Gollancz published a short book entitled *Our Threatened Values* in which he argued for respect in the way in which enemies are treated. He took the Allies to task for their decisions at Potsdam and muddled policy on German restoration; he called for recognition of the 'essential spiritual quality of all human beings'. *Our Threatened Values* attracted a wide readership, although its reception at the outer edges of the political wings was tepid.† Collins, on the other hand, was galvanised. He gave copies to all his students, a group of whom met weekly with him in his room at the top of Staircase 7:

> Mixed in churchmanship, political leanings and personal priorities we nevertheless committed ourselves to being together regularly as fellow Christian believers. John encouraged us to listen to one another and to share our concerns. Debate was far-ranging and vigorous; the times of prayer we kept went deep. Many of us, including John Collins himself, were recently returned from war service, which gave our meetings a certain maturity. There was a strong tide

---

* Gollancz's pamphlet *Let My People Go* (1942) stated that between one and two million Jews had already been slain in Nazi-held Europe and prophesied that without effective action six million more would die in the near future. A coincidence connected the Holocaust with 60 Squadron and San Severo. Some months before my father's arrival, two of his colleagues-to-be flew a sortie to the I G Farben synthetic rubber plant at Monowitz in Poland. As usual, the navigator started the camera running on approach to the objective, to ensure full coverage. When the photo interpreters at San Severo examined the run-in prints, they had before them the first Allied visual evidence for Auschwitz-Birkenau.

† One Marxist reviewer saw Gollancz as just 'the latest in a long line of non-Marxist socialist moralists', while Colonel Thomas Minshall – whose recent book about what to do with Germany (*Future Germany*, Allen & Unwin, 1943) had reached different conclusions – considered parts of it were grounded in discredited historical analysis.

of idealism flowing, a general desire to see Christian values count in the rebuilding of a war-torn world.

From this fellowship, and its interactions with Gollancz, plans were made for 'A Call to Christian Action in Public Affairs'. The accepted medium for projection of an idea in the 1930s and 1940s was a public meeting, and one was duly organised. Early in June Collins wrote to opinion-formers in Oxford and beyond to seek their support for such an occasion. It would be chaired, he hoped, by George Bell, the outspoken bishop of Chichester, who had opposed Allied bombing of German civilians and fostered links with German Christian resistance to Hitler. Oxford Town Hall was booked for the evening of 5 December. A platform of speakers was assembled: Sir Richard Acland (Church of England), Barbara Ward (Roman Catholic), Roger Wilson (Society of Friends), and Gollancz. George Bell, Bishop of Chichester, agreed to take the chair. Refusals came from the moral theologian and Anglican bishop of Oxford, Kenneth Kirk and the classicist Gilbert Murray.

A leaflet explaining the meeting's purpose was drafted and printed. It called for Christian participation in everyday practical life. It urged active involvement in democratic structures, pressure on government 'for a more Christian policy towards Germany', and the promotion of fellowship with German Christians and Churches. My father was among the members of the Oriel fellowship who trekked around the city on grey November afternoons taking posters and leaflets into shops, newsagents, city parishes, and college common rooms. An undergraduate with rooms lower down Staircase 7 recalls the daily and nightly clump of fellowship members up and down the uncarpeted stairs. Collins and his network organised articles and letters in the local and national press in the week before the meeting. There were hitches. As the meeting neared, Bell came close to withdrawal when Collins refused to accept his wish for a simpler resolution. When Bell wished the meeting to begin with prayer, it was pointed out that Roman Catholics were not permitted to join in prayer with other denominations; Roger Wilson, the Quaker, asked if silent prayer would be acceptable; Collins made a trip to the office of the Roman Catholic archdiocese in Birmingham, which agreed to silent prayer, and the Lord's Prayer in which all could join. Somewhere on the edge of things, maybe St Chad was taking an interest.

In the light of what followed, maybe John Henry Newman (1801–1890) was hovering too. Oriel College was the cradle of the movement to revive the Church of England's Catholic roots that took shape around him in the 1820s and 1830s. Newman held a college fellowship for twenty years; from 1828 to 1843, he was vicar of the university church of St Mary the Virgin, with which Oriel had close connections; he acknowledged the influence of Oriel friends like John Keble and Richard Froude; and when he was received into the Catholic Church in 1845, his links with Oriel were the last to be cut. And of course, when Stuart told Brenda about that 'tug at his throat' when the congregation sang 'Lead Kindly Light' at Ludlow in 1942, Newman was the hymn's author.

It rained hard on the afternoon of Thursday 5 December. Nonetheless, by 6.30 pm a queue had begun to form outside the Town Hall. The thorough preparation had paid off. By 8 pm, the hall was jam-packed. 'Crowds Mob Town Hall' ran the headline in the next day's *Daily Mail*: 'Struggling crowds swarmed to a "Call to Christian Action" meeting at Oxford Town Hall last night . . . Despite the rain crowds who could not get in would not disperse until it was announced that the speakers would address an overflow meeting.' Richard Milford, Newman's heir as vicar of the university church on the High Street, offered it as a second venue. St Mary's, too, was soon full. Hundreds were turned away. A double meeting ensued: having addressed one audience, each speaker then walked to the other and did it again. By all accounts, they rose to the occasion.

Around three thousand people either attended the meetings or attempted to do so. A number who were there have spoken of it as life-changing. The impact had a lot to do with the make-up of the audience. As Collins's wife Diana saw, these were not 'innocent idealistic young men full of Utopian illusions: many were ex-Servicemen, and those too young or ineligible to fight would have known loss, fear and disruption of family life. There was no one there who would not, in some degree, have been scarred by six years of war.' In my father's case, it was from this event that much of the momentum of his ministry flowed.

As Christian Action evolved, Britain's economy worsened, and the first hard frosts of the Cold War settled. The following year, Collins visited the British Zone of Occupation in Germany and saw things for himself. Aside from hunger and ill-health, huge numbers of homeless refugees were arriving by the day, while the Allies' policy of destroying undamaged factories stood economic logic on its head. Moving to Berlin, Collins looked for ways to further Anglo-German reconciliation. On an impulse, he invited the Berlin Philharmonic Orchestra to tour Britain.

The tempo quickened. A sold-out meeting at the Albert Hall to rally Christian support for European unity heard from German and French speakers as well as British politicians. A Christian Action Sunday was arranged from which parish church collections were put towards the organisation's work. They campaigned for the accelerated repatriation of German prisoners-of-war, over a quarter of a million of whom in mid 1947 were still in Britain. An anniversary meeting in the Sheldonian again attracted a capacity audience, which once more heard from Gollancz. 'Christian Action is one year old this week,' wrote James Leasor in the *Daily Mail.* 'It was born last December in Dean Collins's study, in Oriel College, where over a century ago Keble, Newman, and Pusey started the great Oxford Movement. A group of ex-Service under-graduates banded themselves together with the intention of making Christian principles mean something in everyday life . . . They are tired of talk and technicalities. They want action.'

The kind of action Stafford Cripps wanted was a national movement to realise his dream of a Christian Socialist Britain in which social justice and personal freedom could flourish side by side. Such a development would require a platform in London, and when a canonry became vacant at St Paul's he saw an opportunity: the post was a Crown appointment; Cripps prompted Attlee to propose Collins for the vacancy. Attlee's suggestion was not welcomed by Archbishop Fisher, who correctly forecast that Collins would devote much of his energy to matters beyond the cathedral, and it irked the dean and chapter because they were not consulted about it at all. But Attlee stuck to his guns, and on 25 June 1948 – around the time Dad was taking his final exams – Attlee wrote to Collins to ask if he would allow his name to go forward.

Collins's wife, Diana, was aghast. Since the end of 1946, they had been living in a college house in a semi-rural enclave off the Cowley Road. Oriel's recreation ground lay to one side, an orchard and meadow to the other; the site had been occupied by a medieval hospital; a fourteenth-century chapel stood in the garden. After separation and disruption through the war, their family life at this place had been 'entirely happy'. The thought of exchanging it for a dark, rundown canonry in the City left her downhearted. Collins hesitated. Having weighed things up, he was poised to decline. However, just as my father was often unable to do justice to his studies while working to heed the prophetic word of his tutor, so was his tutor finding it increasingly difficult to combine his college duties with the furtherance of Christian Action. In his heart, too, Collins had begun to realise that he 'no longer belonged, if ever he really had, in the theological ivory tower of Oxford or Cambridge; he had studied and speculated with the best of them; now was the time to act'. Collins told Attlee that he would let his name go forward. The appointment was confirmed: he would leave Oriel after Christmas.

Attlee's nomination letter to Collins was written the day after the start of the Berlin Airlift. The Soviet blockade of Berlin was but one in a grinding series of hindrances – political, financial, bureaucratic, the Ministry of Labour – that had to be overcome to bring its orchestra to Britain. Among them was an eleventh-hour intervention by the archdeacon of London, who stymied Collins's wish that the orchestra's tour should begin in St Paul's by declaring that it would be wrong to charge for tickets.* By then, programmes had been printed and there was wide advertising in the press. The archdeacon and canons further insisted that the dean and chapter be reimbursed for any costs arising. As a business model, this was not promising. The venue was switched to the acoustically poor Empress Hall in Earl's Court.† The Musicians Union refused to attend, saying that the gesture of reconciliation was unwelcome and that the orchestra's view of the tour as a contribution to the rehabilitation of Europe amounted to scab labour.

The Berlin Philharmonic came with no music (the Red Army had burned it) and only one evening shirt between them. The press encouraged audience members to dress down to avoid embarrassing them. But amid the Empress Hall's glitzy sergeant commissionaires, fancy lighting, ornamental ropes, red-carpeted dais, and the glimmer of smokers' match-strikes, when Wilhelm Furtwängler and Myra Hess turned to face the audience, hand in hand, at the end of Beethoven's Fourth Piano Concerto, everyone in the hall knew that something had changed.

John Collins took up his duties at St Paul's in January 1949. He was already thinking of more cultural exchanges – the Passion Players from Oberammergau, say, or artists from Moscow. Diana records that he looked forward to his first meeting of the cathedral chapter but was downcast when the greater part of it was devoted to a dispute between

---

* The tour itinerary was organised with help from Collins's friend Emmie Tillett, of Ibbs and Tillett. Alongside relatively easily organised destinations like Oxford it included provincial places like Huddersfield, Leicester, and Wolverhampton; regional centres like Newcastle; and national venues in Wales and Scotland.

† *The Times*'s music critic afterwards described the Empress Hall as 'no fit place for music' and reacted to the performance with large artistic reservations.

the archdeacon and the senior canon as to which of them should take precedence in public processions.

My father, meanwhile, had completed his degree at Oxford and moved to prepare for ordination at Westcott House in Cambridge. There were many reasons for going there. Collins had recommended it. Several Oxford friends were either, like Hugh Montefiore, already at Westcott or, like Robert Runcie, about to be. Westcott had a record for placing its ordinands in curacies where they were needed, often in northern industrial and inner-city parishes. There was also the pastoral and theological reputation of Brooke Foss Westcott (1825–1901), after whom the college was named. The college began as the Cambridge Clergy Training School in 1881, when the Church of England was increasingly riven by Evangelical–Tractarian conflict. Westcott had no truck with dogmatism. For him, truth was often greater than our ability to perceive it; it followed that a doctrinal system claiming to know everything must be inconsistent with the spirit of scripture. God-given intellect was for hard thinking, not to be neglected through empty faith or intransigence.

In 1948, there was still plenty of intransigence. Two years before – in fact, just five days before the great meeting in Oxford Town Hall – *Picture Post* carried a feature headlined 'The Battle Within the Church' which reported on the planning of a demonstration against High Church ritual during a service in the church of St Colomb, Notting Hill. The magazine's photographer was duly rewarded when some of the demonstrators were assaulted by members of the congregation. 'For what cause does the National Union of Protestants stage scenes in churches and break up services?' asked *Picture Post*. 'Is it only a quarrel over ceremony, or does it go deeper?'*

It went deeper. One obvious thing about the members of the National Union of Protestants who appeared in *Picture Post* was that they were all men. All the ordinands at Wescott House were men as well. A good many were staunch supporters of the ordination of women, and would live to see this come about – albeit forty-six years later, and even then, leaving unfinished business. The decision to admit women to the priesthood taken in 1992 did not extend to women bishops, and in the ensuing wrangling that lasted – incredibly – for another two decades, the real oppositional heft 'came not from the Anglo-Catholics but from conservative evangelicals who believed that the Bible mandated patriarchy'.

---

* *Picture Post*, 30 November 1946, 21–24.

The idealistic young campaigners for Christian action and social justice half a century before were slow to see the full extent of what was perhaps the largest, at least the most general, injustice of all. But then, if you are up close against something enormous, its outlines are out of sight. At 62 Wharton Road, the disciplined attention that Stuart gave to his studies and led to his first-class degree, and my father's immersion in Christian socialism were enabled by Brenda and Elsie who cooked their meals, tackled the household chores, washed the clothes and nappies, or mended the socks while they were out. Diana Collins enabled her husband to go to St Paul's by agreeing to exchange the house and surroundings she loved for a half-derelict canonry with no electricity above the ground floor. Before that, when Collins came home late in the evening and told her about events at this or that meeting, she yearned to roll up her sleeves and join them. For every parson in a slum parish or a vicarage he could not afford to heat or furnish, as often as not there was a wife who wished either that she could do the job herself or that her family was living somewhere else. In the next chapter, we will arrive in such a place.

16

DOWN JESUS LANE

I was one when we arrived in Cambridge and not yet three when we left. Nothing of it sticks, and since my parents were together for most of the time it was not a period when they wrote many letters to each other. All that survived when we emptied Dad's house were photographs, some lecture notes, and a bundle of letters written during his last term, when he lived in college before his ordination on Trinity Sunday 1950.

Nonetheless, there is still a kind of nearness about the place. References to its people and events kept cropping up. There was a sense that it had been happy: *Always in June* (1949), *Come What May* (1950); in family memory, Westcott House was as cloudless as the days called back in titles of Cambridge's May Week Footlights shows.[*]

Perhaps that had something to do with where it stood. Westcott House is on Jesus Lane, opposite Jesus College, which lies inside a loop of the River Cam that encloses the great adjoining meadows of Jesus Green, Midsummer Common, and Butt Green. Westcott's outlook is thus onto *rus in urbe*, and if the meander of the Cam is taken as a semicircle, for most of its length Jesus Lane runs more or less along its diameter. A walk along it touches familiar themes.

In the thirteenth century, when the University was young, Cambridge on the map looked a bit like a swarm of bees hanging from a branch. The branch was a former Roman road which ran from south-east to north-west.[†] To either side of the bridge over the river the bees cling tightly to the branch, but further south they hang in a plumper, bag-like form

---

[*] Cambridge's 'May Week', actually a fortnight, is a time of inter-college boat races, balls, and other festivities that follows the end of University examinations and culminates in the term's end when undergraduates leave for the summer, or for the rest of their lives.

[†] South of the Cam this was known as the Hadestokweye, which became the Huntingdoneweye to the north.

between the river and the road,* where streets and housing were at their thickest. Jesus Lane struck off from the axial road very roughly at the town's midpoint. A traveller walking along it towards Newmarket in the thirteenth century would very soon leave the town behind. After four hundred yards or so, the road crossed a watercourse and passed out into town fields. To the north, in an area known as Grenecroft, was a nunnery dedicated to St Radegund – which is why the road was then variously known as Nuns' Lane and Venella Radegundis (Radegund's Lane).†

A walker turning into Jesus Lane from Sidney Street today finds Sidney Sussex College in the angle between the two. The college was formed in 1596, on the site of the former Greyfriars: the order of Franciscan friars, who like their founder Francis of Assisi (1181/2–1226) renounced worldly goods and aimed their mission at the poor. Being latecomers on the monastic scene, friaries tended to be on the edge of things – on barren ground, in suburbs, or, as here, on the fringe of a built-up area – where the urban poor scratched their livings and the wealthy dumped their waste. The relationship between the world, its goods, the needy, and salvation looms large in the Gospels and pre-occupied medieval theologians, some of whom arrived at a view in which poverty became idealised. However, moving along Jesus Lane for another four hundred yards, the Wesley House training college on the left reminds us of a different perspective: by the nineteenth century, thinking about poverty had moved on from the distribution of alms to tackling poverty's root causes. Wesley himself was abolitionist; Wesleyan Methodism drew in champions of women's rights, did practical things for social and penal reform, promoted adult education and schooling.

Westcott House comes up on the right after another hundred yards. Before going in, look across the road to the Fellows Garden of Jesus College and recall that the college grew out of St Radegund's nunnery. It did so because John Alcock (1430–1500), bishop of Ely from 1486 to 1500, found the convent in poor shape, had it dissolved, and extended the university by putting a college for six priest-fellows and 'a certain number of boys' in its place. Alcock takes us back, for it was he who in 1486 baptised the infant Arthur, Henry VII's first son. He strove to

---

* The axial road at this point was then known as Condightstrete; today, Sidney Street.

† Radegunda (c.520–587): a princess, wife of the Frankish king Clotaire, founder of the religious house of Saint-Croixe at Poitiers c.560.

renew religion from within rather than through radical reform.* His reputation for self-restraint, keeping vigils, and victory over temptation is interesting to compare with his chantry chapel in Ely cathedral. Like Arthur's chapel at Worcester, it is a stone cage, its stellate vault 'a shower that never falls', intensely personal, delicately cut, and very expensive. None of that was needed for priests to sing daily masses for his soul, so it may be asked: what was its audience? Was it believed that a mass sung in such lavish surroundings would count for more as a unit of merit? Was it for God's pleasure?

Westcott House's tradition was rooted in a belief that close engagement with scripture and sacramental life should be entwined with vigorous, prophetic interaction with the world. The institution started in various premises and rented rooms, and moved to Jesus Lane in 1899. Over the next thirty years, it was provided with a hall (1903), rooms (1914), a chapel and library (1924), and more rooms (1929). The buildings – red brick with stone dressings, of two storeys with attics; a central gatehouse, oriels, courts – hint at Tudors and the sixteenth-century world of Anglican origins.

Without knowing it, my father's arrival coincided with the start of a notable period in the history of Anglican training. Westcott House had a new Principal, Ken Carey, who on the surface was conservative and restrained, in Runcie's view could be 'good company' and was an 'enormous influence on people', and in cynics' eyes was better known for what he was not – neither Anglo-Catholic nor evangelical, unacademic, self-effacing – than what he was. Another student recalls their first meeting:

> His study was at the end of a short passage with a notice on the door which read either 'free' or 'busy'. When I first went in he was standing by the fireplace which had a mantle shelf crowded with a variety of little animals. He was wearing a dog collar, but for the rest, baggy shapeless flannel trousers, a woolly pullover and an old blazer. He had a boyish wrinkled face with a mole, twinkling eyes, a shy uncertain smile, and a cigarette.

Carey, a good listener, had an eye for able staff; under his modest yet

---

* Radical reformers themselves admired his spirituality. The evangelical Protestant controversialist John Bale (1495–1563) described Alcock as one who had 'devoted himself from childhood to learning and piety, made such a proficiency in virtue that no one in England had a greater reputation for sanctity'.

richly networked oversight, he and Westcott House made a noteworthy contribution to the Anglican episcopate of the 1970s and 1980s.

Westcott was pervaded by an 'obviously homosexual atmosphere' of which Runcie professed to be unaware ('I was amazingly ignorant about the gay world'), and which Dad never mentioned, perhaps because for most of the time he was living out on the other side of town in Shaftesbury Road. But other students were very conscious of it. One of them was Vic Whitsey, later to be Runcie's suffragan at St Albans and the Bishop of Chester, who protested in Westcott's termly bulletin, the *Record*: 'Do you belong to Athens or Jerusalem?'

Many of those at Westcott in 1948 had fought in the war. Among them were Patrick Campbell Rodger (1920–2002), future bishop of Manchester and Oxford and ecumenist, who had served in the Royal Corps of Signals; Robert Runcie (1921-2000), wiry, slim, sandy-haired, a gifted mimic, raconteur, future Archbishop of Canterbury, who in 1954 returned to Westcott as its chaplain; and his friend Bill Vanstone (1923-1999), who like Dad had served in the RAF, and not only flown Mosquitos but survived a crash in one. Vanstone, stocky, black-haired, working-class, was regarded as the most academically gifted Anglican clergyman of his day, but evaded all efforts to steer him into an academic post. Instead, following ordination he worked first in Bolton, and then, flat out, on a housing estate at Kirkholt in Rochdale for the next 21 years. Runcie described Vanstone as his 'hero'.

And then there was Simon Phipps (1921–2001), who in April 1945 had been awarded the Military Cross for heroism while leading a company of Guards to capture a canal bridge near Comacchio. As the company moved forward, Phipps stepped on a land mine. While being treated in hospital during the last days of the European war, Dad was overhead, on sorties to photograph the few square miles of the shrinking Reich. Such overlapping experiences made for a special kind of solidarity. Self-discipline learned during military service was rechannelled; the experience of destruction fed desire to build. When Phipps was asked why he had offered himself for ordination, he gave the immediate reply, 'Because I'd loved being a soldier and being a priest was like being a soldier – only more so. I could care for a wider range of people as a priest.'

Phipps, educated at Eton, epitomised the interrelated world of public schools, Oxbridge Colleges, and born-to-rule family connections from which many at Westcott came. Being born to rule also meant being born to serve. His father was a naval officer, who in 1937 was appointed a Gentleman Usher to George VI. Through him Phipps was introduced to the young princesses, Elizabeth and Margaret, and was approved by the then Queen Elizabeth (afterwards, the Queen Mother) as a suitable companion for them. Weekends at Balmoral with amateur dramatics and charades ensued. Following Elizabeth's engagement and marriage to Philip Mountbatten, he became a frequent escort of Princess Margaret at social events and balls. In society pages of local and national newspapers, he can be glimpsed slipping away from Cambridge to join her for a 'quiet informal weekend' with the Duke and Duchess of Buccleuch at Boughton House, or with Peter Townsend and the family of Captain J. H. F. McEwen at Marchmont House in the Scottish Borders. Gossip columnists speculated. Margaret made private visits to see Phipps at Westcott House.

Simon Phipps (right foreground), with Wescott friends Elsie and John Morris (centre foreground) and visiting Princess Margaret, 1949

A likely reason why Phipps and Margaret hit it off is that he was very funny. Phipps was spontaneous, a natural entertainer, and gifted lyricist. By the time my father met him, he was already a legend, having become President of the Footlights while studying history at Trinity. Performance ran in the family – Joyce Grenfell was a cousin; Hermione Gingold used his material in West End shows; *The Stage* reported on his 'witty and pungent lyrics'; the BBC broadcast excerpts from his shows. Julian Slade, then an undergraduate, later known for *Salad Days* (1954), considered him one of the best lyricists of his generation. 'Original sin', written while at Westcott, is an example:

> What can be done that's the least bit new
> That's never been done before?
> Wouldn't it be nice to discover a vice
> That isn't a terrible bore?
>
> I long to break out and make a sortie
> Into the world and be wildly naughty . . .
>
> I've tried them singly and mixed up in a medley,
> But those seven old sins are so absolutely deadly . . .
> Oh there must be another and I just can't wait
> Until I've discovered Number Eight –
>
> Can anyone think of an original sin?
> Can someone please tell me where to begin?
>
> Anger and Avarice have both been tried;
> So have Gluttony, Sloth and Pride;
> That only leaves us with Envy and Lust
> But there *must* be something more amusing! *Really* there must!
>
> Something with a twist that's gay and gorgeous,
> Never even contemplated by the Borgias.
>
> Of course, I suppose that I could –
> Be good.

The composer for most of Phipps's songs was Trinity College's chaplain, Geoffrey Beaumont, around whom undergraduates liked to gather for evening singalongs in the course of which Beaumont thumped the piano 'while cigarette ash tumbled unheeded down his cassock (a spare hand waving one towards a gin bottle)'.* Their best-known collaboration, performed both in West End shows and at college revues, was 'Botticelli Angel', in which a demure young angel, bored stiff in a painting, pleads for release from immortality and demands a noisy night on the town. On stage, Phipps, haloed, in a nightie, with small harp,

---

* Phipps also collaborated with the composer and precentor of Gonville and Caius, Peter Tranchell, who orchestrated some of Beaumont's numbers and wrote music for several more, including 'Heaven' – 'Won't it be heaven in heaven, having a heavenly time!' (1954).

was wont to step out of the picture frame for the upbeat part of the song in which Beaumont's music launches into stride piano. Dad asked Beaumont for a copy of the score. I can visualise it: blue ink, on a sheet of manuscript paper that became ever more fragile and creased as it was curated from one parish entertainment to the next.

Geoffrey Beaumont singing with rock-and-roll musicians in a Soho coffee bar, April 1959

Another of Phipps's projects was a production at Westcott House in 1949 of Shaw's *Androcles and the Lion*, in which Robert Runcie played Caesar and Bill Vanston was cast as Androcles. When Runcie was asked if he thought that the casting reflected Phipps's 'interpretation of their respective characters', he replied: 'Very much so.'

After a three-year curacy in Huddersfield, Phipps was invited back to Trinity to succeed Beaumont as its chaplain. (This itinerary, a kind of convection current – starry undergraduate career, curacy somewhere industrial, back to Oxbridge, on to greater things – is familiar.*) In April 1953, Peter Townsend asked Princess Margaret to marry him. During the ensuing turmoil, it was to Phipps she most often turned for counsel and support. Their friendship lasted. After his appointment as

---

* Beaumont, meanwhile, had gone to be vicar of St George's, Camberwell, where Trinity College had a Mission to which its undergraduates contributed their time in the summer and Christmas vacations: 'Besides undertaking edifying tasks, those of us who came to Camberwell from Cambridge would prepare an entertainment to be given at the Mission at the end of the visit.' Afterwards, Beaumont and Phipps would accompany them from pub to pub around the parish.

industrial chaplain to the Diocese of Coventry in 1958 (a role for which he prepared himself by working in a car factory), his neighbours grew accustomed to the Princess's unannounced arrivals at his council flat, for lunch or supper.*

Stepping back into Jesus Lane, we arrive at one of England's greatest buildings: the parish church of All Saints, built early in the 1860s to the design of George Frederick Bodley (1827–1907).† All Saints is wondrous partly because of what happens when you walk in: as the door opens, you are seared by light, colours, textures, stencilled walls, and roof beams a-gleam with golden suns. The other part is what this means. In 1839, a society had been formed in Cambridge to pursue the idea that Anglo-Catholic reform of the kind being promoted by Newman and his friends could be combined with the virtue inherent in Gothic architecture to recover a lost quality of spiritual-mindedness that had existed in the Middle Ages. The society's founders (John Mason Neal, Benjamin Webb, and Alexander Hope) reasoned that if Catholic ethics had given rise to Catholic – that is, Gothic – architecture, then England could be restored to its former spiritual-mindedness by a reverse-engineered process in which contact with Gothic would restore Catholic ethics. Newman suggested that contemporary architects should develop Gothic, and early essays often did so; here, however, Bodley was moving to a polished historicism, selecting pure English medieval forms that recollected what was going on in the mid fourteenth century. Why?‡ The presence of so much Arts and Crafts work inside (glass, stencilling, woodwork, furniture) invites an answer to do with human scale,

---

* Following the Princess's marriage to Anthony Armstrong Jones, Phipps was a godparent to their first child.

† All Saints began in Cambridge's Jewry, by the junction between High Street and Pylateslane, its tower poised on arches above the street. By the 1850s, it was too small for its worshippers, and its obstructive position led to a decision to remove it to Jesus Lane. Formally, All Saints and Westcott House originally had nothing to do with each other, although it has been pointed out that the college looks like a cloister to the church. The church was made redundant in 1973 (cf. Chapter 5) and is now cared for by the Churches Conservation Trust.

‡ In an important article ('The Rise of Refinement: G. F. Bodley's All Saints, Cambridge, and the Return to English Models in Gothic Architecture of the 1860s', *Architectural History*, 36, 1993, 103–126) Michael Hall points out that the answer did not lie with his patrons, who included William Whewell of Trinity College, and the Master of Jesus, George Corrie, an off-the-planet conservative who was opposed to advanced views of either Tractarian or Evangelical kind, and to university reform.

individuality, and 'a unique link between Anglo-Catholicism and the anglo-aestheticism of Morris and his friends'.

However it came about, All Saints, Jesus Lane, helped to establish a dominant ecclesiological idea of Englishness centred in the imagined world of Edward III. 'Imagined', because no authentic fourteenth-century interior looked like this. As we have seen, much of the terminology used by ecclesiologists and ritualists to describe and analyse the appearance and layout of medieval parish churches was of their own invention, while the Catholic models to which they looked for example were post-Tridentine interiors that in many respects bore no relation to pre-Reformation churches.

Last scene of all. Anglo-Catholicism combined a rarefied upper-class piety with concern for the poor; like the friars and poverty, the two needed each other, and it was to a slum that Dad went for his first curacy. Early in 1950, Ken Carey put him in touch with Ernest Barnes, the eugenicist Bishop of Birmingham, and Barnes introduced him to Martin Cooper, the rector of St George's Great Hampton Row in the Hockley district of inner Birmingham. The area, impoverished before the war, had been badly bombed in 1940–1941, and parts of the parishes of several burned-out churches had been amalgamated with St George's. Cooper was a young rector who had served as a padre in the Parachute Regiment during the latter part of the war.* He and my father got on well, and it was agreed that Dad would join the parish as curate following his ordination in Birmingham cathedral on Trinity Sunday.

Trinity Sunday in 1950 fell on 4 June. The day before, my father took the bus to Wychbold to visit Amphlett. Seven years had passed since their first meeting, and Amphlett had guided many of his steps between. Now the day had come – although, true to form, there was a last-minute crisis. Two weeks before, it was realised that the parsonage on New John Street West which had been earmarked for the newly ordained Rev John Morris and his family was already occupied, and that it would take several months to organise a handover. In the meantime, the rector offered to accommodate us in part of his own rectory. The news threw my parents into depression: for years they had lived as lodgers in other people's houses; they longed to be on their own; what little furniture they had was piling up in Dad's parents' semi in Northfield. There was a

---

* The Korean War began three weeks after my father's ordination. Cooper was still a reservist, and in 1951 became apprehensive that he would be called back.

brief discussion about postponing ordination, but since this would not solve the problem the only real reason for doing so would be to chasten the diocesan administrators for their oversight. Amphlett, meanwhile, had accommodation problems of his own. Wychbold Hall had become run down during the war, his ageing mother and a sister were unable to run it themselves, and he had found it difficult to recruit staff to look after the house and grounds in his absence. Five years later, it was sold, at the same time as Amphlett's marriage to the divorcee Joan Gibbs roused opposition akin to that shown by Archbishop Fisher towards Princess Margaret and Peter Townsend. Amphlett gave up his parish and turned to school-mastering, while helping out as an honorary curate in Edgbaston. Thus did a branch of Worcestershire's gentry and a committed ministry melt away.

The parsonage, when eventually we moved into it, stood on the north side of New John Street West, between Summer Lane and Hospital Street. It was surrounded by courts of back-to-backs (more on these later) and specialised metalworking concerns like the Reliance Spring Company, the Crown and Phoenix Nail and Tube Works (on Brass Street), the Bristol Lamp and Stove Works, and Sheffco Tools and Files. A late-Victorian Sunday school and parish room adjoined the parsonage on one side; on the other was an asphalt yard bordered by the Box Carton factory, from the windows of which, in scenes reminiscent of *Carmen*, friendly girls with their hair tied up in turbans would lean out for a smoke during breaks.

A church stood back from New John Street behind the Sunday school. It was a plain brick building which had been put up as a Presbyterian church in the 1850s, converted to Anglican use as a mission church in 1896, and bombed in 1941. When we left it was still there, open to the sky, awaiting demolition. On some evenings, looking up at its gaunt silhouette, I imagined I could hear singing.

The vicarage had been built earlier in the twentieth century and escaped the Blitz. It was enormous, with vast rooms that seemed all the larger because my parents had so little furniture to put into them. In layout, thinking back, it had features in common with Longbridge and Sanderstead, most notably the public–private interface of a large central hall from which a study and family rooms led off in different directions. Its spaces were almost impossible to heat, and I have clear memories of looking at my hands and seeing them blue. But whereas we had too much space, those around us had too little.

Between New John Street West and St George's, tiny houses were packed around yards known as courts. A court was formed by several houses fronting the street, with more joined together around the three sides of a yard behind which you reached through a narrow tunnel. A yard was usually paved with blue bricks and used by children for games of football (old newspaper rolled into a ball), tipcat, or kick the can. Upwards of a dozen households, around fifty people, lived around a yard, sharing half a dozen outside lavatories and several doorless wash houses (known as 'bruhus'), where water was heated over brick-mounted coppers and women took turns to wash family laundry. A rent man called each week to collect cash from each family. No one knew to whom the rent went. The area was quite rich in shops and trade. There were several butchers, bakers, and greengrocers with open shop fronts nearby, and mobile hawkers sold fruit, vegetables, and winkles (by the pint). For dreams and entertainment, there were cinemas within walking distance in Newtown Row, Snow Hill, and Great Hampton Street, and a music hall: the Aston Hippodrome.

New John Street was within earshot of Big Brum, the clock over Birmingham's council house that told the hours, and Dad made a point of getting to know council politicians. Among them was Frank Price, who was to be a key figure in the modernist redevelopment of Birmingham in the later 1950s and 1960s.* Price was then twenty-eight, a toolmaker and former Young Communist who the year before had been elected to Birmingham City Council for the St Paul's ward – an event to which his employer, who had not expected him to win, responded with his dismissal.

Frank was born in a back-to-back court on New John Street, and while he later showed great affection for Hockley's working-class culture, his concern for social reform was fuelled by a lasting rage at the deprivation and indignity with which he had grown up. His anger extended to the Church of England, following a childhood incident when the incumbent of St Matthias, Farm Street, who made no secret of his dislike for his parishioners, hit him in the face for missing a choir practice. This notwithstanding, he and Dad struck up a working friendship. One of the projects on which they collaborated was the week-long carnival organised in the summer of 1952 to raise funds for the repair of St George.

---

* Shortly after his election as a member of the Public Works Committee, he came to the notice of Birmingham's City Engineer, Herbert Manzoni, who mentored him in planning law, policy, and theory. When the Committee's chairman resigned in 1953, Price was nominated as his successor.

'Carnival Capers' had its own newspaper, the eight-page *St George's Hard Times*, a spoof tabloid with a front-page headline 'PARSONS WHO SAY: "FLOG THE PEOPLE"' alongside caricatures of the rector and curate dressed as spivs:

> While stacking some lead on his barrow, the Rev Martin Cooper said yesterday: 'It stands to reason that in these days you've got to flog something to live. We've tried flogging everything, including the lead off the church roof. Now there's nothing left except the people. So we must flog the people.'
>
> Asked if agreed with this, the Rev John Morris, who was busy sorting nylons, said: 'I'll flog anyfink.'

Five thousand copies were printed by the *Birmingham Mail*, for sale on the street and in pubs. For some days, there were street rehearsals, with a troupe of dancing girls on a lorry, burlesque psalm singing, and a pair of trouserless policemen (the rector and curate) to hustle, harass, and generally hinder the procession. When the main day came, the procession ended at a fete opened by Birmingham's speedway champion.

Advertised as 'the best Church show since Nero threw the Christians to the lions', Carnival Capers prompted a succession of newspaper stories and photographs and a feature on the front page of the *Birmingham News* on the day of the show itself.

The exuberance, involvement of local people, and the sight of two Anglican clergy keen to make fools of themselves caused a stir. It is clear from clerical reaction that nothing quite like it had happened before. Some clergy were aghast. Readers of the Birmingham *Gazette* were told, 'Criticism is mounting against the Hockley clergymen who are responsible for the fundraising revue, "Carnival Capers", which is being staged at Aston Hippodrome on Saturday.' Parsons objected to rehearsals in the street, the enthusiasm, depiction of clergy wide boys in *St George's Hard Times*, and its use of signed pin-up photos contributed by Dinah Sheridan and an eighteen-year-old Joan Collins. One vicar told the press, 'These are cheap-jack methods; they are degrading.' There was talk of disciplinary action, until it was realised that no machinery for such action existed – and that, in any case, the archdeacon of Birmingham was away.

The unnamed clerics who said that laughter was unbecoming and protested at antics in the street had forgotten the Coventry Mystery Plays, and the Gospels. 'Botticelli Angel' was one of the items in the show at the Aston Hippodrome. Alongside Frank Price's socialism, here was another kind of revolution. And looking at the cuttings, I think of that letter, written in the tent at San Severo: 'There is something exciting about an empty hall filled with empty seats, ready for a performance of a play or the holding of a meeting or a religious ceremony. "Give me a village hall and some chairs" I thought, "and I shall be perfectly happy." Think of the things we could do!'

John Morris with his son, Richard, beside the parsonage on
New John Street West, Hockley, 1951

17

EVENING PRAYER

H and sanitiser is the new holy water. Lines of yellow hazard tape run at two-metre intervals across the aisles. A friendly masked lady takes our name and telephone number. It is Sunday 11 October 2020, and the first choral evensong we have attended since March.

We are in the congregation because the choir is limited to six. An ordinary evensong choir would be about twenty strong, but six is the maximum allowed. They stand far apart, which makes performance difficult, because when they sing they can barely hear each other.

The congregation is not permitted to sing at all, but since it is scarcely thrice the size of the choir, it would not make much noise if it did. Anglican congregations are characterised by a kind of magnetic repulsion, whereby the fewer members are present the further away from each other they will sit. On this evening, one gentleman bucks this by putting himself as close to us as he can get. He is the one with the ominous cough.

In summer 1944, this was where Dad came to evensong while he waited to go to war. As 6.30 approaches I wonder where he sat. I think of others like Bill Vanstone, Simon Phipps and Nicolas Stacey who committed their lives to the Church when they came back. I think of George Bell and his work on behalf of German refugees and post-war reconciliation. And I realise that since the 1990s, one by one, their reputations have been trashed. In 2020 Vanstone was censured for failing to ensure the investigation of child abuse allegations against his old Westcott friend, Vic Whitsey, who for all his championing of Jerusalem against Athens at Westcott has since been found to have committed 'appalling acts' against children, teenagers and vulnerable adults; Phipps, for speaking on behalf of a member of his clergy who had admitted indecent assault; Stacey, for his insistence that staff in Kent Social Services refer care home abuse allegations to him before reporting them to the police, and the way this has since mapped onto understanding of the Kendall House scandal; Bell, as victim of posthumous allegations compounded by bungled handling for which the Church has since apologised. Such happenings form a kind of distorting lens through which Vanstone's dedication to equity and fairness, Stacey's pioneering of professional fostering, and Bell's prophetic work for peace are all diminished, while censure and allegation crowd the foreground.

The service starts. There is something odd about a socially distanced, masked choir moving in procession. Whatever it is, the music moves us on. John, our organist, is a musician of exceptional gifts, one of which is the ability to colour the words of psalms and hymns with different voices and textures. I think back to his evocation of the burning chariot in March. He's at it again this evening with Psalm 103, wherein 'the days of man are but as grass: for he flourisheth as a flower of the field. For as soon as the wind goeth over it, it is gone: and the place thereof shall know it no more.'

The psalmist might have had coronavirus in mind with these words, but I guess they are not the kind of thing that those who organise drop-in café churches want to hear. Drop-ins, you recall, are for people who want to connect in a way that 'doesn't mean we have to visit a different planet'. During the *Nunc Dimittis* (Walmisley in D minor), I wonder how replacing liturgy with the everyday helps your search for what lies beyond the everyday.

The Collect for Trinity 18 reminds us how much we have missed the Church's seasons. In the choir stalls, year after year, you get to know these sweeps and moments wherein the history of the world and life of Christ are annually retraced. Trinity is a long haul, a kind of trek across ordinary time towards Advent Sunday when the wheel turns, 'The tortoise stove is lit again', and the Collect asks God to put upon us the armour of light.

The anthem is John Joubert's setting of 'O Lord, the Maker of All Thing'. Its words are from a metrical translation of the Compline hymn '*Te lucis ante terminum*', which is where we began, among the night prayers, where a day can stand for your life, or your life can be the history of the world. Only sixteen years separated the translation (1545) from Thomas Tallis's tune for the final hymn (1561). The Reformation came between and changed the ways in which congregations experienced them.

John the organist often becomes inventive in the last verses of hymns, improvising descants and new harmony – which might be skittish, or daring, or lavish. On this evening, he adds nothing; Tallis's notes speak for themselves. The hymn is another echo of Compline:

> Keep me, O keep me, King of kings,
> Beneath thy own almighty wings.

For a moment, I recall my parents saying Compline together, four thousand miles apart; or myself back in the chapel at Wadderton, with furry moths bumping against the windows, waiting for the verse from Psalm 17:

> *Minister:* Keep me as the apple of an eye.
> *Us:* Hide me under the shadow of thy wings.

Since we were at Blackwell, most of the moths have gone. Oak lutestring, frosted green, brown-spot pinion, flounced rustic, cloaked minor, Webb's wainscot, small waved umber, pale brindled beauty – a terrible requiem is in their names. The ultimate tragedy of Genesis 1.28 is not that God told man and woman to subdue the earth and have dominion over every living thing that moves upon it, but that it set them and nature apart. It still does. When Reinhold Niebuhr wrote that 'Human existence is obviously distinguished from animal life by its qualified participation in creation. Within limits it breaks the forms of nature and creates new configurations of vitality', he was wrong. In his next sentence – 'Its transcendence over natural process offers it the opportunity of interfering with the established forms and unities of vitality as nature knows them' – he was right. However, as the historian Paul Betts points out, where the identification of civilisation with Christianity is narrowed through association with populist conservatism, it brings with it a propensity towards scepticism about secular science, and in particular the science of climate change which challenges the contemporary material culture of Western societies. Diocesan environmental officers and the General Synod's energy footprint tool notwithstanding, until we challenge Genesis 1.27 – 'So God created man in his own image, in the image of God created he them' – ecological collapse is assured.

Nor is all straightforward on the dominion front. Three weeks later, on All Hallows Eve, when families think of their forebears, the Prime Minister again orders the closure of playgrounds, libraries, gyms, pubs, and restaurants. Congregational worship stops. A reduced choir, relayed online, sings to an empty church. Next day is the feast of All Saints, who are held to be close to God, but the ever-agile Covid-19 remains at least one step ahead of them. To judge from the accelerating death rate, a lot of guardian angels are asleep on the job.

Parish volunteers have been energetic during the pandemic's first year – organising deliveries, caring for the vulnerable, feeding the destitute, plugging gaps in others' systems. Nationally, if ever there was a time when Church leaders might have stepped forward to remind people why the Church is here, this might have been it. Instead come rumours, elaborated as the year passes, of proposals to reduce the number of stipendiary clergy, simplify governance, and expand lay-led mission through home, workplace, and digital media. Fears that such steps presage break-up of the parish system are dismissed, although it is not clear how parishes as we know them might be at their heart.

By Epiphany, the virtual choir is restricted to one singer. By Candlemas, the strangely wonderful day in early February when Christmas tips its hat towards Easter, Britain's dead exceed all combatants who died during the three civil wars between 1642 and 1651.

The end of republican rule in 1660 brought another revised Prayer Book. The book of 1662 contained amendments of detail and rubric, and some modernisations of phrase, but its words remained essentially those of Cranmer. It is still the customary worship of the Church of England. The failure to bring it up to date has not been for want of trying. We recall Edward Beckett Denison telling the Protestant Church Alliance in 1889 that 'Nine out of ten of the clergy are High Churchmen, and nine out of ten of the Laity are Low'. Evangelicals in the later nineteenth century believed that reform would be a Trojan horse for Catholicism. Their hounding of clergy who conducted services with gestures they considered inapt, used music in the wrong places, or disregarded the law laid down by the Judicial Committee of the Privy Council on vestments, eventually led to a Royal Commission on Ecclesiastical Discipline, appointed in 1904 to investigate complaints about 'breaches or neglect of the Law relating to the conduct of Divine Service'.

Alb, amice, chasuble, girdle, maniple – meaning is in the eye of the beholder as well as the wearer. 'Many witnesses,' said the Commissioners:

> have ... argued that these vestments are in the public mind so closely associated with the Roman Church that their introduction into the Church of England, where, in fact, they were entirely discarded for 300 years, cannot fail to convey generally the impression that the Roman doctrine and practice are being brought back. They have urged that the attempt to restore such vestments is often accompanied by the restoration of a group of practices discarded at the Reformation.

When the Commissioners turned to music, they noted that the prayer books of Edward VI and Elizabeth hymns had restricted singing in public services to the canticles which are fixed items in Morning and Evening Prayer. However, they also saw that the Crown had used its power to depart from the standard prescribed by the Acts of Uniformity. Elizabeth's injunctions of 1559 had permitted the singing of congregational hymns at the start and finish of Morning and Evening Prayer, and metrical psalters had been published under royal authority. Congregations liked to sing: *The Whole Book of Psalms* (1562) went through 150 editions in Elizabeth's reign alone. Hence, while the Prayer Book's only rubrical direction for music in 'quires and places where they sing' was an anthem after the third collect at Morning and Evening Prayer, there was abundant evidence for the habit of singing metrical psalms and hymns during services. Hymn-singing had further been acknowledged in legal judgements. The Commissioners recalled that in the Lincoln case (1890),* Archbishop Benson had held that while hymns were not explicitly permitted by statute or rubric, 'no Court or authority would consent to declare it illegal, because the prevalent use of it is, by the principles of law, a very safe assurance that it is not illegal'. Commissioners pointed to the practice of making a collection (similarly not provided for in the rubrics) to illustrate what they described as 'non-significant breach of the law'. The Commission concluded that the Church's disciplinary machinery was broken, and that revision of the Prayer Book would be needed to fix it.

The Speaker, a prominent liberal weekly, carried an article about the Royal Commission's report which appears to have been written by someone with his head in his hands. The report's account of 'trivial and irrelevant things about which men are fighting so bitterly' was utterly cheerless. The page upon page of patient investigation that had gone into the direction of a finger or tilt of a head could readily be mistaken for 'an elaborate irony upon the meaning of religion in the modern world'. The report was dismal, too, 'because it is quite certain that nothing will be done. The Secular arm is paralysed; the Spiritual Authority without effective control. Immediately Parliament admitted Dissenters, Catholics, Jews, Infidels, it became evident that the National

---

* An ecclesiastical lawsuit in which evangelicals levelled charges at Edward King, the Bishop of Lincoln, citing him for ritual offences committed in the course of administering holy communion in the Lincoln church of St Peter-at-Gowts, and in Lincoln Cathedral.

Church was impossible.' And so it turned out. Three decades later, a new Prayer Book was approved by the Church Assembly and vetoed by the House of Commons. The Commons rejected it twice, in December 1927, and again the following year when evangelical critics waved away small changes that had been offered to conciliate them.

The MP who led the charge on both occasions was William Joynson-Hicks (1865–1932), Member for Twickenham, Home Secretary in Stanley Baldwin's government, and President of the evangelical National Church League – an organisation which had helped to initiate legal action against a number of Anglo-Catholic clergy. In the first debate, he reminded MPs, 'I want the House to realise that this is not entirely a matter for the Church of England. As long as the Church is established, the final right lies with Parliament.' In the second, he warned that the new Prayer Book represented a drift back to pre-Reformation principles and Romish ideas. Echoing the words of *The Speaker* twenty-two years before, the Liberal MP and Baptist George Thorne (1853–1934) said, 'Why should we and our fathers before us be deprived of the rights and privileges of the Established Church when it appears that the trouble within the Established Church is not due to Nonconformists outside the Church, but is caused by nonconformists inside the Church?'

Stanley Baldwin wound up in the Measure's favour. He addressed anxieties that its rejection might hasten the separation of Church and State:

> I want, before I finish, to say one word on a subject which has been mentioned by several speakers, and that is the question of Disestablishment, which, I think, has much more chance of being brought nearer again into the political sphere by the rejection of the Bill. [*Interruption.*] I am giving my own opinion. We all have our opinions on this subject, and this is what I fear. It is not the loss of income, but the spiritual loss that I fear, and that alone. Under whatever auspices and under whatever conditions the Church of England were freed completely from such State control as exists to-day, I do not believe – I hope I may be wrong – that she will remain long as an entity, with these two streams of spiritual life, the Catholic and the Evangelical, running together. I believe that it is its connection with the State, galling as it may be at times, illogical as it seems to many, that keeps these two streams running in confluence in the Church of England, and I should regard loss of that as irreparable, because if the Church

of England as we know her were to disappear, there is nothing that could be set up to take the peculiar place which she holds.

The question was then put to the House, which rejected it by 266 votes to 220. If only England's MPs had voted, the Measure would have been accepted; the rebuff was decided by the votes of Scots, Welsh, and Northern Irish MPs, many of whom were not Anglicans.

Joynson-Hicks was not one to entertain the idea that imagination might exist to challenge, not support conformity, or its corollary, that however vital or necessary a new idea might look, dynamic interaction with the past remains constant. Instead, he erected a plaque 'in humble thanksgiving for answered prayer' and 'the maintenance thereby in the National Church of the teaching of holy scripture and the principles of the Reformation'.

In customary Anglican fashion, whereby contradictory properties are accepted as co-existent, the bishops agreed to use parts of the new Prayer Book anyway. In 1946, they issued *A Shorter Prayer Book*, which described itself as 'an abbreviated form of the Book of Common Prayer with some additional matter', and in practice consisted of the most commonly used services from the 1928 Prayer Book, with simpler rubrics and alternatives from 1662.

After nineteen years of further discussion and questionable legality, at 4.47 pm on 18 February 1965, the Archbishop of Canterbury rose in the House of Lords to move that the Prayer Book (Alternative and other Services) Measure 1965, recently passed by the Church Assembly, be presented to her Majesty for royal assent. In essence, this allowed the Church to create alternative forms of worship while leaving intact the authority of the 1662 Prayer Book. A number of services that had been revised for the 1928 Prayer Book were printed as the First Series of Alternative Services in the following year. The time taken to achieve this was roughly twice the duration of England's Reformation.

The Church of England's webpage on liturgy takes up the story:

> More periods of experimentation with further Alternative Services (Series Two and Three) began in the mid-1960s; these were followed by the publication of *The Alternative Service Book* (ASB) *1980*. The Series Three services used contemporary English for the first time. The ASB was authorized first for ten years and then for a further ten. From 2000 it was replaced by a new generation of services, under the general title *Common Worship*.

Looked at another way, when the House of Commons put a dam across the Church's streams of spiritual life, the Church responded not by breaching the dam, but by leaving it where it was and flooding the surrounding landscape.

As the waters subside, the dove flying back with a green twig in its beak is widely identified with the movement centred on Holy Trinity Brompton. HTB ('evangelical, charismatic, conservative') promotes the Alpha course that invites you to pose 'life's big questions' in a 'fun, no pressure environment'. The church forms part of the Chelsea Deanery in the Diocese of London, operates through five sites, and has planted offshoots by moving nuclei of believers from thriving congregations to revivify other churches that are ailing. Its PCC is a charity which in 2019 attracted nearly £12 million, mainly in donations and legacies, and 'reimagines ministry'. In doing so, it is vigorous in social activism. It centres on prayer and worship. There is strong web presence, with media-savvy use of tools like Spotify, Instagram, podcasts ('GodPod'), and video/audio downloads. HTB Worship ('a collective of worship leaders and songwriters who seek to lead and write songs that will point to Jesus and resource the church') is headed by young, fit-looking Worship Leaders and Worship Directors. They draw large congregations, engage children, and stir the young. HTB does not do faffy vestments or stuffy liturgy. It has rock-band services with swaying, overhead hand-clapping and arm waving. It also has a very capable Chamber Choir which sings both new music at the Bob Chilcott end of the spectrum and well-arranged cover versions of familiar hymns and carols. HTB is clearly in touch with something.

However, for all the pastoral energy and irrepressible optimism of people who talk to camera about how their lives have been changed, and the Calvinist certainty that hard questions can be sorted in fun environments, HTB seems in some respects a departure from the inherited parish system. For one thing, its charitable registration says it operates 'throughout London': that is, not just within its own bounds. For another, HTB and its offshoots appear to promote themselves on a like-mindedness principle that recruits people who share the same interests and outlook; success might thus come at the cost of the communal tradition in which a parish church is for all. There are more elusive kinds of departure. Where there is an abandonment of liturgy there will be a forgetting of the intricacies of the Christian year, in which time past and future is collapsed into days, months and seasons. A sure answer to everything comes at the price of forfeiture of complexity, contradiction, and doubt.

For some years the Strategic Investments Board of the Church Commissioners (encouraged by Archbishop Welby) has been putting funds towards growth. In 2018, the Church announced a £27 million drive to create over a hundred new churches in coastal areas, market towns, and outer urban housing estates. Some of these involve refits of existing churches; others involve new patterns of ministry, the creation of new 'worshipping communities' outside traditional frameworks as part of an 'ongoing wider church planting initiative'. One feature these all hold in common is that they are taking place within existing parishes. Many of them look less like adjustments to the existing parish system than projects which either seek to compensate for its failure or simply ignore it. There is, of course, no reason to shore up the inherited system as an end itself, or go on doing so if a better model can be found, and church planters might fairly point out that Jesus of Nazareth never set out to create an institutionalised parish system in the first place. But the pursuit of a host of variant new models without agreement on what to do with the legacy of the old one is a path that leads towards fragmentation. In more ways than one, the Commissioners' patronage of 'bold ambitious initiatives' and bids for new formats (like the 'food and magazine-style service based around short interactive activities and input exploring a Christian theme') recalls the sponsorship by magnates in the twelfth century of new religious orders like the Cistercians, Carthusians, and Templars rather than the sustaining of old ones.

The extent to which HTB plants look more like Midwich Cuckoos than rescuers of the parish system can be seen in Lincoln, where in 2014 the church of St Swithin (Victorian, barn-like, 1869–1880) was relaunched by a team sent to the city by HTB at the invitation of the Bishop of Lincoln. St Swithin is lively and growing, but some of those it attracts are said to arrive by car from across the East Midlands and South Yorkshire, while it appears that a number of locals may have moved to other city churches in reaction.

What we see here are signs of the abandonment of the parochial structure. Congregants choose a church in which they feel comfortable, with others of like mind and background, within a reasonable drive-time, and go there. Churches most likely to succeed, at least in terms of attracting congregations, might be those that disrupt the local community – or at least the local parish. (We recall this was what Nick Stacey found in Woolwich in the 1960s.) Will this end in two tiers, drive-to churches for the well-heeled, parish churches for the rest?

A core tenet of managerialism is that the similarities between, say, the Church and a fast-food chain or maker of machine tools are more important than the differences, and hence that the working of any organisation can be enhanced by the application of common skills and processes. Common signs of empty managerialism are worn-out language ('passionate about seeing lives changed'), banality, pointless invented jargon, and repetition. HTB's offshoot, the Churches Revitalization Trust, scores heavily on all four counts in just half a sentence of self-description in which it 'aims to meet demand from dioceses across the country for establishing City Centre Resource Churches (CCRCs) – church plants that will become hubs for resourcing and planting within their diocese – using an effective model of church planting that has grown out of HTB's long track-record of church planting activity over the last 30 years'. The Church is losing its ear.

Alongside the emptying of language has grown an Anglican fashion for doing eccentric things that cannot be readily connected with the words used to describe them. In the summer of 2019, for instance, the Rev Rachel Phillips, Canon for Mission and Growth at Rochester Cathedral, explained the presence of a golf course in the cathedral's nave with these words: 'For over 1,400 years, Rochester Cathedral has been a centre of learning for the community. By temporarily installing an educational adventure golf course we aim to continue that mission, giving people the opportunity to learn while they take part in a fun activity, in what for many might be a previously un-visited building.'

Around the same time, a fifty-five-foot helter-skelter was erected in the nave of Norwich Cathedral as part of a project called 'Seeing It Differently' that aimed to 'give people the chance to experience the Cathedral in an entirely new way and open up conversations about faith'.

And on 22 July 2020, the Dean and Chapter of Sheffield Cathedral announced the closure of its choir. As is often the way when institutions and politicians take controversial decisions, the announcement continued with an explanation which did not logically follow ('we believe this is in the best interests of the long-term mission of the Cathedral'), followed by a cliché (closure was prompted by 'renewed ambition for engagement and inclusion'). The dean himself resigned at the end of the year.

More appropriately, and movingly, the Church was quick off the mark in offering cathedrals and other churches as temporary centres for vaccination against Covid-19. By mid January 2021, three cathedrals – Salisbury, Blackburn, and Lichfield – were in such use. At Salisbury, vaccine patients were given an organ recital while they waited. At

Rochester, educational adventure golf gave way to C-19 testing. But at parish level, incumbents and parishioners were reminded:

> Churches and consecrated church halls will require a faculty, whether or not a lease is granted, as this will be a secular use rather than use of the church as a place of worship. However, Chancellors may issue Additional Matters Orders disapplying the need for faculties in their dioceses but the position will, in each case, need to be checked with the DAC.
>
> The House of Bishops COVID-19 Recovery Group,
> 8 December 2020

This is what comes of having an established Church.

Diarmaid MacCulloch, Cranmer's biographer, has reflected that Cranmer 'would not have known what Anglicanism meant', and that even if it had been explained to him 'he would probably not have approved'. Today, the same can be said for many Anglicans; with HTB at one end of their spectrum and the 1662 Prayer Book at the other, if you identify as a member of the Church of England, what does that mean? MacCulloch goes on, 'without his [Cranmer's] contribution the unending dialogue of Protestantism and Catholicism which forms Anglican identity would not have been possible. Perhaps the most widespread use of his original texts in pure form remains Anglican evensong, where twentieth-century forms have failed to win admirers away from the majestic rhythms of his prose.' MacCulloch points to ironies: Cranmer had little liking for cathedrals, 'no discernible love of complex choral music', and would have disliked the way in which evensong has been appropriated by Christianity's fellow travellers. We can guess, too, that he would have shaken his head in wonder at a process of liturgical writing which involves a Commission, the House of Bishops, the three houses of the General Synod (each voting by a two-thirds majority), and a Revision Committee – or fun environments with no discernible liturgy at all.

It is a question how much of this now matters. With the traditional streams of worship now out of their beds, wandering in a bewildering network of temporary post-evangelical channels, evaporating here, ponding there, how many remember what the 'unending dialogue' was actually about? For last words, then, let us think about William Byrd (1539 x 1543–1623), who was born just before the first English Prayer Book, wrote music for the Elizabethan liturgy, and combined his duties for the Anglican Church with personal Catholicism. In 1943, a few months before his death in action, the twenty-year-old Sidney Keyes imagined Byrd looking back across the Reformation:

> And so I try and remember how it was
> When lovers sang like finches, and the Word
> Was music.
> Lord, I am no coward,
> But an old man remembering the candle-flames
> Reflected in the scroll-work, frozen trees
> Praying for Advent, the willow cut at Easter.
> The quires are dumb. My spirit sings in silence.
> You will appoint the day of my arising.*

---

* Sidney Keyes, 'William Byrd', *The Cruel Solstice*, 1944, 26.

EPILOGUE

ANGELS IN MASVINGO

I was about to put the pen down when I remembered Peter Wagner: the ebullient curate at Longbridge, with his smile, his pipe, the cheery quotation from last night's *Maigret*, who danced the Twist in the youth club, leaning ever further backwards until you feared he would fall over, or more likely collapse into the arms of a girl waiting to catch him. What happened to him? My dad's 1991–92 issue of *Crockford's Clerical Directory* was still on a shelf:

> **WAGNER, Canon Peter Frederick**, *b.33*. Lon Univ BSc56. Westcott Ho Cam. d[eacon]60 p[riest]61. C[urate] Longbridge Birm 60–64. V[icar] Nechells 64–70.

Peter's degree was in chemistry; before that he had been in the Army for eighteen months doing National Service. He used the chemistry to work for a cosmetics company, until, as believers say, he answered God's call. Theological training took him to Westcott House, which no doubt explains his recruitment to Longbridge. But what of his later days at Nechells ('Nee-chells')? Indeed, where is Nechells?

Nechells is in north-east central Birmingham, and since in the early 1960s it lay beyond my teenage cognitive city it might as well have been in Asia. Today, Nechells is the headquarters of the Wing Yip Chinese food emporium (which also offers the little China Town experience, 'with Oriental Architecture and a Chinese Arch'), and Asia has come to it. You might have heard of it too for the Star City entertainment complex (built on derelict land in the 1990s), or Spaghetti Junction, where motorways on stained concrete stilts writhe and coil beside industrial units making car parts, packaging, and welding supplies.

Historians remember Nechells as the backdrop to the finale of the 1972 miners' strike. Britain's electricity was then generated by burning coal, and since the strikers blockaded fuel stocks, they brought the nation's power supply close to shutdown. Two thousand miners came to Nechells to deny access to a large stockpile of coke at the Saltley gasworks, and on 10 February, supported by workers from other industries, they forced the depot's closure. Their success sealed the strikers' victory, humiliated the Heath government, called time on Selsdon Man, and set the scene for Margaret Thatcher's retribution in the following decade.

Nechells before Peter had been a deprived place where decaying Victorian terraces were entangled with canals, railways, and Birmingham's usual plethora of small firms doing specialised things with metal – tubes, nuts, bolts, stoves, thimbles, bicycles, alloy castings, electro-plating. The terraces were cheek by jowl with a tar distillery, chemical and varnish works, two gasworks, and a power station, so everyone's home and washing stank. In 1947, the City Council used powers conferred by the recent Planning Act to acquire five central areas for redevelopment. The areas selected were those where overcrowding was greatest. One of them was Nechells, and by the time Peter arrived most of the old streets had gone. The new tower blocks and houses into which they moved were of lower density, and a lot of the houses were put elsewhere. The grassy spaces and pedestrian underpasses were well intended, but with their blowing litter, graffitied public art, and whiffy shadows, never as progressive as they might have seemed when Frank Price and Herbert Manzoni came to:

> Unveil the dust-wrapped, post-war architects'
> immediate prize-designs in balsa wood,
> excelling fantasies. Sparsely inhabited
> by spaced-out, pinhead model citizens . . .

Probably without much thinking about it, they had emptied his church. And this is where we came in: pastoral reorganisation, church closures, the legacy of Victorian over-provision, and the scattering of poor yet cohesive communities in the belief that tangible links with the past are 'often more sentimental than valuable'.

St Clement Nechells, Peter's church, was designed by J. A. Chatwin (1830–1907), a Birmingham-born architect whose other local works included the city's Greek Orthodox cathedral and a large part of Colmore Row. It was his first church. Contemporaries called it 'handsome' and admired its brickwork, floors of Staffordshire blue-and-red tiles, and galleries for schoolchildren. 'Poor inhabitants of the neighbourhood' subscribed £50 in pennies towards the cost. Optimism was to the fore: it was built to seat over 850 people. Whether it was full even on

the day of its consecration in August 1859 we do not know, but newspapers said the congregation was large and noted the presence of many
clergy, trustees, diocesan officials, and the Bishop of Worcester. At that
point, the manor of Nechells was where it had been since the seventh
century, in the Diocese of Worcester, and St Clement was technically a
chapel of ease in the parish of St Matthew, Duddeston. Duddeston was
a nearby village which had been engulfed by Birmingham's expansion,
and St Matthew was one of ten new churches put up at the expense
of the Birmingham Church Building Society two decades before; St
Clement was St Matthew's first offshoot, and as the bishop explained
in his sermon, the plan was to turn it into a parish in its own right. This
duly happened, and when this part of Warwickshire was transferred to
the new Diocese of Birmingham in 1905, Nechells went with it. A century later, the process went backwards. As community bonds loosened
and neighbours were dispersed, the congregation shrank. St Clement's
was closed in 1975, demolished in 1977, and its parish reunited with St
Matthew whence it came.

However, if the urban Church of England was in retreat, faith was
not: like wildflowers on wasteland, new churches and faith groups
sprang up. They continue to do so. If you look at Nechells on Google
Earth, there they are: the Church of God Prophecy Outreach Centre
(Pentecostal, Bible-centred), the New Jerusalem Apostolic Church, the
Ebenezer Mission Hall in Cook Street. Such non-established groups are
versatile, nimble, not tied to costly buildings, bureaucracies or laws, free
to explore new ways and means, like Balm in Gilead Ministries ('Religious activities through conferences and seminars') or the Redeemed
Christian Church of God which uses the Star City cinema. St Clement,
meanwhile, like the smile of Lewis Carroll's cat which lingered after
the cat itself had vanished, is recollected in the name of a road, a GP
surgery, a school, and a nursing home on the site of the vicarage that
Peter left in 1970.

What then? Back to *Crockford's*:

Rhodesia 70-80; Zimbabwe from 80; Dean Gweru 84-87.

Rhodesia, Zimbabwe, Gweru. What took him there – or who?

The answer is Paul Burrough, whom Peter got to know in the 1960s
during Burrough's term as the Diocese of Birmingham's Chaplain to
Overseas Peoples. In 1968, Burrough was consecrated as Bishop of
Mashonaland, a diocese then in the white-ruled rebel colony of Southern Rhodesia. Two years later, Burrough invited Peter to be Warden

of St Barnabas's Diocesan Centre with a special remit for training Supplementary Clergy. Peter worked here for eight years, mentoring part-time ordinands. When Burrough was forced out in 1981 following Zimbabwean independence, Peter figured there was greater need among Zimbabwe's people than he was likely to find back in England. So he carried on, ministering first in the iron-and-steel town of Kwekwe, then as Dean of Gweru (1984–1987), and finally as rector of a church in Masvingo.

Historians of African Liberation have dealt neither kindly nor always fairly with the episcopate of Paul Burrough. One says that he was 'co-opted by the settlers'. Another claims that he sided with Ian Smith's white-interest government from the moment of his arrival until the elections which brought majority rule in 1980. Burrough's criticisms of those elections as an outcome of appeasement following the vicious bush war endeared him neither to Mrs Thatcher nor to Robert Mugabe, notwithstanding help Mugabe had earlier received from him. In 1981, the writer and teacher Denis Hills spoke for many when he said in *The Last Days of Rhodesia* that in view of Mugabe's 'unimpeachable' commitment to 'peace, non-racialism and racial harmony', Burrough's criticisms were 'puerile and ungracious'. Twenty-two years later, in the light of Mugabe's subsequent record, Burrough's obituarist in the *Church Times* asked 'Who looks puerile now?'

Burrough's pastoral record in Rhodesia–Zimbabwe was strong. He loved its people, among whom he liked to circulate on a scrambler motorbike 'until I broke my leg on the thing 32 miles away from a Church where 510 Confirmation candidates were waiting for me, and which I reached after the worst journey of my life, changing gear with my hands since the leg would not function'. His poor reputation in the eyes of post-colonial historians (or in those of *The Times* obituarist who said that he 'never really came to understand Africans') stems partly from the extent to which many of them have quoted from each other rather than primary sources. More fundamentally it comes from Burrough's refusal to accept the premises upon which politicians of all stripes rested their conclusions. *The Times*'s statement that Burrough 'did not want to upset anyone, least of all those running the country', does not stand scrutiny – he confronted the Smith government on many occasions – while the *Daily Telegraph*'s claim that he had 'counselled moderation, without apparently recognising that, in African eyes, the outlawed regime had, for many, made a peaceful settlement impossible' did not speak to the point. It is the case that Anglicanism 'was peculiarly vulnerable when African nationalism challenged the morality of White supremacy and segregation'. However, such is the extent to which words have been locked up, and contexts frozen, in post-Colonial discourse, that even Anglicans who did speak out against the Rhodesia Front are considered to have been so imbued with supremacism that their opposition sprang from a liberal tendency inside settler thought than from direct concern for Black African members. Burrough's famous criticism of the World Council of Churches ('it is not the function of a World Christian body to advocate force and terrorism') was not because he favoured colonial government but because he stood by the declaration of the 1968 Lambeth Conference that 'war as a method of settling international disputes is incompatible with the teaching and example of our Lord, Jesus Christ'. He declined to define his faith in the context of Cold War binaries. He held that discrimination cannot be ended by political means alone, and that 'states artificially formed out of colonial empires to satisfy world opinion among politicians are beyond the wit of man to govern'. Above all, he refused to argue in language corrupted by conflict. He no more accepted the summary execution of a headmaster by two young ZANLA members, who shot the man through the back of his head in front of his pupils, at point blank-range, within earshot of his wife, as the action of 'freedom fighters', than he accepted as 'security' the actions of Rhodesia Front forces who burned villages in reprisal for help given to insurgents, stacking the villagers' granaries with their furniture and clothing to make the grain burn better.

Paul Burrough knew a thing or two about conflict. After an undergraduate career in which he read theology and rowed for the University of Oxford (in a boat in which the future Dams Raid captain Melvin Young was a fellow crew member), he joined the Royal Corps of Signals, and reached the rank of captain by the time the Japanese captured him at the fall of Singapore in 1942. After some months in Changi prison, where he got to know Leonard Wilson, he was transferred to Japan in the hold of a ship jammed with prisoners, with poor ventilation, little food or water, and no sanitation. In Japan, Burrough husbanded a small contraband radio through which the hopes of his fellow prisoners were kept alive for the next three years with news of outside events. Possession of the radio would have meant immediate death if it had been discovered by their Korean guards. The Koreans were used by the Japanese for their expertise in meting out rough treatment, in the course of which Burrough learned a little of their language. On return to England at the war's end, he entered Ely Theological College, was ordained the following year, and went to serve his curacy at St Michael, Aldershot.

Following the outbreak of the Korean War, Burrough was asked by Geoffrey Fisher, the Archbishop of Canterbury, to go to Korea as a member of the Church of England's mission. Burrough agreed and in 1951 began work in Pusan, 'a sprawling scrap-heap of discarded humanity', where people lived in shacks made of cardboard boxes, in drainpipes, and in the ground. At Pusan's railway station, he found scores of homeless children: 'On a cold night in the assembly hall one could see them lying literally three deep on top of each other to preserve a little warmth. They lived by begging, by every neat trick of robbery and some were forced into various evil forms of selling their small bodies to Western troops.'

On one occasion, Burrough took a small group of children to an eating shop near the station. Even as the food appeared, they reacted to the room's warmth by beginning to rest their heads on their arms and fall asleep: 'The need for sleep was even more urgent than the need for food.'

Burrough worked on among the dispossessed, orphans, and lepers for another eight years. It was the custom for missionaries to be given Korean names. Riding from place to place on a motorbike, he became Father Pak. After his death, a Methodist colleague wrote in perplexity to *The Times* about its claim that Burrough had never come to understand Africans: 'He had understood Koreans well.'

All of which contextualises Leonard Wilson's invitation in 1959 to his old fellow prisoner to become Birmingham's Chaplain to Overseas Peoples. Burrough was at first described as a 'mobile parson' who worked from a caravan and moved every few weeks lest the planners claim that it had taken root. Following his marriage to Bess White, a war widow with whom he fell everlastingly in love, the caravan was exchanged for a house. Small wonder that on a November evening in 1963 Eamonn Andrews stepped forward with a great deal of material under his arm to invite Burrough into the Gosta Green television studios to record *This Is Your Life*.

Thus far Burrough had faced war, imprisonment, poverty, abuse, and destitution. He was now called to contend with racism, fascism, white supremacism, and the views of nearby MPs like Enoch Powell, through whose constituencies the ghosts of former colonial borders now ran. Most challenging of all, perhaps, were the inwardness and anxiety he found among existing Anglican churchgoers, some of whom reacted to immigrants as if they were in some way contagious. New arrivals from the West Indies and Pakistan, quite a number of whom had served with UK armed forces during the war, responded by reading their Bibles at home; many eventually turned away to join or form other churches where they could pray together. It has since been said that such views did 'more damage to the cause of racial integration than all the sneers and blasphemies of their English workmates in factory workshops'.

This, then, was Burrough's preparation for his episcopate in Mashonaland. Seven years after his return to England, he wrote a short book about the experience. It began, 'The story of Rhodesia becoming Zimbabwe has not, nor ever will, be accurately related. Too many entrenched positions make it unbearable for the holders of them to face evident facts.' To which one would like to reply that this is what historians are for – save that, so far, many of them, too, have occupied entrenched positions and failed to face evident facts.

Burrough called his book *Angels Unawares*. He took the title from a verse in Hebrews:

> Be not forgetful to entertain strangers:
>   for thereby some have entertained angels unawares.
>
>   Hebrews 13.2

Aquinas believed angels to have no bodily existence; they are simply energy and take on human shapes to make themselves apparent to mortals.

The last sentence in Burrough's book builds on a challenging statement further up the page: 'Justice and Peace without love and without that untranslatable Shona quality of "kunzwana" or listening acceptance, are never enough in themselves' – 'In some distant relationship, untroubled by political ideologies, angels must be entertained and enjoyed for themselves in a new kind of undemanding hospitality.'

Which brings us back to Peter, whom we have followed for several years in a parish in Harare, then as dean of the cathedral of St Cuthbert at Gweru in central Zimbabwe. (At this point there could be another chapter, about why the cults of seventh-century Irish-trained Northumbrian saints introduced by colonial missionaries took root in Zimbabwe, especially when Zimbabwe has impressive saints in waiting of its own. Will there be a day when Anglican churches in Surrey or Norfolk are dedicated to figures like Arthur Shearly Cripps (likened by many to Francis of Assisi) or the martyr Bernard Mizeki (1861–1896)?)

Cuthbert (d.687) was the subject of several early medieval biographies; we have already glimpsed the tiny gospel of St John, Europe's earliest surviving intact book, that was placed in his coffin. Images of archangels were delicately traced on that coffin, together with symbols of the four evangelists, depictions of the twelve apostles, and of the Virgin and Child – in other words, a depiction of the names invoked in the Litany, a graphical representation of their perpetual prayer around him. The first *vita*, written around AD 700, is probably the earliest life of an English saint to come down to us from Anglo-Saxon England. In its second part, the young Cuthbert is given the job of greeting visitors to the monastery of Ripon. On a freezing winter day, he meets a traveller whose feet he warms. Having no bread to hand, Cuthbert goes to the monastery's bakery but comes back empty-handed because the bread is still a-baking. On return, Cuthbert finds the visitor gone, and three warm loaves. Looking out, there are no footprints in the snow. Cuthbert realises that he has been entertaining an angel.

Peter's later years look increasingly Cuthbert-like. By the later 1980s, he was giving most of his small income and belongings to others. After a spell as rector of St Martin's, Kwe Kwe, in 1997 he became archdeacon of the province of Lundi and rector of St Michael and All Angels in Masvingo. By then he had ceased to draw his stipend, asked that it be diverted to needier causes, and lived on part of his small UK pension.

On Monday 26 February 2001, he rose, as usual, just before sunrise, and went into church to say matins – one of the offices of personal devotion that Cranmer put in the foreground of Anglican liturgy. The Old Testament reading that morning was from Chapter 5 of the Book of Amos:

18 Woe unto you that desire the day of the LORD! to what end is it for you? the day of the LORD is darkness, and not light.

19 As if a man did flee from a lion, and a bear met him; or went into the house, and leaned his hand on the wall, and a serpent bit him.

20 Shall not the day of the LORD be darkness, and not light? even very dark, and no brightness in it?

At some point, Peter became aware that others were in the church. It is not known if anything was said – whether Peter attempted to entertain strangers, for instance, or indeed whether they were strangers; we can reconstruct events only from their results. Peter had an appointment later in the day which he did not keep. The churchwardens went to look for him. He was not in the rectory, which had been broken into. They looked next in the church, and eventually found him lying behind the belfry door. He had been dead for hours. The visitors had beaten him about the head and body, bound him hand and foot, broken his neck, and pulled off his socks and stuffed them into his mouth. The socks made it impossible for him to breathe; he died from asphyxiation.

The funeral was held in his own church of St Michael, on 3 March 2001. It was conducted by Rt Rev Ismael – Ismael! – Mukuwanda, the bishop of Gweru, and the former bishop of Harare, Jonathan Siyat-ichema. No proper explanation for the killing has appeared, although by the time of the funeral one man had been arrested. The other, still at large, was believed to be a former caretaker, who had recently com-pleted a prison sentence for thefts from the rectory and had since been responsible for assaults on two elderly women in Peter's congregation. The motive was assumed to be robbery; indeed, after the funeral, the same man was held responsible for a break-in to the office of the church treasurer, presumably in search of the proceeds of the funeral's collec-tion. It is a question how any of that might relate to the vigour and extent of the violence.

Two of Peter's brothers travelled to Zimbabwe for the funeral. After-wards, one wrote:

> Because these incidents are not overtly political, they do not attract media attention in this country. However, they are political in that they reveal how years of petty official racism have in the past few months given way to a callous indifference to the safety of one part of the community, and to the official condoning of such acts of violence.

The claim by Masvingo's police that they had launched a 'massive man-hunt' was at odds with their further reported comment that their chief suspect had so far eluded them 'because he was never at home when they called'.

St Michael's churchwardens consulted bishop Ismael about the possibility of declaring Peter Wagner a martyr. The bishop agreed that he had died for his faith. But there were no canons of the diocese that covered martyrdom. In the absence of a process, he was not empowered to act.

The last words in the allotted reading on 26 February, perhaps the last words he read, were:

> But let judgment run down as waters, and righteousness as a mighty stream.

Amos 5.24

Peter, by now, will know what we cannot know, if there is anything to be known. For the rest of us it can only be a matter of faith.

NOTES

Abbreviations used

BCP   Book of Common Prayer
HMSO   His/Her Majesty's Stationery office
JRM Collection   Letters and papers of John Morris
LPL   Lambeth Palace Library
ODNB   *Oxford Dictionary of National Biography*
TNA   The National Archives

Preface

p. 1   On decline and numbers: the most recent British Social Attitudes Survey
of religion and belief (released in 2018) found that the proportion of
citizens identifying themselves as belonging to the Church of England
was at a record low and had more than halved in the last fifteen years.
Decline was sharpest among those between forty-five and fifty-four.
On numbers, trends and analysis generally, see Trevor Cooper's valuable
presentation to the All Party Parliamentary Group on Churches and
Chapels, 'Churches and chapels: the long view', 2012 (https://www.
hrballiance.org.uk/wp-content/uploads/2012/05/2012-01-7-APPG-
trevor-coopers-presentation.pdf) and its parent, Trevor Cooper, 'How
many seats in church?' in Trevor Cooper and Sarah Brown, eds, *Pews,
Benches and Chairs: Church Seating in English Parish Churches from the
Fourteenth Century to the Present*, Ecclesiological Society, 2011. See also
Clive D. Field, *Religious Statistics in Great Britain: An Historical Introduction*, University of Manchester, 2010.

p. 1   Secularisation and the rate of decline: Jeremy Morris, 'The strange
death of Christian Britain: another look at the secularization debate',
The Historical Journal, 46:4, 2003, 963–976.

p. 1   Confessional state: J. C. D. Clark, 'England's Ancien Regime as a
Confessional State', *Albion: A Quarterly Journal Concerned with British
Studies*, 21:3, 1989, 450–474.

p. 2   'Anglicanism, coming from an establishment position . . .' William J. Wolf, ed., *The Spirit of Anglicanism: Hooker, Maurice, Temple*, T. and T. Clark, 1982, 158; Kevin J. Gardner, 'Anglicanism and the Poetry of John Betjeman', *Christianity and Literature*, 53:3, 2004, 361–383, at 365. Gardner identifies four key Anglican qualities – a communal tradition, wariness of absolutism, mysticism, an awareness of God in the everyday world – at the heart of Betjeman's verse.

p. 2   Conservatism, populism and Christianity: Paul Betts, *Ruin and Renewal: Civilising Europe after World War II*, Profile Books, 2020; and its review by Richard J. Evans, 'Staying alive in the ruins', *London Review of Books*, 43:8, 22 April 2021, 27–29, at 29.

p. 3   'Half of our churches, 8000 of them, have 26 adults or fewer on a Sunday. If you had 26 people to form a Christian presence in a community, you wouldn't start from here': from David Keen commenting on the Church of England's statistics for mission, 2019, in Ian Paul, 'What is happening to church attendance?', *Psephizo*, 22 October 2020: https://www.psephizo.com/life-ministry/what-is-happening-to-church-of-england-attendance/

p. 4   Influence of English Reformation on survival of medieval churches: Martin Renshaw, 'The place of the organ in the medieval parish church', *Journal of British Institute of Organ Studies*, 37, 2013; reissued 2014 with additions: http://soundsmedieval.org, 7–8.

p. 5   A. N. Wilson's opinion of Stuart Blanch: *Our Times: The Age of Elizabeth II*, Arrow Books, 2009, 246.

Prologue

p. 9   Henry Tudor, Arthur, and Tudor destiny: Steven Gunn and Linda Monckton, 'Introduction: Arthur Tudor, the Forgotten Prince' in *Arthur Tudor, Prince of Wales: Life, Death and Commemoration*, eds Steven Gunn and Linda Monkton, Boydell Press, 2009, 1–6.

pp. 9, 18   Arthur's tomb: Mark Duffy, 'Arthur's Tomb and its Context', in *Arthur Tudor, Prince of Wales: Life, Death and Commemoration*, eds Steven Gunn and Linda Monkton, Boydell Press, 2009, 77–89.

p. 13   *Life* of David: Richard Sharpe and John Reuben Davies, 'Rhygyfarch's Life of St David', in *St David of Wales: Cult, Church and Nation*, eds J. Wyn Evans and Jonathan M. Wooding, Boydell Press, 2007, 107–154.

p. 13   *Portus Magnus* and nearby object distribution: see user-generated digital mapping of finds from the Portable Antiquities Scheme (https://finds. org.uk/); Mark Redknap, 'St Davids and a new link with the Hiberno-Norse world', in *St David of Wales: Cult, Church and Nation*, eds J. Wyn Evans and Jonathan M. Wooding, Boydell Press, 2007, 84–89.

p. 13 St Patrick's chapel: K. Murphy, M. Shiner, H. Wilson and K. Hemer, 'Excavation at St Patrick's Chapel 2016', interim report from Dyfed Archaeological Trust.

pp. 15–16 Particulars of Arthur's funeral: Ralph Houlbrooke, 'Prince Arthur's Funeral', in *Arthur Tudor, Prince of Wales: Life, Death and Commemoration*, eds Steven Gunn and Linda Monkton, Boydell Press, 2009, 64–76.

pp. 15–17 Account of Arthur's funeral at Worcester and presentation of the horse: Julian Litten, 'The Re-enactment of the Funeral of Prince Arthur', in *Arthur Tudor, Prince of Wales: Life, Death and Commemoration*, eds Steven Gunn and Linda Monkton, Boydell Press, 2009, 167–180. Cf. Anna M. Duch, 'The Royal Funerary and Burial Ceremonies of Medieval English Kings, 1216–1509', unpubl. PhD thesis, University of York, 2016.

p. 17 Thomas Cooke's will: TNA PROB 11/17/347; Henry Weyman, 'Chantry chapels in Ludlow church', *Transactions of the Shropshire Archaeological and Natural History Society*, vol. 27, part 3, 1904, 337–370.

p. 18 Uvedale's will: TNA PROB 11/23/53.

pp. 18–19 Absence of image: Duffy, 'Arthur's tomb', 84-5. Arthur's chantry: Christopher Guy and John Hunter, 'Prince Arthur's Chapel and Tomb: An Archaeological Analysis', *Arthur Tudor, Prince of Wales: Life, Death and Commemoration*, eds Steven Gunn and Linda Monkton, Boydell Press, 2009, 90–111; Julian Luxford, 'The Origins and development of the English "Stone-Cage" Chantry Chapel', *Journal of the British Archaeological Association*, 164:1, 2011, 39–73. Cf. Sarah Schell, 'The Office of the Dead in England: image and music in the Book of Hours and related texts', unpubl. PhD thesis, University of St Andrews, 2011.

p. 20 Angela Tilby, 'Why choral evensong is so popular', *Church Times*, 2 November 2018.

p. 20 Cranmer, BCP and evensong: Diarmaid MacCulloch, *Thomas Cranmer: A Life*, Yale UP, 1996, matins and evensong, 510–511; rhythms of prose, evensong, 629–630.

p. 21 Kingswood and the 'Sunday sesh': http://www.kingswoodcofe.com/sunday-sesh

p. 22 Church closures: Trevor Beeson, a former dean of Winchester Cathedral, wrote to *The Times*: 'I find it deeply disturbing that the Archbishops of Canterbury and York, yielding to government pressure, have suspended until further notice the offering of public worship in the Church of England. This is unprecedented and was not considered necessary even in the darkest days of our national history . . .'

1   **Longbridge and Before**

p. 25   'The new vicarage is nearing completion': *Contact*, Longbridge Church Monthly, April 1956.

p. 26   Vicarage and rectory: Anthony Jennings, *The Old Rectory. The Story of the English Parsonage*, Sacristy Press, 2 edn, 2018. On later twentieth-century parsonage design see Church Commissioners, *Parsonage Design Guide*, 1953.

pp. 27–9   Stuart Blanch and Eynsham: Dick Williams, *Stuart Blanch: A Life*, SPCK, 2001, 63–64; personal knowledge.

p. 32   Malcolm Williamson on Beaumont: Obituary, *The Times*, 26 August 1970, 10.

pp. 32–3   Literary merit of Awdry's railway books: Belinda Copson, 'Awdry, Wilbert Vere', ODNB, 2007. Cf. Trevor Beeson, *Priests and Prelates: The Daily Telegraph Clerical Obituaries*, Continuum, 2002, 152–154.

p. 33   US visitors' opinions of British Railways: *Contact*, Longbridge Church Monthly, August 1956.

p. 35   Stuart's voice and humour: John Morris, MS memoir for Dick Williams, JRM Collection.

pp. 35–6   Blanches at Blackhall Road: Dick Williams, *Blanch*, 70–71; personal knowledge.

pp. 39–40   Career and character of Leonard Wilson: Roy McKay, *John Leonard Wilson: Confessor for the Faith*, Hodder & Stoughton, 1973.

pp. 42–4   John Collins and ANC: Diana Collins, *Partners in Protest: Life with Canon Collins*, Victor Gollancz, 1990, esp. 183–227; Diana Collins, 'Origins and achievements of the Defence and Aid Fund for Southern Africa', in *Christian Action 1946–96*, ed. Eric James, 9–11.

p. 43   'Church of England was still run by men who smoked pipes': Andrew Brown and Linda Woodhead, *That Was the Church That Was: How the Church of England Lost the English People*, Bloomsbury, 2016, 1.

p. 43   Claim that racial segregation is founded on biology: James Plowden-Wardlaw, letter to *The Times*, 17 January 1955.

p. 44   Trevor Huddleston, letter to *The Times*, 10 December 1956. Cf. Rob Skinner, 'The Moral Foundations of British Anti-Apartheid Activism, 1946–1960', *Journal of Southern African Studies*, 35:2, Liberation Struggles, Exile and International Solidarity, 2009, 399–416.

p. 44   Geoffrey Fisher and 'Roman Catholic apartheid': *The Times*, 5 July 1956; letters to *The Times* from B. C. Butler and C. Scott-Paton, 7 July 1956.

pp. 44–6   *The Church and the Atom*: Martin Wight, review, *International Affairs*, 25:1, January 1949, 74; editorial, *Manchester Guardian*, 16 April 1948; Tina Alice Bonne Reeh, 'The Church of England and Britain's Cold War', 1937–1948, unpubl. PhD thesis, University of Oxford, 2015.

More discussion and contextualisation: Dianne Kirkby, 'The Church of England and the Cold War Nuclear Debate', *Twentieth Century British History*, 4:3, 1993, 250–283; Dianne Kirby, 'Ecclesiastical McCarthyism: Cold War Repression in the Church of England', *Contemporary British History*, 19:2, 2005, 187–203; Andrew Chandler, *George Bell Bishop of Chichester: Church, State and Resistance in the Age of Dictatorship*, William B. Eerdmans, 2016, esp. chapter 3; Dianne Kirkby, 'Christian Faith, Communist Faith: Some Aspects of the Relationship between the Foreign Office Information Research Department and the Church of England Council on Foreign Relations, 1950–1953', *Kirchliche Zeitgeschichte*, 13:1, Katholizismus und Protestantismus während der NS-Diktatur und in der Nachkriegszeit, 2000, 217–241.

p. 45   Ernest Barnes, science and eugenics: Patrick T. Merricks, 'God and the Gene: E.W. Barnes on Eugenics and Religion, Politics', *Religion & Ideology*, 13:3, 2012, 353–374. Cf. 'Inferior stock "increasing far too rapidly": Dr. Barnes on Problems of Overpopulation', *Manchester Guardian*, 4 September 1950.

p. 45   International Research Department: Hugh Wilford, 'The Third Force revisited: the British Left and the IRD', in *The CIA, the British Left and the Cold War: Calling the Tune?*, Taylor & Francis, 2003, 48–81.

pp. 45–6   H-bomb: Matthew Grimley, 'The Church and the Bomb: Anglicans and the Campaign for Nuclear Disarmament c.1958–1984', *God and War: The Church of England and Armed Conflict in the Twentieth Century*, eds Stephen G. Parker and Tom Lawson, Routledge, 2012, 149–164. Fisher quotation: Lambeth Palace Library, Fisher Papers, vol. 204, f. 246, Fisher to Philip Toynbee, 3 January 1958.

pp. 46–7   Moscow congress: John Morris, 'Peace mongering in Moscow', *Birmingham Post*, 18 July 1962.

pp. 47–8   CND: Christopher Driver, *The Disarmers: A Study in Protest*, Hodder & Stoughton, 1964, 228–269; Diana Collins, *Partners in Protest*, 228–269.

p. 47   Security significance of CND membership: TNA CAB 21/6026, Memorandum 5 May 1962.

p. 49   Clergy voice: see comments from 'An Anglican vicar' in 'Why do (some) Anglican vicars use "sing-songy" voices?': https://christianity. stackexchange.com/questions/33997/why-do-some-anglican-vicars-use-sing-songy-voices. Cf. 'Clerical malady', *Birmingham Gazette*, 11 August 1954.

pp. 49–50   Personal costs of ministry: Harriet Sherwood, 'A bit of you is always on duty': the vicars struggling with stress, *Guardian*, 1 February 2018; personal knowledge.

p. 50   'You can't go around carrying people's burdens': Dick Williams, *Blanch*, 61.

2   A Coventry Carol

p. 51   'A stocky water tower ... now legendary dust': Geoffrey Hill, *The Triumph of Love*, Penguin, 1998, VII, 2–3.

p. 54   Coventry redevelopment: Jeremy and Caroline Gould, *Coventry Planned: The Architecture of the Plan for Coventry 1940–1978*, English Heritage, 2009. Gibson quotation: *Journal of the Royal Institute of British Architects*, 17 March 1941, 76–77.

p. 55   Steps towards a new cathedral: Provost R. T. Howard, *Ruined and Rebuilt: The Story of Coventry Cathedral 1939–1962*, 1962, 3 edn 2019, Coventry Lord Mayor's Committee for Peace and Reconciliation.

p. 56   Competition for new cathedral: Louise Campbell, 'Towards a New Cathedral: The Competition for Coventry Cathedral 1950–51', *Architectural History*, 35, 1992, 208–234.

p. 57   Cloudsley-Shovel criticism: *Daily Mail*, 20 August 1951, 2.

pp. 59–60   Coventry cycle discussion: Pamela M. King, 'The York and Coventry Mystery Cycles: A Comparative Model of Civic Response to Growth and Recession', *Early Theatre*, vol. 22, no. 1, 1997, 20–26; R. W. Ingram, *Coventry, Records of Early English Drama*, University of Toronto Press, 1981.

p. 60   Why plays stopped: Bing D. Bills, 'The "Suppression Theory" and the English Corpus Christi Play: A Re-Examination', *Theatre Journal*, 32:2, 1980, 157–168.

pp. 62–3   Witness account of burning cathedral: Howard, *Ruined and Rebuilt*, 32–37.

p. 63   Wall painting discovery: 'Bombing reveals a painting', *Birmingham Post*, 22 March 1941.

3   Sanderstead Man

p. 67   Godfrey Talbot quotation: audio clip, Second World War Experience Centre, 'Godfrey Talbot War Correspondent'.

p. 69   Discussion about Monty Python's *Life of Brian*: BBC TV, *Friday Night, Saturday Morning*, 9 November 1979.

pp. 69–70   Mervyn Stockwood: Michael De-la-Noy, 'Stockwood, (Arthur) Mervyn, bishop of Southwark', ODNB, 2011; Trevor Beeson, *Priests and Prelates*, 122–124.

p. 70   John Robinson: Eric James, 'Robinson, John Arthur Thomas, bishop of Woolwich and biblical scholar', ODNB, 2004.

p. 71   C. S. Lewis review: 'Must our image of God go?', *Observer*, 24 March 1963, 14. Cf. review by Christopher Driver, 'A bishop breaks the moulds', *Guardian*, 19 March 1963.

p. 71   Heresy trial: *Guardian*, 25 March 1963.

p. 72   *Observer* article: John Robinson, 'Our image of God must go', *Observer*, 17 March 1963, 2.

p. 72   Reactions: 'Must our image of God go?', *Observer*, 24 March 1963, 11.

p. 72   Sense of before-and-after moment: Keith Robbins, 'Contextualizing a "New Reformation": John A. T. Robinson and the Church of England in the early Sixties', *Departures and Adaptions – Church Reform in the 20th Century*, Vandenhoeck & Ruprecht, 2010, 428–446.

pp. 73–4   Brian Hope-Taylor and Farthing Down: David Mitchell, 'The Secrets of Farthing Down', *Picture Post*, 23 October 1948, 19–21.

p. 74   Yeavering: Brian Hope-Taylor, *Yeavering: An Anglo-British Centre of Early Northumbria*, HMSO, 1977.

p. 75   For Hope-Taylor's papers: Papers of Brian Hope-Taylor, archaeologist, Cambridge, England, CANMORE (National Record of the Historic Environment, Historic Environment Scotland): https://canmore.org.uk/collection/1176323

pp. 75–6   Medmenham: Christine Halsall, *Women of Intelligence: Winning the Second World War with Air Photos*, History Press, 2017.

p. 76   John Betjeman quotation: *Survey of London: Battersea*, vols 49–50, eds Andrew Saint and Colin Thom, Yale UP for English Heritage, chapter 3.

4   Journeys and Margins

p. 79   Context of Becket's shrine: Paul Binski, *Becket's Crown: Art and Imagination in Gothic England, 1170–1300*, Yale UP, 2004.

pp. 79–80   Glass in Trinity Chapel: information from Anna Eavis; 'Discovery of earliest known image of pilgrims on the road to Cantebury': https://www.medievalists.net/2018/09/discovery-earliest-known-image-pilgrims-canterbury/

p. 80   Becket-relics: Julian Luxford, 'The Relics of Thomas Becket in England', *Journal of the British Archaeological Association*, 173:1, 2020, 124–142.

p. 80   Reassessment of Pilgrims' Way: Derek Bright, 'The Pilgrims' Way revisited: the use of the North Downs main trackway and the Medway crossings by medieval travellers', Kent Archaeological Society e-Article, 2010.

pp. 80–1   Taking on Becket: Kay Brainerd Slocum, *The Cult of Thomas Becket: History and Historiography Through Eight Centuries*, Taylor & Francis, 2018.

p. 81   'Large perceptive qualities': C. F. Routledge, 'The Bones of Archbishop Becket', *Archaeologia Cantiana*, 21, 1895, 73–80.

pp. 81–2   Survival of angels as popular figures in Reformation England: Peter Marshall and Alexandra Walsham (eds), *Angels in the Early Modern*

World, Cambridge University Press, 2006; for further survey of beliefs and apparition of angels in early modern England, Alexandra Walsham, 'Invisible Helpers: Angelic Intervention in Post-Reformation England', *Past and Present*, 208:1, 2010, 77-130.

p. 82   Carlo Carretto, *Letters from the Desert*, Darton, Longman & Todd, 1972.

p. 85   Trewarren Gardens and context: Cadw/ICOMOS Register of Landscapes, Parks and Gardens of special historic interest in Wales, ref. PGW (Dy) 65 (PEM).

p. 86   Ismael, St Ishmaels, *cantref* in kingdom of Dyfed: T. M. Charles-Edwards, 'The Seven Bishop-Houses of Dyfed', *Bulletin of the Board of Celtic Studies*, 24:3, 1971, 247–262.

5   Battersea and Afterwards

p. 89   Advice from Douglas Jay: recollected in memorial address for Douglas Jay, 11 March 1996, JRM Collection.

p. 89   *Batriceseg*: P. H. Sawyer, *Anglo-Saxon Charters: An Annotated List and Bibliography*, Royal Historical Society, 1968, nos 1246, 1248.

p. 90   Heathwall: Jon Newman, with illustrations by David Western, *The Heathwall: Battersea's Buried River*, Backwater Books, 2019.

pp. 90–1   Parish development: *Survey of London: Battersea*, vols 49–50, eds Andrew Saint and Colin Thom, Yale UP for English Heritage, chapter 3; John George Taylor, *Our Lady of Batersey: The Story of Battersea Church and Parish Told from Original Sources*, George Whice, 1925.

pp. 91–2   Wandsworth as laboratory for privatisation: Simon James, 'The Cradle of Privatisation: Wandsworth Borough Council 1980–87', *Britain and the World*, 4:2, 2011, 294–302.

pp. 93–4   Coleraine as forerunner of Thatcherism: Kevin Hickson, 'Lord Coleraine: the neglected prophet of the New Right', *Journal of Political Ideologies*, 14:2, 2009, 173–187.

p. 94   Richard Law: J. Enoch Powell, 'Law, Richard Kidston, first Baron Coleraine', ODNB, 2011.

pp. 94–5   Arnold Taylor biography: 'Arnold Joseph Taylor 1911–2002', *Proceedings of the British Academy*, 138, 2006, 363–381.

pp. 95–7   Narrative of repairs and archaeology at York Minster: B. M. Feilden, 'Why is an archaeological excavation being carried out in York Minster?' Memorandum to Dean & Chapter, 26 June 1967, York Minster Library, D&C Archives, E8; Brian Hope-Taylor, *Under York Minster: Archaeological Discoveries 1966–1971*, Dean and Chapter of York, 1971; D. J. Dowrick and P. Beckmann, 'York Minster structural restoration', *Proceedings of the Institution of Civil Engineers*, Paper 7415, supplement vi, 1971, 93–156; B. M. Feilden, 'The restoration of York Minster', in *The*

Noble City of York, ed. A. Stackpole *et al.*, 1972, 409–446; Derek Phillips, *The Cathedral of Archbishop Thomas of Bayeux: Excavations at York Minster Volume II*, HMSO, 1985, esp. 21–46; statement by Alan Richardson, Dean of York, that the Minster would not be closing: BBC TV News, 7 April 1967.

p. 98   'the flowering of medieval culture upon the highest plane . . . better blood': John Harvey, *The Mediaeval Architect*, Wayland, 1972, 13; 'well-bred biological caste', ibid., 45; on Harvey, fascism and extreme anti-Semitism: Graham Macklin, 'The two lives of John Hooper Harvey', *Patterns of Prejudice*, 42:2, 167–190. For security service reports via observation of Arnold Leese, TNA KV 2/1365-1367.

p. 100   'Stockwood was never a serious contender . . .': Michael De-la-Noy, 'Stockwood, (Arthur) Mervyn', ODNB, 2011.

6   Getting Lucky

pp. 102–3   Relationships between church-building and capacities in later nineteenth century: Trevor Cooper, 'Churches and chapels: the long view', 2012.

pp. 102, 104   White elephants: 'Churches seek ecclesiastical "Dr Beeching"', *The Times*, 30 December 1963, 10.

p. 103   'Great towns will never be evangelised by the parochial system': John Henry Newman, 'Home thoughts from abroad', *British Magazine*, vol. 9, 1836, 365.

p. 103   'It doesn't matter that there's no-one here': John Betjeman, 'A Passion for Churches', BBC2, 7 December 1974; printed in John Betjeman, *Coming Home: an Anthology of Prose 1920-1977*, ed. Candida Lycett Green, Vintage, 1998.

pp. 103–4   Southwark report on the future of parishes: John Robinson *et al.*, *Tomorrow's Parish*, report from policy subcommittee of Southwark Pastoral Reorganisation Committee, Outwood Press, n.d. (1967/8).

p. 104   'Clergy clinging to their freeholds': *The Times*, 30 December 1963, 10.

pp. 105–6   Stacey narrative, 'which we converted into a multi-purpose centre for worship shared by the United Reformed Church . . .': Nicolas Stacey, 'A crisis of credibility in Dr Carey's church', *Guardian*, 27 February 1993. Cf. British Library Sound Archive, interview with Nicolas Stacey, ref. C1155/07, Track 3, 48–70, 4 August 2006.

p. 106   'We no longer accept that the Science of God is an exact science': Nicolas Stacey, 'How the Church could survive', *Observer*, 23 May 1965, 21.

p. 108   'Turmoil that hits at the heart of going to church': Terry Chinery, 'The doubting bishop', *Daily Mail*, 30 April 1984, following ITV broadcast of *Credo*, 29 April 1984.

p. 108 Centralisation: Stuart Blanch, *The Burning Bush. Signs of Our Times*, Lutterworth Press, 1978, 14.

p. 109 First archaeological consultants: Margaret Jesson, *The Archaeology of Churches: A Report from the Churches Committee of the CBA Presented to the Conference on the Archaeology of Churches Held at Norwich on April 13–15 1973*, Appendix III A, list of Diocesan Archaeological Consultants.

p. 109 Extra-mural education and cultural studies after the Second World War: Janet Coles and Paul Armstrong, 'Researching the legacy of Richard Hoggart the adult educator', paper presented at the 39th Annual SCUTREA Conference, 7–9 July 2009, University of Cambridge.

p. 111 Pastoral Measure 1968: Andrew Chandler, *The Church of England in the Twentieth Century: The Church Commissioners and the Politics of Reform*, Boydell Press, 2006, 202–203, and chapter 8 ('Reforming the Parish'), 211–240. For changing perceptions and attitudes towards church closure, see Steven Saxby, 'The rise and fall of the "redundant church": urban church closure and the Church of England from 1833 to 2011', unpubl. PhD thesis, King's College London, 2020.

pp. 111–12 Conceptions of sacrality: John Alfred Thomas, 'Theory, Meaning and Experience in Church Architecture', PhD thesis, University of Sheffield, 1994, esp. section 1.3, 'Sacralism – Church Buildings as Holy Places', 14–88.

p. 113 Church Commissioners: *Supporting the Work and Mission of the Church of England. The Church Commissioners Annual Report 2018*, 2019.

p. 113 Asset managers' remuneration: 2018 *Annual Report*, 63; clerical stipends, 48th Report of the Central Stipends Authority, Archbishops' Council 2020.

7   Hear Me When I Call

p. 119 Early day motion for Big Ben to chime on day of Brexit: UK Parliament Early Day Motions, 19 December 2019. Iain Duncan-Smith, 'arguably the biggest decision . . .' *Catholic Universe*, 24 January 2020. Appeal to ring church bells: Leave.EU website, 10 January 2020; 'vast majority of churchgoers are patriotic people . . .' and 'We've just about had enough . . .'

p. 120 Inscriptions on bells are taken from county volumes ('The Church Bells of . . .') published by archaeological, architectural and historical societies from the later nineteenth to mid twentieth century. For towers, frames and bells generally see *Towers and Bells. A Handbook compiled for the Central Council of Church bell Ringers by the Towers and Belfries Committee*, ed. Alan J. Frost, 1990.

p. 121 St Michael and funeral ritual: David Stocker and Paul Everson,

Summoning St Michael: Early Romanesque Towers in Lincolnshire, Oxbow Books, 2006.

p. 124   Baptism and ordination of bells: Professor Christopher Page, 'Medieval music: the lands of the bell tower', Gresham College, transcript of lecture given at St Sepulchre without Newgate, 5 May 2016.

p. 127   Report on conference to 'maintain the principles of the Reformation': *The Times*, 21 June 1889, 8.

p. 127   John Betjeman, 'Pershore Station, or A Liverish Journey First Class'. On the context: Candida Lycett Green, conversation with author, December 2009.

8   Postcards from Kellington

p. 129   Ur-heraldry: Nigel Saul, *Lordship and Faith: The English Gentry and the Parish Church in the Middle Ages*, Oxford UP, 2017, 45.

pp. 130–1   Meeting convened by British Coal: Malcolm Webb, *Unearthing the Story of the Church of St Edmund King and Martyr Kellington*, West Yorkshire, privately printed, 2006; personal knowledge.

p. 132   Kellington in Domedsday: Great Domesday Folio 316r TNA E 31/2/2/5608; E 31/2/2/5636; E 31/2/2/8994.

p. 133   Humphrey de Ruhale: William Farrer ed., *Early Yorkshire Charters*, III, 1916, Lacy Fee, 286–287. Cf. Linsey Forsyth Hunter, 'Charter diplomatics and norms of landholding and lordship between the Humber and Forth c.1066–c.1250', unpubl. PhD thesis, University of St Andrews, 2012.

p. 135   Making of the structural record: Caroline Atkins, 'Recording before dismantling and re-erection: St Edmund's church, Kellington', in *Buildings Archaeology: Applications in Practice*, ed. Jason Wood *et al.*, Oxbow Monograph, 43, 1994, 219–234.

p. 141   Carved stone under threshold: for recognition that the stone derives from a cross-shaft, and information on its likely artistic context, I am most grateful to Professor David Stocker.

p. 142   Dismantling methodology: Atkins, 'St Edmund's church'.

p. 145   Fullest excavation of church in use? For interim accounts: Harold Mytum, 'Kellington Church', *Current Archaeology*, 12:1, 1993, 15–17; Harold Mytum, 'Parish and people: excavations at Kellington church', *Medieval Life*, 1, 1995, 19–22. Professor Mytum's substantive report on the project is forthcoming.

9   Anglicans, Celts, Coincidences

p. 147   Trullae: British Museum database: https://www.britishmuseum.org/collection/object/H_2005-1204-1; Ralph Jackson, 'The Ilam pan', in

David J. Breeze ed., *The First Souvenirs: Enamelled Vessels from Hadrian's Wall*, Cumberland and Westmorland Antiquarian and Archaeological Society extra series, 37, 2012, 41–60.

p. 148 *'Ego Patricius, peccator rusticissimus'*: *The Book of Armagh*, Dublin, Trinity College, MS 52, folio 22r.

pp. 148–9 Locating Banna: Diarmaid MacCulloch, 'Who kicked them out?', review of Roy Flechner, *St Patrick Retold: The Legend and History of Ireland's Patron Saint* (2019), *London Review of Books*, 41:15, 2019.

p. 150 Archaeological reassessment and analysis of Glastonbury: Roberta Gilchrist and Cheryl Green, *Glastonbury Abbey: Archaeological Investigations 1904–1979*, Society of Antiquaries of London, 2015.

pp. 154–5 Concepts of cultural areas: E. G. Bowen, *Saints Seaways and Settlements in the Celtic Lands*, University of Wales, 2 edn 1977 (repr. 1988), chapter 4, esp. 81–82.

p. 156 Caherlehillan: J. Sheehan, 'Caherlehillan: ritual, domestic and economic aspects of a Corcu Duibne ecclesiastical site', in C. Corlett and M. Potterton eds, *The Church in Early Ireland*, Dublin, 2014, 247–258; J. Sheehan, 'A Peacock's Tale: Excavations at Caherlehillan, Iveragh, Ireland', in *The Archaeology of the Early Medieval Celtic Churches*, ed. N. Edwards, Society for Medieval Archaeology Monograph, 29, 2009, 191–206.

p. 158 Discoveries at Lastingham: Richard Morris, 'Landscapes of Conversion Among the Deirans: Lastingham and its Neighbours in the Seventh and Eighth Centuries', in *Places of Worship in Britain and Ireland, 300–950*, ed. P. S. Barnwell, Shaun Tyas, 2015, 119–152.

pp. 160–2 Consecration of St Chad's Cathedral: *The Freeman's Journal*, Dublin, 26 June 1841. Dating of bones: Angela Boyle, 'Report on the bones kept in St Chad's Cathedral, Birmingham in M. Greenslade, St Chad of Lichfield and Birmingham, Archdiocese of Birmingham Historical Commission No. 10, Stafford, 1996, 25–26.

pp. 162–3 David Woods, 'Gildas and the mystery cloud of 536-7', *Journal of Theological Studies* (new series), 61:1, 2010, 201–234; Isaiah discussion at 233.

p. 163 M. Sigl *et al.*, 'Timing and climate forcing of volcanic eruptions for the past 2,500 years', *Nature*, 30 July 2015, vol. 523, 543–560; Ann Gibbons, 'Why 536 "was the worst year to be alive"', *Science*, 15 November 2018; M. G. L. Baillie, 'Dendrochronology raises questions about the nature of the AD 536 dust-veil event', *The Holocene*, 4:2, 212–217.

p. 164 Andrew Breeze, 'The Historical Arthur and Sixth-century Scotland', *Northern History*, 52:2, 2015, 158–181; 'Arthur's Battles and the Volcanic Winter of 536–37', *Northern History*, 53:2, 161–172.

p. 164 Welsh Annals transcription from British Library, Harley MS 3859, ff.

1901–1931, Henry Gough-Cooper, 1 edn, 2015, published online by the Welsh Chronicles Research Group: http://croniclau.bangor.ac.uk

10   Jarrow Crusades

p. 166 *'Gens'* in its earlier Roman sense signified people who shared the same *nomen* and a common ancestor.

p. 166 The politics of the houses' association are complicated and were probably reasoned backwards: Ian Wood, 'The origins of Jarrow: the monastery, the slake and Ecgfrith's minster', *Bede's World Studies* 1, 2008.

pp. 167–9   Rosemary Cramp recollections: 'Rosemary Cramp: on celebrating the stone sculpture of the Anglo-Saxons', interview with James Rivington, *British Academy Review*, spring 2019, 26–33, at 26, 27, 29.

p. 169 Rosemary Cramp, *Wearmouth and Jarrow Monastic Sites*, English Heritage, 2005 (vol. 1) and 2006 (vol. 2).

p. 170 Evolution of concept and its challenges: Peter Fowler and Miriam Harte, 'The Genius of the Place: Managing a "Min-National Park" at Bede's World', in 'Archaeology and the National Park Idea: Challenges for Management and Interpretation', *The George Wright Forum*, 16:4, 1999, 91–106; Peter Fowler, 'Bede's World, UK: the monk who made history', in *The Constructed Past: Experimental Archaeology, Education and the Public*, eds Peter Stone and Philippe G. Planel, One World Archaeology, Routledge, 1999, 245–257.

pp. 174–5   New kind of visitor: Fowler and Harte, 'The Genius of the Place', 102–104.

p. 179 Nomination document: Sunderland City Council and Wearmouth-Jarrow Partnership, *The Twin Monastery of Wearmouth-Jarrow: Nomination As a World Heritage Property: Nomination Document and Management Plan*, 2 vols, 2011.

p. 180 Initial reaction: 'The Twin Monastery of Wearmouth-Jarrow', letter from UK State Party to World Heritage Centre, 15 May 2012, reference CLT/WHC/5007/GB/PA/PT.

p. 180 Further response to ICOMOS: Commentary of the ICOMOS evaluation of the Wearmouth–Jarrow World Heritage Site nomination. Final draft following discussion at Wearmouth–Jarrow drafting group, September 2012.

p. 182 Bede's bones: Joanna Storey and Richard Bailey, 'The skull of Bede', *The Antiquaries Journal*, 95, 2015, 325–350.

p. 182 Joseph Barnard Davis and John Thurnham, *Crania Britannica: Delineations and Descriptions of The Skulls of the Aboriginal and Early Inhabitants of the British Islands* (1856–1865).

11 Quires and Places Where They Sing

p. 183 Wetheringsett find and report: Timothy Easton and Stephen Bicknell, 'Two pre-Reformation organ soundboards: towards an understanding of the form of early organs and their position within some Suffolk churches', *Proceedings of Suffolk Institute of History and Archaeology*, 38, part 3, 1995, 268–295.

pp. 183–4 Organ specifications: http://www.goetzegwynn.co.uk/

p. 184 The Early English Organ Project, Royal College of Organists: https://www.rco.org.uk/library_tudor_organs.php/

p. 184 How many organs were there in England in 1500? Question posed by Peter Williams (1937–2016) in February 2008.

pp. 184–5 http://soundsmedieval.org – discovering the origins of English music.

p. 185 Late medieval organs: Martin Renshaw, 'Investigating the archaeology of the late medieval organ', lecture, Barber Institute, Birmingham, 25 Feb 2012: http://soundsmedieval.org

pp. 186–7 Mainly post-medieval terms, need for less anachronistic terminology, analysis of design layout of churches: Martin Renshaw, 'Beyond Ecclesiology: some implications which arise from considering medieval chancels as buildings designed for music', essay, 2015: http://soundsmedieval.org

pp. 186–7 Chaunsell geography, use and implications: Renshaw, 'Beyond ecclesiology'.

p. 187 Musical graffiti: Rebecca Hiscott, 'The permissibility of the practice of inscribing graffiti in Beverley Minster, with specific reference to the eastern side of the reredos', PhD thesis, University of Hull.

p. 187 Kirby Hall is an Elizabethan and 17th-century prodigy house, owned for a time by Sir Christopher Hatton (1540-1691), England's Lord Chancellor (1587-1591). Part of the upper board of a chamber organ, dating perhaps from the 1630s, was recognised in its collection in 2021. Domestic organs of this date are known also from great houses at Hunstanton, Norfolk (now at St Luke's Smithfield, Virginia) and Staunton Harold. It is suggested that they were used to play in ensemble with viol consorts and singers: Peter Holman, 'Evenly, softly and sweetly according to all: the organ accompaniment of English consort music', in *John Jenkins and his time*, eds Andrew Ashbee and Peter Holman, Oxford University Press, 1996, 354–382; John Bryan, '"Choice consorts . . . (*rare chests of viols*)": the evidence of the repertory', in *Early English Viols: Instruments, makers and Music*, eds Michael Fleming and John Bryan, Routledge, 2016, 31–81.

12   Intensive Care

p. 191 Runcie told him that Humphrey Carpenter, in his biography, had been 'somewhat selective' in reporting Runcie's views of his days at Westcott; 'there were characteristics of the system which did not appeal to me and he rather over-emphasised them'. Robert Runcie to John Morris, letter, 17 April 2000, JRM Collection.

p. 192 Obituary: 'Canon John Morris: Much loved Left-wing Vicar of Battersea who had early created a new parish for workers at the Austin plant at Longbridge', *Daily Telegraph*, 6 June 2000.

13   Amphletts and Itineraries

p. 196 Postings and dates: John Morris's service record, AM Forms 1406, 543.

p. 198 'I was conscious of the difference in rank . . .': John Morris, MS memoir for Dick Williams, JRM Collection.

p. 199 William Blanch death and inquest: *Gloucester Citizen*, 1 and 4 September 1923.

p. 199 Blanch at Christmas: Williams, *Blanch*, 35–39.

p. 200 Navigator streaming: C. G. Jefford, *Observers and Navigators and Other Non-pilot Aircrew in the RFC, RNAS and RAF*, Airlife, 2001, 161–163, 165–174.

p. 200 Amphletts and Wychbold: Landed families of Britain and Ireland, 'Amphlett of Hadzor House, Wychbold Hall, Clent House and Four Ashes Hall', 28 May 2014: https://landedfamilies.blogspot.com/2014/05/124-amphlett-of-hadzor-house-wychbold.html

p. 202 Navigation training at Mount Hope: John Hill and Pamela Howarth, *We Did What We Had To*, Matador, 2018, 25–26.

pp. 202–3   *Fourth Wall*: Elsie Morris (Wearne), MS memoir; *Mount Hope Meteor*, Geoffrey Baker Collection, Hamilton Central Library, 779.092016.

p. 204 'Buses were celestial . . .': John Morris to Elsie Wearne, letter, November 1944, JRM Collection.

p. 206 'Yesterday afternoon I arrived in Birmingham . . .': John Morris to Elsie Wearne, letter, 10 June 1944: JRM Collection. Further letters to Elsie Wearne in this chapter are from this collection.

p. 207 Traherne verse: *Christian Ethicks, Or, Divine Morality. Opening the Way to Blessedness, By the Rules of Vertue and Reason, 1675.*

p. 209 'Oh yes! And you must get to Fountains Abbey . . .': Maurice Cohen to John Morris, 7 September 1944: JRM Collection.

p. 212 No. 1 Overseas Aircraft Despatch Unit, Portreath, Cornwall: TNA AIR 29/471/1.

14   Italy and the Testing of Hearts

pp. 215–16   Work of 60 Squadron, tactics, details of operations: 60 Squadron SAAF Operations Record Book, January–July 1945, TNA AIR 27/572.

p. 229   'If it is true the dead return . . .': Louis Ginsberg, 'The Room', *Collected Poems*, Northern Lights Publishing, 1992, 162.

p. 232   'I am much in need of intercessory prayer . . .': Richard Amphlett to John Morris, letter, February 1946, JRM Collection.

15   Church Militant

p. 234   'He would wait a bit in case I could take a rare chance to shine . . .': John Morris, MS memoir for Dick Williams, JRM Collection.

p. 235   'He arrived, looking lean, keen and rather formidable . . .': Recollected in memorial address for Douglas Jay, 11 March 1996, JRM Collection.

p. 235   Church Reform Group: Diana Collins, *Partners in Protest*, 142–144.

p. 237   Christian Action beginnings and letter proposing meeting: MS John Collins Papers, MS 3289, LPL. Recipients included George Bell, E. L. Mascall and C. S. Lewis. Bell's unavailability in October may explain why the meeting was put back to December. For the involvement and eventual stepping back of C. S. Lewis: Gregory Anderson, 'Lost Letters of Lewis at the Lambeth Palace Library, Sehnsucht', *C. S. Lewis Journal*, 10, 2016, 33–50.

p. 237   Platform refusals: Collins Papers, MS 3289, 19, LPL.

p. 237   Leaflet and slogging the pavements: John Morris, 'As it was in the beginning', in *Christian Action 1946–96*, ed. Eric James, 6.

p. 237   George Bell, MS Collins Papers, MS 3289, 25; 40 John Collins, MS Collins Papers, MS 3289, 28, LPL.

p. 238   'A Call to Christian Action in Public Affairs': 'Resolutions before Oxford meeting', *The Times*, 29 November 1946; 'Crowds mob town hall', *Gloucester Citizen*, 6 December 1946, 4. 'In all about 2,500 people attended' and passage of resolutions: John Collins, 'Christian Action', letter to *The Times*, 12 December 1946; Diana Collins, *Partners in Protest*, 150–155; Diana Collins, 'Origins and major activities of Christian Action', in *Christian Action 1946–96*, ed. Eric James, 2–5.

p. 239   James Leasor, 'A Church militant', *Daily Mail*, 1 December 1947, 2; '3,000 at Oxford meeting', *Manchester Guardian*, 1 December 1947. A capacity audience in the Sheldonian, with standing, would be c.1,600.

p. 239   Diana Collins's regrets at leaving Oxford: *Partners in Protest*, 165–173.

p. 240   Berlin Philharmonic itinerary: Christopher Fifield, *Ibbs and Tillett: The Rise and Fall of a Musical Empire*, Routledge, 2018, 268–269.

p. 241 'Is it only a quarrel over ceremony, or does it go deeper?' 'Battle within the Church', *Picture Post*, 30 November 1946, 21–24.

p. 241 Main opposition to women bishops 'not from the Anglo-Catholics but from conservative evangelicals who believed that the Bible mandated patriarchy': Andrew Brown and Linda Woodhead, *That Was the Church that Was: How the Church of England Lost the English People*, Bloomsbury, 2017, 201.

16 Down Jesus Lane

p. 243 Topography of early Cambridge: M. D. Lobel with W. H. Johns, 'Cambridge', *The Atlas of Historic Towns*, vol. 2, Scolar Press & Historic Towns Trust, 1976.

p. 245 Westcott House description: Historic England, list entry, 1967.

p. 245 'good company' and 'enormous influence', Robert Runcie, quoted in Humphrey Carpenter, *Robert Runcie: The Reluctant Archbishop*, Sceptre, 1997, 108.

p. 245 Carey and his predecessor Cunningham: Canon Trevor Shannon, 'The priest as parson', *Bradwell Papers*, 5, 1997.

p. 245 'His study was at the end of a short passage with a notice on the door which read either "free" or "busy"': Michael Fisher SSF, *For the Time Being*, Gracewing: Fowler Wright Books, 1993, 89.

p. 246 Robert L. Glover, 'Man, meaning and ministry: the question for the historical Vanstone', *Theology in Scotland*, 11.1, 2004, 5–32.

p. 246 'Because I'd loved being a soldier . . .': Eric James, 'The Trinity Years', in *Simon Phipps: A Portrait*, collected by Caroline Gilmour and Patricia Wyndham, ed. David Machin, Continuum, 2003, 7.

p. 247 'Witty and pugent lyrics': review of 'La Vie Cambridgienne', *The Stage*, 10 June 1948.

p. 248 Original sin: Adam Fergusson, 'The Songs', in *Simon Phipps: A Portrait*, 43.

p. 248 'while cigarette ash tumbled unheeded down his cassock': ibid., 39.

p. 249 Casting of Caesar and Androcles: Carpenter, *Robert Runcie*, 108–109.

pp. 250–1 All Saints Jesus Lane and the move towards English models in nineteenth-century Gothic: Michael Hall, 'The Rise of Refinement: G. F. Bodley's All Saints, Cambridge, and the Return to English Models in Gothic Architecture of the 1860s', *Architectural History*, 36, 1993, 103–126. Ecclesiology and Gothic: James F. White, *The Cambridge Movement: The Ecclesiologists and the Gothic Revival*, Cambridge University Press, 1962. Piety and beauty of the Middle Ages as source of ethical restoration: J. M. Neale, 'The Place Where Prayer Was Wont to be Made: Re-introduction of the System of Private Devotion in Churches', considered in a letter to the venerable The President of the Cambridge Camden Society, John Thomas Walters, 1844, 20.

p. 253 Birmingham courts and life around New John Street West: Sir Frank Price, *Being There*, Upfront Publishing, 2002, 20–31.

p. 254 *St George's Hard Times*, June 1952, Carnival Committee of Parish Church of St George, Birmingham; printed by *Birmingham News*.

p. 254 1952 carnival press coverage and adverse clerical reaction: '"Best Church show since Nero" stops traffic', *Birmingham Despatch*, 27 May 1952; 'Curate parades dancing girls', *Birmingham Gazette*, 27 May 1952; 'Rector and Curate Run their Own Theatre Show', *Daily Mail*, 28 May 1952; clerical coppers: *Birmingham News*, 29 May 1952; '"Policemen" parsons will upset carnival', *Birmingham Despatch*, 29 May 1952; 'Curate tries on angel's wings between sermons', *News Chronicle*, 2 June 1952; 'The show will be great fun', *Birmingham Mail*, 5 June 1952; 'Parson puts on song and dance show', *Weekly News*, 7 June 1952; 'Hatchet will chase curate – Hockley fun begins today', *Birmingham News*, 7 June 1952, 1; 'Curate mimes a prima donna' and 'Curate stars in church "capers"', *Birmingham Gazette*, 9 June 1952, 1, 5; clerical criticism: 'Church capers', *Birmingham Gazette*, 5 June 1952; 'Hard times', *Birmingham Gazette*, 9 July 1952.

17 Evening Prayer

pp. 256–7 Vanstone: David Pearl *et al.*, 'A Betrayal of Trust. The independent report into the handling of allegations that have come to the attention of the Church of England concerning the late Hubert Victor Whitsey, former Bishop of Chester', 2020; Stacey: S. Proctor, S. Cohen and R. Galloway, 'Report of a review of Kendall House, Gravesend, 1967–1986', 2016, qualified by Tim Wyatt, 'Kendall House campaigner finds more links between Kent social services and notorious C of E children's home', *Church Times*, 13 October 2017; Phipps: *The Times*, 9 February 1985, 3; Bell: Lord Carlile of Berriew, 'Bishop George Bell: the independent review', 2017; Statement of apology from Archbishop of Canterbury, Justin Welby, 24 January 2019. Cf. Professor Alexis Jay, Professor Sir Malcolm Evans, Ivor Frank and Drusilla Sharpling, *The Anglican Church Case Studies: 1. The Diocese of Chichester: 2. The Response to Allegations Against Peter Ball*. Investigation Report May 2019, a report of the Inquiry Panel.

p. 257 'The tortoise stove is lit again': John Betjeman, 'Christmas', *A Few Late Chrysanthemums*, 1954, 10.

p. 258 'Human existence is obviously distinguished from animal life by its qualified participation in creation. Within limits it breaks the forms

of nature and creates new configurations of vitality': Reinhold Nei-
bhur, *The Nature and Destiny of Man: A Christian Interpretation. Volume
1: Human Nature*, Westminster John Knox Press, repr. 1996 (first publ.
1941), 26.

p. 258 Identification of civilisation with Christianity and alignment with conservatism: Paul Betts, *Ruin and Renewal: Civilising Europe after World
War II*, Profile Books, 2020.

p. 259 'Many witnesses have … argued that these vestments are in the public
mind so closely associated with the Roman Church that their introduction into the Church of England': *Report of the Royal Commission on
Ecclesiastical Discipline*, HMSO, 1906.

p. 260 'trivial and irrelevant things about which men are fighting so bitterly':
The Speaker, 7 July 1906, 308.

p. 261 'I want, before I finish, to say one word on a subject which has been
mentioned by several speakers': Stanley Baldwin, *Hansard*, Prayer Book
Measure, 1928, vol. 218, debated Thursday 14 June 1928, col. 1, 319.

p. 262 'More periods of experimentation with further Alternative Services
(Series Two and Three) began in the mid-1960s': Where the Liturgy
Comes From, Church of England website: https://www.churchof
england.org/prayer-and-worship/worship-texts-and-resources/
where-liturgy-comes

p. 263 HTB and like-mindedness marketing principle: Andrew Brown and
Linda Woodhead, *That Was the Church that Was*, 131–132.

p. 263 HTB trustees and area: at the time of writing (1 July 2021) the Charity
Commission Register of Charities records one trustee cross-membership
between Holy Trinity Brompton and the Church Commissioners, and
that the charity operates 'throughout London'.

p. 264 Strategic Development Funding was established in 2014. In 2018,
it awarded £61.9 million in response to project bids; projects run for
terms of up to six years. Church Commissioners' Annual Report 2018,
14–16. For survey of projects, *Resourcing the Future: Projects and Progress*, Church Commissioners, 2019, aiming at 54,000 'new disciples',
over 1,600 church plants ('Fresh Expressions of Church'), and a further
52,000 disciples.

p. 265 'aims to meet demand from dioceses across the country for establishing
City Centre Resource Churches': Churches Revitalisation Trust, 'Our
Work': https://crtrust.org/work. The opening of the self-description has
implications for the parish system: 'In line with the Church of Eng-
land's strategy for growth and working in close partnership with the
Bishop of Islington …' This seems to imply either that HTB is part
of Anglican strategy or else that Anglican strategy is congruent with
HTB. The Bishop of Islington (Rt Rev Ric Thorpe) is described by the

Diocese of London as 'free from territorial responsibilities and focuses on supporting newly established worshipping communities both within London and at a national level, serving as a resource for the whole Church of England.'

p. 265 'For over 1,400 years, Rochester Cathedral has been a centre of learning for the community . . .': 'Adventure golf at the cathedral, Rochester Cathedral, 1 July 2019'.

p. 265 'we believe this is in the best interests of the long-term mission of the Cathedral': 'Sheffield Cathedral Choir', statement by Sheffield Cathedral Chapter, 22 July 2020.

p. 265 Cranmer 'would not have known what Anglicanism meant' and 'unending dialogue': Diarmaid MacCulloch, *Thomas Cranmer: A Life*, Yale UP, 1996, 629–631.

Epilogue: Angels In Masvingo

p. 269 'Unveil the dust-wrapped. post-war architects' . . .': Geoffrey Hill, *The Triumph of Love*, XXV.

p. 271 Mugabe's 'unimpeachable' commitment to 'peace, non-racialism and racial harmony': D. Hills, *The Last Days of White Rhodesia*, Chatto & Windus, 1981.

p. 271 'until I broke my leg on the thing 32 miles away from a Church where 510 Confirmation candidates were waiting for me': Paul Burrough, *Angels Unawares*, Churchman Publishing, 1988, 130–131.

p. 271 An example of cross-quoting is Thomas Mhuriro ('Theology of Empire and Anglicanism: Replicating Eusebius of Caesarea in the Diocese of Mashonaland (1890–1979)', PhD thesis, University of South Africa) who bases many of his discussions and assessments on verdicts taken from secondary sources, such as Michael Lapsley (*Neutrality or Co-option? Anglican Church and State from 1964 until the Independence of Zimbabwe*, Mambo Press, 1986) and Joram Tarusarira ('Christianity, Resistance and Conflict Resolution in Zimbabwe', in *Handbook of Global Contemporary Christianity*, ed. Stephen J. Hunt, Brill, 2015, 264–284) which variously put Burrough on a spectrum between Rhodesia Front collaborator and enthusiast for white supremacy. In result, Burrough emerges as one who at best failed to see what was wrong with Rhodesia's white establishment, and thereby forfeited the right to be a true shepherd of indigenous Anglicans ('He identified with those who had the power and not with those who stood in need of being defended.' (636)), and at worst was actively complicit with the Smith government. Behind this and similar statements is the view that Burrough put his care 'not to offend those who were running the country' before Gospel imperatives, whereas Burrough, arguably, considered that he was putting Gospel imperatives before mapping himself onto a political spectrum dictated by others.

p. 271 'did not want to upset anyone, least of all those running the country': 'Rt Rev Paul Burrough', *The Times*, 31 January 2003, 39; replies from Canon Richard Rutt, Rev R. G. Forrest, Rev S. J. Davies, *The Times*, 13 February 2003, 39.

p. 271 'counselled moderation, without apparently recognising that, in African eyes, the outlawed regime had, for many, made a peaceful settlement impossible': 'The Right Reverend Paul Burrough Bishop who had to lead Anglicans through the turbulent early years of what was to become Zimbabwe', *Daily Telegraph*, 28 January 2003, 23.

pp. 271-2 Anglicanism 'was peculiarly vulnerable when African nationalism challenged the morality of White supremacy and segregation . . .': Prosper Muzambi, 'Kenneth Skelton versus Nolbert Kunonga in Light of Responsible Citizenship Discourse', in *Religion and Development in Southern and Central Africa Vol. 2*, eds James N. Amanze, Maake Masango, Ezra Chitando and Lilian Siwila, Mzuni Press, 2019, 51-85, at 65.

p. 272 'it is not the function of a World Christian body to advocate force and terrorism': Norman H. Murdoch (*Christian Warfare in Rhodesia-Zimbabwe: The Salvation Army and African Liberation. 1891-1991*, Lutterworth Press, 2015, 190) describes Burrough as 'a Smith supporter' and claims that he 'spoke for white Anglicans who voted for the Smith regime's new constitution and Land Act aimed at continued white rule'. *The Catholic Herald*, 8 October 1976, described Burrough as being 'not known' for opposition to Smith. Burrough's vote against the rest of the fifty-member Anglican Consultative Council in 1971 on a resolution denouncing racism was in the context of the Council's earlier approval of the WCC's grants to ZANU and ZAPU.

p. 272 'states artificially formed out of colonial empires to satisfy world opinion among politicians are beyond the wit of man to govern': Burrough, *Angels Unawares*, 134.

p. 273 'On a cold night in the assembly hall one could see them lying literally three deep on top of each other to preserve a little warmth': Burrough, *Angels Unawares*, 64.

p. 274 'more damage to the cause of racial integration than all the sneers and blasphemies of their English workmates in factory workshops': David Muir, 'From Tilbury to the pew and pulpit: how the Church met the *Empire Windrush*', *Church Times*, 22 June 2018.

p. 274 'The story of Rhodesia becoming Zimbabwe . . .': Burrough, *Angels Unawares*, 17.

p. 274 'In some distant relationship, untroubled by political ideologies, angels must be entertained and enjoyed for themselves in a new kind of undemanding hospitality': Burrough, *Angels Unawares*, 134.

p. 274 Arthur Shearly Cripps (1869–1952) was an Anglican priest and writer who spent most of his life in what is now Zimbabwe, lived among the Shona, opposed colonialism and gained a reputation akin to that of Francis of Assisi. His shrine in Maronda Mashanu has become a place of pilgrimage.

p. 276 Murder of Peter Wagner: Hugh Wagner, 'My brother was a good man. Why was he killed?', *Guardian*, 20 March 2001.

p. 276 'Because these incidents are not overtly political, they do not attract media attention in this country . . .': Hugh Wagner, 'My brother's murder', letter, *Guardian*, 13 March 2001.

ACKNOWLEDGEMENTS

Warm thanks go to Amy Levene for her maps of parish neighbour-hoods and to Emily Taylor for help tracing images. Chapter 11 draws substantially on the work and generosity of Martin Renshaw, whose recent studies of later medieval church musical culture and the perform-ative geography of the buildings in which it flourished are to be found in ground-breaking lectures and essays accessible through Sounds Medieval.org.

For permission to quote from the work of others, the author and publishers thank Oxford Publishing Limited (Academic) for lines from *The Triumph of Love* by Geoffrey Hill (© Geoffrey Hill 2013), for extracts from entries for Richard Law (by J. Enoch Powell) and Mervyn Stockwood (by Michael De-la-Noy) in the *Oxford Dictionary of National Biography*, all of which are reproduced with permission of the Licensor through PLSclear; Canon Angela Tilby and the *Church Times* for the extract from 'Why choral evensong is so popular'; Pro-fessor Christopher Page for extracts from his Gresham College lecture 'Medieval Music: the Lands of the Bell Tower'; *The Stage* for a passage from its 1951 review of the Coventry medieval guild plays; Ian Paul and Rev. David Keen for the extract from David Keen's discussion of 'Statis-tics for Mission' published in Ian Paul's 'What is happening to Church of England attendance' in his blog Psephizo; Professor Diarmaid MacCulloch and the *London Review of Books* and Yale University Press, respectively, for quotations from the review of Roy Flechner, *St Patrick Retold* (2019), and *Thomas Cranmer*; Dr David Woods for the extract from his paper 'Gildas and the Mystery Cloud of 536-37'; The British Academy for extracts from James Rivington's interview with Professor Dame Rosemary Cramp; Professor David Brown and Oxford Univer-sity Press for sentences from *Tradition and Imagination*; and Gracewing for the quotation from Michael Fisher's *For the Time Being*. Lines from John Betjeman's poem 'Pershore Station' from his Collected Poems are reproduced by permission of John Murray Press, an imprint of Hodder and Stoughton (© The Estate of John Betjeman 1955, 1958, 1960, 1962, 1964, 1966, 1970, 1979, Betjeman 1980, 1981, 2001. Introduction Andrew Motion © 2006). The lines from 'A Passion for Churches', broadcast by the BBC on 7 December 1974, printed in John Betjeman's *Coming Home: An Anthology of Prose 1920–1977* (edited by Candida Lycett Green), published by Vintage, are quoted with the permission of Random House. Sidney Keyes's poem 'William Byrd' appears in his Collected Poems and the extract is reprinted by kind permission of Carcanet Press, Manchester, UK.

LIST OF ILLUSTRATIONS

List of plates

Longbridge 1935 (Historic England)

Artist's impression of new church and vicarage at Longbridge, 1956

Ascensiontide at Longbridge, 1958

Sanderstead rectory, 1964

Pilgrim graffito, Beverley Minster (Rebecca Hiscott)

Battersea church and bridge c.1796, by J. M. W. Turner (Tate)

Ringers' rhyme board in tower of St Brevita's church, Lanlivery, Cornwall (Mick Sharp)

Church of St Edmund, Kellington, North Yorkshire, under repair, 1991 (Alamy)

Shrine of St Melangell, Pennant Melangell, Powys (Mick Sharp)

Soundboard of sixteenth-century organ, found at Wetheringsett (Suffolk Institute of Archaeology and History)

Reconstructed Tudor organ (Goetze and Gwynn)

Cuthbert Gospel, produced early in the eighth century (British Library Add MS 89000)

St Peter, Monkwearmouth, 1946 (Historic England)

Decorated door jamb in west entrance to porch of St Peter's monastic church, Monkwearmouth (Mick Sharp)

Monastic church of St Paul, Jarrow (Mick Sharp)

Returning crew at San Severo, April 1945 (JRM Collection)

Masked procession at San Severo, Good Friday, 1945 (JRM Collection)

Westcott House and All Saints, Jesus Lane (Historic England)

Scene from *Androcles and the Lion*, Westcott House, 1949 (JRM Collection)

Carnival Capers, 1952 (*Birmingham Mail*/JRM Collection)

St George's Hard Times – carnival newspaper, June 1952 (JRM Collection)

List of illustrations in text

Maps

INDEX